RELIGIOUS
AND
SPIRITUAL GROUPS
IN
MODERN AMERICA

RELIGIOUS and SPIRITUAL GROUPS in MODERN AMERICA

ROBERT S. ELLWOOD JR.
University of Southern California

PRENTICE-HALL, INC., ENGLEWOOD CLIFFS, NEW JERSEY

Library of Congress Cataloging in Publication Data

ELLWOOD, ROBERT S.
   Religious and spiritual groups in modern America.

   Includes bibliography
      1. Cults—United States.   2. Religions.   I. Title.
BP603.E55 1973   200.973   72–4371
ISBN 0–13–773317–8
ISBN 0–13–773309–7 (pbk.)

For my mother and father

Prentice-Hall International, Inc., *London*
Prentice-Hall of Australia, Pty. Ltd., *Sydney*
Prentice-Hall of Canada, Ltd., *Toronto*
Prentice-Hall of India Private Limited, *New Delhi*
Prentice-Hall of Japan, Inc., *Tokyo*

contents

fOREWORO

When I first visited Los Angeles in 1961, by chance I drove past the plain but dignified building which houses the meetinghall and headquarters of the United Lodge of Theosophists. Located at 33rd and Grand, it is only a few blocks from the University of Southern California. The Lodge is on the "wrong" side of the Harbor Freeway from the campus, though, in a neighborhood now sadly given over to warehouses, marginal manufacturing, and the sprawling East Los Angeles multiracial slums. Once, long before the freeway, smog, and the postwar population explosion, these broad streets, imperial with palms, had rejoiced in the townhouses of the prosperous. It is said that in the twenties half the wealth of Los Angeles lived on nearby Adams Boulevard in the vicinity of St. John's Episcopal Church. Now, the great mansions are mostly schools and institutes of various sorts, St. John's conducts a noteworthy ministry to the disadvantaged out of its striking baroque edifice, and across from the May Company's main warehouse, busy with the comings and goings of delivery trucks, the clean rectangular house of the United Lodge of Theosophists posts its lectures on karma, reincarnation, or the mystic path of the Masters.

Intrigued, I parked my car in front of the building and walked up to it. Unfortunately, it was Saturday and the hall was closed. But I walked past it two or three times. To me, a small-town midwesterner displaced to southern California by military service, something about the spindly yellow-green trees by the legend, "United Lodge of Theosophists," and the large lighted sign reading Theosophy Hall over the structure, evoked a Los Angeles quite other than the freeways and Orange Leonards. I thought of how they spoke of California back in Nebraska: A land where movie stars lived better than princes, where young men came to make love or fortunes, and the old came to die, homesick under palms and lemon trees by the sea. Our California friends reported the stunning power of lady evangelists, or the persuasiveness of lecture hall meta-physicians whose minds scanned realms of which we had scarcely dreamed. The pieties of the plains were as often as not dried up by the fierce deserts which lay between the heartland and the Golden State— or else were reborn with a desert intensity.

Was this United Lodge of Theosophists a lingering stage prop from these fairy tales of an American youth? Or did the fairyland really exist somewhere under or between the noisy freeways? Were these now-sealed portals perhaps magic gates which might have opened to it? Unfortunately, a young man about to be shipped for service to the Far East has many things on his mind, and I then never found out.

Several years later, after graduate study in the history of religions, I returned to Los Angeles, to the same neighborhood, to teach at the University of Southern California. Very soon one of my favorite avoca-tions was the careful reading every Saturday of the religion pages of the *Los Angeles Times.* These remarkable sheets are more than the sedate promulgation of the time of women's circle meetings and the sermon topic in Dr. So-and-So's fashionable Wilshire Boulevard church. They instead serve up a gourmet feast well worth the careful attention of the connoisseur of spiritual matters. Virtually a full page is devoted to the advertisement of denominations which were, to say the least, not known in Nebraska. The first week after my return to Los Angeles I detected on this page a small square announcement containing the words, United Lodge of Theosophists, a lecture time and topic, and the address which I knew to be within walking distance of my apartment. I deter-mined to attend the next Sunday evening.

I was not entirely ignorant of Theosophy. I had long before read a rather unsympathetic biography of its cofoundress, Madame Blavatsky, and a few snippets about the Theosophical movement in books on American cults. I knew that Theosophy had been one of the most influential and least understood cult movements of the last hundred years. It was well known, at least by name, to our parents and grand-parents by reason of a hundred sensational newspaper articles. Its leaders, more often than not strong-willed ladies of the (first) feminist era, titillated a generation with what seemed a never-failing stream of scandals, schisms, bizarre psychic phenomena, and egregious claims to superhuman contacts. But now, I gathered, Theosophy's institutional life burnt with a low flame. Yet beyond a doubt the sort of ideas early and pervasively introduced to the West by Theosophists—reincarnation, mystical monism, a new birth of the *ex oriente lux* mood—has now a greater hold than ever before. Theosophists have never been alone in promulgating them in the West, and today represent only a small sector of the Asian spiritual invasion. But give credit where credit is due. When their lecturers went, as some still do, even to the smaller cities of Europe and America, when the lurid publicity was in full flower, Theosophists must have made their arcana visible to millions unlearned in academic philosophy or orientalia. The clubwomen who chat of previous lives, the old men who haunt the secondhand bookstores specializing in esoterica, the messiahs of a dozen cults have all drunk lightly or deeply of the ponderous learning of Theosophy.

But I had little notion of where the United Lodge stood in the movement, or what to expect at a meeting. I found a cavernous old-fashioned lecture hall virtually bare of symbolism inside the mysterious building. At the back were tables covered with books and magazines and tracts, presided over by a couple of smiling fiftyish ladies. I purchased two or three magazines (*Theosophy, The Aryan Path*) and a booklet on the U.L.T. to read while I waited for the lecture to begin. Glancing through them, I learned that the U.L.T. is not the original Theosophical Society of Madame Blavatsky, but was founded by a Robert Crosbie in 1909 as a "reform" movement in reaction against the leadership squabbles and alleged embellishments of teaching which had already divided the original organization in two. It is now in a sense the most conservative of the lodges, for its theme has ever been loyalty to the theosophy of Blavatsky herself and of William Q. Judge, an early American disciple, and not to any of the later apostles of the movement.

But almost sixty years after its founding, the U.L.T. did not give an impression of a dynamic reform movement. The great hall was peopled with only a pathetic sprinkling of listeners, mostly elderly. The decor, the clientele, the strictly intellectual lecture hall format all suggested something from the Chatauqua rather than the "hip" epoch in American life. If the medium is the message, I asked myself, what story is told by this puritan-plain hall, these neat old people, this communication by heavy books and high-minded lectures?

A few weeks later, I went to the Wilshire-Ebell Theater to hear the Maharishi Mahesh, then at his popular height, address an overflowing crowd of enthusiasts in paisley shirts, beads, long hair, and bare feet, and to see the Maharishi himself with his hair and beard knotted like old vines, his cherubic smile, his spectacular white robe, and tiger skin pallet. Sixty years ago, the greats of Theosophy like Annie Besant and Katherine Tingley commanded similar crowds and headlines, lecturing in the then-current style between bunches of flowers in water-filled bowls.

The speaker at the U.L.T. was also a son of India. But unlike the vivid Maharishi he was dressed in a dark business suit, white shirt, and dark tie. He was clean-shaven and his hair was neatly cut. He was, I later learned, a professor at the University of California in Santa Barbara. So careful is the U.L.T. to avoid the alleged personality cults of other Theosophical organizations that the names of speakers are never given in announcements. The lecture I heard was on "Cyclic Evolution and Karma." It was a most competent exposition of the doctrine of karma in philosophical Hinduism, without—a little to my disappointment, I am afraid—any allusion to the more exotic beliefs ascribed to Theosophy, such as the trans-Himalayan "Masters" and the "precipitation" of letters from them.

I had come, I confessed to myself a little sheepishly as I left, ears tingling to hear of occult initiations and bizarre signs. I stayed not indeed to pray, but to marvel that the ambiance of a simple style and high thinking worthy of the New England of Emerson should reappear under such unlikely auspices. The doctrine was, to be sure, not a particularly warm gospel. I felt slightly oppressed by the contemplation of almost countless aeons of progress by the soul through life after life, cycle after cycle, on world after world, goaded by the inflexible cause and effect of moral and spiritual karma, until it finally reaches its eternal home in reunion with the divine ground. The rationalism, the cool infinity of space and time in which this drama was laid no less than its monistic soil, the avoidance of devotional fervor, hinted at an odd alliance of the enlightenment and India.

Later I had the opportunity to visit a number of other new religious groups in the southern California area. The exploration of this scene became almost an avocation. At the suggestion of a colleague, I turned a hobby into a professional matter by starting a course named "New Religious and Philosophical Movements in Southern California." Preparation for it led to more systematic investigation and cataloging of such groups. This research in southern California is the foundation of the present book, although attention has also been given to historical and national aspects of the field.

More and more, in the course of preparation of this study, the conviction has grown that the contemporary American religions of the "cult" type are more than mere curiosities or byways of spirituality. They are of major importance to the phenomenology of religion since they represent in America one of its principle types, the faith based directly on mystical or shamanistic experiences, and the kind of world view that goes with that foundation. They represent a religious style which Max Weber saw as based on an "exemplary" rather than an "emissary" or "ethical" charisma. The "exemplary" prophet is filled up from within with a divine fullness because he is in perfect harmony with the cosmos, having been successful in a great quest in which he has subdued all demons, all corners of the unconscious. He is fundamentally in search of the Platonic source of religion, wonder, rather than the envoy of a sure, burning message he must deliver. Plato, the source of that great tradition which leads to Western mysticism and Theosophy, and indirectly to the "journey to the East," made wonder and amazement, not conceptual revelation, the root of the love of wisdom: "Yes, Socrates,' said Theatetus, 'and I am amazed when I think of them [i.e., of the significances of things], by the gods, I am, and I want to know what on earth they mean, and there are times when my head swims with the contemplation of them!' "

The resoundingly vast cosmos of the Theosophical lecturer worked by its infinite number of fine karmic springs comes out of this kind of consciousness because he senses the cosmos to be continuous with his own intellect in the mood of deep illumined wisdom: unlimited, unbroken, wondrous, yet subject to subtle law. The Maharishi's spirituality too, in which the mind is allowed to go to "the place of greatest joy" at the depths of its being in "transcendental meditation," is eminently of this type. The more usual Western style, the "emissary," has made central the charismatic individual as bearer or receiver of a *message* from God for repentence, obedience, or social reform.

In the East, the "exemplary" style prevails, and wisdom is the final inner goal of the spiritual path. This was the goal of the highest spirituality of our primitive ancestors and of all peoples outside of historical consciousness. In the West, it has not been without witness. But it has usually been a minority voice, almost a subversive voice, in a cultural history dominated by the message and its deliverers, whether prophet, preacher, or professor. In the process, the ideal of the harmony of man, his mind, and his cosmos has been subordinated to dualisms: God versus man, mind versus body, man versus nature, contemplation versus social duty. In the same way the message and the message giver, except for Christ, have been different things. The message giver learned his message by listening, or study, or analysis, not so much by intuition, participation, and mystical identification.

The ideal of powerful cosmic harmony attained by interior illuminative breakthrough born of wonder was well known in antiquity by gnostics, neoplatonists, and mystery teachers. It was heard again in the mouths of Renaissance savants and kabbalists like Ficino, Mirandola, Agrippa, and Paracelsus, before it was fairly drowned out by the voices of the Reformation and modern science and technology. Occasionally the cosmic wonder tradition has emerged again, always in new guise, whether in New England transcendentalism or in the strange tales through the centuries of European fellowships of Rosicrucians and Illuminati.

The modern American cults are not its only voice today, nor are they dominated by minds of the caliber of those cited here. Yet they do embody a full-blown *religious* expression of this alternative vehicle of spiritual reality. In this respect they are of symbolic if not numerical importance. This is true whether we are speaking of a cult which is an import from the Orient, or one of the "occult" type, which usually means the Hellenistic-Renaissance line of neoplatonism, hermeticism, and kabbalism. Like Spiritualism and UFO cults, they display the richly peopled supernatural world of the old shaman in modern dress.

The United Lodge of Theosophists, with its lecture hall format, reminds us that the cults have not avoided compromise with Western styles which really grew out of a different view of religious communication. This was inevitable, though it is now changing, as in the case of the Maharishi. Yet collectively these groups stand for another kind of religion than that known to the main Western traditions, and in this they have behind them a great part of the humanity which has walked on this planet.

The study of cult groups is important for what it shows us of religious typology. It enables us to see that there are two basic types of religions: those grounded in cosmic wonder and communicated by the exemplary personalities, and those grounded in revelation within history and emissary communication. Such a study also provides opportunity for isolating many subtypes and combinations. It allows a laboratory experience in religious dynamics. The birth and childhood crises of each cult is a reenactment of the origin of every religion. Once again we see the role of the revelation, the founder, the disciple, the called band of believers, unveiled in human flesh and form. We see the hurdle of transition to the second generation met and either failed or passed.

Nor can these tableaux be gazed upon as remote, as though taking place on another world and observable only through a telescope. Few readers can be unaware that the America in which these events are transpiring is in the midst of a profound spiritual crisis in which the struggle of these two concepts of the meaning of religion is a deep theme. The cult scene, especially in the youth culture, is important because it is a barometer of changes in the psychology of significant segments of society. We sense a new spiritual type emerging in contemporary America. The new spiritual man is more like the kind of person we have heretofore associated with the East—or with cultists. He presumes without question that God or spiritual reality, if it is to be found, is to be found within through expanded states of consciousness which penetrate like searchlights toward the deep floor of being. Interior exploration is his main concern. He is suspicious of words and verbal communication. He is disenchanted with sermons, lectures, and disquisitions, but is highly sensitive to nonverbal communication and the lessons of meditation. He is susceptible to the exemplary person, one who by subtle, often nonverbal means shows he is "turned on" and is able to "turn on" others just by the radiance of his presence. The new spiritual man's social concern is for an organic, ecological harmony of humankind with the cosmos in subtle interaction. His moral values center around openness, sincerity, and love.

Not all persons with these kinds of feelings choose to express them by joining a cult. Some are able to find scope for them in the normative religious institutions, others just by themselves or in *ad hoc* groups. The visible cults are only the top of the iceberg. But in a culture as obviously fragmented and rapidly changing as ours, it is meaningless to regard the cultists simply as hopelessly alienated "oddballs," as one might consider nonconformists in a more stable and integrated culture. In the present situation, not knowing what the pattern of the future will be except that it will be immensely different from the past or present, we cannot afford to discount any cult. We cannot be sure what is "just a cult," and what may be, even if in wildly grotesque fetal shape, a harbinger of the mystic future. The cults are tokens of what we feel in the air, a new Hellenistic era, in which all is changing, all in flux, all is protean in the world of the spirit.

It is hoped this book will provide a panoramic view of this world, at least insofar as it has concretized itself in groups which are definitely religious cults. (Of course a number of very important things are happening in other fields of social and spiritual creativity: communes, new kinds of art, the new politics, etc.)

This book is not intended to be a work in sociology or cultural anthropology of the more technical sort. The writer is trained in the history of religions rather than in these fields, and begs the forgiveness of specialists in these and other areas for failure to deal with all the questions they would ask.

Rather than a social science study, this book is intended to be a quest for *verstehen*, understanding from within, of the spiritual experience of each group. It tries to detect it through appropriate clues in group history, structure, and symbol. But ultimately any such quest, the writer believes, involves a more intuitive than analytic appreciation of the social, practical, and ideological matrix out of which spiritual experience is born. I believe a survey of this kind is valuable (1) as an exercise in comparative religion, since half the religious world and its history may be represented *in parvo* in the American cult world; (2) as an indicator of directions of change; and (3) as a confrontation with certain little-understood types of religious personality and dynamics.

If this book provides the reader with information that will help him in assessing the meaning of contemporary cults for himself and with some sense of participation in the enjoyment and excitement with which I have explored this world, it will have served its purpose.

Acknowledgments

I would like to express my deep gratitude to the many persons and institutions whose assistance has made this book possible:

To my wife Gracia-Fay for much initial encouragement and many valuable suggestions; to my colleague Professor Gerald A. Larue for suggesting that I explore the area covered by this book as a field for study and teaching; to the publishers, institutions, and individuals, too numerous to list here by name, who have kindly given permission for the use of material quoted or presented as Reading Selections.

Above all, I would like to thank the great number of men and women associated with the groups discussed in this book who generously devoted hours of time in talking with me. Invariably, I have found these people courteous, appreciative of my interest, open, and helpful. I alone am responsible for the contents of this book. In a few cases members of groups discussed may find reason to regret wording or emphases I have chosen. I sincerely hope, however, that most readers who are affiliated with one of the groups discussed will feel that the tone of my effort reflects the gratitude I feel for the wonderful conversations and experiences my time with them has given me, and for the hours of time they have sacrificed.

R.S.E.

RELIGIOUS and SPIRITUAL GROUPS in MODERN AMERICA

one

in quest of new religions

1. The Scope of the Book

Dr. Krister Stendahl, Dean of the Harvard University Divinity School, once suggested that a new "world theology" may be in the making from the "shambles" of modern Christian theology. In contrast to the past tendency to ask what the traditional church or biblical teaching is, he says, "We come to a point where theologians have started to become much more bold, expressing 'straight' theology out of religious experience, rather than the historical approach. This will lead to where contemporary religious experience will be allowed once again to inform theology. Ultimately it will bring us to give much more serious attention to other religious experiences than Christianity alone." This does not mean, Dr. Stendahl explained, that distinctively Christian truth will be lost, but that religious truth will be sought wherever it may be found. "Truth cannot take adjectives. There cannot be a Methodist truth, or a Lutheran truth or a Catholic truth. There can be only—truth."[1]

If this is the case, where do we find these "other religious experiences"? It is not necessary to make Herman Hesse's paradigmatic *Journey to the East* by literally travelling to India or Japan. Nor need we content ourselves with the highly vicarious experience of reading.

We have, in America, a subculture which has long lived to taste these exotic spiritual experiences. Indeed, it has not satisfied itself just with reproducing more or less successfully export versions of the great non-Western faiths. It has also given birth to religious expressions otherwise not known that may also cast a light on some facet of nonadjectival truth.

1

Our quest in this book will be to investigate many of these religious movements. Sometimes it may be a tour no less strange than the exploration of another planet or a fairyland from out of the mists of childhood memory. But it is also a tour which requires all the discipline of social analysis one can bring to it. This is necessary to see not simply a reflection of one's own fantasy in a movement, but also what it is in itself— why it arose where and when it did, how it works, what sort of people are attracted to it. Only by recreating in this way the world of the movement can we really comprehend what it is in itself, and thus get outside of ourselves and into it for the sake of understanding.

Yet this task simultaneously requires sympathetic human empathy. We need that peculiar, almost indefinable quality which enables one individual to have a flash of insight into what it would *really* feel like to be someone else. We need to be able to make a jump from seeing a member of a cult as an intriguing human-sized object "out there" with certain bizarre beliefs and behavior, to saying, "He has the same feelings inside as I do—though he's looking at things with a different pair of spectacles, he could be me and I could be him. By learning about where he is, I'm not just expanding myself intellectually, I'm expanding my *humanness*—my ideas, my feelings, my life style, everything." If we cannot perceive in this way what total human experience, and so what human truth, lies inside a cultic experience, how can we contribute to the quest for nonadjectival truth? The question to ask is always, "How would it feel from within to be a part of this religious movement?"

What is a religious movement? To many, the term calls up the image of an unusual wild-eyed individual in the mountains or desert hearing the voice of some new god, and then returning to the city and shouting that it is the divine will that people wear only one shoe or build a temple of pure isinglass. Vast crowds become so possessed as to return the seer's fervor with mob enthusiasm and money.

To others, a religious movement may suggest activity within the institutional religious tradition: the effect of a popular evangelist, the splintering of denominations. On the other hand, there are those who speak of political causes like Fascism and Communism as "religious" in some very important sense.

In this book we will be looking at a number of groups which fall into a certain category. They may be called *new, not normatively Judaeo-Christian, religious movements in America.* The borderlines of any such definition are inevitably hazy. It may help to make a brief preliminary examination of the terms used.

New means groups which have arisen or taken root in America within the last 150 years and are extant today. This time span, going back to the early nineteenth century, may seem overly long. But it is necessary to include in our general purview the beginnings of Swedenborgianism —actually eighteenth century—Spiritualism, New Thought, and Theosophy. These movements have all had continuing interaction to the present day with the cultural milieu of the type of groups we are studying. All are still of some importance today. Groups which have arisen only in the last century and a half, of course, are very "new" in comparison with Judaism and Christianity, even though major American demoninations and schools of both are no less recent.

Not normatively Judaeo-Christian means that the group's central symbols or teachings are not directly derived from mainstream interpretations of Jewish or Christian sources. They obviously have a different focus from the Bible, the creeds, and what is considered normal in the church or synagogue down the street. Some of the groups consider themselves Christian according to their own lights. They may claim, as Spiritualists do, that the Bible verifies their views. But here we are mainly concerned with the similarity or dissimilarity of the central teaching (and spiritual experience) which called a group into being to that of the synagogues and churches in the group's actual setting.

The purpose is not to cast doubt on any group's right to the use of Christian or any other term, but to set up categories for comparison. In the case of Spiritualism, for example, the central *raison d'être,* the practice of communication with the spirits of the departed through a medium and belief in the importance of this practice, is obviously at great variance with the Christianity and Judaism found elsewhere. In the same way, even the most Christian-oriented groups in the Theosophical and occult traditions, such as Anthroposophy and the Liberal Catholic Church, seem better understood as a part of an alternative to the ordinary Judaeo-Christian tradition than as a part of that tradition.

The principal test for determining whether a group is not normatively Judaeo-Christian will be the historical continuity of its central teaching and experience with the Judaeo-Christian religion of its actual American setting. Similarity in worship format, symbolism, or type of organization to other American religion will not, however, exclude a group from our study. There is much variation in these matters in groups with non-normative teaching. In some New Thought churches, like the Church of Religious Science, the structure of Sunday morning worship is barely distinguishable from that of any liberal Protestant church. But the teaching, coming down as it does to a "mind is all" philosophical idealism, is really not very dissimilar from that of the Maharishi Mahesh Yogi, the colorful Hindu guru whose involvement with the Beatles and other entertainment figures a few years ago led to considerable publicity for his movement. The Maharishi's cultus, with the offering of fruit and flowers to the teacher, the guru's tiger skin pallet, and secret initiation and silent meditation of adherents, is wildly different from the ambiance of Religious Science. Obviously, followers of Religious Science prefer, in their new teaching, to experience general symbols of continuity with the worship and organization of the churches of their forefathers. In fact, the victory of those with such a preference was an important milestone in the history of that denomination. The generally younger and more "alienated" adherents of the Maharishi's movement clearly want to express their profounder dissatisfaction with much of the whole Western religious tradition by rejoicing in an atmosphere of exoticism.

We thus determine whether a group is or is not normatively Judaeo-Christian by comparing its "reason for being" teaching with "ordinary usage" meanings of "Judaism and Christianity." We ask whether it expresses continuity or discontinuity with its cultural setting. This means asking such questions as, "Does it have a clear lineage in denominational history?" "If most churches emphasize salvationist doctrine and experience, does it emphasize something else?"

A *religion* means a group centrally concerned with "the means of ultimate transformation," which has simultaneous expression in three areas: *theoretical* or *verbal* (myth and doctrine); *practical* or *worship* (ritual, cultus, and other special behavior); and *sociological* (a structure of interpersonal action which enables a continuing group life).

The terms of this definition will be discussed later. It is a definition not so much concerned with the *kind* of teaching or practice of the group (whether about God or not, whether ritualistic or not) as with the *value* and *goal* of the teaching or practice. Does the idea seem to be to work toward an unqualified transformation of oneself and/or society and the cosmos into a final and perfect state in line with the nature of absolute reality? Does one experience in the teaching and practice of the group *means* to accomplish this change? Or is it thought of as just a moderate reform movement, or as interesting and entertaining ideas and activities?

A religion is not just a teaching, like the philosophy of Plato. It produces a corporate expression. In a religion persons are regularly in contact with each other to study, discuss, celebrate, and practice the teaching; these people would presumably not otherwise associate. Probably the group of persons brought together around the teaching—or more precisely, no doubt, around the teacher—come to have some sort of structured interaction. They develop patterns for calling meetings, making decisions, and determining whose words are most weighty.

A real religion—a "means of ultimate transformation"—always takes this kind of social expression. It always manifests a verbal, a worship, and a societal vehicle. It is never just an idea or an inchoate assembly. If it is genuinely concerned with the *ultimate,* it seems to require vehicles for expression in all these areas. Their presence or absence, then, is a good test (and one employed in this book) of whether a group is really a "religion" or not. One can quibble about what is or is not a religion. Some groups included here do not care to be called religions, associating that word with some other definition than the one we have employed. But it has been necessary to establish a yardstick and apply it impartially.

Almost all the groups treated here are also cults. *Cult* is of course a subcategory of religion. We will speak of it as a group derived from the experience of one or a few individuals who are able to enter (or are fascinated by the possibility of entering) a superior, ecstatic state of consciousness in which contact and rapport with all reaches of a non-historical and impersonal universe are possible with the help of inter-mediaries. And in a cult, an outer circle of members experience the presence of the sacred in these individuals, and seek to participate in their experience. Because these premises are widely deviant from those of normative Judaism and Christianity in America, the scope of the definition seems to be practically coextensive with that covered by the somewhat more negative definition above, *new non-Judaeo–Christian religions*.

2. Means of Ultimate Transformation

In order to have a clear idea of what kind of general phenomena we are dealing with, it may be helpful to digress a moment to further discuss our understanding of the nature of religion. In this section we will also look at some dynamics of religious change relevant to understanding new movements today against their background in the nature of religion.

We have indicated that some political movements, like Fascism and Communism, have been spoken of as "religious," and that religion is defined as a "means of ultimate transformation." If this is the case, it is evident that no particular metaphysical idea, such as the existence of a heavenly god, is necessarily involved in the definition. We in the West tend to forget that there are vast numbers of persons in the world who observe practices involving temples, altars, priests, offerings, scriptures, meditation, and festivals which in all respects look like religion, yet do not make a personal God central. I speak of most Buddhists, many Hindus, and many followers of the Chinese religions. A definition of religion which said it necessarily had to do with God or gods would seem very odd in these cultures. But religion does have to do with some-thing which wants to come out simultaneously in the three forms of expression we mentioned. It has to do with something which impels people to relate certain stories, perform certain stylized actions which would seem quite odd in any other context, and organize themselves into certain groups. This approach on the basis of what looks like religion, judged by similarity to universal patterns, after observing simply the "forms that appear," is called the phenomenological.

Some groups object to being called religions because to them the word implies that they accept their beliefs on authoritarian grounds, rather than out of rational philosophical reflection. Yet this too is a matter which varies greatly in different cultures, despite the consistent appearance of what looks like religion. Our definition is concerned not so much with the basis of the authority of the teaching as with what is done with it—how it is symbolized, how it is acted out, how ultimate its position is, what type of group forms around it.

It seems that religion first of all implies a distinction between two kinds of activity: the ordinary, which we do because we must and look forward to its end; and the special, in which we are joyous and fulfilled in a condition which seems complete and sufficient in itself. An anthropologist once asked an African tribe what they did. They said, "We work and we dance. But we work in order that we can dance." Undoubtedly dancing exhausts as much energy as working. But it *feels* different. Dancing is not drudgery; it creates a glorious, ecstatic, timeless mood.

Mircea Eliade and others have spoken of these two poles of activity as the sacred and the profane.[2] The sacred indicates place, time, or state of consciousness in which a person feels as totally real and sufficient as he conceives the gods were at the beginning. In this condition he wishes to dwell, but it is hard to bear, and he cannot stay in it all the time. There is also a frightening dimension to the sacred; it may reach out to slay those who presume too much upon it. And one must save time to do the work of the world. The profane is the opposite of the sacred. It is the common everyday world with its dull, continuing sense of enervating meaninglessness.

Religion involves the experience of space, time, or aspects of self as polarized by the sacred and profane. This makes the world of religious man nonhomogeneous. Religion is the process by which man tries to express in symbol, story, and experience this polarized quality of his life and to make as much of it as possible sacred. He builds temples as sacred centers, celebrates festivals which recapitulate sacred time, and endeavors to achieve ultimate identification with the sacred by internalizing it within himself through mysticism.

Frederick Streng proposed "means of ultimate transformation" as a definition of religion which adds an element of dynamism to the sacred and the profane.[3] It is also reminiscent of Paul Tillich's "ultimate concern," of reflection on the deepest questions of meaning one can ask, as the ground of religion. But religion is not just individual musing, or even passionate existential commitment. It is intended to do something.

The Buddhists speak of their faith as *yana,* a ferryboat. It is intended to carry believers from here to the farther shore where the Buddha himself went. That "shore" is not, of course, a geographical place, but a totally transformed state of consciousness as infinite and unconditioned as our present consciousness is limited by our being able to think of only one thing at a time. The journey on the *yana* is thus a radical reversal, an ultimate transformation of man's present state. The "ferry" by this definition is a religion.

The means Buddhism uses are a set of stories the believer hears (about the Buddha and his saints—verbal expression); a set of actions he performs (meditation practices, the cultus of the Buddhist temple—worship expression); and a set of persons he groups himself with (a Buddhist order or denomination—social expression). By these means he builds around himself a sacred world, a world in which everything is conducive to the journey toward ultimate transformation, and operates like a foretaste of it. He puts himself into the middle of that sacred world.

Religion is a set of symbols, words, acts, and social groupings which have this thrust toward *ultimate,* unconditioned transformation of self and/or world. It does not aim for mere reforms, though these may be part of the path, but for a total, exhaustive change which leaves not the slightest margin for more. Religion is the means of movement between the two poles, the conditioned and profane and the ultimate or sacred or unconditioned. It is the individual's attempt to create in and around himself the sacred.

Depending upon the world view of the culture, the individual immerses himself in the sacred in many ways. For those primitive and archaic cultures whose outlook is what is called "cosmic religion," the occurrence of the sacred is associated with the turning of the seasons. The harvest and new year festivals, thought of as times when the world turns back again to its beginning, when the gods are near and the dead return, is the pivotal point for the breakthrough to the sacred. The proximity of the gods, the return of the dead, the joy of harvest—all these suggest radical reversal of the ordinary conditions of death-limited life, of the anxiety of agriculture, and of estrangement from the joy of creation, and hint at ultimate transformation for a brief season. We retain remnents of this mood in Halloween and Christmas. It is as though the turning of the year opens up a momentary crack through which eternity can shine.

After the discovery of agriculture, probably the most significant event in man's spiritual development was the discovery of the historical nature of time. Man discovered that time not only moves around the same course year after year, but also has an irreversible linear direction. He began to realize that things change and do not change back; he could not tell what was coming next. This realization was arrived at only very gradually, and was at first heavily veiled in myth and symbol. Something in man is terrified of the inflexibility and irreversibility of time and seeks to deny it. Yet sooner or later the realization comes. We learn that time does not really begin and end with each year. New things happen, new human discoveries are made of things never known before.

The discovery of historical time creates a crisis for religion. Religion is intended to create an experience of the sacred. Yet very often the forms of religion do not actually do this for many people, and ostensibly nonreligious situations may actually do it better. At best religious forms only teach good morals and sanctify the social order—they provide no special ecstasy. This is partly because religion, as ultimate custodian of the experience of total joy, must in practice perform two functions: (1) to make ecstasy available, and (2) to conserve the social order so that lives of nothing but ecstasy do not tear society apart and destroy everything for everyone. For this reason, religion restricts ecstasy to certain times and places or persons, hedges it about with ethical and moral conditions, and associates images grounded in the ecstasy with the duller parts of social life—political order, work, and duty—to give an alleviating aura of the sacred to the ordinary. When these two functions of religion are both genuinely felt and are in balance, there is a stable and integrated society. But if a religion gets too far from its source, if it seems to have only constraints to offer and no joy, then it is in trouble. Competitors will arise, probably seeming at first to be unbalanced toward ecstasy.

The rise of the world religions—Zoroastrianism, Buddhism, Confucianism, Taoism, Christianity, Islam—must be seen against the background of the discovery of the historical nature of time. They are at once the result of the discovery of historical time—they stem from unique and dateable persons—and they are struggles to deny or control the absolute reality of that historical time. In these religions, the sacred becomes localized at a point in the historical stream which gives history a center. This point unveils once and for all what was formerly thought to turn open once a year—the gateway to eternity. Because history becomes a vortex rather than a stream, its absolute terror, its quality as the absolute profane, is denied. The center is probably the founder and his work, or else the final consummation of which he tells. Through the center time is finally defeated.

Emphasis on the final consummation, rather than on a more interior kind of salvation through identification with the past founder, is typical of times of social stress and rapid change. In our own day, we have seen examples of this kind of teaching in the so-called Cargo Cults among colonial peoples. In America, UFO cults have stated almost exactly the same scenario in more technological language. The talk of the coming Aquarian Age illustrates the same placing of a trans-historical absolute in the future.

To illustrate, here is a typical Cargo Cult story. A myth in the East Indies had it that the hero Mansren would return to bring in the Golden Age. To do so, he would plant a tree which would touch the sky; then the tree would lean toward the island which was Mansren's birthplace. A marvellous child named Konor would run up its trunk. Then the aged would find youth again, the sick health, and the dead would return to life. The arrival of this *puer aeternus* would in fact reverse the whole order of creation. Underground crops like yams, potatoes, and roots would grow on trees; coconuts and fruits would grow underground.[4] All this indicates a total reversal and renewal of creation, an ultimate transformation. Mansren was said now to be living in Java, Singapore, or even Holland.

Many other Cargo Cult prophets, influenced by missionaries, predicted that Jesus would return on board the cargo ships of the white man, or even identified themselves with him. It was a common theme that God and Jesus were really natives, or on the side of the natives, but that the white men had deceivingly kept this fact from their native wards, and had also kept from them quantities of goods brought on the great cargo ships. But God, in a radical reversal of the usurperous state of affairs, was about to change all this. In preparation for the great event, present conventional modes of life, the prophets said, and indeed all traditional native society, being of the old order, must be destroyed. In many cases all household goods were thrown away or put out on the road, all work was stopped, nudism was practiced; everyone worked up to a frenzy of expectation.

In more sophisticated circles, philosophies like those of Hegel and Nietzsche and Teilhard de Chardin, not to mention Marx, promise the same final defeat of the terror of history. They indicate that history is not meaningless but an evolution, a rope, leading to the revelation of pure absolute spirit, or the "true man," at the end of time. We see in all of them a striving for ultimate transformation, for a reversal of the historically conditioned state.

In this case, the *means* indicated may be called religion. One can speak of *means* when the process is in part accessible to human control or response. Evolution as a purely naturalistic force is indifferent to man, and is not religion. But we may speak of submission to evolution as a *means* of transforming one's life from something separate and ephemeral to something meaningful, a part of a great process. Or we may say, as have Julian Huxley and Teilhard, that through our scientific and spiritual lives we can begin to guide the course of evolution and make it into a *means* to transform the human state into a paradisical condition. In both cases, we would be speaking religiously. We would be saying things parallel to what mystics and prophets of the past have said in the language of their symbols.

New religious movements usually originate in periods of great social stress, frustration, or transition. They employ symbols from the prevailing culture, but the symbols are radically rearranged. Symbols—the word is used very broadly to include language, art forms, subjective experience with special meaning, and so forth—are scrambled into new constellations. Perhaps formerly nonreligious symbols—political, technological—will be discovered to have religious meaning, while formerly religious symbols will have lost it. Symbols imported from elsewhere will be discovered to have meaning within the culture. In any case, the use of symbols in the new movement will not be the established usage, since the intention is to express alienation. But the symbols do not spell out the social situation, or the alienation, in a one-to-one way; as soon as they are "released" they acquire a life of their own.

Usually a new movement has a single individual who actually or symbolically sums up in himself and his gestures its meaning—like Madame Blavatsky of Theosophy,[5] Bapak of Subud, or UFO contactees. The founder expresses the rearranged symbol system and "style" in his personality. Like the symbols, the founder is not one utterly different from his culture, as though descended from an angelic sphere. He is a man or woman who lives in the context of his time and place, and may well wear more conventional clothes than traditional religious leaders. (The latter also have to serve as symbols of continuity with earlier cultural eras.) Religious founders and leaders are those who call into conscious expression the deepest latent spiritual intuitions of which their hearers are potentially conscious and can understand. This evocation is possible only because a commonality of experience exists between the founder and his audience. This common experience seems to take into account areas of life as it is now actually lived which the traditional religion leaves out. The way is open for a word which will crystallize a new pattern, a new religious gestalt.

To invent totally new religious notions, to fit new pieces into the puzzle, is usually precisely what is not very successful. The founder is one who can reintegrate a cosmos which is shattered, which already holds too many extra notional and experiential fragments. His genius is to see the possibility of a new pattern which will give integrated value to everything which now has independent value—not merely by rearrangement but by opening a window which casts new, and now harmonious, patterns. A new principle, a different focus, is drawn, but in a way which leads men to say, "This was really true all the time, but we did not realize it." An example is Mary Baker Eddy, who devised in

Christian Science a tightly integrated system from pieces of transcendentalism, the Calvinist struggle of light against darkness, and the prestige of science. She had that sort of impact on some of her contemporaries. Christian Science provided, as do all religions, a new means of ultimate transformation.

Saying that once the new symbol is released it acquires a life of its own is not saying that the structural form it takes is entirely unpredictable. There are really only a few basic religious symbols which appear over and over again in many forms. In the center will be the main means of ultimate transformation, hedged about with appropriate signs of special numinosity. One may find an *axis mundi* (central pivot of the world), like the palm tree in the Mansren myth, or the cross in Christianity, or the bodhi tree under which the Buddha found enlightenment in Buddhism. Behind it, as in these cases, may be the even more powerful symbol of the individual who has attained ultimate transformation and bears it to others. Further common symbols are waters of rebirth, an initiating female, the wise old man, the moon as token of regeneration.

The religious group provides foretastes of ultimate transformation as a part of the means to attain it. The group will demarcate sacred time and space as occasions and places where the winds of the ultimate are felt most strongly—in all likelihood, places and times of worship or gathering. In some cases these experiences may be highly individualized. The means of transformation—the *axis mundi*, the sacred space and time—is within the individual's heart. So it is with groups stressing mental transformation, like Christian Science, or those centered on yoga or meditation. But even so, such symbols as it has, or even the very absence of symbol considered as a symbol, is a corporate support of the internalization process.

The new symbol system—the new cosmic constellation of meaning orbiting around the founder and the group—will probably be both external and internal, though the "outer" or "inner" may be stressed. Neither is absolute. One may be given an actual sacred center (mountain or temple), or a metaphorical–internalized one, or both. The symbol system begins by expressing the individual discovery of alienation and goes on to articulate its own cosmos centered on the new means of ultimate transformation. It then winnows out the absolute nature of reality implied by those means.

3. Shamanism

One of the most important religious phenomena is *shamanism*. It is essential to give this phenomenon particular attention when examining aspects of religion relevant to understanding the dynamic of new religious movements. In certain important ways the genius of the primitive shaman is reborn in those individuals, called magi, adepts, masters, mediums, or magicians, or by no such special name, who have been the centers of cults. The example of an illumined and empowered magus offering individual initiation into his mysteries is no new thing, but has roots far back toward the dawn of religion. In many archaic societies, alongside the regular means of initiation of young boys and girls into the sacral matters of adulthood, a few individuals may receive special admission into unusual practices connected with the sacred. They will be those who become shamans.

G. K. Nelson has suggested that, of all religious institutions, the one which most resembles modern spiritualism is primitive shamanism.[6] It has striking parallels not only to spiritualism, but also to all the groups under consideration in this study. The cult phenomena could almost be called a modern resurgence of shamanism. It is important, therefore, that we examine some of its characteristics.

Many kinds of religious specialists inhabit the world of primitive society—priests who offer sacrifices, heads of households who perform the family cultus, old men who supervise initiations, sorcerors who cast spells for luck or love, witches who curse, medicine men who heal the sick by natural or supernatural means, sacred kings, and so forth. In the midst of them may be a person who, having probably passed through a severe emotional ordeal, now communicates with gods or spirits by ecstatic means—he is called a shaman.

Not all of these vocations, of course, are necessarily found in all primitive societies. There may also be considerable overlap. The religious life of primitive man is a vast welter of little things which do not easily lend themselves to idealized structural concepts. Clifford Geertz writes that primitive and archaic religions

> consist of a multitude of very concretely defined and only loosely ordered sacred entities, an untidy collection of fussy ritual acts and vivid animistic images which are able to involve themselves in an independent, segmental, and immediate manner with almost any sort of actual event.[7]

This may be as true of role as of rite and symbol. Eliade has pointed out that

> the shaman is also a magician and medicine man; he is believed to cure, like all doctors, and to perform miracles of the fakir type, like all magicians, whether primitive or modern. But beyond this, he is a psychopomp, and he may also be priest, mystic, and poet.[8]

Although healing may not be the main function of the shaman in all societies, and the mere acquisition of healing powers may not exhaust the shaman's spiritual quest, yet broadly interpreted healing is probably the ostensible purpose of the majority of shamanistic seances—and of many spiritualist seances. In both cases, even though many may actually be more interested in the ecstatic or psychic phenomena which attend the affair, it is not considered good form to desire that for its own sake; one must have a proper reason for calling upon the supernatural, such as desire for a cure. Thus G. K. Nelson, continuing on shamanism and spiritualism, is not amiss to write:

> The shaman is a medicine man whose prime function seems to be the cure or causing of disease. In order to carry out this function he must communicate with the spirits, either the spirits of the dead or nature spirits, although in some cases there are other reasons for communicating with the dead. Communication with the spirits is often carried out under conditions that closely resemble those at a Western spiritualist seance. The shaman goes into a trance state, usually in a dark hut, and produces spirit voices and sometimes physical phenomena.
>
> Shamans are mediumistic persons, often of an unstable type, who are chosen solely because of their peculiar gifts, although there are doubtlessly fake shamans as well as fake mediums, and probably more of them, for shamanism is a source of social prestige in many primitive societies.[9]

The definition of shamanism varies considerably among students as they endeavor to fasten labels to this confused and changing background. Naturally, whether the shaman is looked at in terms of his psychological, functional, or mythological role will determine the nature of the definition. Some see no significant difference between the shaman and the healer, who together with a stock of medicines uses the aid of trance and attendant spirits to extract the evil power causing illness or to catch and restore the patient's soul. Most would perhaps agree, however, that while most shamans may function as medicine men, not all medicine men are shamans, for the latter also have have special qualities of vocation, mystical experience, and technique unshared by mere craftsmen of healing.

Mircea Eliade believes that the word *shaman* should be limited to those who are masters of techniques of ecstasy. "A first definition of this complex phenomenon, and perhaps the least hazardous, will be: shamanism = *technique of ecstasy*."[10] Even so, not any ecstatic is a shaman; the shaman specializes in a trance during which his soul is believed to leave his body and ascend to the sky or descend to the underworld. Moreover, a shaman is different from a "possessed" person in that the shaman controls his spirits without becoming their instrument.[11]

Eliade writes, "The shaman begins his new, his true life by a 'separation'—that is...by a spiritual crisis that is not lacking in tragic greatness and in beauty."[12] The shaman typically passes through an initiatory psychopathy. It will probably begin with a "call" from a god or spirit, perhaps the primordial master shaman, communicated by a seizure, an involuntary trance, dreams, or visions. Thereafter the novice is disturbed by these things until he controls them by acquiring the techniques of shamanizing. This means, as Eliade points out, that the process is not a happenstance matter but follows a traditional model in the culture. There is "no question of anarchical hallucinations and of a purely individual plot and dramatis personae."[13]

Generally the candidate will be guided by a senior shaman. He will go through a crisis, a death and rebirth experience, a capture of the spirits who have been tormenting him. He will acquire the traditional shamanic techniques, names of spirits, mythology, and secret language. Sometimes a public ritual is involved, but the initiation and part of the instruction may just as well be given directly by spirits in dreams.[14]

Lommel has described the process in this way:

> The future shaman, the young man suited for shamanizing, is a sick man. He suffers from psychopathic or epileptic states and is very often also physically ill. He cannot escape the demands of the spirits, which drive him deeper and deeper into the illness, although he very often tries to resist. He gets into a situation, into a mental illness, from which he can find no way out but death or the assumption of the office of shaman.
>
> Part of the shaman's activity consists in the trance. During initiation and during artistic creation the essential thing for the shaman is a displacement of the plane of consciousness. Clear consciousness is eliminated. Images are activitated on another plane of consciousness. These images are always taken from the world view, mythology, and religion of the tribe or culture in question. But instead of these images being given form in a conscious state, this takes place in an unconscious or subconsciousness state. The shaman sings, dances, mimes—he may even paint and draw in a trance, from which he then awakes. Once awake he often no longer remembers, or remembers only dimly, his actions while in the trance. If the calling to be a shaman may be described as a kind of self-cure of a prolonged psychosis, "shamanizing" consists in a repetition of this healing process.[15]

Recent anthropological work has brought to light the importance of hallucinogenic plants in creating these states of consciousness in the shamanism of many cultures.[16]

What does the shaman do after initiation? The shaman is prepared by his ecstatic gifts to be the bearer of communication between individuals or the community and the gods. For example, among the Altaic peoples of Siberia, the shaman, beating a drum to induce ecstasy, climbs a tree trunk. At each of several levels he is believed to be in the heaven of one of the gods, and he shouts down to the people what transpires in conversation with that deity. Finally at the apex he communicates with the High God himself, interceding on behalf of the tribe. Among other peoples, the shaman may in spirit dive through the earth to the under-world, or go out beyond the woods to confront the Master of Animals.

The shaman has under his control a band of spirit helpers whom he acquired during his initiation. He may have a spirit wife; union with her may also have been a part of his initiation. The shaman is no doubt the original singer, dancer, poet, and artist. He can do performances in these areas which far exceed those of the ordinary person. He is believed to know the language of birds and other wildlife. His vocabulary generally is much greater than that of ordinary tribesmen, and he is the main custodian of myth and lore. His ceremonial garb is elaborate, often including helm, bow and arrows, feathers (symbol of flight), metal discs, and drums and other musical instruments.

The cultural role of the shaman is not to be despised. Sick he may be by ordinary standards, but he has conquered his sickness and made it a vehicle for the exploration of realms far beyond the everyday perimeters of the human spirit. In him lie the seeds of later culture, seeds of a meaning to human life beyond the struggle to meet basic needs. Indeed, general culture has as yet only begun to claim some of the spiritual terrain marked out by shamanism. Dante in his *Divine Comedy* recapitulated the shaman's journey and made it part of the Western literary heritage. But the *angakok,* or enlightenment-giving spirit, obtained by Eskimo shamans during initiation, suggests an ecstatic opening which is harder for our uninitiated concepts and expectations to deal with.

> The *angakok* consists "of a mysterious light which the shaman suddenly feels in his body, inside his head, within the brain, an inexplicable searchlight, a luminous fire, which enables him to see in the dark, both literally and metaphorically speaking, for he can now, even with closed eyes, see through darkness and perceive things and coming events which are hidden from others: thus they look into the future and into the secrets of others."

> The candidate obtains this mystical light after long hours of waiting sitting on a bench in his hut and invoking the spirits. When he experiences it for the first time "it is as if the house in which he is suddenly rises; he sees far ahead of him, through mountains, exactly as if the earth were one great plain, and his eyes could reach to the end of the earth. Nothing is hidden from him any longer; not only can he see

things far, far away, but he can also discover souls, stolen souls, which are either kept concealed in far, strange lands, or have been taken up or down to the Land of the Dead."[17]

Certainly this is an experience of ultimate transformation. Probably this kind of experience of ecstatic vision and power is the very origin and ground of all religion, and the gods themselves are patterned on the model of great shamans. This is not a matter we can pursue here, but it may be worthwhile to point up the similarities of the shamanistic to the "peak experience" described by Abraham Maslow. While the shaman's ecstatic trance is usually active and dynamic, leading to great nervous exhaustion, it, like the more contemplative "peak experience," must seem a state of absolute being, sufficiency, wholeness, effortlessness. It is a state in which all things have a self-contained power of being, and in that sense is the epitome of human life at equilibrium with the cosmos and its forces.[18]

Such a state is in one sense conservative, for it gives rise to a joy which accepts the world as it is as charged with wonder. It provides a resolution of feelings of discontent not in social change but in moving down to deeper and stiller planes of consciousness. In primitive societies, the shaman's role is highly routinized and affords its holder an important place in the social hierarchy. He is thus identified with religion's role as the conserver and teacher of moral norms. He prophesies what it is expected he will prophesy—or at least uses conventional language. He may demand that this temple be levelled or another built, but he will not ask that the *kind* of temple, the *kind* of religion favored in his society, be modified. His ecstasies are the expected ecstasies available to man.

There is, however, always something about a role involving continual diving into the unconscious which is potentially discordant with following the same pattern eternally. For centuries and millennia, shamans may have served as safety-valves to release psychic energy and keep primitive society stable. But when times of spiritual upheaval came, shamanistic activity found it could break out of these bonds and glide into the radically different role of founding new faiths. This period of change, called the axial age by Karl Jaspers, was the period of the discovery of historical time. In Zoroaster and the Hebrew prophets, a vine with roots obviously reaching to the subterranean pools from which shamanizing draws life, suddenly grew in another direction. Rather than keeping fretful society on a steady keel with mutterings from the ancient tribal gods about taboo or the paths of the dead, the ecstatic seems to tip the balance unexpectedly the other way toward careening change. He hears new words that, in radicality, trump the new experience time is forcing upon his people. He says the change you have seen so far is nothing: war

and destruction will be worse, social changes more unsettling, the subsequent earthly paradise more glorious, than anything so far.

But although movements based on such shamanistic activity are likely
to emerge in times of historical change, they are really antihistorical. Like
the Cargo Cults, they wish to deny the terror of actual historical time
and establish a paradise beyond its reach through radical reversal. Or,
like yogins, they wish us to interiorize the religious cosmos sufficiently
that the individual is beyond the reach of external time. There are, in
other words, two uncompromisingly extreme ways in which religion tries
not merely to harness and control time, but to demolish it entirely. The
first is mysticism, which creates an interior psychological time so divorced
from exterior clock or historical or ordinary human time that ideally it
does not move at all, but remains in an eternal now of bliss. The second
is apocalyptic, which lives for a moment when, by divine intervention
from without, time in all its destructive aspects will be demolished, and
a paradisical condition established which is in effect without time because all potentialities are realized.[19]

The followers of movements based on ideas like these which emerge
along with the terrifying experience of historical time do not wish to
confront directly a history in which great changes are taking place—
neither do most of the new religious movements we are discussing. They
too speak mostly mystic or apocalyptic language. Significantly, most of
the new movements reject more vehemently than anything else the
Judaeo-Christian concept of a personal God. They are antihistorical and
conservative in the same sense as science and mysticism. They wish
instead to live in rapport with absolute ontological states and unchanging
natural law. Nonetheless they profoundly reflect and impel history.

But contemporary non-normative religious movements are not identical
with primitive shamanism. The most obvious difference is that the primitive shaman is part of an integral culture whereas the modern cultist is
expressing a sense of alienation. Sometimes, like the primitive psychopath
who is potentially a shaman, he may be going through a half-ritualized
process of self-realization with a number of visible precedents. But the
modern cultist also has much in common with those founders of historical religions whose alienation was based not only on existential
factors but also on historical experience—a sense that time moves irreversibly and that therefore some symbols are more in tune with the
present than the conventional symbols of ultimate transformation. For
this reason, unlike the shaman, the cultist has no role sanctioned by the
established world view. He is a fragment of a pluralistic culture, not a
major prop of an integrated one.

Nonetheless, some of the new movements like to compare themselves
to shamanism in one way or another. Perhaps they are looking for roots

in those ages when man was not aware of history, because that is the kind of consciousness they would like to have today—and believe is still valid. Theosophists think of themselves as perpetuating the teachings of "ancient mystery schools" which are said to be preserved in many traditional cultures, such as the Maori, Hawaiian, African, and Mayan. In all of these, the bearers of lore would be shamanistic types of individuals. Indeed, Theosophists talk of dream initiations, expanded states of consciousness, and other mainstays of shamanism. Spiritualists like to call their faith the "oldest religion in the world," which expresses certainly a desire to identify with the mediumistic functions of the shaman. The affinity the "hippie" counter-culture feels with the American Indian is well known. Its ephemeral psychedelic "churches" have posed as recoveries of the spirituality of the Amerindian. They have in common with the Amerindian shaman a reaching for states of consciousness, aided in both cases by such things as peyote, which transcend and defeat time and history, and bring treasures out of the unconscious. Theodore Roszak writes of the free-flowing poetry of Allen Ginsberg, a major voice of this culture:

> Far from being an avant-garde eccentricity, Ginsberg's conception of poetry as an oracular outpouring can claim an imposing genealogy that reaches back to the rhapsodic prophets of Israel (and beyond them perhaps to the shamanism of the Stone Age). Like Amos and Isaiah, Ginsberg aspires to be a *nabi*, a mutterer: one who speaks with tongues, one who permits his voice to act as the instrument of powers beyond his conscious direction.[20]

But like the prophets of Israel, Ginsberg expresses not the adhesion of the tribe to its god but a howl of indignation. We do not speak of a new primitive shamanism today, but of a rediscovery of certain motifs of shamanism as effective counters to the values of a technological, rationalistic culture in historical time. The charismatic leaders of the new movements in question have in common certain elements of the shamanistic typology. The elements are, of course, detached from archaic integration, and serve as major constituents of a new constellation with a life of its own.

Whether spiritualist medium, Theosophist, UFO contactee, witch, or orientalizer, on one level of language or another, an experience of initiation into a new ecstatic consciousness is found against the background of a nonhistorical universe of cosmic and spiritual law, through the mediation of personal supernormal helpers. The new shaman's role is to serve as charismatic center of a cultus, around which a new symbolic cosmos, and ultimately transformed world (through processes really mystical or apocalyptic rather than historical), will form itself.

4. Sect and Cult

Mystical or apocalyptic groups growing up around ecstatic experience and communication comparable to that of shamanism and often obviously composed of people "opting out" of historical processes correspond to those commonly referred to as *cults*. The exact sociological definition of this term and other common generic terms for types of religious organization like *church* and *sect* has been a matter of discussion. Assuming that most of the groups discussed in this book are cults, and that collectively they represent a fair sample for phenomenological analysis of this type of group as it exists in contemporary America,[21] the following will serve as a working definition. A *cult* is a group derived from the experience of one or a few individuals who are able to enter (or are fascinated by the possibility of entering) a superior, ecstatic state of consciousness in which contact and rapport with all reaches of a non-historical and impersonal[22] universe are possible with the help of inter-mediaries (human and/or supernatural). In a cult an outer circle of members experience the presence of the sacred in these individuals, and seek to participate in their experience. Because these premises are widely deviant from those of normative Judaism or Christianity, in our society these groups are highly eclectic in temperament.[23]

Virtually every religious group in America which cannot be called Judaeo-Christian (apart from ethnic-based organizations, like Japanese Buddhist temples) is a cult which fits the above definition.

Regarding the relation of this definition to shamanism, these words of G. K. Nelson might be kept in mind:

> The term shamanism has been selected as an omnibus term covering all forms of psychic and mystical experience because in primitive societies shamanism does in fact cover this wide range of experience of the "sacred," the "numinous," and the holy. Shamans have experiences that vary from the mediumistic to the mystical. . . . The category of shamanism is useful in drawing a distinction between those religious practitioners whose authority is based on a direct contact with the sacred who are shaman, and priests whose authority is derived from other sources.[24]

The precise definition of types of religious organization has been a matter of debate at least since the work of Ernst Troeltsch and Max Weber. In *The Social Teaching of the Christian Churches,* Troeltsch traced three types of Christian organization: (1) the church, which operates with the priestly type of authority to administer grace to the world, is universalistic (one is generally born into it rather than entering by independent decision), and supports the existing social order, tending to be strict in matters of faith and relatively lax in moral discipline; (2) the sect, a society of those who have made a voluntary decision which rejects compromise with the world, stressing individual perfection; and (3) mysticism—closest to what we have regarded as the shamanistic ground of cult movements. It is "simply the insistence upon a direct and present religious experience"[25] in such a way as to have no need for existing forms or organization. It would seem to be like the self-sufficient peak experience which is one with the type of experience around which cults form. Troeltsch associated his mysticism more with Protestantism than Catholicism. It existed in the latter, but never stood alone. Protestant mysticism could see itself as the logical outcome of Protestant ideas: laicism, the priesthood of all believers, individualism.

The sociological consequences of the sect and mystical impulses were very different for Troeltsch. Sectarians, such as Anabaptists, shared some of the same premises but sought to realize them by highly rigid structures based on a literal, perfectionist following of the "Gospel Law." Protestant mystics were interior, knowing nothing but the Spirit, its freedom and inward impulse. They had no use for doctrine or sacraments —the church, the return of Christ were all meant to be inward. It might seem that such extreme interiorization and individualism would lead to no social expression whatsoever, but such is not the case. According to Troeltsch, although mystical fellowships do arise, they are held not to be absolute, but more or less temporary works of the divine Spirit.

As many writers have pointed out, the typologies of Troeltsch are of limited use because they relate only to a particular cultural setting— Christian history up until about 1800. Since his "mysticism" refers actually only to Christian mysticism, it might appear that the category has no relevance to cults outside the main Judaeo-Christian stream. That would not be entirely true. Christian mysticism in Troeltsch's sense does not seem to be producing historically important phenomena today. But the same ground—that of meeting the needs of the individual who desires a religious stance based on deeply internal ecstatic experience, and who desires religious social expression only with those who share his temperament—is taken by the cults today.

A case could be made that in recent centuries the Christian consensus has moved more and more in the direction of historicism, and the uneasy but positive marriage which existed in the Middle Ages and up through the days of Thomas Traherne and Henry Vaughan between Christianity and mysticism has more and more fallen apart. The same has happened in Judaism. Thus persons of mystical temperament have been more and more forced into non-Judaeo-Christian forms of expression.

For this reason, though, the great stress Troeltsch laid on the individualistic, almost anarchic, character of mysticism, and the ephemeral character of its fellowships, has led astray some later observers who have seen the parallel between the ground of his mysticism and the modern cult. The cult is by no means necessarily ephemeral or unstable, even though it is still clearly distinguishable from the sect. Troeltsch indicated that the mystic took for granted the objective forms of the normative religion of his culture even though he was far more interested in inward experience. Hence he had no need to create forms. But now that much mysticism does not accept Judaeo-Christian forms, and does not need to in a pluralistic society, it has created its own parallel structures. In some cases it has done a reasonably good job of creating structures which perpetuate its collective and teaching life without doing complete violence to the ideal of inward ecstasy as the major focus of religious meaning.

Later writers like Leopold von Weise, Howard Becker, and J. Milton Yinger (in *Religion, Society, and the Individual*) have added refinements to Troeltsch's categories. Yinger's categories are: (1) the Universal Church, most successful in integrating society and meeting the needs of the greatest number of individuals, like the Catholic Church of medieval Europe; (2) the Ecclesia, which attempts this task less successfully and on a smaller scale, like the Church of England; (3) the Denomination, which while in harmony with the existing social order has only a class, racial, or regional base, like the Congregational or Methodist churches; (4) the Established Sect, a group which, like the Quakers, achieves a stable and probably middle class mode of being yet does not display that acceptance of the social order, professional leadership, and so forth which marks a denomination; (5) the Sect; and (6) the Cult.

The sect is basically understood in Troeltsch's terms. Yinger divides sects into three categories according to their reaction to undesirable circumstances: (1) acceptance (middle class sects which, like most cults, do not interpret the serious individual problems its members may feel in terms of a bad society); (2) aggression, the attitude of total antagonism to the present evil social order; and (3) avoidance, the most common sectarian attitude.

ⵗ Cults are small and ephemeral groups developing around the charisma of a leader, having beliefs greatly at variance with those of the broader community, and being basically concerned with individual problems. Spiritualistic churches are perhaps the best examples. More specifically, Yinger's discussion brings out the following traits of the cult: small size, search for "mystical experience," lack of organizational structure, presence of a dominant charismatic leader, a sharp break *in religious terms* (not social) with society, short life, often of local character, great problem with succession, wide deviation in rite and belief, and concern almost wholly with problems of individuals rather than the social order. They are, Yinger says, religious "mutants."[26]

The cult seems to appear in this classification mainly as "a group that is at the farthest extreme from the 'universal church.'" This lowly status seems to force a rather schematic treatment of it; it is almost by logical necessity "small, short-lived, often local." The quest for mystical experience, Yinger asserts, is a criterion which is not actually appropriate to the classification scheme. The schema does not entirely meet with ours, which because it is more fundamentally oriented to the type of religious experience characteristic of a group, is able to focus on the notion that mystical or ecstatic experience is the *raison d'être* of the cult.

G. K. Nelson indicates that this schema does not do full justice to the cult. While Yinger gives Spiritualism as a good example of the cult, Nelson points out that far from being short-lived, some of its institutions have found a way of both depending on charismatic personalities and surviving for over a century.[27] Individual spiritualist circles and churches may come and go, but the movement, though dependent on charisma, has been able to replenish itself through "medium development," as it is termed, just as primitive shamanism is replenished after established models. One might call such movements "established cults."

Yinger is right, of course, in indicating that the cult tends to break up easily, especially on the local level. That is only half the story, since in the cult world new movements usually spring up to take the place of those which collapse, often with approximately the same clientele. There is a stable cult population, in a manner of speaking, whose affiliations bear an ever-changing series of names. This is not entirely true either, however; some groups, like Theosophy, have survived institutionally for almost a century—but with a rather wildly fluctuating membership. Most of the many people who have been in and out of Theosophy have gone on to other "occult" movements.

The problem of the second generation, of the perpetuation of a spontaneous and ecstatic experience in institutional forms, is naturally a major crisis for any religious group based in this way. It is the problem of achieving what Max Weber called the "routinization of charisma." S. G. F. Brandon spoke of religion as the "ritual perpetuation of the past." The more ecstatic and non-normative an experience is, of course, the more difficult is the quest for ways to perpetuate or reproduce it at will. Many movements fail due to an inability to come to grips with this crisis, especially in the second generation. On the other hand, the fundamental dynamic of the creation of these new movements is the occurrence of experience which is not allowed for in the normative categories of religious expression. Since there is a body of people oriented toward such experience, there is a continual replenishment of the cultic fountains. The psychedelic drug experience today has been especially formative of such experience. Many new cults are largely attempts to perpetuate by nondrug means the initiatory drug "high."

This perpetuation process may take one of two forms or both together. There is the actual continuing creation of new charismatic personalities and phenomena, as in Spiritualism. Then there is the use of a secondary device similar to posthypnotic suggestion, which will hopefully trigger a response in the believer comparable to that evoked by the original experience, even though the technique may be superficially different. Examples are chanting, liturgical drama, even lectures which employ suggestive rhetorical images. These are really the same as sacred space and time symbols, for the latter were archaically intended to re-create the time of origins and the world as it was originally made. The cult endeavors to do this in terms of its own moment of origin when its experience was pure.

On the basis of his study of religious groups in Alberta, Canada, William Mann has added material to the problem of definitions. He states that the sect is essentially a withdrawal phenomena within the normative tradition characterized by ascetic morality, other-worldliness, literalism, and highly selective membership. Examples are the Salvation Army, Church of God, Church of the Nazarene, and Jehovah's Witnesses. These groups are normatively Christian in the central teaching that justifies their existence. Indeed, it is intense separatist commitment to it which sets them apart and makes them sects rather than cults.

The cult, on the other hand, is syncretistic, combining traditional and alien religions with elements of modern science. These are all blended with Christian doctrine to obtain a more adequate or modern faith. The services of cults generally lack "stirring emotional manifestation," says Mann. They are opposed to elaborate ceremony—with a few exceptions —preferring to win new members by reasoned arguments. They are thus "pseudorational," accepting the validity of science and a rational cosmic system. But in a sense they are postscientific, "metaphysical," a word they much enjoy, protesting a merely materialistic world view. They are not ascetic in most respects, coming to terms with the world, wealth, and so forth, and show condescension to ordinary churches. Their goals are harmony, happiness, success, wisdom—not emotional salvation.

Examples of cults Mann found in Alberta are Christian Science, Unity, Theosophy, Rosicrucianism, I Am, Spiritualism, and Divine Science. He observed that there is a "cult world" distinct from that of church or sect, inhabited by many drifters from one to another, the most conspicuous of which are sometimes called "metaphysical tramps." Anglo-Saxons predominated, with women much outnumbering men, and there was a scarcity of family groups. The typical cultist had more schooling than average; most were avid readers, especially in the weird and bizarre. "Field workers who went into the homes of cult members invariably discovered a number of serious books scattered about." They were of comfortable means, but seemed to lack full middle class acceptance and showed a high mobility.[28]

Mann's typology distinguishes well enough between groups like the Mennonites and Jehovah's Witnesses on the one hand, and Divine Science and Theosophy on the other. But other cultisms visible in America today, like Krishna Consciousness, Witchcraft, and Neo-Paganism, seem unaccounted for since they include ceremonialism and high group consciousness as well as syncretism. J. A. Dator, for example, notes that on this reckoning Nichiren Shoshu (Soka Gakkai) "has structural, dogmatic features of a cult and the sociological features of a sect."[29]

Benton Johnson has made some suggestions which may be of help. He argues that the church-sect typology of Troeltsch is of limited use because it is applicable only to a specific historical context. In Troeltsch's world it was inevitable that sectarian alternatives to the establishment (inseparable from the established church) would have a protest character growing out of unrest and alienation. In the U.S. this is not necessarily true; there is no official religion, and hence few radical protest religions.

In the course of this argument Johnson points out that the church-sect typology can only be employed within the Judaeo-Christian-Islamic tradition because there is a basic difference in the role of the charismatic personality in these religions from the religions of Eastern Asia. Using Max Weber's terms, he indicates that the Western religions make central the role of the emissary or ethical prophet, the agent of a personal God who makes ethical demands. In the East, the charismatic personality is rather an exemplary prophet. This personality, like the Buddha radiant with complete integration into a wondrous but impersonal cosmos, does not so much deliver a message as manifest a life style through which his followers can attain individual holiness and enlightenment.[30]

It would be too much to say that the exemplary type of prophet has been unknown in the West, but like St. Francis he has generally been able to exist within the existing structures. Johnson employs only a single variable in this church-sect distinction—acceptance or rejection of the social environment in which it exists. His placing this distinction in the Western tradition, and showing it to be a result of the emissary prophet type, is valuable to us. The sect, like the emissary role, is related to a verbal and historicized concept of religious truth, for that has been the supreme burden of Judaism, Christianity, and Islam. The sect, like these faiths in general, understands its existence as a response to belief that God, through preachers, can at any point in time break new light out of his Word. When this is done, in irreversible time, it may be a clear mandate to form a new group centered around adherence to the Word of that time, for no social structure is more important than response to it. At the same time, the notion helps us to understand the contemporary upsurge of cultic activity in a way congruous with the increasing and instinctive rejection of Judaeo-Christian symbols and emphasizing what seems more and more to be really distinctive—a new style of religious communication.

What is it that groups as diverse as Western Zen, Nichiren Shoshu, Theosophy, Spiritualism, Witchcraft, and UFO groups really have in common? That they have something more in common than rejection of Judaeo-Christian norms is evident from a considerable overlap of membership and, for many, a common vocabulary. How do we understand the search for ecstatic experience in our culture?

Troeltsch said that mysticism is, above all, individualistic. While this may not be quite as prejudicial to institutional formation as he thought, it must be reflected in the nature of the institution. David Martin says that in the cult, "the highest level of interpersonal action is a 'parallelism of spontaneities,' more particularly of the kind involved in the common pursuit of psychological techniques or therapeutic discussion."[31] In contrast, in the sect, group consciousness replaces the individual conscience. He goes so far as to say that the "sectarian rarely experiences religious tranquillity or devotional communion"—he is rather wrapped up in the expounding of God's plan, which may or may not be comfortable.[32]

This seems to lead in the right direction. We have spoken of the cult as a movement grounded in ecstatic experience (rather than doctrinal message, social protest, or the like), concerned with perpetuating that experience. Such an experience will be ultimately nonverbal, like Maslow's "peak experience," though it may give rise to shamanistic or mediumistic muttering. But in both cases the verbalization, like Theosophical doctrine, is essentially not taken literalistically but as symbolic of the richness of the ecstasy. The banality of most Spiritualistic communication is well known, like the unintelligibility of most glossalalia. Neither is important for what they say, but for what is said by the fact that supernatural communication happens at all.

The individuality of cultism needs to be rightly understood. It does not mean members are more strongly affirmative of theological freedom than, say, Unitarians. Indeed there may be a very close communion and participation mystique in the group. In organizations like Scientology, it may take highly centralized structural forms. To some this closeness may prove the cult's greatest attraction. But it does mean that the unity is to be based on individual experience, not on family or social factors, or on verbalized doctrinal conformity.

The cult stems from the exemplary type of personality possessed by an ecstatic experience, or even by the symbolized or verbalized suggestion of the possibility of such an experience.[33] This central figure "turns on" others to the experience. They seek both to have it as a means of ultimate transformation, and to trigger or perpetuate it by direct or symbolic means. It is important that each individual's interest be maintained by the experience itself. If the group begins to show other reasons for continued existence—simple friendship among members, social reformism—to that extent it ceases to be only a cult in the strict sense. This is well expressed in Martin's phrase, "parallelism of spontaneities." However conditioned and prepared for, ecstatic experience always *feels* spontaneous. A group discovering it together feels a sense of mutual wonder. But the object is the experience, not the group as such.

The recent rise in cults seems to herald a new style of personality in the West, one which is more like the Eastern personality which responds to the exemplary prophet. This new type of American character has been delineated by Robert Jay Lifton, John B. Orr, and F. Patrick Nichelson. Lifton speaks of the new type as "Protean man." His life style is "characterized by an interminable series of experiments and explorations—some shallow, some profound—each of which may be readily abandoned in favor of still new psychological quests."[34] In other words, the truth which gives central meaning to life is not an objectified word from God, or if so, access is sufficiently difficult to make the quest itself a life style.

Orr and Nichelson have developed this image further in employing the term "expansive man."[35] This type inhabits a region (really more a state of mind or life style domain than a geographical place) called "the radical suburb," and it is here that the real creation of a new culture in our society is taking place. Expansive man views the self as process created out of a series of experiences. Experience is for him the highest good. It is the medium which creates whatever message there is. Expansive man is sensual and somewhat anti-intellectual—the "meaningful experience" must be total, not simply verbal or conceptual. He is eclectic, drawing his experiences from things new and old with whimsical freedom, even displaying a remarkable capacity for nostalgia (camp and pop art) in his aesthetics.

Clearly "Protean" and "expansive" man have much in common with "cult" man as he seeks an experience beyond words through a fluid variety of vehicles and disdains the traditional Western emissary, historical, verbal doctrine bias. All of the latter is a part of the concerns of Orr and Nichelson's "conscientious man," the traditionalist opposite of "expansive man." These writers have explicitly pointed to the vogue for Zen, the *I Ching,* and other Eastern religious imports as illustrative of the eclecticism and experience orientation of expansive men now influencing our culture. We can certainly validly relate the expansive or Protean style to the popularity of exemplary, ecstatic experience religious styles and cults which seem to embody them—even though many churches and synagogues are desperately striving to achieve the same image.

Marshall McLuhan is talking about the same cultural break when he calls television a "cool" medium—multisensory, allowing participation. It is an experience one moves in and out of and which does not demand violent, one-pointed reaction to words and ideas, as do radio and the phonetic printed page—the "hot" media. This may be the same as speaking of media appropriate to exemplary as compared to emissary concepts of communication.[36]

5. General Characteristics of Cults

The main thrust of this discussion is that the contemporary American cult is a movement based on the hope of ecstatic experience. Like primitive shamanism, it seeks to perpetuate itself through a technique of ecstasy. Like shamanism it will draw strange images and associations from the depths of the unconscious in the course of this quest: the often bizarre visions, doctrines, and rites of cults. The shaman has a ready-made group in his tribe where he has an accepted and prestigious role, so he generally does not need to form a withdrawal group.

In American society, the pluralistic model is accepted; it is not necessary that any particular experience be at a disadvantage when compared to a uniquely established institution in giving itself a structured collective form. "Metaphysical" and "occult" and "spiritualist" churches are formed as readily, as legally, and as officially as Methodist or Baptist. The Hindu ashram, the Buddhist monastery should remind us that, Troeltsch to the contrary, there is nothing in the mystical or exemplary religious style which makes it inherently incapable of taking institutional form. It is just that it will be different in shape from the church or sect based on the Western emissary religious dynamic. It may seem more fluid, in a sense more fragile, than the Universal Church, but both it and its forms of expression recur with some sort of interior continuity. The Buddhist *samgha* or monastic order is probably the oldest continuing nonfamilial institution in the world. Compared to the Universal Church or denomination, the cult and what lies behind it is like the amoeba compared to the whale—far more ephemeral yet in a sense far more immortal.

Yet the ecstatic-experience-based group without verbalized norms of doctrine and polity is a novelty. Except for some of the newest groups, all cults have felt constrained to put forth statements of belief or principle and constitutions. Those deriving from the nineteenth century do so with full Victorian aplomb. Even so, a new orientation, a new style seems to be breaking through. Nonverbalism, free orientation toward "the experience," may represent the real assumptions of Protean and expansive man, but it does not have established models for group expression in our religious tradition. Those who express this experience in religious terms (as a means of ultimate transformation) can do so only through an objective break with the religious traditions of their society.

The distinction of sect and church remains useful in ecclesiastical history. But we are now dealing with a third force foreshadowed by Troeltsch's mysticism, but now becoming capable of establishment. Third force groups today have of course varying relationships to the Judaeo-Christian tradition, but we can distinguish between the church-sect continuum—a few or even one variable implied—and the cult type which is moving toward a different pole of religious expression, the exemplary, mystical, or shamanistic. The former will share characteristics of the "Great Tradition" of our culture—verbal orientation, historical and personalistic consciousness, emissary style—and may boast of avenues of access to the American past not shared by the cult. The cult shares with shamanism not only the general typology of the charismatic seer, but to a remarkable extent details of the pattern, including the spirit band, learned or spontaneous ritual, antihistoricism, bringing wisdom from faraway geographical or supernatural places, healing, and above all, techniques of ecstasy.

Here are some general characteristics of modern American cults.[37] Different cults will, of course, stress or interpret certain characteristics in different ways.

1. A founder who has had, or at least seems to know the secret of, nontemporal ecstatic experience. (It is often not really so much having ecstatic experiences, as being fascinated with their techniques, literature, and meaning, which activates cults and even their founders. It is that which seems faraway which people are driven to quest for.) The founder may be a personality of the magus type.

2. An interpretation of the experience as possession or marvellous travel. This familiar motif of archaic shamanism is strikingly renewed in Spiritualism and UFO cults and less obviously perhaps in the symbolism of interior mystical exploration and lore from faraway places.

3. A band of supernormal helpers. Again, in Spiritualism, there is a literal re-creation of this shamanistic motif, and scarcely less so in the Theosophical "Masters" and the UFO "space brothers," in the spirits evoked by Witchcraft and the gods and goddesses of Neo-Paganism. If the psychological meaning of this phenomena is the subduing of uncon-

trolled fragments of the psyche, it indicates the emphasis on the under-standing and control of subjectivity typical of the whole movement. Its equivalent can be found in other cultic groups which prefer not to use such mythological modes of expression.

4. A desire to be "modern" and to use scientific language. As we have indicated, there is something postscientific about the mood as well, a tendency to disdain as materialistic science and technology for their own sake. But there is an instinctive realization that, in the battle against the historical and emissary style, something in science—especially the broad confident assertion of unchanging natural law more typical of Victorian than of contemporary science—is congenial with the cultist's experience of timeless absolute reality and can be used to strengthen it intellectually. However, when scientists attack the cultist's use of his language, he does not hesitate to respond in kind; the alliance is quite unstable and one-sided. Like the scientist, the cultist also has felt a bitter alienation from much of the West's religious past, and hence much is made of modernity and the hope of a better future.

5. A reaction against orthodoxy. Hard language is often used in opposi-tion to the established churches, and also, when occasion suits, against scientific orthodoxy.

6. Eclecticism and syncretism.

7. A monistic and impersonal ontology. It is impressive how common this metaphysical characteristic is. The cults may populate the "inter-mediate" cosmos between man and the absolute with any number of spirit guides, masters, space brothers, and other quasideities, but the absolute itself is not the personal Judaeo-Christian God, but some more abstract entity, usually capitalized, like "Infinite Intelligence," "Principle," etc.

8. Optimism, success orientation, and a tendency to evolutionary views. This is no doubt a part of the "scientific" and "modern" mentality, rein-forced by a feeling that orthodoxy is too much devoted to other-worldly benefits (although the orthodox are also inconsistently accused of praying in church for selfish ends), and that a faith based on present ecstatic experience ought to be able to produce benefits in this world, here and now, and a better world to come. This is a major argument of groups as sociologically divergent as Religious Science and Nichiren Shoshu. They say that other groups promise pie in the sky after you die; only we can deliver the goods here and now and tomorrow on this earth. Sectarian groups may tend toward apocalypticism; cult groups toward a slower and more evolutionary change for the better under the influence of better thinking, though in times of crisis their language too, as in current talk of the coming Aquarian Age, may move in an apocalyptic direction. The cult groups are usually nonpolitical, and do not do much to advance

the course of social evolution by direct political or reformist action. They may use utopian rhetoric, but because they require only tolerance, they function well in a capitalist society because today capitalism usually implies religious pluralism.

9. Emphasis on healing. This is another characteristic of shamanism picked up by modern cults. No doubt it grows out of the sense of total power and vision engendered by the ecstatic experience. Most cults provide some means for charismatic power to be applied to the healing of mind and body.

10. Use in many cases of magic techniques. Nelson defines magic as the use of nonempirical means for empirical ends, in contrast to pure religion's nonempirical means and ends and science's empirical means and ends.[38] The final purpose of the cult may be ultimate transformation, but there is generally a spin-off which can be applied to secondary, finite transformations. Ceremonial magic, another shamanistic motif, is becoming popular. Of course ceremonial magic has also an ultimate transformation usage as a means to mental concentration to attain an altered state of consciousness.

11. A simple but definite process of entry and initiation. The importance of this is obvious. Whatever they say, most cults want a large membership. They also recognize the clear psychological importance in a group based on a sense of alienation of making membership seem a privilege not lightly granted, involving a definite act of separation, commitment, and study.

12. In some cases, the establishment of a sacred center. Perhaps because of the strong reaction toward universalism, this has been less a feature of new American cults than those elsewhere, but some groups do speak of places of special spiritual power, and afford imposing temples which are like Mecca to scattered members.

13. Emphasis on psychic powers. This is another shamanistic trait which is no doubt taken as evidence of access to the places of ecstatic transformation, although not all psychics are ecstatics.

14. Tendency to attract isolated individuals rather than family groups. This is an obvious but important characteristic of any cult. Some older groups like Theosophy and Spiritualism maintain this characteristic even after virtually a century of continued existence. With it we may cite the typical predominance of older women of white, Anglo-Saxon background, except of course in the newer youth culture cults.

15. Increasing emphasis on participation by all members in the ecstatic experience through group chanting, meditation, and so forth. The ecstasy is not just a display trance by the central figure, but a corporate act. This is of course a result of the emergence of Protean or expansive man and

a reaction against the Protestant church style of the older cults in which the expansive quality of mysticism was only embryonic.

6. Forms of Religious Expression

If religion is the means of ultimate transformation, of transforming a profane life and environment into a sacred life, then these means must take tangible form. Joachim Wach defined the three major categories of expression as theoretical (myth and doctrine), practical (worship and cultus), and sociological.[39] Here we shall regard Wach's pattern as normative. A human phenomenon in which we see the quest for ultimate transformation, and the means to it articulated by use of *all three* of these categories, will be considered a religious phenomenon. Contrariwise, expression in only one or two of the categories is not a religion. Doctrine without worship or sociological expression, whether about gods or not, is not a religion, but a private metaphysical system. With social expression, but without worship or cultus, it becomes a philosophical school but is still not a religion. A form of worship without doctrine, or even with doctrine but without relation to any social unit, is only private magic or at best a personal devotion or mysticism. (This is probably not really possible; like Troeltsch's mysticism it represents an individualized pole of spirituality which is religious because it is still in a dialectical relationship to the objective forms of religion in its cultural background and presumes their existence. When they recede, as is the case today, mysticism asserts its religious character by creating its own objective forms to fill up the void.) A social group without either or both of the other categories is a club, not a religion.

It is important to insist with some firmness, at least for the purposes of this study, upon a strict definition of what is considered a religious phenomenon. This is particularly necessary in the hazy world of cults, whose denizens use the word "religion," as well as other words like "metaphysics," "church," and "mysticism," mostly according to individual taste. On the other hand, there are social scientists who find no valid descriptive use for the word. While a word in itself, of course, is nothing, and another could as well be invented or substituted, yet it seems that there exists a particular set of social phenomena embracing both the presentation of a means of ultimate transformation *and* all three of Wach's categories of expression for which a descriptive term is useful. Any notion which is genuinely conceived of as a means of ultimate transformation, in the absolute sense of each of these words, will soon enough manifest expression in each of the categories. The two sides of our definition, means to ultimate transformation, and something which finds

simultaneous expression in doctrine, worship or cultus, and social grouping, are mutually corrective. The value of a definition like this is apparent
in comparing, for example, Platonism and Buddhism. The former is only
doctrine and occasionally a school; the latter more clearly sees itself as
a means of ultimate transformation and has obvious expression in each of
the categories. Quite apart from doctrinal similarities and dissimilarities,
which in themselves are not really relevant, Buddhism is clearly a religion
and Platonism is not, except as it is adopted by a religious system like
Catholic Christianity.

By the same token, we can see why the Theosophical Society (despite
its claims to the contrary) needs to be considered a religion for the
purposes of a phenomenological study, while transcendentalism and positive thinking, despite their generous use of sacred language and their
advocacy by clergymen, are not. In this study, considering cult as a
subdivision of religion, we will treat only phenomena which meet this
definition of religion, and will look for its expression in each of these
areas. Let us examine more closely the three categories.

A. Theoretical Expression

The first includes any kind of verbal and conceptual expression
of the means, or experience, of ultimate transformation. It will exist
on several levels. The most primordial may be the shaman's ecstatic
description of his visions and ghostly wrestlings. Then, when a religious
world view derived from this muttering, or from another source, is
accepted by a community and is expressed in narrative form, it becomes
myth. A myth is a story, but it is not just any story about gods and
heroes giving a prescientific explanation of natural phenomena. It must
be a story which sums up the attitudes, values, and concepts which are
most important to the conceptual framework of the community. In
primitive societies this means the major myth generally has to do with
the creation and the origin of man, death, and agriculture—if we know
where things came from, the feeling is, we will know how to deal with
them. In historical religions, on the other hand, the major myth will
have to do with the *renewal* of the pristine glory of the world through
the mighty acts of the founding hero. In modern cults, the functional
myth is generally the story of the experience of the founder which
establishes his ecstatic (shamanistic) capacity and his access to a new
means of ultimate transformation such as Madame Blavatsky's initiation
by the Masters and Daniel Fry's ride in a UFO.

At a later stage comes verbal expression in doctrine. It does not intend
to say anything different from what was said by myth, but to generalize

from it, to state in abstract form the truth about the gods and the world implied in the myth. It asks the question, If such-and-such is how God has acted on this and that occasion, what can we say about him that is true all the time?

While many cults profess to have only doctrine—"metaphysics"—it appears that unless there is also a mythical, narrative account connected with the movement validating the authority of the teaching or the teacher, it has difficulty attaining the other forms of expression and so falls short of being a real religion. If there is no story of the supernormal origins of the teaching, at least there will be reverent accounts of the struggles of the founder in getting the world to accept it, or else validating stories of remarkable conversions, healings, and psychic phenomena. Cosmological matters—the creation, etc.—will, in modern cults, probably be expressed in doctrine, heavily larded with scientific language, rather than in myth.

In connection with verbal expression, then, we would look for:

The functional myth and its validating role

The nature of the doctrinal expression

The world view implied by each

What is communicated by the style of language—abstract or concrete, personal or objective, and so forth

The supportive relation of verbal expression to the means of ultimate transformation

B. PRACTICAL EXPRESSION

Practical expression (worship and cultus) means simply what is done physically to actualize the experience of ultimate transformation. It is related to both verbal and social expression; it acts out the former, it gives reality to the latter. Most worship is a mythical scenario in a broad sense, re-creating over and over the crucial moment of the unveiling of the new means of ultimate transformation. It is, in other words, a presentation of the most important thing the group has to offer as that means. The analysis of what the group does when it is together, however, requires some degree of acumen. Very often the corporate activity will not be understood as worship, much less as mythical scenario, by the group itself. They will often say, "We just come together to hear a lecture, or meditate, or talk—there is really no worship."

Let us consider, however, a meeting of a Theosophical Society. Usually little more transpires than a lecture on a theosophical topic. But in the first place, the formal lecture in America—with the introduction of the speaker, the flowers and water on the table, the discussion period—is actually a highly ritualized affair. It is not recognized as such mainly because it is a part of the Chautauqua tradition growing out of that New England Protestantism which considered itself almost by definition anti-ritualistic. But in most non-Western cultures this particular performance would be as exotic as a shaman's dance in ours.

Nonetheless, as surely as the remotest ritual of sacrifice and dance, this ceremony says more by what is *done* than by what is *said*. The fact that it is a lecture says more about Theosophy than the words uttered. It expresses its continuity with a particular tradition in American society. It expresses a primacy of verbal expression, quite different from the non-verbal and somewhat anti-intellectual message of the corporate work of those groups which meditate or chant together. The lecture in Theosophy is also a reenactment of the primacy of words in the talks and books of the great founders of the group—Blavatsky, Besant, Leadbeater.

Thus the formal lecture is practical expression in that it does exactly what any practical expression—from High Mass to Quaker meeting—does. It re-creates the most pristine moments of Theosophy, places the present in the largest possible context, and says what the means of ultimate transformation are. That is, it says: "What we rejoice in is the discovery of tremendous and mind-expanding ideas in the words and books of the Theosophical founders (rather than directly in their or our immediate mystical experiences). Hence we see ourselves in continuity with those to whom the word is the central vehicle of transformation, and we wish to hear and read to continue the transforming effect the words of Theosophy have." Any familiarity with Theosophy, with its unceasing atmosphere of excitement about books, lectures, writing, discussion, classes, and libraries will bear out the meaning of these observations.

The basic point is that the nature of the corporate life of any group bears a message. That message may or may not be superficially consistent with the doctrinal expression, but it is equally important and equally real. The corporate life is, in a religious group, as sure a guide to understanding what the group's means of transformation are as the doctrine, and often far more so. Verbal expression meets certain needs, but they often are symbolic and compensatory.

It seems axiomatic that if a group has doctrinal and social expression it will have expression in the second category, the practical. Any expression in this area is equally important as a clue to the meaning of the group's life: a simple meeting, or even a free-form discussions, says as much as an elaborate ritual It is only that the message is different.[40] Negative data tell as much as positive.

In the practical or worship category we will look for variables in areas like these:

Formal–informal structure
Multisensory–unisensory expression
Rational–nonrational leadership,[41] and other leadership aspects
Conformity–individualized expression

C. Sociological Expression

The study of social expression is the observation of what message is communicated by the organization of the cult, the interrelation of the members, the type of persons attracted to it, and the cult's relation to the outside world. The type of experience enjoyed by the members will obviously be conditioned by such factors as whether the group has a tight and centralized structure, like Scientology and Nichiren Shoshu, a traditional parliamentary organization like Theosophy, or an unarticulated kind of local charismatic leadership like the Meher Baba groups. Even more, perhaps, experience will be conditioned by the kind of persons associated with in the group—their age, education, personality types, and their reasons for joining. This is especially the case in cult groups where the dynamic is to be "turned on" to a particular ecstatic experience by what one experiences in and through the group, which of course means its leadership and the other people in it.

The three categories are interlocking, like three intertwined rings. It is meaningless to ask which comes first. The social group creates the doctrine and myth as a narrative justification of its drama; the verbal expression creates the social group as a body held together by talk about its tenets. The relationships could equally well be read in the other direction. But it should be recognized that the popular idea that a religious group is formed around verbal expression, that is, around a particular "belief," is misleading. Many people, especially those who, like most cult members have made conscious adult choices in religion, may interpret their choice as being essentially on the basis of doctrine. But the sort of analysis indicated here may show that the messages communicated by the style of worship and the type of people in the group and its structure have made equally compelling appeals, whether or not their messages are totally consistent with the doctrine. There is also the attraction to people an individual wants to be like, the need for authority or egalitarianism, the ability to identify with a certain style of worship.

Behind all three categories is a unifying essence which is closer than any of these to the means of ultimate transformation in an absolute sense. It is often difficult to articulate the unifying essence since it is a sort of combined experience. Words must begin somewhere, but we cannot posit any of the categories as primary. The unifying essence, then, may be almost an impressionistic thing when written out—the low sweet roar of the Latihan in Subud, the proverbial "taste of tea" in Zen. (In Western Zen centers, tea is customarily served after a long period of silent *zazen* or seated meditation.) Finally, nothing is more important than to express this flavor or aura, for no doubt it is this, rather than something more rational, which often effects the persuasion of converts.

Notes

1 "World Theology Move Seen by Harvard Dean," *Los Angeles Times*, Sunday, May 31, 1970. Copyright 1970, *Los Angeles Times*. Reprinted by permission.

2 Mircea Eliade, *The Sacred and the Profane* (New York: Harper & Row, Publishers, 1961).

3 Frederick J. Streng, *Understanding Religious Man* (Belmont, Calif.: Dickenson Publishing Company, Inc., 1969), pp. 4–5.

4 Mircea Eliade, *Mephistopheles and the Androgyne: Studies in Religious Myth and Symbol* (New York: Sheed & Ward, Inc., 1965), pp. 135–36.

5 The puzzling and yet human quality of the founder is suggested by these words about the Theosophist Madame Blavatsky by her close associate Colonel Olcott:

> Just because I did know her so much better than most others, she was a greater mystery to me than to them. It was easy for those who only saw her speaking oracles, writing profound aphorisms, or giving clue after clue to the hidden wisdom in the ancient Scriptures, to regard her as an earth-visiting *angelos* and to worship at her feet; she was no mystery to them. But to me, her most intimate colleague, who had to deal with the vulgar details of her common daily life, and see her in all her aspects, she was from the first and continued to the end an insoluble riddle. How much of her waking life was that of responsible personality, how much that of a body worked by an overshadowing entity? I do not know." Henry Steel Olcott, *Old Diary Leaves, Second Series, 1878–83* (Madras: Theosophical Publishing Co., 1900, 1954), p. viii.

6 Reprinted by permission of Schocken Books, Inc. from *Spiritualism and Society* by Geoffrey K. Nelson. Copyright © 1969 by Geoffrey K. Nelson, p. 44.

7 " 'Internal Conversion' in Contemporary Bali." Mimeographed, 1961, p. 3. Cited in Robert N. Bellah, *Religion and Progress in Modern Asia* (New York: The Free Press, 1965), p. 176.

[8] Mircea Eliade, *Shamanism, Archaic Techniques of Ecstasy,* trans. Willard R. Trask, Bollingen Series LXXVI (Copyright © by Princeton University Press, 1964), p. 4.

[9] Nelson, *Spiritualism and Society,* p. 44.

[10] Eliade, *Shamanism,* p. 4.

[11] Dominik Schröder, however, argues that there are two types of shamanism, that of the "travelling" shaman such as Eliade makes normative who goes in ecstatic trance to the heavens and the underworld, and that of the "possession" shaman who, without losing control of the spirits, allows them to enter him and speak through him, calling them down from the spirit realms like a medium. In either case, the constant would be a technique of trance or ecstasy. Dominik Schröder, "Zur Struktur des Schamanismus," *Anthropos,* L. (1955), 848–81.

[12] Eliade, *Shamanism,* p. 13.

[13] Eliade, *Shamanism,* p. 14.

[14] For useful and striking comparative material on shamanistic initiation and practice, see Mircea Eliade, *From Primitives to Zen* (New York: Harper & Row, Publishers, 1967), pp. 423–45.

[15] Andreas Lommel, *Shamanism: The Beginnings of Art.* (New York: McGraw-Hill Book Company, 1967), pp. 11–12.

[16] See for example Carlos Castaneda, *The Teachings of Don Juan: A Yaqui Way of Knowledge* (Berkeley: University of California Press, 1968); and R. Gordon Wasson, *Soma: Divine Mushroom of Immortality* (New York: Harcourt, Brace & World, Inc., 1969).

[17] Eliade, *Shamanism,* pp. 60–61. Based on and quoted from Knud Rasmussen, *Intellectual Culture of the Iglulik Eskimos* (Copenhagen: Report of the Fifth Thule Expedition, 1930). Compare the following statement by an individual who had reached the initiatory state of Clear in Scientology:

> I am CLEAR! It's really out-of-sight! Distances have no significance to me anymore. I can just see as far as I can see and that's quite a distance. When it happened, going Clear that is, I looked at the stars and the moon. They were within reach of my arm. And oh my gosh, I just realized—it's forever!! (Church of Scientology of California, *Clear News,* May 11, 1970.)

[18] From *Toward a Psychology of Being* by Abraham H. Maslow, Copyright © 1968 by Litton Educational Publishing, Inc., pp. 103–14. The basic characteristics of the person in the peak experience as described by Maslow may be summarized as follows:

1. He feels more integrated than at other times.
2. He feels more able to fuse with the world.
3. He feels at the peak of his powers.

4. He has a sense of effortlessness and ease of functioning.

5. He feels himself the "responsible, active, creating center of his activities."

6. He is free of blocks, fears, inhibitions.

7. He is more spontaneous and natural than at other times.

8. He is more creative in the sense that what is in him flows out freely.

9. He is more intensely individual, himself, noninterchangeable with anyone else.

10. He is more "here-now," "free of the past and of the future."

11. He is "more a pure psyche and less a thing-of-the-world living under the laws of the world."

12. He feels non-needing, non-striving, and unmotivated in the sense of "having transcended needs and drives of the ordinary sort. He just is. Joy has been attained which means a temporary end to the striving for joy." In this respect he is "godlike."

13. Expression (as with the shaman and seer) tends to become "poetic, mythical and rhapsodic."

14. The state is a "completion-of-the-act," like a total catharsis or consummation, in contrast to states like only half-satisfied hunger.

15. There is a certain kind of playfulness, a "happy joy," a good-humor transcending hostility of any kind.

16. "People during and after peak-experiences characteristically feel lucky, fortunate, graced. A not uncommon reaction is 'I don't deserve this.' Peaks are not planned or brought about by design. We are 'surprised by joy.'"

19 More precisely, "apocalyptic" (literally, uncovering or unveiling) means a teaching, such as that found in some parts of the New Testament, that the world we know will end through a sudden, dramatic divine intervention. There will be a final judgment and reconstitution of the world as paradise. Very often it is taught that times will only get worse and worse until that day, and that the climax may be accompanied by Armegeddon-like battles between the forces of good and evil.

20 Theodore Roszak, *The Making of a Counter-Culture* (New York: Anchor Books, © Doubleday & Company, Inc., 1969), p. 128.

21 The "New Thought" churches, like Religious Science, Divine Science, and Unity, and groups with a membership mostly limited to ethnic minorities (black, oriental, American Indian, etc.) are given less attention in this book than their numbers would warrant. New Thought has been given more study elsewhere than most of the groups described here—especially in the work of Charles S. Braden and J. Stillson Judah.

[22] The Krishna Consciousness movement does understand its supreme and absolute God, Krishna, to be personal.

[23] W. W. Sweet has written: "A cult is a religious group which looks for its basic and peculiar authority outside the Christian tradition. Generally, cults accept Christianity, but often only as a halfway station on the road to a greater 'truth' and profess to have a new and additional authority beyond Christianity. This new authority may be a revelation which constitutes additional 'scriptures' or it may be an inspired leader who announces that he or she has gained additional insight into 'truth.'" *American Culture and Religion* (Dallas: Southern Methodist University Press, 1951), p. 93.

[24] Nelson, *Spiritualism and Society*, p. 230.

[25] Ernst Troeltsch, *The Social Teaching of the Christian Churches*, trans. Olive Wyon (New York: The Macmillan Company, Publishers, 1931), Vol. 2, p. 730.

[26] J. Milton Yinger, *Religion, Society, and the Individual* (New York: The Macmillan Company, Publishers, 1957), pp. 142–55.

[27] Nelson, *Spiritualism and Society*, p. 220. In a more recent book, *The Scientific Study of Religion* (New York: The Macmillan Company, 1970), pp. 279–80, J. Milton Yinger discusses Nelson's criticism of this earlier treatment of cult, accepting the latter's suggestion that some cults can be long-lasting and the seedbed of new religions, especially in the context of social anomie.

[28] W.E. Mann, *Sect, Cult, and Church in Alberta* (Toronto: University of Toronto Press, 1955), pp. 5–8, 37–40.

[29] J.A. Dator, *Sōka Gakkai: Builders of the Third Civilization* (Seattle: University of Washington Press, 1969), p. 126.

[30] Benton Johnson, "Church and Sect," *American Sociological Review*, 28, No. 4 (August 1963), 539–49.

[31] Reprinted by permission of Schocken Books Inc. from *Pacifism: An Historical and Sociological Study* by David A. Martin. Copyright © 1965 by David A. Martin, p. 194.

[32] Martin, *Pacifism*, pp. 188–89. Martin offers a few paragraphs regarding the relation of the cult to the emissary style, society, mysticism, individualism, and organization which illuminate the above discussion and are worth quoting.

> Since the cultural context within which these groups [cults] appear is Judaeo-Christian it is necessary to point out that the major monotheistic religions, like Judaeo-Christianity and Islam, include an expression of the social totality. The sense of the objectivity of the divine which they celebrate is logically related to a fundamental group principle as well as to the dependence of all creation upon God. This means that monotheism has been rarely hospitable towards the more extreme forms of individualism, particularly as exemplified by the solitary mystic.
>
> Christianity and individualism are compatible only in the denominational type of religion where individualism is sharply inhibited by group solidarity, even though the group concerned is not coextensive with the

social totality. While it is true that the denomination may in one form or other diminish the objective reality of God to an abstraction of the individual reason or to an emotional sense of individual salvation, it never reduces the area of the divine simply to the self-exploration of the gifted individual. However, it is precisely this process of reduction which typifies the cult. The result is an emphasis on self-sufficiency which is logically associated with a hierarchy of spiritual conditions. Where religion is concerned with self-cultivation there can be no equality by virtue of God's unconditional grace.

Clearly many aspects of the modern situation present opportunities for a radically individualistic type of religion. Because the Church has striven to incarnate the divine through history and within society it is seen as compromised by innumerable social evils. Mysticism enables the individual to opt out of such evils. At the same time the mystic is not a member of a group suffering from oppression and is therefore not primarily interested in passing a sectarian judgment on society. He is more likely to be a creative personality, perhaps separated from forces of social integration, without suffering from class domination...

The fundamental criterion of the cult is therefore individualism. It is neither a worshipping community, like Church, order, and denomination, nor is it the closely-knit separated band of the elect...The most characteristic form of face-to-face relationship is that of teacher (or *guru*) towards initiate, although in many cases communication is restricted to correspondence and the circulation of books. . . .

Reprinted by permission of Schocken Books, Inc. from *Pacifism: An Historical and Sociological Study* by David A. Martin. Copyright © 1965 by David A. Martin, pp. 193–94.

33 It should not be presumed that the ecstatic or peak experience is necessarily common in cult life. In some cases it may be that no one, not even the leader, has actually had such an experience in all its intensity. The point is rather that these are people who are *fascinated by the possibility* of ecstasy, and for whom its attraction is a more powerful magnet than any other type of religious expression. It is more appealing than the logic of doctrine, or the pull of family or community religious loyalty, or traditionalism.

34 Robert Jay Lifton, "Protean Man," in *The Religious Situation: 1969,* ed. Donald Cutler (Boston: Beacon Press, Inc., 1969), p. 816.

35 John B. Orr and F. Patrick Nichelson, *The Radical Suburb: Soundings in Changing American Character* (Philadelphia: Westminster Press, 1970).

36 Marshall McLuhan, *Understanding Media: The Extensions of Man* (New York: Signet, 1964), pp. 36–45. Compare the following statement with emissary and exemplary styles: "Any hot medium allows of less participation than a cool one, as a lecture makes for less participation than a seminar, and a book for less than dialogue. . . . The hot form excludes, and the cool one includes."

37 Some items in this list are suggested by the characteristics of the New Religions of Japan given in Harry Thomsen, *The New Religions of Japan* (Rutland and Tokyo: Charles E. Tuttle, 1963), pp. 20–29.

38 Nelson, *Spiritualism and Society,* p. 132.

39 Joachim Wach, *Sociology of Religion* (Chicago: University of Chicago Press, 1944), pp. 17–34. The word "cultus" is a somewhat broader than "worship" in the sense of a service. Cultus refers to all the outward forms and ceremonies of religious practice: rite, formalities, verneration of images, pilgrimage, stylized private and public devotion or meditation, etc.

40 Some writers like Huizinga and Caillois have commented on the intriguing parallels between religious rite and play. In both cases there is the establishment of an artificial place and time—the temple and festival, the playing field and game—in which conditions of life are controlled by rules, by special kinds of dress and gesture, and the disorganized world of chaos and absolute freedom is excluded. At the same time in some games an interior, creative, unconditioned freedom, like that of Maslow's peak experience, can come out: masquerade, make believe. It is as though play were a charade, or better a concealed but real, form of religion. It is in this way, in fact, that expansive man may be religious.

Roger Caillois, in *Man, Play, and Games* (New York: The Free Press, 1961), says that play is (1) free, not obligatory; (2) separated in time and space from "ordinary" life; (3) uncertain in outcome; (4) unproductive of goods and wealth (though there may be exchange, as in gambling); (5) governed by rules; (6) fictive, imaginary, make believe. The types of play are competition, chance, simulation (mimicry, pretending), and those which aim at creation of vertigo, dizziness, and disorder. When one considers that both run on a scale from organized to spontaneous (rite to mysticism), one can see that all of these characteristics could be applied to religious as well as play phenomena. (In many cultures one finds various sorts of ritual combat and competition.) In play (as in rite) perhaps everything is ultimately designed to produce those states of consciousness detached from deprivation and "serious" striving which can move into the all-sufficient eternal now of the peak experience, the closest imitation of its being perhaps in that play which creates vertigo and dizziness.

41 These are Max Weber's terms. "Rational" leadership means that based on constitutional or regularized arrangements; "nonrational" is that grounded in the personal charismatic power of the leader.

two

the history of an alternative reality in the west

1. Two Views of Reality

The various typologies and criteria presented in the first chapter provide tools for gaining the understanding we want of contemporary American cults. In Chapter three we will begin to examine present-day groups selected on the basis of these criteria. But the cults of today have not suddenly appeared from nowhere. Not only do they have parallels in the phenomena of primitive and Eastern religion, but lines of influence can be traced over many centuries, and across many miles, to modern American groups. It is impossible to understand them without an understanding of the historical heritage they bear. In this chapter we shall trace the long history of movements and teachings related to modern cults from the Hellenistic period to the present. We shall then examine the immediate roots of contempory groups in the eighteenth and nineteenth centuries, and survey briefly the present scene before examining individual groups.

Although it is an oversimplification to do so, the historical background of the modern cults can be understood by thinking of Western spiritual life as divided into two camps. These are the same two realms we have spoken of as employing emissary and exemplary modes of religious communication. On one hand, there was, both among the ancient Hebrews and the Greeks of the Homeric era, an assumption that men or tribes are each separate entities living and acting in the stream of world history and dominant over nature. This orientation, different from that of the East, led to the unique contributions of Western man to world culture, and as well to certain evils of the West.

On the other hand, the West has also known a view, traceable to early contact both with India and Asiatic shamanism, developed in Platonism and Neoplatonism, which is like the cultist perspective. Grounded in Platonic wonder and amazement at Being itself, it sees the soul as separate from the body, and man as a part of nature in a monistic cosmos. A man's task is to attain to individual initiatory expansions of consciousness and awareness until he becomes mentally one with the whole cosmos.

In Christianity the two sides have been to some degree reconciled, but the first usually predominates if conflict arises. Science takes from the first view the idea that man is to analyze or exploit nature (not just attain mystical unity with it), and from the second derives monism, which it assumes means universally valid natural law, and expansion of awareness, which it takes to mean acquisition of valid knowledge.

But just as there have been adamantly conservative Jews and Christians who have tried to hold firm to the first view without allowing any contamination of it by science and philosophy, so also there has always been in the West a minority which has veered so far in the other direction that it rejects both Christianity (or orthodox Judaism) *and* normative science in favor of taking the second alternative whole. They live in a monistic, mystic world full of occult initiatory laws. It is out of this stream that the world view of modern cults comes. But because this option has never been entirely absent in Western history, we may call it the alternative reality tradition, meaning an alternative view and experience of reality.[1]

2. The Hellenistic Period

The exuberance of cult activity in modern America has a precedent, one that has profoundly affected the shape it has taken here. Ours has not been the only period in which a struggle between the hectic pace of history, disturbing in its rapidity and ruthlessness, has thrown up a radical reaction in the form of movements dedicated to living with a different focus. In this other period, too, these movements were watered from Eastern wells or fed by shamanistic springs.

We speak of that period of Mediterranean culture known as Hellenistic. The term embraces the time from Alexander the Great to the fall of the Roman Empire. It is the culture which grew up out of the confrontation of Greek letters and philosophy with Egyptian and Near Eastern life. The sort of mystical, syncretistic, cosmopolitan culture to which this label is attached flourished in the cities of the eastern Mediterranean such as Antioch and Alexandria.

It was a time when wandering philosophers–Diogenes in his tub, Apollonius of Tyana with his magic, Neoplatonists with their gaze lost in the One Eternal, Cynics, Sceptics, Stoics, Epicureans—enlivened the markets and groves of dozens of towns with their lectures and schools. Here one might be declaiming that nothing exists, and that if it did it could not be known; another that the best life is found in the pursuit of pleasure; another that one can only submit to destiny and bear all things with equanimity; another that man's only true end is to unite with the Eternal like two concentric circles merging into one. These philosophers were their own men, and their followings often could not be called continuing religious groups in any real sense. But for some people the philosophical schools—actual or figurative—which sprang up around them or in their wake must have played the role that cults play today.

The traditional gods of Olympus and Rome held little persuasion for an increasing number of these people. But philosophies of the more mystical sort, while partially compatible with their rites (Pythagoreanism and Neoplatonism), offered spiritual insights or techniques which certainly meet the test of means of ultimate transformation. In the close, almost monastic Pythagorean communities the three forms of religious expression can be found. The founder of Neoplatonism, Plotinus, seems to have been content to preside over an academic school and to keep his mystical practice private. But the later theurgic or magical Neoplatonism of Iamblichus and Proclus involved students in practice as well as doctrine. These academies are more or less the "ancient mystery schools" so much celebrated by some modern cults as their authoritative precedents.

Besides the philosophers, the other vital force in Hellenistic spiritual culture was the Egyptian and Near Eastern gods. It seems that even as the native deities of the Greeks and Romans faded into inconsequence, almost any exotic import from the East had an uncanny power to fascinate and create a cult around itself. One thinks of Isis, Serapis, Cybele, Mithra, Christ. Cut loose from the ancient cultures which had nurtured them, devotion to them spread from one port to another in the free communication and open atmosphere of the new empires. No longer were they the gods or cultus of a tribe, a little people here or there. Suddenly these gods became the centers of cosmopolitan religions. Persons of different traditions freely and individually chose to undergo the initiation and plead the favors of foreign deities, often at missionary temples in their hometowns.

If the air about the philosophers was one of dignified academic reserve

and private occultism, that of the Eastern religions was quite different. The devotees probably received initiation under conditions of great secrecy. Yet the general display of the cult was visible enough. For example, the priests of Isis, white-stoled, carrying bells, symbols, sacred water from the Nile, and a model of a great ship, would process their way to the shore each spring. Women in linen would scatter flowers and perfume on the way, while music of flute and pipe floated on the breeze. The mother of the stars, Isis, would be honored with tapers and torches. At the beach, the sacred ship would be consecrated with hymns and chants and litanies, and set to sail with the vows and offerings of the faithful for the succor of those on the deep.

This was a time of spiritual emptiness and fullness. Like the inside of a balloon being inflated, the spiritual sphere seemed both hollow, waiting for something to fill up the void, and expanding to embrace all things near and far. As in any vacuum, everything on the widening perimeter cluttered in toward the center to try to fill it. And much was shaken loose.

The armies of Alexander marched east through Persia and into India. Then the Seleucid and Ptolemaic Empires welded together in an uneasy combination the ways of Greece and the Orient. Finally Rome sent her armies, highways, and governors around the Mediterranean world. The soldiers, merchants, and administrators not only went out, they also came back, making, in the process, a collection of provinces into a world. What had been the ancient faiths of integral cultures became detached *options* for the whole known world.

In our day, practices like Zen and Nichiren Shoshu have been brought to America in large part by soldiers returning from the occupation of Japan or from American military bases overseas. Likewise, some Roman legionnaires far from home became fascinated with the faiths of Isis, Mithra, or Christ. At the same time, the peoples of the far places—Jews, wandering philosophers, Greek traders, slaves, missionaries from the Nile —swarmed freely toward the centers, even as teachers of Hinduism and Buddhism today walk the streets of American cities.

This was the foreground of that lurid and luminous age. The spiritual background, the old gods of Homer and Virgil, were fading more and more into clear air and infinite starry space. It was a time of the death of the Olympian gods, not from violence or persecution, but from apathy. It was, in other words, a time of the discovery of historical time. The old was inexplicably discovered not to fit, even though only externals of human life had seemed to change—as has happened at many junctures before and after.

Hellenistic religion, then, had these characteristics: it was a reaction to the discovery of historical time, hence it saw time as the great enemy to be defeated; it was cosmopolitan, bringing together gods and rites of many places and worshipping deities without regard for place; it was individualistic, requiring each person to make an individual choice and holding out the ideal of religion centered on individual religious experience and initiation; it was a faith searching for one God, for a unity behind the many unsatisfying atoms of historical time, place, and polytheism.

The plenary power of Isis in her cult points toward what is perhaps the most profound of the spiritual drives of the age, this desire for one God. A near second, also offered by her cult, was the desire for initiation, for mystic death and rebirth. What was wished was initiation into a universal, divine state of consciousness. It was a desire to transcend both the real but fearful experience of individualism through return to the One, and the sequential atomistic particulars of history through finding them to be all aspects of the One. This one God was alike the impersonal Absolute of the philosophers, and the Lord of starry heaven of the initiates, for whom the way to union was lit by the bright torch of a savior who knew the way—an Orpheus or Osiris.

The Hellenistic cults, therefore, had many things in common with the cults of our own day. Both center on ecstatic personal experience; both use syncretistic symbols. The background of both is often an ultimately impersonal universe against which all sorts of lesser spirits and saviors operate. Very often at the center of both is a charismatic personality like Apollonius of Tyana or a powerful philosopher. Apollonius was indeed a model of the exemplary type; he spoke not a word for five years, swaying the hearts and souls of men to good by his silent presence.

On the other hand, there are differences. While, like modern cults, the ancient ones seized upon the terminology of the science of the day (the four elements, etc.), the modern concept of progress was lacking. Instead the mood was the opposite of that worldly optimism which pervades many cults today. Hans Jonas has compared the psychological mood of Gnosticism to that of twentieth century existential despair.[2] For Gnostics, nothing could check the passions except the transcendent and trans-historical.

We will now look briefly at several of the most important of the Hellenistic cult movements. Those involving secret initiations promising salvation are often called mystery religions. This list is not exhaustive, but it is important to have some familiarity with them, since both in style and content they have influenced the whole history of Western cult activity. They are what the Western world might have become spiritually had it not been for Christianity, and they are the ever-flowing fountain which feeds Christianity's and science's alternatives in every generation.

THE ORPHIC RELIGION

Orphism was the first known separatist Greek religion with a founder and scripture of its own—even if mythical. Moreover, its goal is obviously ultimate transformation—blessed immortality on the other side—and it clearly had the three forms of expression. In a real sense it could be called the first known cult in Europe.

Orpheus, who came from Thrace, was a fabulous singer and magician able to charm animals and even rocks and trees to follow him. After crazed jealous women had torn him apart his severed head was said to have continued to sing. He was also said to have undergone initiation in Egypt, to have conquered the world of shades, and to be able to bring his initiates into immortality. This was the main theme of the Orphic cult, whose followers believed themselves strayed citizens of a better world who, through the mystery, could be led home once again. On arrival in the other world, devotees were to say

> I am a son of earth and of starry heaven...By good fortune I have escaped the circle of burdensome care, and to the crown of yearning have I come with swift foot; I bury myself in the lap of the Lady who rules in Hades...[3]

THE RELIGION OF THE GREAT MOTHER

The Magna Mater or Great Mother religion, popular across the Mediterranean, was basically Syrian though the goddess went by innumerable names—Astarte, Ishtar, Cybele, etc. She was notable for the frenzy she created among her devotees, particularly the eunuch priests.

> They danced about fanatically with a sinuous motion of legs and necks; they bent down their heads and spun round so that their hair flew out in a circle; now and then they bit their own flesh; finally, everyone took his two-edged knife and slashed his arms in various places.[4]

Here we see ultimate transformation and the three forms of expression. The self-mutilation is evidently a way in which the devotees as individuals try to make themselves children of the Great Mother (denying their adult sexuality), and a non-natural group is formed by those who do this.

THE RELIGION OF ISIS

Isis represents the Great Mother of a thousand names in a more benign form as a protecting and rejuvenating force. Like the Roman novelist Apuleius, many in her initiation

> drew near to the confines of death...at the dead of night, saw the sun shining brightly...approached the gods above and the gods below.[5]

Here is another cult of individual salvation through an unforgettable experience of initiation, and one well furnished with richly robed celibate clergy and majestic rituals.

THE RELIGION OF MITHRA

The cult of Isis brought the sacred to many in the guise of the eternal feminine, while another cult, very popular among the Roman soldiers, presented it in masculine image. This was Mithraism, the cult of the Persian sun god who made the world by sacrificing a bull, and who brought his followers into immortality through a kind of baptism with the blood of bulls. This faith has left temples from Britain to the Near East. It had a number of grades of initiation, and taught a rough code of honor and justice.

JUDAISM AND CHRISTIANITY

Of course the faiths from this period we know best today are Judaism and Christianity. The importance of their role in the ancient world is not to be minimized, even without benefit of retrospect. Perhaps as much as 10 percent of the population of the Roman Empire was Jewish, and Jews dwelt not only in Palestine but in all the major cities. Particularly at Alexandria, a Jewish intellectual life richly flavored by Platonic philosophy flourished. At the same time, Judaism with its one God and its recognition of individual moral choice had a deep appeal for many. It seemed to be an ancient tradition which, despite some very odd laws and customs, spoke to those concerns which were at the heart of the Hellenistic spiritual quest. This was a situation which led to the rise of mediating movements on the borderline between the world of the Jew and the Greek. On one level, Judaism could be made essentially a symbol system which expressed Platonism, as it was by the Alexandrian Jew, Philo.

On the level of a full religious life, Christianity provided an opportunity for non-Jews to feel "grafted into" the great Jewish tradition without having to undertake those parts of the Law which were alien to them. At the same time they could participate in a saving death-and-rebirth experience as profound as that of any Mystery. This was to prove the most powerful mix of all.

GNOSTICISM

Superficially Christian, but at heart Judaism-Platonism combinations, the schools called Gnosticism offered saving knowledge concerning the destiny of the soul—its fall from the Primal Light, its imprisonment in the world of matter by lesser lords including the planets and the Old Testament God, its way back. What sort of cultic and social life Gnosticism had is not clear. Probably it consisted mainly of theological positions held by certain teachers within or peripheral to the Christian movement, except for Manichaeanism. Unlike the purely Greek mysteries, Judaism, Christianity, and Gnosticism offered the idea of cosmic as well as individual ultimate transformation. The impressive array of movements in and around emerging Christianity has been treasured by modern occultists, who have frequently revived Gnostic and Alexandrian interpretations of the Bible and of Jesus Christ as a "higher" wisdom of which the normal Christian teaching is only a veil. But the main Christian tradition, convinced that it had a proclamation about the potential for ultimate transformation of a unique and particular historical event, the work of Jesus Christ, proceeded to orient the Western world toward that emissary style of religious communication to which a message like this is suited.

THE MAGUS

The world of the ancient charismatic philosophers, exemplary in style, is more continuous with that of the modern cults. Such groups as Pythagoreans, Hermeticists, and Neoplatonists, as well as later personages such as Cagliostro and Madame Blavatsky, offer splendid examples of a type of person who may be called a magus. This manner of spiritual personality has been helpfully isolated and examined by Eliza M. Butler.[6]

The magus is the old shaman revamped to flourish within the context of the civilized world. E. R. Dodds has shown, following the Swiss scholar K. Meuli, that in the late archaic period the Greeks came into contact with peoples of Scythia, and probably also of Thrace, who possessed a central Asiatic type of shamanistic culture. From this time on there appears in Greece "a series of *iatromanteis*, seers, magical healers, and religious teachers, some of whom are linked in Greek tradition with the North, and all of whom exhibit shamanistic traits."[7] There was Abaris, who came riding upon an arrow as do shamanistic souls in

Siberia and who banished a pestilence and taught the worship of his god. Aristeas travelled north on a fabulous journey replete with creatures from central Asiatic folklore. He was also credited with the shamanistic powers of trance, being able to appear at two places at the same time, and out-of-the-body travel. His soul could take the form of a bird and travel wherever it wished. By the time of Sophocles, who alludes to them in the *Electra,* tales like this of appearing and disappearing shamans were common. Orphism also had roots in Thrace (the region north of Greece). Dodds goes so far as to consider Pythagoras a great shaman. The Scythians and Thracians knew cannabis; the hallucinogenic drug experience may have had no small part in creating this tradition.

In any case, Dodds shows that the whole concept of the soul as separable from the body, having a separate destiny—preexistence, perhaps many lives, postexistence, the ability to leave the body, which was so important to Greek thought from Pythagoras and Plato onwards—was no more known to Homeric and archaic Hellenes than to the ancient Hebrews. For them, the only meaningful life the soul enjoyed was with and in the flesh. The separate *psyche* or soul does not appear until after Orphism, Aristeas, and the like have introduced it. The idea is clearly based on the logic of the Asiatic shaman's trance and ecstasy, with all its fateful and immeasurable impact on Plato and the whole train of Western thought and religion. The world of this thought is also the world of the shaman-in-civilization, the magus.

The magus tradition presupposes, like shamanism, not only the ultimate inseparability of valid teaching from the initiation of ecstatic experience, but also the inseparability of experience and life style for such a profoundly initiated and "different" man. In civilization, many may discourse metaphysically upon the doctrine of the soul. But when one appears who incarnates the whole kit of proofs which the shamans knew regarding the powers of the soul—initiatory experience, strange psychic abilities, extraordinary travel, mastery of spirits—he is no longer an integral part of the culture, but comes as a mysterious visitor to civilization, offering an alternative reality. This is the magus. Persons like Pythagoras, Apollonius, Iamblichus, certain medieval wizards and alchemists, Paracelsus, Saint-Germain, Cagliostro, Madame Blavatsky all are in this tradition.

While some genuine saints and mystics may have had comparable experiences, the magus is neither a saint, nor a savior, nor a prophet, nor a seer. He is a shaman-in-civilization. Like most shamans, he is part fraud, part showman, part myth, and part extraordinary ecstatic. The magus's story is always half legend, even in modern times, but the plot, like all real myths, follows a similar line.

The story of the magus will typically make contact with many of the following points—or all of them. The magus is of unusual birth and of strange and deep intellectual powers from early childhood. He travels very widely as a young man, often in Asia. He crisscrosses the world to meet sages and receive esoteric initiations. When he enters his public work, he amazes the world with fabulous magical powers, but he feels his teaching is his most important work. His teaching will be of a universe of intricate and subtle spiritual–physical forces and planes within the One, which he grasps by initiated intuition, and of a separate destiny of the soul—the "ageless wisdom." He will be able to put these forces into play in seeming miracles. The magus gathers about him both a band of disciples and invisible attendants. His disciples, however, find him puzzling, for he unpredictably appears and disappears. The magus has always about him a certain "lightness," like a shaman's. Often no one knows where he is, and he turns up unexpectedly in odd places. He has a shimmering grace and uncanny persuasive power, but unlike the saint he may not be moral or ascetic by ordinary standards; he may even be given to drink or luxury, at least sufficiently to baffle those who thought they understood him. He never, though, loses his magic or his dark, luminous wisdom. He seems not to age in the usual way, and no man knows his age. His end may be as mysterious as his life; he may finally just disappear.

The magus, with his personal mystery, is an exemplary figure, potentially the center of a cult type of group. He is a personified symbol of the "otherness" which the cultist seeks to lay hold of for himself. The magus appears like one who has been through ultimate transformation, yet is visible here. As a visible phenomenon, he may serve as focus for the three forms of expression and stimulate desire for initiation into his world.

One of the first western examples of the magus is Pythagoras (died around 495 B.C.). As a young man, he travelled to Egypt and Chaldea, then established a school at Krotona in southern Italy where he and his disciples, divided into esoteric and exoteric sections, studied philosophy and lived a life of asceticism. They were apparently vegetarian and abstained from sacrificial rites. Pythagoras was deeply influenced by Orphism (or, if E. R. Dodds is correct, it may have been as much the reverse[8]), with its teaching of a purification process by which the soul could recover its original godlike character and return to its eternal home. To the populace, he was a magician; it was said he appeared simultaneously in Italy and Sicily, and tamed a bear by whispering in its ear. Like the Orphics, he taught transmigration or the movement of the soul from one body to another life after life. The basic teaching was that the universe is a great unity which begins with the One, and unfolds in mathematical ratios comparable to those of geometrical forms and solids. Modern Theosophists have named their principle school in America Krotona, and the influence of Pythagoras is evident on almost every page of Madame Blavatsky's work.

A later Pythagorean, Apollonius of Tyana, also exemplifies the magus. He is said to have been no ordinary infant, but an appearance of Proteus, the same shape-shifting god after whom Lifton named his Protean man. He followed the Pythagorean discipline scrupulously, and after Pythagorean custom, wandered for five years keeping absolute silence. He spent four years as a sort of initiation living in the temple of Asclepius at Aegae. He was said to know all languages, including those of birds and beasts. He travelled to Babylon and Susa to talk with the Magi, and thence to India, where he discoursed on philosophy with the Brahmins. Extraordinary cures and miracles were attributed to Apollonius everywhere. After triumphantly responding to interrogation in Rome by the Emperor Domitian, he is said to have suddenly vanished away from the court. He lived to a very great age, and then disappeared. Some say he walked into a temple and did not come out, others that he ascended into heaven. A cult built around Apollonius continued into the fifth century.

THE HERMETIC BOOKS

Much "ancient wisdom" type of teaching and magic has gone under the name of Hermeticism. It is not clear to what degree Hermeticism was a cult in ancient times; there are some allusions in its literature to devotions to the sun and initiations as well as to instruction. But the name derives from the *Book of Hermes Trismegistus*, which was composed in Alexandria in the third or early fourth century A.D., probably on the fecund borderline between Judaism and Hellenism, though (typically of the culture) a few Egyptian and Christian terms are employed.

The book's prestige derives from the fact that in medieval and early modern Europe it was universally believed to be the oldest book in the world, dating at least back to the Deluge. This status has influenced many modern cultists who have taught what they call "Hermetic science" as the oldest accessible human wisdom. Hermeticism has been used both then and now to embrace not only the contents of the book, but also broadly to cover an ill-defined mass of magic, Gnostic and Neoplatonic philosophy, astrology, theurgy, and so forth deriving from the same Alexandrian milieu, but presented as much older.

The *Book of Hermes Trismegistus* centers around the instructions of the thrice great Hermes (the Greek god who became, among other things, guide of the souls of the dead and revealer of wisdom) to his son Tat (the Egyptian god Thoth, lord of wisdom and regeneration). It begins with an impressive initiatory experience, and continues with material on the creation of the world through personified emanations, and presentation of the way of salvation through lofty morals and meditation.

NEOPLATONISM

The intellectual spine of that world was Neoplatonism, the new construction of the Platonic philosophy by Plotinus (204–70 A.D.) and his followers. In brief, Plotinus taught that the cosmos is made of emanations from the One, and that man's goal is to return to the One by mystical experience through which he transcends the limitations of matter and the intervening mental emanations—the world soul, the archetypes. One can see the roots of a system like this in the Greek shamanistic tradition. Later Neoplatonists like Porphyry (234–305), Iamblichus (approximately 250–325), and Proclus (410–85) became more and more fascinated by the practice called theurgy, the evocation of gods, who often personified various planets or points in the emanational scheme.

A basic text for them, and one indicating at least the commonly accepted source of much of the magic, was the *Chaldean Oracles,* a turgid prophetic text of obscure origin taken very seriously by the later Neoplatonists. It seems to have provided prescriptions for a fire and sun cult and for theurgy. The sun, and the gods, were made into the lords of various levels of emanation, or of segments of the cosmos, and so were fitted into the more serious Platonic tradition. Systems like this were given official encouragement in the days of the Emperor Julian the Apostate (reigned 361–63), because they were considered crucial to the emperor's attempts to save Paganism.

Dodds delineates two types of theurgy. The first was concerned with consecrating magic statues by use of formulas, animals, plants, and minerals "sympathetic" to the god involved. The seven planetary gods were the most important. The second type of theurgy was the mediumistic trance. According to Iamblichus, the most suitable people for mediums are "young and rather simple persons." The characteristics of these trances seem quite comparable to those of modern spiritualism. At times the god seems to appear in a shape formed of a luminous substance not unlike the ectoplasm of today.[9]

A third practice which might have been thought theurgy, invoking a spirit or demon visibly by incantation, perhaps into a magic triangle in the manner of the "high magic" of later ceremonial magicians, seems to have been less developed by the Neoplatonists than the use of oracular statues or spiritualism. The latter are, after all, both long-standing Hellenic traditions. There were the many magic statues of the public cults of Greece and possessed oracles like that of Delphi. All of the basic principles of the later tradition of incantational evocation were developed in the first four centuries A.D., but, though not unknown to classic Greece, largely in Egyptian, Chaldean, and Hebrew circles. The names and magic words of the tradition prove as much, as do the perenniel legends of Solomon, archetype of the evocational magician, who trapped demons in jars and made them do his will. The question of the origin of modern ceremonial magic is not a simple one, however, for its practitioners work both mediumistic evocation and invocation into an exterior space or object.

The Neoplatonists and Hermeticists offered teaching and cultic activity, but their social expression is not clear. The Neoplatonists tried both to be public academic philosophers in the classic tradition—spokesmen of a wisdom compatible with the official temples and, ideally, the heritage of the total community—and at the same time custodians of very personal initiations and esoteric lore. However, only the exemplary teacher, because he leaves much unsaid, can sustain such ambivalence. But he can function only in a society which is attuned to his kind of interior spirituality. A society like the late Roman, individualized, battered by the "terror of history," threatened, haunted by the ghosts of too many dead gods, could not be reached by silent illumination so much as by a new cause which could bring it out of the past, and which was best communicated by emissary fire.

3. The Middle Ages

The expansive Hellenistic age, willing to try to tolerate any vagary of the spirit, did not suddenly turn into what we call the Middle Ages with the victory of Christianity in the fourth century. Nor was the spiritual life of the Ages of Faith nearly as monolithic as that term would suggest. Circles of dissent, sometimes flaring into vast movements like the Albigensianism of southern France, broke out upon the disputatious and always-changing face of Catholic Europe. The dissent often took the form of movements of the cult type, and those of the more intellectual sort were like long-lingering shadows of the very different Hellenistic world. Albigensianism, for example, had its ultimate inspiration in the Gnostic Manichaean religion.

WITCHCRAFT

Hellenism, however, was not all that went into the medieval alternative reality tradition which countered what the dominant vision had built. The pre-Christian faiths of northern Europe had also survived. If survivals of Hellenism have produced cults of the Theosophical and occult type, so somewhere behind Witchcraft lies the old faith of northern Europe. It has been much twisted by its unfortunate subterranean role of opposition, and much influenced by the non-northern tradition of incantational evocation. There yet lingers within it the faint trace of another path to the world of the paleolithic shaman, and of that science of soul its practicioners are pleased to call *wicca* or witchcraft—the word is related to "wit," "wisdom," and "Veda."

Perhaps its roots lie, as Margaret Murray believed, in a Stone Age cultus of a horned god, at once the Moon and Master of Animals, the patron of a hunting people. He was celebrated at full moon, and was personified by a dancing shaman in an animal skin and deer horns, like the famous "sorcerer" painted on the walls of the cave at Dordogne, France. In some way, enough forms from this old religion survived in folk beliefs and customs to provide a frame of reference for both the persecutors and alleged practitioners of Witchcraft in the days of its persecution. Clearly some of what was then called Witchcraft derives from the Hellenic alternative reality tradition and ceremonial magic, and some from pre-Christian north European belief preserved in folkways.

The evidence concerning the nature of this tradition in the Middle Ages through the eighteenth century is very difficult to assess, coming, as most of it does, by way of the passions of exaggerated fear and hatred which fired the notorious witch trials. Allegedly there were some kind of organized groups, "covens," of practitioners of the cult. According to Miss Murray, they had initiatory rites and weekly meetings. Their great quarterly Sabbats were held at the same times as the four great festivals of the Druids had been. Remnants of this faith survive in the home traditions of certain families in Britain to this day, as well as in certain folkways. But most of the contemporary Witchcraft circles are of independent origin, like the modern revivals of Druidism.[10]

THE KABBALAH

Witchcraft was not the only medieval counter-culture. Another minority was the Jews. Judaism's most profound mystical statement of the period, and its major contribution to later cultism, was the Kabbalah.[11] Kabbalism is an intricate symbol system for expressing spiritual knowledge, drawn from the premise that the Hebrew Bible is also a symbol system which expresses such knowledge through allegory and the numerological and occult meanings of words and letters. The Kabbalah predicated that as man looks toward God, he faces into the infinite darkness of God's absolute self, the *En Soph,* and between this Abyss and himself, like flashes of lightning from out of a dark cloud, the seer observes a chain of ten brilliant attributes of God. These are in male–female pairs, and range from the conscious mind of God (Kether) to the Malkuth or Shekinah, the heavenly archetype of the city of man which is in a continual love affair with human society.

Clearly the system has a connection with Neoplatonism. But the Sephiroth, as the ten attributes are called, should not be regarded merely as emanations. The Sephiroth are a freer and more reversible system. On the Last Day they will be turned on their head, so that the world of man will be raised to the top, closer to God's essence than is God's own conscious mind! The Sephiroth are ultimately coequal attributes of God which man sees as a living system, portrayed as something like a diagram of a molecular structure. Many of its key ideas entered the stream of non-Jewish thought through Renaissance Christians like Pico, Paracelsus, Boehme, and Fludd who were learned in the Kabbalah.

Alchemy and Magic

Another medieval tradition which should be mentioned is alchemy, if only because it also is part of the Hellenistic wing of the alternative reality tradition, and many of its practitioners were deeply involved in Kabbalah and magic. As Jung and Eliade have shown, alchemy was by no means merely a practical science of metallurgy.[12] The serious alchemist regarded his craft as a spiritual venture, a ritual done with retort and crucible. The procedures were of two basic types: the *coniunctio*— or marriage of opposites—a statement of the quest for wholeness; and the *transmutatio,* the transmutation of base metals into higher metals. The secret of the latter was that it was not really the metal which was changed, but the alchemist himself; he was making himself the philosopher's stone. A third procedure was that of making a *homunculus,* or small artificial human being, in the laboratory. Of course, as in any mystic path, the way was beset with temptation, and one could leave aside the higher and be diverted into metallurgy and magic for wealth.

Again, there was the tradition of ceremonial magic. Its main vehicle is the group of books called *grimoires,* of late medieval and early modern Europe, which tell how to evoke and bind demons, or even planetary gods, to the magician's will, and how to perform various minor magic. The tradition uses techniques basically the same as those of the Hellenistic Greek-Egyptian magic papyri, and even Babylonian magic, but the vocabulary is full of Hebrew names, as well as Christian invocation. Perhaps the tradition derives from the fringes of the Hermetic tradition which had become the fringes of Kabbalistic Judaism and alchemistic

Christianity. Legend assigns grimoires both to Solomon and Pope Honorius. In any case its continuity is with the classical world rather than with Witchcraft, although in time these two lines found their natural affinity for each other.

Together, all these lines presented an alternative vision of reality to that of orthodox Christianity for medieval man—one that was nonhistorical; dealt with spiritual levels or entities above man but below God; induced changed states of consciousness through festive pleasure (witch's sabbat), or concentration on alchemical or magical rites; and declared its experiences were more real than the formal baptism and repressive social order of the dominant culture. Yet this alternative reality was a perpetuation of late Hellenistic experience, the last religious phase before Christianity. It refused to die, but has lingered as an underground alternative to the present, almost breaking through to a second victory in the Renaissance.

4. The Renaissance

As the Renaissance dawned, many of these traditions rose to the surface as a reaction against the medieval system. Sages like Pico took up Neoplatonism as a counter to scholastic Aristotelianism. The Kabbalah was used by orthodox and mystical Jews alike to oppose the Aristotelianism of philosophers such as Maimonides. Neoplatonism, occultism, alchemy, astrology, and the like flourished in Europe as never before or since. The minds who took up these things were among the most independent and intelligent of the age. It was by no means a reaction into mindless superstition, but rather a plunge into the depths of the unconscious and its symbols, and into the past, in order to integrate all of man and his story in preparation for the imminent mighty leap into the modern world. For most, Neoplatonism was soon transmuted into belief in the eternality of the laws of nature upon which science is based. Alchemy became chemistry, astrology became astronomy, and finally, perhaps, Kabbalah became psychoanalysis.[13]

But teachers of the occult tradition have treasured the seminal Neoplatonism and occultism of the Renaissance for its own sake. They hold that its ideas, far from being outdated, are a deeper seed wisdom which the world is privileged to experience only once in centuries at the moments of its great turnings. It is a mental *prima materia,* a primordial half-conscious symbol-flux on the perimeters of what is graspable by man, but out of which all that is truly new and creative must come.

Renaissance occultism is a deep and complex matter; the dust that lies on its Latinate tomes is disturbed only by historians of science and

religion, who trace its role in making the modern world; Jungian psycho-
analysts, who see the profundity of its symbols; and cultists, who affirm
its continuing truth and worth.

For the Renaissance savants, Neoplatonism and occultism made cause
against the realism and rationalism of the Aristotelian Schoolmen, who
in that day seemed part of the cramped world of the passing age. The
new men wanted experience in the daring, open-ended world of mystical
Platonism with its use of the deepest affects and symbols, rational or not,
of all planes of mind and feeling. Whether Jewish or Christian in background, they wanted to let go of the past and soar into the infinite. It
was no wonder the work of such unfettered minds in both camps should
influence each other.

Their cosmos offered an unbroken graded sequence descending from
God to man and nature. God was not above, but as Nicholas de Cusa put
it, a circle whose circumference is nowhere and whose center is everywhere. Therefore God is in man and man is in God. Moreover, man in
a special way mirrors God; the mind of man is an image of the divine
mind. It is able to reflect on God in nature and also on God in himself
just as God knows nature and also himself. A popular concept was that
of man as microcosm—a miniature reproduction of the whole cosmos,
with the brain in the place of God, the various organs in the place of
sun, moon, and planets, and so forth. Naturally, the external entity had
correspondence or mutual influence upon its internal equivalent, and
with related stones, plants, and so forth, as the theurgic Neoplatonists
had taught.

Man can also influence the great cosmos. "As above, so below"—and
vice versa. The man of wisdom need not be merely a slave to the stars
and fate. Through knowledgeable manipulation of metals, elements,
thoughts which are in special rapport with planets, spirits, and archetypes personifying the higher realms which control vast ranges of the
cosmos, it was believed that man could, by small magical events, precipi-
tate great results.

In the Christianized Kabbalah and occultism of the Renaissance there
was almost a revival of the end of the Hellenistic period. Ideas like
allegory, magic, demonology, transmigration, and Pythagorean numer-
ology were again discussed in their ancient forms. It is not surprising
that, in this Renaissance milieu, the magus enjoyed a vigorous revival.
Indeed, that ideal was vigorously defended. Marsilio Ficino (1433–99),
a priest, was moved to ask the question, "What has a priest to do with
medicine? What again with astrology? Why should he, a Christian,
interest himself in Magic and Images, and the life animating the whole
of the world?"

The answer he gave, defending his own interests, drew significantly
from pre-Christian precedent. The Chaldean, Persian, and Egyptian

priests were also physicians as well as astronomers, serving charity as well as piety. A sound mind and body were to be maintained together by the same person—a cultured restatement of the integrative function of the shaman.

Perhaps the most striking example of the Renaissance magus is Paracelsus (1493–1541). His life was an attack on the educational "establishment" of his day—Aristotle in science and philosophy, Galen and Celsus in medicine. They were to him "so many high asses." While medicine was his field, Paracelsus (an assumed name, meaning "going beyond Celsus," the great Roman physician) seems to have had no regular degree. But, in the magus pattern, he travelled very widely, going even as far as Russia at the invitation of the Grand Duke of Moscow. There he was captured briefly by Tartars. One biographer writes of this experience, "Their primitive psychic—*shamanistic*—techniques made such a deep impression upon him that, in later years, their central principle became the kingpin of the Paracelsian teaching."[14]

This Paracelsus, bombastic, fiercely and principially independent, brilliant, erratic, went about learning what he could from shamans, gypsies, and workingmen as well as the wise, testing and doubting everything, teaching and practicing where he could. He made some discoveries of importance in science and medicine. He practiced alchemy according to a system of his own—he wanted to obtain the "genius" or essence of each element and metal, a personification which would incarnate its power. He wrote a famous formula for the production of a *homunculus*. He was much given to drink, but had no use for women. He always carried with him a great sword, which some said was his magician's staff, but others that he carried in its hilt laudanum, the drug made from opium, which he discovered and may have used often. He anticipated Mesmer and first used the term "magnetic" for the force by which the stars influence men and their imaginations.

Indeed, what seems to be the most interesting idea in the vast mass of medicine, alchemy, occultism, and bold independent speculation on all sorts of things Paracelsus has left is his exaltation of imagination. For him the power of thought was central, and imagination its highest ratio. He writes, as it were on behalf of all the magi:

> Perfect Imagination is the Great Arcanum. All arcana belong to Medicine. All Medicines are arcana. All arcana are volatile, without bodies: they are a chaos, clear, pellucid, and in the power of a star... Man is a star. Even as he imagines himself to be, such he is. He is what he imagines... Man is a sun and a moon and a heaven filled with stars...
> ...Imagination is Creative power. Medicine uses imagination strongly fixed. Phantasy is not imagination, but the frontier of folly. He who is born in imagination discovers the latent forces of Nature. Imagination exists in the perfect spirit, while phantasy exists in the body without the

perfect spirit. Because Man does not imagine perfectly at all times, arts and sciences are uncertain, though, in fact, they are certain and, by means of imagination, can give true results. Imagination takes precedence over all. Resolute imagination can accomplish all things.[15]

Paracelsus was far too much an independent to form any group, though he did have awestruck students and disciples, certain of whom in time turned against him. Yet a passage like the above might have been articulated by a modern New Thought teacher, or for that matter by any occultist or magician who had penetrated his art to its core.

But it was not long before his tradition, and the pattern of his life, gave rise to the idea of arcane orders of initiates, even as the mainstream of science was beginning to move away from affiliation with occultist and mentalist philosophy.

5. The Rosicrucians

In 1614, the town of Cassel in Germany was surprised by the appearance, from where no one knew, of a pamphlet entitled, *The Fame of the Fraternity of the Meritorious Order of the Rosy Cross Addressed to the Learned in General and the Governors of Europe*, usually called for short (it being written in Latin) the *Fama Fraternitatis* or *Fama*. It proposed that men of learning should band together to undertake a reformation of science comparable to that which religion had recently undergone, and that this should be done with the assistance of a hitherto hidden brotherhood of light—the Rosicrucians.

The old ideal of the magus is brought into play in connection with this esotericism and modernism. The *Fama* tells of a noble German knight, Christian Rosencreutz (Rosy Cross) who lived from 1378 to to 1484, and who as a young man had travelled to the Near East, and to Fez in Morocco, where he had been greeted by great initiates. He was instructed by them in all the occult sciences, including the invocation of spirits and the preparation of the elixir of life. Returning to Europe, he gathered about himself a secret order. After Rosencreutz' death, his order continued in secret for more than a hundred years. Then, the *Fama* relates, his hidden burial place was discovered with the body in perfect uncorrupted condition, surrounded by certain marvellous documents and instruments all bathed in mysterious light. This led the order to consider it was time to make itself known; hence the appearance of the pamphlet. A year later another pamphlet, *Confession of the Rosicrucian Fraternity*, offered initiation to selected applicants. Aspirants were to declare themselves by publishing writings so that the mysterious brothers could get in touch with them.

But although many philosophical and alchemical treatises were written, none seemed worthy of the attention of the hidden elect, and would-be initiates were frustrated in their efforts to obtain access to the mysteries of the East. More sober critics pointed out wild discrepancies in the documents. The *Fama* and *Confessio* soon came to be regarded by most as either hoaxes or fantasies.

Modern Rosicrucians claim that the traditional history of Rosicrucianism makes it part of a great secret order of the wise of all ages, among whose lights in the past have been Ikhnaton, Solomon, Jesus, Plato, Philo, Plotinus, the Essenes, the early Christians, the Kabbalists, Francis Bacon, and Benjamin Franklin. There is little real evidence to connect most of these with such an order. The name "Rosicrucian" and the symbols of the rose and the cross do not appear before about 1600 in connection with occultism, although they are on the arms of Martin Luther. It seems overwhelmingly unlikely that any such person as Christian Rosencreutz ever lived. Many have pointed out that his life, as well as his alleged teachings, seem to parallel those of Paracelsus in some ways.

Of course, the idea of an alchemical fraternity need not be regarded as wholly fictional. Many alchemists flourished at that time, and probably there were various gatherings and associations among them. But the Rosicrucianism of the *Fama* does seem to propose the first known modern association ostensibly devoted to the perpetuation of the alternative reality tradition we have been endeavoring to delineate. The Rosicrucian appeal was in effect to stand for that tradition against its transmutation into naturalistic science on the one hand and orthodox Christianity on the other.[16]

If the Order had actually existed, it would have been the first true modern cult. At least it had a sort of archetypal value. Even after the initial Rosicrucian sensation died down, it left a residue in the form of a string of emulations, some equally unrealized, some of a certain substance even in the phenomenal world. In England, persons like Robert Fludd (1574–1637), John Heydon (1629–?), and Thomas Vaughan (1626–66) took up the name and cause of Rosicrucianism. They flourished on the more occultist fringe of Cambridge Platonism, writing strange disquisitions on astrology, numbers, psychic arts, and the creation.

BOEHME

A very influential person from this period was the German mystic Jacob Boehme (1575–1624). A simple shoemaker by trade, he took the tradition of the Neoplatonists and the Renaissance savants, especially Paracelsus, and shaped it with his Protestant Christianity and his own powerful spirit. Boehme had influence on persons as diverse as George Fox and Madame Blavatsky. He taught that the soul is a magic fire derived out of God's Essence, but imprisoned in darkness. Man, as microcosm, is thus a mingling of fire and darkness. The soul is in anguish so long as it shut up in darkness, but when striving to reunite with the primal light it becomes a flame of love. The soul fire cannot die; it must either hunger, or love, eternally. Heaven and hell, thus, are always in man.

6. The Eighteenth Century

It is in the eighteenth century that we see the first appearance of substantial sociological entities connected with the alternative reality tradition which have clear continuity with American cultism today. Examples of this are Freemasonry and its more occult imitations, and the influential movements or enthusiasms connected with such persons as Swedenborg, Saint-Germain, Cagliostro, Saint-Martin, and Mesmer. If the century of the Enlightenment was the century of the triumph of sceptical reason, it was also a century of almost unprecedented success for the magus and the purveyor of mystic initiations. It has been said the age was skeptical regarding everything except occultism. In fact, the period was one of increasing polarization between several parts of man —belief and feeling, reason and fascination. In such a situation, each side must have its due turn; as each enjoys the light it may be dangerous without the restraining presence of its opposite. It was the age of Mozart's *Magic Flute,* with its light yet sympathetic treatment of Masonic and Egyptian Mystery themes, and of Weishaupt's still-controversial Order of the Illuminati, which beneath Masonic rituals and occult jargon promoted revolutionary republicanism, and may have had no small role in fomenting the revolution of 1789 in France.

FREEMASONRY

The most important of these eighteenth century phenomena for the dissemination of alternative reality ideas (and other ideas too) was Freemasonry. Eventually it became, especially in the United States, sociologically different from what it was in eighteenth century Europe. Those serious about occult ideas moved on to establish "lodges" of Theosophical, Rosicrucian, and other persuasions in the nineteenth and early twentieth centuries. But the structure, ritual, and even concept of an initiatory and degree lodge in the midst of the modern city is largely borrowed from Freemasonry.

Freemasonry was the happy combination of two strands of the early eighteenth century: the ancient English guild of working masons, and the Rosicrucianism of the seventeenth century, which had plenty of lodge theory but little functioning institutional life. All of the traditional craft guilds had rituals for the induction of members and the inculcation of moral and spiritual teaching in a language appropriate to the lore of that craft, but the guild of masons seems to have been richer in this respect than others. Its proud old guild halls appeared suitable bases on which to build something new, and yet old, in the way of ritualized wisdom of the Pythagorean-alchemical or Rosicrucian sort, well tempered with rationalistic ethics. An enigmatic hint of longstanding connection between the two strands is found in the fact that the distinguished antiquarian Elias Ashmole (1617–92) has been linked to both the Guild of Masons and the Rosicrucians.

The modern history of Freemasonry begins on June 24, 1717, when the Grand Lodge of England was inaugurated by several old guild lodges under the obvious guidance of outsiders who wished to use the old lodge halls with their fantastic rituals as vehicles for partially new teachings. The endeavor seems to have had the support of the House of Hanover, which had recently acquired the British throne, and of many of its Whig supporters. The spiritual leader of the new Masonry was a French Huguenot clergyman living in England, John Theophilus Desaguliers (1683–1744). He was a close friend and zealous apostle of Sir Isaac Newton. The project bore the stamp of the great physicist's remarkable combination of rational science, Rosicrucian occultism, and biblical literalism.

The new Freemasonry was at base an attempt by the more responsible element of the upper classes to counteract a very real tendency toward moral and spiritual disintegration in backlash against the previous century's excessive and often sanguinary religious polemics. The Freemasonry of the craft lodge with the Rosicrucian type of lore added to it seemed an apt instrument. It taught rectitude in the most solemn manner; at the same time its ethos was not at odds with the new veneration of science and reason. It was only supportive of the discreet anticlericalism and Deism of many Enlightenment gentlemen, yet it did not disdain the British flair for ceremony which remains even in the most unpromising times. Indeed, with its unlikely but auspicious marriage of the virtues of solid British craftsmanship to an aura of the immemorial and mystic usages of oriental temples, Masonry supported both the patriotism and the yearnings of those who desired more than the flat unceremonial religion of the day.

Freemasonry spread quickly from England to the continent, as well as to America and other parts of the British world. Before long Europe was honeycombed with Masonic organizations, the most prominent of which was the famous Grand Orient of France. Its honorary Grand Master was a member of the Bourbon royal family, and its membership embraced both prominent aristocrats and eminent clergy. The liberal Joseph II of Austria (reigned 1780–90), a patron of Mozart, encouraged Masonry, as did Frederick the Great. But not all Masonic organizations were of such exalted standing. There was no unity of rite or structure among groups using that title. The name was immensely popular, and so was adopted by any sort of society with a secret handshake and pretension to ancient lore. These ranged from the Swedenborgian rite lodges, based on the teachings of the Swedish seer, to the Egyptian Masonry of the inimitable Cagliostro.

A good example of Masonic type organizations is the Order of the Illuminati, established in Bavaria in 1776 by Adam Weishaupt. It did not make much headway until a Baron von Knigge entered it in 1780. A man of powerful imagination, von Knigge had been initiated into most of the secret and Masonic orders of the day. The occult possessed a deep fascination for him. Under his leadership the Order of the Illuminati progressed rapidly among the wealthy and educated and those in positions of governmental power in Germany. It established an elaborate structure of degrees and an organization modeled on that of the Jesuits. The Order attracted progressive-minded people, and was accused of advocating political revolution. Thus the conservative, clericalist Bavarian government took steps to suppress it.

SWEDENBORG

Perhaps the most pivotal and influential individual figure from the eighteenth century is Emmanuel Swedenborg (1688–1772). He is the major bridge between the old medieval alchemist or Rosicrucian in his dark laboratory, and the Spiritualist seance on the American frontier or the modern Theosophical lecture. Swedenborg, a man of superb intellectual gifts, was the son of a Lutheran bishop. As a young man he found himself drawn to science. Certain of his writings in mathematics, engineering, physics, cosmology, politics, and even psychology were definitely in advance of their time. But explorations of these fields were not able to answer his deepest questings, and he began to turn more and more to philosophy.

Then, when he was about fifty-five, a remarkable series of visions began to manifest themselves to him. According to him, the spirits of the departed, and even God himself, appeared before him with perfect visual reality. Moreover, the Swedish mystic was taken on lengthy journeys through the realms of heaven and hell, which he describes with fullest detail as to housing, civic organization, economic life, and so forth. He provides us with current interviews of notables of the past, from Plato to Luther and Calvin.

Swedenborg's writing, after the onset of the revelations, was extraordinarily prolific. In addition to his descriptions of the supernatural spheres and their activities in such works as *Heaven and Hell* and *The Last Judgment*, he produced doctrinal works like *The True Christian Religion*, as well as bulky commentaries on Genesis and the Apocalypse. A survey of this literature reveals his continuity with the alternative reality tradition, even though he, like some of the Spiritualists he influenced, was at pains to keep a Christian façade.[17]

Swedenborg was more effective than anyone else in popularizing ideas that come out of the alternative reality tradition in the modern world. Even though he is not too well known today, most cult and metaphysical movements, except direct Eastern imports, are greatly indebted to him. There is even a Swedenborgian church—the Church of the New Jerusalem. Swedenborg had such influence because he dealt not directly with recondite Kabbalistic puzzles, but from his concrete visions he gave answers to the sort of questions ordinary Christians would ask, such as, What is heaven like? What really goes on in hell? How do spirits live? But his method, apart from the direct visions, is Kabbalistic, as are his ultimate concepts. As Sir Isaac Newton's theological writings indicate, there was in the eighteenth century an almost Kabbalist Protestantism rife with interpretations of the words and numbers of the book of Revelation.

Swedenborg spoke of a "Lost Word," at once a primitive innocence and a Philosopher's Stone of transformation. He mentioned an arcane superancient scripture preserved in central Asia.

> The ancient Word, which existed in Asia before the Israelitish Word, is still preserved among the people of Great Tartary. In the spiritual world I have conversed with spirits and angels who came from that country. They told me they had possessed from the most ancient times and still possessed a Word; and that they performed their divine worship in accordance with this word which consisted of pure correspondences.[18]

Correspondences, as we have seen, are the Neoplatonist and Paracelsean idea of "magnetic" relationships between specific planets, stones, organs, etc., as well as allegorical interpretations of scriptural words. This idea of an ancient scripture in central Asia was also used by Madame Blavatsky.

In addition, Swedenborg as precursor of the modern new religions has contributed:

1. The Gnostic, Kabbalistic, and Pythagorean idea of pre- and post-existence in a spiritual state.
2. The Spiritualist idea of talk with persons on the other side.
3. A monistic idea of God.
4. A Gnostic idea of events of great importance transpiring in the invisible spiritual world known only to initiates.
5. Most significantly, the Second Coming of Christ, which Swedenborg said happened spiritually in 1757. His emphasis on this invisible consummation must be a precursor of modern "New Age" and "Aquarian Age" ideas.
6. The idea of the plurality of worlds, each with its own spirits and angels.
7. The Renaissance idea that God's consciousness is continuous with man's.

Swedenborg, with his mysterious travels to the other side, was a real magus or shaman. His rich and literalistic mysticism has been attractive to America. John Chapman, "Johnny Appleseed," was a Swedenborgian. He lived as something of an itinerant and thoroughly American Saint Francis, in love with all life here and beyond this world. As he wandered about the frontier, he left Swedenborgian literature in cabins everywhere, planting not only apples but also the Spiritualist enthusiasm of the 1850s, for Spiritualism was just a practical frontier application of the Swede's visions.

SAINT-GERMAIN

Before coming to Spiritualism, however, we must first look at a few habitués of the European courts of the *ancien régime*. The individual who called himself the Comte de Saint-Germain (approximately 1710–85) was the talk of high society in the middle of the century. He combined mystical conversation concerning ancient initiations and Masonic rites with a pleasingly flippant character. He served as a diplomat (and spy) for several monarchs. His birth and death (as he no doubt wished) are shrouded in mystery; some say he was a Portuguese Jew, but he talked knowingly of kinship with Transylvanian royalty, and above all loved to further the rumors that he had lived for millennia, and would for many more. This is the view that Theosophists have taken of him. They believe Saint-Germain to be one of the Masters of the Seven Rays, an adept of benign magic who lives in his ancestral palace somewhere in eastern Europe. The "I Am" movement has made him virtually its central figure. In the eighteenth century he was reputedly much involved in spreading mystical and Masonic rites.

CAGLIOSTRO

Cagliostro (died 1795) is a man of whom much more has been written, but of whom perhaps no more is known. He too appeared in the middle of the century in the courts of Europe, from England to St. Petersburg, claiming to be an alchemist, master of spirits, and healer. In coming to France, he struck up a friendship with the prominent and wealthy Cardinal de Rohan. He moved into the highest social circles. In the eighteenth century ancient Egypt was beginning to be appreciated anew as the Greeks and Romans had appreciated it—a darkly fascinating land of immemorial mystery and wisdom and occult initiations. Cagliostro admitted many people into a rite he called Egyptian Masonry, which he claimed was the oldest ceremonial in the world and was founded by Enoch. It received both men and women; Cagliostro was its "Grand Copht," his wife "Grand Mistress." Much has been written about its ridiculous pretensions, and there have been allegations of scandalous behavior and chicanery in connection with it. But probably it was actually no more than an enhancement of the magus's magnetic personality with a hodgepodge of alchemical and occult jargon.

Cagliostro seems to have been a complex personality, with strands of deep sincerity interwined with opportunism. He honestly sought to make his healing gifts available to rich and poor alike. He quietly gave much of the wealth he accumulated to charity, and strove tirelessly to spread his Masonic organization both in favorable times and in the face of adversity. Unfortunately, he was implicated with his friend de Rohan in the celebrated diamond necklace affair. Though he was acquitted, the enmity of the king and queen ruined his career. Not for the first time, malicious enemies pounced upon him. Some said, as some still do, that he was actually a certain Peter Balsamo from Sicily, a charlatan and confidence man with the assumed name of Cagliostro. Regarding his origins, Cagliostro himself told an elaborate story of his having been born of Christian parents in Arabia. He had, he said, travelled throughout the kingdoms of Asia and Africa, and in the usual way of the magus, attained to esoteric wisdom. But his end was dismal. After his fall from the light in France he unwisely went to Rome, where the Inquisition seized him, tried him for his Masonic activities, and sentenced him to the dungeon of San Leo where he perished a few years later.

MESMER

Yet another famous eighteenth century figure is the Austrian doctor Franz Antoine Mesmer (1733–1815), who also flourished in Paris just before the Revolution. From his name comes the word *mesmerism,* but Mesmer was not himself a practitioner of induced trance. Rather, his technique was the manipulation of "animal magnetism," a supposed health-giving substance he thought was conveyed by iron rods from a tank to patients seated around it. It is evident that what we would call suggestion, what Paracelsus called imagination, was in operation. Background music created an atmosphere. The patients frequently went into strange convulsions and finally lethargy, all of which often had an apparently cathartic effect. Some of Mesmer's followers explored suggestion further, finding that "animal magnetism" could be passed also from operator to patient. In the process, modern hypnotism developed. Hypnotism is a subject not far removed from the tradition of theurgy, magic, and spiritualist trance. Many magi have undoubtedly been successful because they have been able to make people believe they were powerful healers and transformers. And indeed, this is not far from the honest principle of most of them, that mind is all, the universe itself only the vibrations of thought.

SAINT-MARTIN

A final figure, typical of another eighteenth century type, was Louis Claude de Saint-Martin (1743–1803). Although he called himself *le philosophe inconnu,* Saint-Martin is among the best known of French occultists. He was a mild and saintly person, almost a divine fool, although of aristocratic background. While in Bordeaux as a young army officer, he met a Martinez Pasqually who had introduced new rites into the Masonic lodge there and who practiced a sort of theurgy. This interested Saint-Martin, though he was more concerned with the philosophic implications than the evocations themselves. He read Swedenborg, and found him congenial, as he later did Jacob Boehme. His own writings reflect especially the teaching of Boehme—that man has within him a divine principle too often dormant, but which he can develop to great capacities by disdaining attachment to the material.

Saint-Martin was not overly original, but he did much to popularize such thought in France, and to separate magic from occult philosophy.

He saw the Revolution as a sort of vindication of his principle that, because of the divine within, "all men are kings," almost in anticipation of the political mysticism of certain modern revolutionaries. His ideas are reminiscent of Chinese Taoism, which contained mystical, magical, and revolutionary wings. He called the Revolution the "Lost Word," that is, the philosopher's stone of spiritual transformation. When it came, he said, it was "the miniature of the Last Judgment."

7. Spiritualism and the Nineteenth Century

The nineteenth century was a period of tremendous change and growth in the alternative reality tradition, just as it was in the political, industrial, and scientific life of mankind. The alternative reality tradition is not just a conservative persistence of something grounded in an obsolete age, wanting only to undo the work of history. Its dynamic cannot be fully understood if one considers it merely a negative reaction to the dominant culture of the day. The alternative reality tradition has a life of its own and its own kind of creativity which interacts with the dominant culture—not just responds to it.

Yet it is true that the dominant mood of an era calls forth, as an undertow, its opposite. Often in society the alternative reality tradition is able to fill this role, and is thereby given opportunities to surface. The religious excesses of the seventeenth century called into being that rationalistic science which finally broke up the Renaissance alliance of physical science with alchemy and occultism. But against the background of the common sense of the Enlightenment, there was an uncontained fascination with the marvellous and mysterious which appeared in the wilder side of Masonry and the careers of such men as Saint-Germain and Cagliostro.

The eighteenth century mind envisioned a clockwork music box universe in which there just might be a secret spring which, if touched, would cause delighted handclapping by making the works run backwards or set off an amazing fireworks display. But the great passion of the nineteenth century was for infinity, and hence for totality. Gothicism, romanticism, science, and revolution had shown there were more facets to man's experience and potential than accounted for by the boxed-in universe of the earlier age.

There was also a new feeling that man could exalt in sensation, passion, and the experience of expansive time in history and the infinite void of space. Under the tinkling of teacups in the hands of duchesses, the earth spun dizzily in blue space, friend of meteors and wan nebulae, held in place only by the fine strings of Newtonian law. Below, heroes and lovers suffered death and transfiguration while the poor awaited a freeing springtime.

At the same time, the nineteenth centry was an era of extreme individualism, with its accompanying loneliness, and the suffering resulting from its social blindness. Finally, it was a time moved by the discovery, or rediscovery, of the East, not only as the land of spices, but as home of wonder and philosophy.

The unlimited passion for expansiveness attached itself to a variety of vehicles. Connected with the gothic past, it became Catholic romanticism or the Theosophical delight in "ancient mystery schools." In metaphysics, it expressed itself naturally in the transcendental monism of Fichte, Emerson, and Quimby, which ended in the "mind is all" idealism of New Thought of today. Attached to a future orientation, this expansiveness became utopian socialism and evolutionary optimism, which set the stage for all sorts of experimental societies and reformist causes—many with a cultist character. In politics, it became imperialism and nationalism and revolution. In science and philology, it was the quest for origins and for the comprehensive system.

Against this backdrop the claims of the alternative reality tradition were at once more serious and more precarious—more serious because their real impulse could be better understood, more precarious because there were so many rival offerings of infinities.

Yet for all that, the ordinary contemporary view of the age—an age in which, after all, poets died young while ruthless industrialists grew fat—was that it was a time of dead materialism and wingless thought. The alternative reality tradition, revamped in new dress, was able to make some appeal. Every age needs some frontier of mystery, and if the usual rites are no longer mysterious, it will discover new—or old— mysteries. In the Victorian age, wonder (the heart of the alternative reality tradition) took for some the form of passion for psychic phenomena, for ghosts and spirit communication.

Spiritualism as a definite religious movement is a product of that century. It provided a direct experience of the marvellous, in a way that goes back to archaic shamanism. The "other side" is revealed through a remarkable individual who, having been initiated, can control spirits, travel to their world, or allow spirits or ancesters to communicate. Edward Burnet Tylor, the greatest nineteenth century anthropologist, defined the remote savage beginnings of religion as animism, a belief in souls distinct from their physical bodies or vehicles. Of course, Victorian man felt that his own scientific rationalism or ethical monotheism was entirely separate from these rude origins.

At the same time, a view of the soul not greatly different from animism, and a use of psychic display reminiscent of shamanism, became popular in the drawing rooms of Victorian Europe and America. From the Court of the French Emperor to the frontier villages of the Great Plains, in Russia and Brazil, tables rose and turned, rappings sounded out occult messages, and the voices of the dear departed gone over to the "Summerland" spoke through trumpets marvellously floating in the air. The mood of the Empire parlor, with its wealth of greenery, its overstuffed chairs, its crillioned pianoforte, in which the spirit-entranced circle would gather in near-darkness, may have been different from that of the central Asian shaman with loud bells and drum and birdfeathers, shaking with trance amid his leather-clad tribesmen. But it was the same altar, and Spiritualists with some right boasted that theirs was the oldest religion in the world.

It is to what was then one of the newest nations in the world, the United States of America, that the credit must go for the reemergence of this most ancient of faiths in its modern form. Its institutional birth can be pinpointed quite precisely to the evening of March 31, 1848, in the home of John Fox at Hydesville, in upstate New York. (It had been preceded by spirit communication through rapping among the Shakers of Watervliet, New York.)

The Fox family had two daughters, Margaretta (then eleven) and Kate (then eight). Since moving into the house three months before, they had been hearing puzzling noises, mostly rappings like imitations of the recently invented Morse Code. On the night of March 31, the younger daughter, Kate, is said to have snapped her fingers at the rappings and said, "Here Mr. Splitfoot [the devil], do as I do!" She then proceeded to work out a code with the rappings. The Foxes were told that the noises were caused by the spirit of a peddler who had been murdered in the house four or five years before. A skeleton which seemed to confirm the story was allegedly found in 1904 after a cellar wall collapsed.

In 1848, the story of the Hydesville occurrence was an immediate sensation. A circle began meeting in the Fox home to discuss and experience the phenomena. Committees of ministers and others from nearby Rochester investigated it and disputed their results amidst great publicity. An enthusiasm for spirit manifestations spread rapidly. Circles met everywhere to reproduce, if possible, the remarkable events. Lecturers and publications followed. Soon not only rappings but voice mediumship from the spirit world, table tilting, and other such phenomena were reported. The Fox sisters aided the growth of the Spiritualist movement by their traveling, lectures, and demonstrations. The speed with which Spiritualism grew, however, indicates the nation must in some way have been in remarkable readiness for such a breakthrough; it was like a field dry and ready for the torch.

Prominant supporters of Spiritualism included Horace Greeley, James Fennimore Cooper, W. C. Bryant, Governor Talmadge of Michigan, and, by 1857, Abraham Lincoln. In the early 1850s six or seven Spiritualist newspapers and magazines were published, and sensational stories in the secular press also whipped the enthusiasm to greater and greater heights. In 1857 it was reported the majority of the inhabitants of Cleveland and the Western Reserve section of Ohio were Spiritualists. In many places the regular churches were forced to close; Spiritualist meetings were packed.

One of the most significant aspects of the spiritually restless early nineteenth century in America was the establishment of many utopian communities, whether based on socialist or religious principles. It was not long after 1848 that a number of such communities appeared with Spiritualist connections. Sometimes, as in the case of the Mountain Cove community in Virginia, the whole enterprise was directed by the spirits (in this case such exalted biblical figures as St. Paul, St. John, and Daniel) through the medium. Both the Rappite and Owenite communities in New Harmony, Indiana, ended amid an effusion of psychic phenomena.

Brook Farm, Hopedale, and Ceresco were well-known utopian communities which developed Spiritualist practices after their founding. These three had been established before 1848, but they experienced spirit manifestations after the enthusiasm began, submitted to important guidance from the spirits (in the case of Hopedale, from the shade of the founder, Adin Ballon, after his death in 1852, and did much to help advance Spiritualism. Other Spiritualist communities, like Harmony Springs, Mountain Cove, and Kiantone, through bizarre excesses of free love, crank teaching, and flagrant claims, brought discredit to the movement.

In America Spiritualism suffered wild fluctuations in its support. At times it received spectacular accolades, at times vehement ridicule. But the ridicule grew stronger. The enthusiasm of the fifties proved a passing fad. The movement was hurt by a series of exposures of fraudulent mediums, by the follies of the fringe, and by the opposition of the churches and important segments of the academic world. Finally, the passions of the Civil War swallowed up all other national emotions.[19]

While many fell away after 1860, a remnant carried on Spiritualism, and it was to enjoy later moments of comparative fame, especially in the period between the two World Wars. Moreover, the seed of the movement was carried in the fifties from America to Europe, where it experienced less meteoric but more stable success.

Why did Spiritualism emerge when and where it did? The upstate New York territory in which it started has been called the "Burnt-Over Country." It was a region that had experienced a surfeit of revivals during the first decades of the century. After these had exhausted the potential for evangelical Christian conversion, other alternatives moved in to fill the void. But the revivals had also helped pave the way, for the phenomena they had manifested such as speaking in strange, rapturous ways, made the trance process in mediumship less unfamiliar.

On the other hand, the frontier experience also worked in favor of unorthodoxy. The frontiersman was an individualist, cut off from his roots. He believed he was creating a new and far better civilization out of the wilderness. As the same time, hardship and death were his constant companions. Both his individualism and his nearness to death cemented the appeal of Spiritualism. He would phrase spiritual issues in terms of "Have those I loved survived physical death *as individuals* with whom I can communicate? Will I so survive? Can this be proven in ways concrete enough to convince a hardheaded, practical American who still desperately wants to believe?" The fact that the teaching was new and denounced as unorthodox would have only enhanced its appeal for many frontier Americans. The freedom to form new churches allowed by the religious liberty of the American nation, the institutional flux and lack of any long-established churches on the frontier, and the idea of a new age with new ways being born, all combined to permit Spiritualism to find ready expression in all three of the forms of expression, and Spiritualist churches to spring up rapidly.

Certain intellectual influences also paved the way such as Swedenborgianism, which people like John Chapman had spread through the frontier. A generation was already familiar with the idea of investigating the lives of those who had gone beyond. The "animal magnetism" of Mesmer had also become known in America and had made the phenomena of trance and clairvoyance familiar.

All these influences are evident in the career of Andrew Jackson Davis (1826–1910), the "Poughkeepsie Seer" who became the most important American Spiritualist writer. With little formal education, Davis was put into trance by a Poughkeepsie tailor who had heard a series of lectures on "animal magnetism." Davis became a professional clairvoyant. In 1844 he said that he had fallen into a trance while alone and conversed with Galen and Swedenborg.

Later he gave a series of trance lectures which were published in 1847, just before the Fox sisters' experience, as *The Principles of Nature, Her Divine Revelations, and Voice to Mankind.* Fundamentally Swedenborgian, this work presented an evolutionary view of nature. It held, moreover, that the earth is surrounded by a series of spiritual planes. The soul naturally gravitates to its own level, and remains on that plane until it is ready to evolve to the next higher; the progress is always upward, whether fast or slow. In social thought, Davis, like many early Spiritualists, was a radical. He predicted a new utopian dispensation preceded by a social revolution.

The other most important Spiritualist philosopher was the Frenchman Hyppolyte Léon Denizard Rivail (1803–69), who wrote under the name of Allan Kardec in the 1860s. He differed from Davis in holding to reincarnation, which could occur periodically as decisive events in the career of the soul until it reached a very high level. To this day there is a large and influential Kardecist church in Brazil. The argument over reincarnation has been a major issue among Spiritualists ever since.

The idealism of a system like Davis's carries into occult dimensions the Transcendentalism of Emerson. The belief that consciousness is the fundament of existence, creates its own world, and is continuous with an evolving world spirit is of course a steady component of the alternative reality tradition. It rolls like a great river through the fields of early nineteenth century philosophy. Later the river was dammed by a new realism and scientific positivism, but dribbling streams continued to trickle on.

Finally, proximity to the shamanism and spiritism of the American Indians may have influenced the movement. Descriptions of the evocation of spirit guides by the native American shamans had been published early in the century by pioneer ethnologists like Henry Rowe Schoolcraft. The popularity of the Indian guide theme in later Spiritualism suggests a half-conscious tribute to those who were the first American Spiritualists, and who, despite the frontier wars, have always been much respected by their white imitators. In nineteenth century Spiritualism there was a great enthusiasm for the "Shawnee Prophet" (1768–1837), brother of Chief Tecumseh, who became a legendary seer.

There is also the influence of the European occult tradition. Masonry, Witchcraft, and Rosicrucianism had all been imported to America. The Salem witch trials of 1692 and the Anti-Masonic Party of the mid-century bear them ungrateful witness. But essentially Spiritualism is a folk, home-centered movement. It was not founded by a single magus and does not boast mighty initiations or proud lodges. It is what becomes of the occult tradition when processed through the minds of a literalistic Swede and an American original like Davis, and then potently mixed with the wild, open society of the frontier with its direct exposure to an archaic shamanistic people, its enthusiasm, and its hope of building a new order.

8. Theosophy

The return of the magus is the theme of the next great nineteenth century movement, Theosophy. This is a movement which has behind it one of the most memorable of those who have played the role of magus, Helena Petrovna Blavatsky.

Madame Blavatsky, or H.P.B. as her friends and followers affectionately call her, was a lady of great mystery and complexity. She was clearly composed of several personalities, all of them extreme. Whether she is considered a fraud and confidence artist, or a sage of sages, or a compulsive liar, or a rare psychic and intimate of supernormal entities, or a gluttonous and overbearing old tartar with a fishwife's tongue— whatever she was, or if she was all of them together, she was that to an unrivalled degree. When her public career began, she was already, or seemed, impossibly old, fat, ugly, profane. Yet she was laden with the exotic aura of a lady of Russian aristocratic background. She seemed an exile from a world of monarchical splendor. Moreover, she told tales of long intervening years of fabulous travel and initiations by members of a secret occult order in Greece, Egypt, and Tibet. The "Masters" and the Order were not unlike those portrayed in the then popular novels of Bulwar-Lytton such as *Zanoni*. H.P.B. had eyes of a singularly opaque, yet piercing, hypnotic quality, as though she penetrated everything while revealing nothing of herself except sheer, burning psychic power. Nor could any equal her public work, whether in mysterious phenomena produced, in fascination of conversation, in mass of pages written expounding the philosophy of the "ancient wisdom," or in travel and fame.

The real H.P.B. was born in Russia in 1831 and died in London in 1891. Her family was of high nobility. As a child she was unusual—headstrong, secretive, imaginative. She would hide in strange places reading myths and legends for hours while her family searched desperately. She would tell her brothers and sisters marvellous tales of the fossils and animals in the manor's zoological museum, describing not only the animal's immediate life, but also its previous incarnations.

She was a quite an uncontrollable child—at once obstinate, of a terrifying temper, and fanciful and mystical. She was married at the age of sixteen to General Blavatsky, Vice-Governor of Erivan and a man in his forties. Less than a year before she had plunged her leg into scalding water rather than attend a fancy ball at a Viceroy's. She later said that at that time if any young man had dared to speak to her of love, she would have shot him like a dog who bit her, and on another occasion said, "I wouldn't be a slave to God Himself, let alone man." It seems her sudden and surprising decision to contract the marriage was but another example of her strong-headed contrariness, and was apparently in response to taunts that no man would want such a strange and graceless young lady. Also marriage at least made her independent of her family. In any event, the marriage did not last long. Whether the ill-matched couple remained together less than three weeks, as H.P.B.

asserted, or longer as others have said, she managed to flee her older husband and her native country very soon. Apparently she was supplied with some funds by her family.

In 1851 she was in London with her father, and here she says she first viewed her "Master," a striking turbaned man of the East. (Perhaps she saw a member of a Nepali delegation which was in the capital at that time.) During the later Russian period, she amazed her family and social circle with remarkable displays of psychic and magical powers. H.P.B. then virtually disappeared from sight for almost thirty years, with the exception of 1858–64 which she spent again in Russia with her family and, it seems, in part with General Blavatsky.

As for the balance of years, if we take her word for it, H.P.B. ranged widely and wildly over the world, contacting shamans and masters of arcane lore in places as far apart as Egypt, Mexico, Canada, and inner Asia, always seeking her ultimate goal, Tibet. She finally achieved it, spending 1864–67 there undergoing initiations with her Masters. Thus she fulfilled the archetype of the magus—remarkable birth and childhood, wide travel, esoteric initiation, enigmatic personality, supernormal powers.

She came to America in 1874 and met a successful agricultural scientist and lawyer who was also keenly interested in investigation of Spiritualist phenomena, Colonel Henry Steel Olcott. Madame Blavatsky was then practicing as a medium. Through her, higher and higher figures from the spirit world—Masters—began appearing to Olcott. The mysterious Russian lady and the American man of affairs became inseparable. Together they were the real founders of the Theosophical Society in 1875. With the help of the Masters, and of Olcott, H.P.B. wrote her first book, *Isis Unveiled*, published in 1877.

The Theosophical Society was founded to discuss ideas regarding ancient lore, supernatural phenomena, and the expansion of human powers of mind and spirit. Its nucleus was a group which had gathered in H.P.B.'s apartment to hear a lecture putting forth curious Egyptological speculations. The group included a Unitarian minister and General Doubleday, the inventor of baseball, but seems to have been composed mostly of persons of the artistic and literary sort, probably rather Bohemian.

Olcott's fascinating *Old Diary Leaves* vividly recalls the New York days. There is an impression of a Victorian Haight-Ashbury. The room where H.P.B. held commerce with her Masters, wrote *Isis Unveiled*, and entertained Olcott and others with visions and apports, was heavy with smoke from incense and her imported cigarettes. Olcott and H.P.B. held legendary parties replete with thrillingly serious discussions of the enigmatic Madame's latest "phenomena" and exciting theories, or else put on uproarious charades which might spoof Theosophy first of all. The fantastic apartment in New York was the center of something at once dangerously avant-garde—the first cremation in America was under Theosophical auspices—and full of whispers of ancient caves and tombs. Above all there was the presence of H.P.B., defiant of society, talking in exotic accent of mysteries far outside its purview. There was the aura of her Spiritualist antecedents—the arcane books and pictures in the room with its bizarre decorations, one wall plastered by a jungle scene made of colored leaves. There was the independence of the principals regarding social convention. It is not surprising that the early Theosophists quickly won a notoriety like that of the "hippies" in 1967.

The New York period ended in 1878, when Madame Blavatsky and Colonel Olcott sailed to India. That land, and beyond it enigmatic Tibet, had become the magnet of their spiritual adventure, surpassing Egypt, the Kabbalah, and the old Rosicrucians. Those Western sources had been the major inspirations of *Isis Unveiled,* which does not make much mention of reincarnation. But the author had been talking increasingly of India and Eastern Masters. By the time she and Olcott arrived they were heady with the classic quest of the westerner for spiritual light from the East. Olcott wrote that upon landing in Bombay

> the first thing I did on touching land was to stoop down and kiss the granite step; my instinctive act of pooja! For here we were at last on sacred soil; our past forgotten, our perilous and disagreeable sea-voyage gone out of mind, the agony of long deferred hopes replaced by the thrilling joy of presence in the land of the Rishis, the cradle country of religions, the dwelling place of the Masters, the home of our dusky brothers and sisters, with whom to live and die was all we could desire.[20]

Eventually a Theosophical headquarters was established at Adyar in Madras, India. The society spread throughout Europe and America. The respect Theosophists showed for the indigenous religions of Asia played a role leading to cultural revival, national self-consciousness, and finally the independence movements of the present century which should not be underestimated. For his work in promoting Buddhism, Colonel Olcott is regarded as a major national hero in Ceylon—he was recently portrayed on a beautiful commemorative stamp of that nation.

The history of the Theosophical Society was never smooth, however. In the early 1880s, certain Theosophists, particularly A. P. Sinnett, had been receiving letters signed by one of the Masters. He would find them in unexpected places—tucked in the inner fold of a napkin, or among the papers on his desk. When Madame Blavatsky returned to Europe in 1884, a Mr. and Mrs. Coulomb, who had been left in charge of the Adyar buildings, charged that they had been given instructions by H.P.B. to produce the letters fraudulently. The matter was investigated by the Society for Psychical Research, together with other of H.P.B.'s "phenomena," and the ensuing report did much damage to the Theosophists.[21]

After the death of Madame Blavatsky, the American society broke with the Adyar headquarters. The lady who became head of the American society, Katherine Tingley, established a remarkable Theosophical utopia at Point Loma, in San Diego, California which survived over forty years. The Adyar society, which soon recovered its ground to embrace most American Theosophists, was dominated during the first three decades of the twentieth century by Annie Besant and C. W. Leadbeater. During their time the concept of the Masters was refined into a schematic hierarchy. A young Indian boy, Krishnamurti, was advanced as likely to become the World Teacher for this era. This caused considerable excitement until he renounced the claim in 1929.

Theosophy was successful in the middle and upper classes of American society before the First World War and in the 1920s. It was a time when after-dinner lectures were popular, and the magnetic personalities, both European and Indian, who represented Theosophy provided sensational and thought-provoking presentations.[22]

Theosophy occupies a central place in the history of cult movements, for the writings of Madame Blavatsky and some of her followers have had a great influence outside of her organization. They represent an interesting and significant attempt to interpret the alternative reality tradition. The notion of hidden Masters, far ahead of the rest of mankind in spiritual evolution and secret holders of earth's destiny, is not new in that tradition. It had been suggested by theurgic Neoplatonism, Rosicrucian lore, and earlier in the nineteenth century by the Polish philosopher Hoene Wronski, the French writer on magic Eliphas Levi, and Bulwar-Lytton the novelist.

But the Theosophists developed the "Masters" idea more fully than anyone else, and, connecting it with similar Eastern ideas such as the role of the transcendent Rishis in Hinduism and the Bodhisattvas in Buddhism, made it the foundation of a world view. In her greatest book, *The Secret Doctrine* (1888), Madame Blavatsky brings together planetary and individual initiation. Both move from the consciousness of the atom to planes far beyond our scan—animals, man, and the Masters are on a great ladder. This makes initiation, expanding one's consciousness to move from one rung to a higher one, central. It suggests what we may call a psychological view of the nature of reality in contrast to a mechanical or even biological one. Matter is, with spirit, an original production of the One and is not rejected. But areas of experience, planets, the solar system, all have behind them high minds who control them. It is perhaps a bold way of saying that the most adequate way to describe reality is to say its expressions are expressions of chains of consciousness—the minds of individual men are like embodied archetypes, fantasies, memories, or ideas in the vaster mind of the planet, and in turn parts of the mind of the solar system, and on up. The "White Lodge" Masters are intermediate figures who prepare themselves and others for planetary and cosmic initiations.

In a cosmos like this, the important thing is to move from one level of consciousness to another—from an animal's to man's, a man's to a Master's, and Master's to a planet's or a solar system's. This would mean being able to include things within one's awareness which were not included before. The great moments of a mind are when new connections are seen, like a gestalt, and are emotionally and subjectively realized. These would correspond to the great moments of initiation into a "higher plane" with a wider scope of activity or understanding so celebrated by Theosophists.

9. New Thought

Belief in the supreme reality and power of mind is fundamental to another late nineteenth century development, New Thought. It is not so much a cult or church in itself as a type of teaching which has influenced a number of groups. Certain churches, like the Church of Religious Science, Church of Divine Science, and Unity, are based on its tenets. But a vast variety of what is called "metaphysical," or even "positive thinking," derives from this tradition and its major writers—Phineas Quimby, Ralph Waldo Trine, Horatio Dresser, Thomas Troward, and Ernest Holmes.

New Thought is a modern Western adaptation of the assumption that mind is fundamental and causative. This means that the real cause of every event is an internal, nonmaterial idea. Like Theosophy it holds the inner reality of the universe to be mind and idea. It does not point to Masters as the minds which make things happen, but to the mental potential of every individual. New Thought teachers have always striven to show how, in very practical ways, thoughts of health, wholeness, and success can create their corresponding material realities. If mind is the ground of the physical world, then changing one's thoughts ought to change the physical world. Even if one concentrates on particular objects, for example a needed sum of money, this act will draw corresponding physical realities into being. New Thought has always put special emphasis on healing—both of mind and body. It has generally taken a style similar to that of liberal Protestantism and has thus emphasized verbal expression and forming congregations. Its atmosphere is optimistic, theologically liberal, extravertive, generally nonradical in life style and social opinion.

The remote roots of New Thought may lie in Hegal and Emerson— German idealism and New England transcendentalism—but the real originator of the movement is Phineas P. Quimby (1802–66). J. Stillson Judah has shown that there are large areas of agreement between Quimby and the Spiritualist Andrew Jackson Davis, which in turn shows how pervasive the influence of Swedenborg has been.[23] Both agreed that God (pure mind or spirit) is wisdom and man's real nature. But while Davis, like Madam Blavatsky, was interested in world evolution and life after death, Quimby was concerned with healing. Disease, he taught, has its roots in mind. Behind every illness is an erroneous idea. It is the false idea that matter has a reality and power of its own that cause disease. Actually matter comes into being at the behest of God, and God, as wisdom, continuous with one's own wisdom, knows it to be nothing but a thought. To regard matter as a possible source of discomfort is the result of ignorance.

Quimby, functioning as a hypnotist, healed Mary Baker Eddy of serious ailments by the power of mind, or so she believed. She later discovered Christian Science, based on the belief that the mind of God is all. New Thought teachers have, however, developed independent positions.

Despite its American pragmatism and its relative success, it is interesting to observe what New Thought has in common with cult movements like Theosophy and Spiritualism. All three have been much more open than the major churches to feminine leadership and have had women as important founder figures. Usually the women had been dissatisfied in marriage. Perhaps the spirit of these movements is closer than the Western norm to the feminine psyche, too, and perhaps the whole alternative reality tradition is really a more psychologically feminine view of the cosmos than the obviously masculine values which exist in the dominant culture—or have until recently.

Like Spiritualism and Theosophy—and the whole tradition—New Thought too has shared the basic presupposition that the mind is capable of transcending all limitations the world seems to place around it, because mind is ultimately sovereign, or is all that is. Mind can enjoy communication with those who have seemed to die; mind can expand through initiations to embrace the cosmos; mind can create by its own direct force all desirable conditions of life.

10. Eastern Imports

Fundamentally, the sovereignty of mind has always been the position of the alternative reality tradition. But it has seen several changes in methods of communication of this principle. It was changes of this sort which overtook it as it went into the twentieth century. Two important things happened: it was reinforced, if not almost swallowed up, by the direct importation of Eastern religions; and it later found verbal communication giving way in large part to nonverbal communication, as it moved into the world of expansive man. It is as though it finally wanted to express the mind's independence of everything, even words.

The introduction of oriental religion in explicit institutional form into America can be dated from the World Parliament of Religions held in Chicago in 1893. The most memorable address given was that of a man from India, Swami Vivekananda, a disciple of the great Hindu saint, Ramakrishna. Vivekanada had been a brilliant student and had received a Western scientific education, but, finding it did not answer his deepest needs, had turned to the ancient spiritual path of his native land as exemplified in his God-realized master. Then he had sought—a radical notion in those colonialist days—to bring the spirituality of the East to the West, in exchange for the technological and political sophistication and the Christianity Europe was confidently exporting to Asia. He brought it in the form of Vedanta philosophy. This is the most important school of Hindu thought, and he no doubt rightly considered it Hinduism's most universal form, more applicable to man at large than particular devotional deities or yoga techniques. Vedanta holds that the only reality is Brahman, the Absolute One, realized in profound meditation. The phenomenal world is *maya*, illusions of mistaken identity, or *lila*, the games the One plays with himself, which are all that is seen by a person in a state of ignorance.

The mission of Vivekananda inspired the establishment of Vedanta Societies dedicated to the study of this teaching in the major cities of Europe and America. Usually the spiritual leader was a *swami* from India of the Ramakrishna Order. Typically he interprets his message in such a way as to minimize discontinuity with the spiritual traditions of the West. There is a service with sermon at the usual hour on Sunday morning, and homiletical emphasis on passages in the Bible congenial to Vedanta. The Vedanta Society has generally attracted the most intellectual of those westerners who have been persuaded by the wisdom of the East; persons such as Aldous Huxley and Christopher Isherwood have been among its adherents.

Other Eastern groups and teachers followed Vedanta. In the 1920s another missionary from India appeared in America. He was called Paramahansa (the title of a supreme yoga master) Yogananda, and he was the founder of the Self-Realization Fellowship. His dramatic *Autobiography of a Yogi* is well known. The Self-Realization Fellowship, now large and successful, also retains definite elements of syncretism. The newer import groups have been incrasingly less syncretistic until one comes to the Western Zen institutions and Krishna Consciousness. The adherents of these two seem to delight in reduplicating down to details of dress and diet the traditional life of their coreligionists in Japan or India. But in all cases, the tendency is toward preserving authentically the symbols, worship, and methods of transmission of the Eastern faith. The Eastern missionaries are today less apologetic about the Asiatic cultural packaging of their teachings, and westerners seem more than eager to experience it whole.

11. Conclusions

In visiting cults, one notices typically even more stratification and segregation as to age, social class, and life style than in ordinary churches. They fall in fact into three groups: those founded before the First World War, those founded between the wars, and those founded after the Second World War.

Those in the first group—Theosophy, New Thought, Spiritualism, Vedanta—put heaviest emphasis on verbal communication. They employ lectures, books, and discussions. The format generally emphasizes symbols of continuity with the dominant Protestant culture. The individual member expects only deferred spiritual reward as compensation for study, service, or vicarious participation in the spiritual power of another, such as a medium or master. The worship and ideology is syncretistic, but centers on words, and in format emulates liberal Protestantism. The social group is quite structured, at least on paper, with a constitution and a federalist rational polity.

Between the wars, a new set of groups arose, like Self-Realization, the Krishnamurti enthusiasm in Theosophy, "I Am," and the Meher Baba movement. These groups work more or less from the basic premises of groups of the older type. But they represent freer, more expansive developments, usually centered on flamboyant, charismatic personalities. Their systems in theory take the comprehensive philosophies of Theosophy or Vedanta whole, but in practice are much less interested in discursive thought. Rather, like all personality devotionalism, they show how a person can mystically rather than intellectually attain ultimate transformation by opening himself to the contagion of a personality and enthusiasm which is close to the center of things. In this experience there is, in fact, likely to be much more immediacy. One no longer need postpone realization until after one has read a number of books. The new teachers used language more adapted to triggering immediate awareness of the riches of Vedanta or Theosophy by intuition.

X Finally, after the Second World War, and especially in the sixties, another style set in. A new generation took the tendency of the twenties and thirties much further. At the same time, the cosmopolitan mood of the postwar world was ready to accept unadulterated Eastern imports. The new generation was more concerned with expressing alienation from the cultural tradition than continuity with it in religious format. It was a period which saw the introduction of Nichiren Shoshu, Zen, Subud, and Krishna Consciousness, faiths which almost rejoice in their foreignness.

Both in this and in their teaching, the new groups seek to permit everyone a direct experience, not one deferred until after much listening and study, not one only vicariously felt. A *real* experience may require a total special environment, different from the ordinary, and therefore productive of wonder or shock. This is one result of the use of symbols of discontinuity. The experience will perhaps be multisensory. Once the strange Puritan idea that hearing is the most religious of the senses, and religious communication through any others (except visual reading) rather suspect, has been abandoned, it becomes obvious that the more senses involved, the more reinforced the communication. Thus one uses light, color, incense, music, touch. Many of the Asiatic faiths, of course, have effective enough multisensory techniques. On the other hand, there is an equally strong presumption that no external sensory communication can really achieve religious transmission. At best, it can only produce an atmosphere conducive to internal realization.

Thus the new groups tend to take to an extreme the basic alternative reality idea that the only God one can find is within and known only by expansion of interior awareness. Words are of secondary importance, since there is nothing to be *said* that is an actual *communication* of divine reality, although of course, like incense or a holy touch, certain words may be conducive to an atmosphere which ignites the interior experience.[24]

In teaching, then, the new generation of cults presents words which are obviously not so much the communication of content as the evocation of a mood or the catalyst of an experience. This is very clear in the chanting religions and the Zen koan and the scientistic language of

Scientology. The cultus will likely seem unfamiliar in format to one accustomed to the usual Western religious body, whether the cult displays a lavish and exotic ritual, or an almost disconcerting informality. In the same way, the social expression will seem both more democratic and more authoritarian—the first in witness to a feeling that the only important thing is inner experience for all, the second because the group is likely to have a charismatic leader at the center, and no one now is as concerned about parliamentary procedure as our Victorian forebears.

The new groups are fully in the alternative reality tradition going back to Alexandria and India. Indeed, they represent a great and pure revival of it, one strong enough to challenge the main pillars of Western spiritual culture. Their real triumphs will probably not come in numbers of direct converts, but in the changes they make in the tone of the whole culture, not least within the traditional churches and synogogues themselves.

Notes

[1] I do not speak of alternative reality *culture*, since the word *culture* implies a set of symbols and structures held in common by a group of people sharing all main areas of life—the political, economic, spiritual, etc.—which children of the community learn by growing up with them. Although the word is sometimes used loosely—"drug culture," etc.—to mean a group within a society centering around a particular experience or rite, this is really a different social phenomenon. I feel the word *tradition* is most appropriate for what we are attempting to deal with historically in this chapter. That term suggests something whose main extension is in time. This *tradition* is never especially widespread at any one time—synchronically—but seems to persist unquenchably in history diachronically. It usually does not determine all the symbols, words, actions, and relationships of a person since he must live within the human context of the general culture. But it may determine them so far as he is voluntarily able to allow it. Probably most people involved in the tradition take it on as a choice rather than on the basis of the natural relationships—home and family—through which culture is learned. Yet there is definitely a long-term transmission from person to person.

[2] Hans Jonas, *The Gnostic Religion* (2nd ed., rev.) (Boston: Beacon Press, 1963), pp. 320–40.

[3] Frederick C. Grant, ed., *Hellenistic Religions* (New York: The Liberal Arts Press, 1953), p. 108–9. Hymns from two Orphic gold plates are combined here.

[4] Grant, *Hellenistic Religions*, p. 121. The passage is from Apuleius, *Metamorphoses*, VIII, 27.

5 Grant, *Hellenistic Religions,* p. 142. The passage is from Apuleius, *Metamorphoses,* XI, 23.

6 Eliza M. Butler, *The Myth of the Magus* (New York: the Macmillan Company, Publishers, 1948).

7 E. R. Dodds, *The Greeks and the Irrational* (Berkeley: University of California Press, 1951) pp. 140–41.

8 Dodds, *Greeks and the Irrational,* pp. 143–44.

9 Dodds, *Greeks and the Irrational,* pp. 283–311.

10 Margaret Murray, *The God of the Witches* (New York: Anchor Books, Doubleday & Company, Inc., 1960). First published 1933. Miss Murray's intriguing theory of a continuing survival of the "old religion" with organization structure and uninterrupted devotion to the "horned gods" is not accepted by most historians on the grounds of lack of evidence of Witchcraft's explicit practices in what little is known of pre-Christian religion in northern Europe, and on the grounds of the lateness of the witch persecutions. It is however believed devoutly by modern practitioners of the "craft." Some scholars would be willing to concede survival not of a particular god or ideology, but of *forms* of rite and celebration, such as folk divinations, agrarian magic, and perhaps even the keeping of nonecclesiastical festivals carried over from pre-Christian days. With these relatively innocent folkways, other strands of the alternative reality tradition, especially evocational magic, were blended, particularly in the minds of persecutors, in the late Middle Ages, and the whole was held to be maliciously anti-Christian. The process would be a good example of the axiom that second of Wach's three categories, expression in rite or form, is much more conservative than the other two, and can last through several revaluations of a practice's ideological and sociological meanings—even of changes of the names of its gods. Other scholars would hold that virtually the whole of the Witchcraft mania of the fifteenth through seventeenth centuries was a figment of the pathological minds of the persecutors, and the general public seems to wish to believe this so. As in any case as complicated as this, the truth probably lies somewhere between the extremes of opinion.

11 See Gershom G. Scholem, *Major Trends in Jewish Mysticism* (New York: Schocken Books, Inc., 1967), and by the same author, *On the Kabbalah and its Symbolism* (New York: Schocken Books, Inc., 1969).

12 See *The Collected Works of C. G. Jung* (Princeton: Princeton University Press), Vol. 12, *Psychology and Alchemy* (1968), Vol. 13, *Alchemical Studies* (1968), Vol. 14, *Mysterium Coniunctionis* (1963): and Mircea Eliade, *The Forge and the Crucible* (New York: Harper & Row, Publishers, 1962).

13 See David Bakan, *Sigmund Freud and the Jewish Mystical Tradition* (New York: Schocken Books, Inc., 1965).

14 John Hargrave, *The Life and Soul of Paracelsus* (London: Victor Gollancz, Ltd., 1951), p. 72. Italics in original.

15 Hargrave, *Life and Soul of Paracelsus,* p. 102.

16 The Rosicrucians have, however, always insisted upon their Christianity,

and more than other cult groups, have sought to employ Christian verbal and graphic symbols, giving them their own interpretation.

[17] A curious book exists, obviously by a writer steeped in the Theosophy of Blavatsky and A. P. Sinnett, endeavoring to show that Swedenborg was actually a Buddhist (at least, in the sense that Sinnett used the term in his *Esoteric Buddhism,* a partisan of the "ancient wisdom"). It is Philangi Dasa, *Swedenborg the Buddhist* (Los Angeles: The Buddhistic Swedenborgian Brotherhood, 1887).

[18] Emmanuel Swedenborg, *The True Christian Religion* (London: Everyman's Library, 1936), p. 335.

[19] Geoffrey K. Nelson, *Spiritualism and Society* (New York: Schocken Books, Inc., 1969), see Chapter 4. Slater Brown, *The Heyday of Spiritualism* (New York: Hawthorne Books, Inc., 1970).

[20] Henry Steel Olcott, *Old Diary Leaves, Second Series, 1878–83* (Madras: Theosophical Publishing House, 1900, 1954), pp. 13–14.

[21] *Proceedings of the Society for Psychical Research* (London: 1884) Vol. III, part ix. For the Theosophical response, see Adlai E. Waterman, *Obituary: The "Hodgson Report" on Madame Blavatsky* (Madras: Theosophical Publishing House, 1963). Certainly some of the accusations made against Madame Blavatsky, such as that she may have been a Russian agent, are dubious. On the other hand, it seems likely that, as even some Theosophists are able to concede, the answer to the mystery of the Mahatma Letters lies somewhere in the fabulously complex personality of H.P.B.

[22] A fascinating picture of the world of the early Theosophists is given by Mrs. Rosa Praed, herself a Theosophist, in her novel, *The Brother of the Shadow.* The incident which inspired it is related in her biography by Colin Roderick, *In Mortal Bondage: The Strange Life of Rosa Praed* (Sidney, Australia: Angus and Robertson, 1948), pp. 125–33. In 1885 a rumor spread through the esotericist set that a Dugpa, a "black magician," was abroad in London. A certain *chela,* named Mohini—a Hindu follower of H.P.B. living in London and much in demand for after-dinner lectures—explained at lunch with Mrs. Praed that this was true, and that he could be known by his red cap, which by occult law he had to wear. His goal was the satisfaction of sensuous desire, and could create by diabolical means passions contrary to the purity of heart required of adepts; they must therefore be in special devotion to the good. The same biography contains another episode typical of the Theosophical mood, a vision of a deva or nature spirit (pp. 177–91).

[23] J. Stillson Judah, *The History and Philosophy of the Metaphysical Movements in America* (Philadelphia: Westminster Press, 1967), pp. 149–54.

[24] The new religious mentality of this generation may be partly attributed to changing methods of childraising. Traditionally, East and West have followed opposite principles. In the West, the young child was restricted and attained freedom only by maturation. Becoming an adult meant that he could choose whom he would marry, what type of work he would do, where he would live. He would be able to replace his father in the world of men. Hence

freedom was equated with achieving adulthood, acceptance in the "real" world of interpersonal verbal communication and individuation.

In the East, to the contrary, most of these decisions are made for one by means of the caste system or an extremely totalitarian family system. Traditionally young children have been given considerable freedom, and even made objects of erotic love by their mothers. Thus the Eastern child would have the opposite experience of the Western. Maturation is not a process of acquiring greater and greater freedom, but lesser and lesser. Freedom would become instead an idealized internal memory of a childhood paradise deep within oneself, which could only be reentered through withdrawal from the oppressive "real" world, as in meditation.

It is interesting, then, that the Eastern and Western concepts of God and especially of means of attaining valid information from and about him correspond to the milieu of the arena of greatest freedom. In the West, God is outside man in principle, and communicates by word as do free adult men. In the East he is an interior state which one has once had, and which is one's true being, but which one has lost and can recover only by going into the depths of the self.

But we in the West now have a new generation which seems in very important aspects to have the Eastern rather than the traditional Western psychology. Is this because Western methods of childrearing have changed to become more like the Eastern—more permissive in early childhood, hence creative of the Eastern kind of internal nostalgia, and so of a generation oriented toward meditation and the internal quest? The only authority would be within, since there sounds the voice that can call one to the lost world of freedom. If so, our experience with this kind of person will be a new one, since our society does not have the external constraints of Eastern society which have compelled that this quest be conducted only through meditation and devotion within the context of a traditionalist society.

three

new vessels for the ancient wisdom:

groups in the theosophical and rosicrucian tradition

Out of respect for their venerable place in the tradition we are exploring, we will begin with Theosophical and Rosicrucian groups. At first glance they may not seem to represent that tradition in its fullness. The magus and the mentalist philosophy are certainly evident, but it may seem there is more talk about initiation into states of expanded consciousness than experience of it. The mood may seem dry and intellectual, or at best liturgical rather than spiritually active like yoga camps or Zen meditation halls. It must be kept in mind that the cultic tradition is defined as much by *fascination with the possibility of entering* ecstatic and cosmic states of consciousness as by techniques. The era in which these groups took modern shape was one dominated by verbal communication and deferred reward presuppositions. If the realization of ecstasy beyond words, study, and waiting was not anticipated until after many years or many lifetimes (not always the case), it was still the object of the faith.

Each of the groups we are studying is best understood through the portal of one of the three forms of religious expression. For Theosophy, it is certainly the verbal, both myth and doctrine. It is through the word, more than ritual or social interaction, that most Theosophists are drawn toward the gates of transcendent joy. Though the other forms exist, especially in the Full Moon Meditation Groups, the Liberal Catholic Church, and "I Am," they pale beside the vast richness of Theosophical lore and wisdom. To understand Theosophy one must understand this wisdom's fascination, its ability to warm those to whom it appeals to a certain inner ecstasy here and now, and its focus on the ultimate joy of cosmic harmony and consummation.

Some of the groups treated in this chapter consider themselves Christian, but most make central the "ancient wisdom" contained in many cultures and faiths, and speak of Christianity as just a symbol language expression of it suitable for our culture. A few might consider the Christian expression of it absolute, but even so interpreted it is Christianity understood in a way most Christians today would probably regard as unusual, and in a way quite in the alternative reality tradition. For these reasons, it is fair to regard even Anthroposophy and the Gnostic churches .as not normatively Judaeo-Christian.

Around Theosophical institutions one always has a rich sense of age. The weight of a halcyon past seems almost too burdensome for the plain halls and cheerful but unspectacular folk. There is now a palpable calm after the storms of supernatural excitement and schism, gorgeous hope and grim disappointment, of Theosophy's first decades. The staid gray photographs of Madame Blavatsky, Annie Besant, and C. W. Leadbeater on the walls call to mind, for the informed, flamboyant personalities and colorful incidents now locked in the past. Behind these figures there is the dusty weight of millennia of books. Behind the books stand temples and loremasters, their ranks stretching down the centuries.

Inland from Ventura lies the small California town of Ojai, famous in Theosophical as well as regional history. Here in the 1920s, the golden days of Hollywood and of Theosophy, Annie Besant and Krishnamurti summered with movie stars. Krotona, a major Theosophical school, is also situated in the Ojai valley. In California Spanish names like Ventura and Ojai mix with English ones like Oxnard and Hollywood, and with such esoteric epithets as Krotona, originally the title of Pythagoras' ancient academy.

Toward the front of the Krotona complex of buildings is a library with high shelves reached by ladders, and spotless polished reading tables. It is presided over from one to four every afternoon by a sequence of elderly ladies. The schedule is posted near the door. When I visited the library, I was taken to see one of the main lecture halls, a striking room. Around the walls are a set of "mystical" paintings, ghostly representations in pastel blues and silvers of lakes, mountains, and faces. One feels in the presence of a reality not yet quite solidified, or else so far beyond the physical as to leave only a shimmering trace behind.

The director of the Krotona school was a retired professor of biochemistry from the University of Texas. To his mind, materialism, the equation of the physical with the totality, is the fundamental error, the error with which Theosophy is in mortal combat. It is not necessary, he said, to accept any one of the traditional teachings of the Theosophical Society. But one can recognize that their purpose is to open up a world in which matter is an expression of mind rather than the other way around. To read the Theosophical classics, he remarked, is like listening to great music; one is carried, as on waves, to where one's own mind and imagination seize new intuitions unconstricted by conventional horizons. The rejection by some youth of those over thirty, he added, is the epitome of materialism, for it equates life and mind with the moment of greatest flourishing of the physical body.

The rejection of materialism, though not of natural law, is a key to the understanding of the many varieties of Theosophical experience. The world-wide movement has never counted more than twenty or thirty thousand members. But it has produced a fantastic array of religious forms, from the liturgical to the messianic, though it generally falls back in the end upon the lecture hall and verbal expression.

Theosophy really has two sides. First, there is what amounts to a cult of the marvellous, a delight in wondrous psychic phenomena, and of apparitions of the Masters. Second, there is a vast and deep mentalist philosophy squarely in the alternative reality tradition. Both are egregiously represented in the life and work of Madame Blavatsky. Both have in common a rejection of the ordinary presuppositions of materialism. The two sides are appropriately linked together, for the same tradition which sees mind as the basis of all is also rooted in that shamanistic ecstasy which sees the spirit as separable from the body. The mentalist and the marvellous in Theosophy may both seem off-base to the empiricist, but they are not really inconsistent. Nor, if our hypothesis of an alternative reality tradition is correct, is Theosophy's boast of representing the "ancient wisdom" empty. That wisdom is the knowledge of mental powers and supernormal entities and strange initiations which the old shaman knew.

These two sides are also evident in the development of the concept of the Masters, those great mediating figures who represent individuals much more highly evolved than the ordinary person. Allegedly, they live both in East and West and are heirs to the wisdom of Egypt, India, and other ancient cultures. Just as they unite East and West in the mind of the Theosophist, so the Masters are evidently the unifying experience in Theosophy itself. Their appearance and the individual's contact with them is a marvel—their message is deep wisdom.

In the last chapter, the journey was described which Helena Petrovna Blavatsky and Colonel Olcott made to India in 1878–79 after the publication of *Isis Unveiled*.[1] The impressively described advent of the occultist pair in the mysterious East is a watershed in Theosophical history, and, in a certain sense, in the history of East–West relations. Once in India contacts with the Masters, especially those of the Himalayan lodge, naturally multiplied. Through psychic contact with them, H.P.B. was seemingly able to work miracles. Most important, epistles (the famous Mahatma Letters) from the Masters explaining important points of Theosophical doctrine were given to members and prospective members. Sometimes they came by ordinary post, but often they materialized in enigmatic ways. Soon, as a sort of routine correspondence, they were "precipitated" regularly in response to queries in the "Shrine Room" of the Theosophical headquarters in Adyar.[2]

Allegations of fraud in the production of the letters in 1884, instigated it seems by Christian missionaries, led to investigation by the Society for Psychical Research whose conclusions were critical of Madame Blavatsky. Afterwards, a near split between H.P.B., who had returned to Europe, and Olcott occurred over the establishment of an Esoteric Section of the Society to supervise its study of arcane doctrine. Despite all this, Madame Blavatsky managed to publish her major work, *The Secret Doctrine,* in 1888.[3]

After the death of H.P.B. in 1891, a schism occured between the American lodges, under the leadership of William Q. Judge, and those in most of the rest of the world which followed Olcott's presidency from Adyar. Disputes arose over further letters from the Masters, this time supposedly produced by Judge, and other matters. The division took place in 1895. Subsequently each of these leaders was succeeded by a remarkable woman. Katherine Tingley took the place of Judge in America shortly after his death in 1896. Annie Besant followed Olcott in 1907.

New manifestations shaped the character of each of these branches of Theosophy. In 1899 Mrs. Tingley established a great utopian Theosophical community at Point Loma, in San Diego. After summoning the leading spirits of her tradition of Theosophy to Point Loma, she dissolved the other lodges in her association, leaving the field to Annie Besant and Adyar. The Point Loma community, complete with heroic architecture, schools, notable musical and dramatic groups, and model agricultural programs, survived until 1942.

Adyar Theosophy, under Mrs. Besant and C. W. Leadbeater, took a more speculative direction. Leadbeater, who possessed remarkable clairvoyance or imagination and a facile pen, described in pleasant detail the lives of the Masters, and the past existences of many living Theosophists in Atlantis and the ancient world. Charges of homosexuality brought adverse attention to Leadbeater, yet he still exercised a powerful influence on Adyar Theosophy in the first three decades of this century. His writings emphasized, besides the lives of the Masters and the apocryphal past, occult initiations. Persons who were to be initiated to new levels were believed to be taken out of the body to the abodes of the Masters, usually at night, where remarkable gifts would be imparted.

Feeling a need for a liturgical and sacramental expression of Theosophy, Leadbeater, a former Anglican priest, entered the Liberal Catholic Church. This body, established in 1916 by the Theosophist James Ingall Wedgewood, employed a liturgy very similar to that of the Roman Catholic or Anglican mass. But an interpretation was given of ceremonial worship, especially in Leadbeater's writings, based on Theosophical concepts of the meaning of the life of Christ and the nature of man's relations with the divine.

Finally, Leadbeater and Mrs. Besant came to believe, on the basis of Leadbeater's psychic reading, that a certain young Indian boy, Jiddu Krishnamurti, was destined to be the next vehicle of the World Teacher, the Christ. The boy was brought up by devoted Theosophists with care worthy of a crown prince. But in 1929, when he was expected to enter fully into his mission, the young Krishnamurti instead caused Theosophy to suffer yet another shock by renouncing any special claims and totally disaffiliating himself from Theosophy. He has subsequently become a notable lecturer and writer, advocating his philosophy of life lived wholly in immediacy, and is today probably better known than Theosophy itself.

In 1912 the Adyar lodge opened a school and community under the name Krotona in the Hollywood Hills, which moved to Ojai in the twenties. While it was in Hollywood, an Englishwoman, Alice Bailey, joined the community and began to produce writings purporting to come from one of the Masters. Not all Theosophists, however, accepted her claims, and after certain personality conflicts, Mrs. Bailey left Krotona to become the leader of her own movement. Never an organized institution, it has been held together by the Alice Bailey books and correspondence courses based on their teachings issued by the Arcane School and the School of Esoteric Studies, both in New York. It adherents are characterized by the practice of meditating together at every full moon. The movement offers standard speculative Theosophy, but has become more eschatological in orientation. The full moon meditations are considered to create channels for force which will aid in the return of the Christ or World Teacher.

This and the other devolutions from Theosophy fall into two general classes. On the one hand, there are what might be called the "right wing" groups, which reject the alleged extravagance and orientalism of evolved Theosophy, in favor of a serious emphasis on its metaphysics and especially its recovery of the Gnostic and Hermetic heritage. These groups are Western in orientation, and feel that the love of India and its mysteries which grew up after *Isis Unveiled* was unfortunate for a

Western group. In this category there are several Neo-Gnostic and Neo-Rosicrucian groups. The Anthroposophy of Rudolf Steiner is also in this category. On the other hand, there are what may be termed "left wing" Theosophical schisms, generally based on new private revelations from the Masters not accepted by the main traditions. In this set would be Alice Bailey's groups, "I Am," and in a sense Max Heindel's Rosicrucianism.

The fountainhead text for all these developments is still Madame Blavatsky's *The Secret Doctrine*. This massive and remarkable work is a description of the genesis of the solar system by emanation from the One, in accordance with tremendous cosmic cycles of divine rest and activity, and of the evolution of man through several worlds and races. The whole is allegedly based on very ancient but hidden learning, communicated to the author by the Masters. The book ends with an elaborate display of the cryptic expression of these teachings in ancient symbolism.[4]

The Secret Doctrine is a book not easily forgotten, even by those who despise it or who, like many outside the Theosophical orbit, find it almost impossible to read. As the modern classic of occultism, it represents a certain pinnacle, either of profundity or absurdity. To understand what it has to offer, one must learn how to read it. *The Secret Doctrine* is not a text book, but is like an ocean with waves and currents and eddies and whirlpools and quiet caves. It calls for suspending one's normal mode of conceptual progress until one has discovered where the tides and techniques of this new medium will carry him. Water is, to man, a distorting element, and probably whatever he sees in it will not be seen as it really is. The ecstatic surges in his body as he rides the swells will not be forgotten after he has found his feet once again on the sand. Like riding the waves, or like listening to great music, this book wafts one to where he can perceive reality in new configurations that unite the subjective and the objective. It does not so much convey specific fact as arrange science, myth, philosophy, and poetic narrative in peculiar combinations which can generate remarkable experiences—or so it has been with Theosophists.

The very terminology of *The Secret Doctrine* is exciting, for it unites names and concepts from many systems, East and West. Any system appearing venerable enough to be regarded as a legitimate custodian of primordial vision is taken into account in the synthesis which sets forth the contours of that range of perception. But it seems that while Eastern terms, especially Sanskrit, are most favored, the actual concepts still are more of the Hellenistic heritage than anything else (except the notion of karma), particularly the Kabbalah, Manichaeanism, and Proclus.

As one grows into the world of *The Secret Doctrine*, one understands more and more that it presents a psychological model of the cosmos.

The more its vision is comprehended and interiorized, the more the reader shares the workings of universal consciousness. Levels of Theosophical initiation take in wider and wider sweeps of the thought processes of the cosmic mind. Each level—man, Master, world—is more subtly attuned than those below to the whole scale of vibrations. As a person evolves, he is at once more invisible to lower levels—more a part of the background—and more powerful, sharing in the strength of that background. This is the mode of being described for the Masters.

The fully developed Hierarchy of spiritual rulers was not worked out until the second generation of Theosophy. A little surprisingly, it seems to have been first presented in Alice Bailey's earliest book, *Initiation Human and Solar* (1922), but was quickly expounded by C. W. Leadbeater in *The Masters and the Path* (1925), and then by Annie Besant and others. Most of the leading figures in the Hierarchy and their interrelationships had, of course, been given by H.P.B., A. P. Sinnett, and Olcott, but the full pattern had yet to be schematized.[5]

The developed Hierarchy found a place for adepts of all national lines, symbolizing thereby the syncretism. The personal "God" is the Solar Logos, ruler of the solar system. At the terrestial summit is Sanat Kumara, Lord of the World, the supreme guide of earthly evolution of mind who came from Venus some eighteen million years ago. He resides in Shamballa, a mysterious paradise in the Gobi desert. Under him the Buddha is spiritual head and the goal of interior development. There is under the Buddha the Bodhisattva, or future Buddha, and under Sanat Kumara the Manu, the archetypal man and future world Lord.

On the next plane we find the earthly expression of the Seven Rays, seven lines of activity emanating from above, governing seven broad areas encompassing the spectrum of terrestial life. Each is governed by a Master. The Masters of the first and second, respectively, are directly under Sanat Kumara and the Buddha. The other five are under a sort of Prime Minister called the Mahachohan. The First Ray, of rulership and the founding of nations and of analysis and science, is thus under the governance of the Lord of the World. Its Master is Morya, a special familiar of H.P.B.

The Second Ray, of wisdom (in the sense of *prajna*, that direct intuitive nonverbal understanding necessary to enlightenment), is ruled by the Buddha, and its Master is Kuthumi (or Koot Hoomi). He was also a special companion of Madame Blavatsky, and is familiar to readers of the Mahatma Letters.

The Third Ray is that of service to mankind and also of astrology. The common meeting-point of these two is the idea of right timing, of skill-in-means in the matter of human service involving above all a subtle and precise penetration of the humanistic meanings of time. The illuminati of this Ray grasp the deep but inescapable organic unity of the tides of human affairs with the forces and periodicities of the cosmos as a whole, which is the profoundest meaning of astrology. Its Master is called the Venetian.

The Fourth Ray, of harmony and beauty, is under the Master Serapis, of vaguely Alexandrian-Egyptian background.

The Fifth Ray is guided by the Master Hilarion. He was once the Neoplatonist Iamblichus. More recently he produced (apparently through automatic writing) two Theosophical classics by Mabel Collins, *Light on the Path* and the fictional *Idyll of the White Lotus,* and also a story or two published by H.P.B. But despite this literary excursus, Hilarion is particularly concerned with exact science, though he includes in his science laws and forces little known to conventional savants. He may be considered the paragon alchemist.

The Sixth Ray is that of devotional religion and is epitomized by the Master Jesus. He was next incarnate as Apollonius of Tyana, then as the medieval Hindu theologian of *bhakti* or devotion, Ramanuja.

The Seventh Ray is that of one of the favorite Theosophical heroes, and the special patron of the "I Am" movement, the Master Rakoczy, also called the Comte de Saint-Germain, identified with the famous eighteenth century courtier and elegant mystagogue. He has an impressive list of previous appearances, however, having been Francis Bacon, Lord Verulam, Robertus the Monk, Hunyadi, Janos, Christian Rosencreuz, Roger Bacon, Proclus, and St. Alban. His is the realm of mysteries and ceremony and of European politics. "I Am" makes him the patron of America, a land which has a particular vocation in this age. They tell of his appearing in visions to Washington and Lincoln, and helping to write the American Constitution.

The Theosophical expansion of consciousness, then, was not limited to the apertures of the Infinite and the Indic, but was turned outward by Western romance as well. Theosophists rejoiced in pictures of the Master Prince Rakoczy's castle, an edifice of the most elegant gothic imagination supposed to be somewhere in Transylvania. The very image of the sanctuary of this Master calls up to the inner ear the blare of chivalric trumpets and the mutter of alchemic incantations. One envisions the guarded ceremonial hall deep within, the weighty vellum grimoires, the retorts, the pentacles, the richly robed white wizard with his glittering wand of power.

Were this not enough, the same Master was also the enigmatic Comte de Saint-Germain, that bewigged ornament of the *ancien régime,* he of mysterious quasi-Masonic initiations, unexplained appearances and disappearances, parlor tricks which hinted of more, and reputed immortality.

Then there are those Masters of vaguely Alexandrian color, Hilarion, Serapis, perhaps the Venetian, with their singing priests of the celebrated "ancient mystery schools." In fact, only Kuthumi and Morya (the only two names of the seven totally unheard of before Madame Blavatsky) are actually Indian, though the higher figures—the Bodhisattva, Manu, Buddha, and Sanat Kumara—bear titles from Hindu and Buddhist lore. Yet higher is the Hellenistic Logos.

The general schema of the Rays is subtle and majestic. The Logos, which is the fundamental constituent of our world as an expression of the Solar Logos, boasts three aspects: Lordship, the First Ray of Sanat Kumara and his lieutenant Morya; Wisdom, the Second Ray of the Buddha and his lieutenant Kuthumi; and the variegated third aspect of the Mahachohan and his five under-Masters which can be summed up as activity. The seven rays, like the colors of a spectrum, play over the world.

Different persons, as well as different historical periods, may have aptitude for one or another of them. Cultural or religious history can be interpreted in their light. Individuals may find themselves especially drawn to the *ashram* or school of a particular Master. The vision of the world is that of a diversified university of many, or to be precise seven, courses of study. Each will illumine a particular epoch, and cycles of epochs will recur until each ray is brought historically to the epitome of its own potential. It was said that we are now moving into a seventh ray period, dominated by Saint-Germain and ceremony; this notion was very important to the founding of the Liberal Catholic Church and the "I Am" movement.

But wisdom and rulership have special roles as goals beyond goals. The highest historically incarnate initiate is the Buddha. His successor, the Bodhisattva, has already appeared twice, in Krishna and Christ, and will soon appear again—the driving idea, of course, behind the Krishnamurti and Full Moon Meditation Groups movements. During this coming incarnation he would receive full Buddha initiation, so would not again come in human form, but the Master Kuthumi would become the next Bodhisattva. (The Christ of Palestine as an incarnation of the future Second Ray Lord of Wisdom should not be confused with the Master Jesus who governs the Sixth Ray of devotion, although in the first century they were one and the same person. The Master Jesus whose mind and body the Bodhisattva filled to add grace upon grace to that ministry was the same one who, in his next incarnation as Apollonius of Tyana, attained the initiation of adepthood which made him the Master of devotion.)

These notions, so deeply stirring to persons of a certain temperament, have inspired a variety of cultic expressions. In general, whether in the Liberal Catholic high mass or Theosophical meditation, the object has been to open lines of force to the great figures of the Hierarchy to make it easier for their benign influence to penetrate the world. But, by and large, Theosophy has been more concerned, at least collectively, with exposition and spontaneous experience of the Masters than with corporate work; the lectures and books, verbal expression, have been most conspicuous.

Social expression, therefore, has in Theosophy been most lastingly oriented around verbal expression. The many ventures centered about ritual—Co-Masonry, the Liberal Catholic Church, and others—have, like the utopian experiments at Point Loma, not seemed as adequate to the task of Theosophy today as the lecture hall and study group. However, the Full Moon Meditation Groups of Alice Bailey lineage have continued to prosper quietly, and some offshoot Gnostic and "I Am" groups have had substantial ritual expression.

The importance of Theosophy in modern history should not be underestimated. Not only have the writings of Madame Blavatsky and others inspired several generations of occultists, but the movement had a remarkable role in the restoration to the colonial peoples of nineteenth century Asia their own spiritual heritage. We have mentioned Colonel Olcott's work in Ceylon. It is said that Gandhi was first given an English copy of the *Bhagavad Gita,* the Hindu scripture which became virtually his bible, in London in a Theosophical translation. In those days few outside of closed Brahman and academic circles except Theosophists were interested in Eastern scriptures. No European was more effective in advancing Indian education, unity, and independence than Annie Besant, who led in the establishing of the Home Rule League in 1916, and whose support greatly strengthened the radical wing of the Congress Party during the First World War. She was, in fact, briefly imprisoned by her own countrymen for her activities on behalf of independence for India.

In the West, Theosophy's most important cultural impact was doubtless in the "Irish Renaissance." Writers like W. B. Yeats and "A.E." (George Russell) were sometime members of the Theosophical Society and deeply affected by its vision. In the hands of such persons as these, Theosophy was a vehicle for a deeply visionary presentation of the alternative reality tradition, the ancient wisdom, to the modern world. Perhaps its essence, and the flavor of its inward and initiatory way back, was never caught more movingly than in the poetry of "A.E.," a writer and economic activist who treasured Madame Blavatsky's *The Secret Doctrine* above all other books. Here is one of his verses:

Ancient

The sky is cold as pearl
Over a milk-white land.
The snow seems older than Time
Though it fell through a dreaming and
Will vanish itself as a dream
At the dimmest touch of a hand.

Out of a timeless world
Shadows fall upon Time,
From a beauty older than earth
A ladder the soul may climb.
I climb by the phantom stair
To a whiteness older than Time.[6]

1. The Theosophical Society in America

American Theosophy today is comprised of three groups—the Theosophical Society, the descendent of the Point Loma community and the Judge-Tingley tradition; the United Lodge of Theosophists, founded in 1909 by Robert Crosbie, essentially representing the stance of those who were disenchanted with Mrs. Tingley's experiment, but who also resisted the claims to universal legitimacy of the Adyar leadership; and the Theosophical Society in America, which is the United States branch of the world organization headquartered at Adyar.

The first, the Theosophical Society, now has little sociological or cultic expression. Informal meetings are held regularly, but the main link is an attractive inspirational magazine, *Sunrise*, published at the headquarters in Altadena, California. The Headquarters also issues correspondence courses, and sees as one of its main missions the maintenance of a fine library of some 20,000 volumes in theosophy, religion and philosophy. Leadership in this Theosophical Society, in the tradition of Judge and Tingley, is emergent rather than formally elective; the present leader is Grace F. Knoche.

The United Lodge of Theosophists, on the other hand, represents a conservative interpretation of Theosophy. It holds close to the writings of Blavatsky and Judge, rejecting even Olcott's undue humanizing of the great lady in *Old Diary Leaves*. The group's scattering of lodges and discussion groups, headquartered in Los Angeles, maintain a highly austere and intellectual Theosophy.

Undoubtedly most active Theosophists today belong to the Theosophical Society in America. In 1970 the Society reported 5,436 members, of whom 943 were new members. Lodges or study groups may be found in most cities. Growth seems to be greatest not in places like New York and California, but in parts of the country such as the south central states where most groups in the alternative reality tradition have not penetrated, but into which Theosophy has long been able to send lecturers. American headquarters are at Olcott House in Wheaton, Illinois. Here also is the Theosophical Publishing House, which has recently won widespread interest in Theosophy through its "Quest Books," a series of widely advertised paperback editions of Theosophical classics. The Krotona school in Ojai and three summer camps in different parts of the country are also part of the Society.

The typical Theosophical lodge is an older, somewhat plain building with pictures on the walls. It will have a fairly large lending library and bookstore. On the stage in front may be a podium and a table with a vase of flowers or even potted palms. A Theosophical symbol, such as a serpent-entwined tau cross, may be hung behind the podium. Lectures are likely to be on one of the major Theosophical books, karma, reincarnation, an aspect of astrology, psychic phenomena, meditation, or an oriental work such as the *Bhagavad Gita* or *I Ching*. I have an impression that difficult matters such as the Masters and the several stages of evolution of the world and its races are giving way to more popular topics in orientalism and extrasensory perception. The developed view of the world hierarchy of Besant and Leadbeater is definitely not in favor today except as a general symbol of spiritual evolution. To a great extent, Theosophical lodges seem to be coming to play the role of forums where speculative spiritual ideas can be freely presented by all sorts of speakers. Among lecturers who definitely represent Theosophy, I have heard some who found most appealing the sense of security and self-reliance given by confidence in the law of karma, some who loved to dwell on the colorful history of Theosophy, and some who emphasized such antimaterialistic concepts as the Solar Logos. There is little current talk of contacts with Masters. Particularly in more staid parts of the nation, this function doubtless meets a felt need. Each lodge is democratically self-governed, and the national organization operates on the federal principle.

In some places young people have been brought into Theosophy through general interest in the occult. But the typical Theosophist is middle-aged, white, and middle-class. Programs attract the sort of serious, neat old men never seen without tie and vest, and women loaded with rings and bracelets and earrings. But the majority of attenders at most public lectures are not members. One sees very few blacks, although Spanish-speaking lodges flourish in the U.S. as well as in Latin America.

The sometimes controversial inner circle of Theosophy, the Esoteric Section, still continues its work, headquartered in Ojai. Its members, who must have been Theosophists three years to be admitted, do not partake of tobacco, alcohol, or meat. They practice a definite secret meditation method to attune them with the Hierarchy. They also follow a study regimen, and in larger places meet periodically. The National leader of the E.S., a delightful middle-aged lady, merely laughed when I discussed with her the bizarre rumors one sometimes hears that the E.S. constitutes a sinister secret inner government of the Theosophical Society (of course, much of the leadership does belong to it), or that it is in some sort of continuing occult communication with the Masters, discussing with them the fate of the Society and the world. The E.S. is apparently no more than what it seems to be, a devotional and study confraternity of persons who take upon themselves a certain way of life.

The Theosophical Society in America, then, is a group teaching that there is a "secret doctrine," knowledge known to a few but which could be known widely, which explains why things are as they are and how one can evolve beyond his present state. These teachings are mainly presented verbally. The Society is oriented more to knowledge than to mystical or yogic practice; it is a body of occult intellectual activists. Even in India, and rather more in America, it draws people who are Western in temperament but Eastern, or Gnostic, in spiritual sympathies, and who sense themselves called out to set their feet to the endless path.

Reading Selection: Theosophy

I have chosen two selections to represent the central tradition of Theosophy, one from Madame Blavatsky's The Secret Doctrine, *to indicate its philosophical wing, and one from C. W. Leadbeater's* The Masters and the Path, *to illustrate the marvellous and hierophanic experiences which have attended those living in this tradition. The Secret Doctrine is certainly the book considered most authoritative by most Theosophists. The lines below summarize concisely the basic points of Theosophical teaching which are elaborated in the rest of the book. The passage from Leadbeater in a sense takes up where the Blavatsky quotations end, for the Masters, appearing and helping the Theosophical Society, are of course beings in the transhuman states of evolution suggested by her words.*

The Secret Doctrine establishes three fundamental propositions:

(a) An Omnipresent, Eternal, Boundless, and Immutable PRINCIPLE on which all speculation is impossible, since it transcends the power of human conception and could only be dwarfed by any human expression or similitude. It is beyond the range and reach of thought—in the words of the Mandukya Upanishad, "unthinkable and unspeakable."

(b) The Eternity of the Universe *in toto* as a boundless plane; periodically the playground of numberless Universes incessantly manifesting and disappearing, called the manifesting stars, and the sparks of Eternity. The Eternity of the Pilgrim [the "Pilgrim" is the Monad or immortal principle in each individual] is like a wink of the Eye of Self-Existence. The appearance and disappearance of Worlds is like a regular tidal ebb of flux and reflux.

This second assertion of the Secret Doctrine is the absolute universality of that law of periodicity, of flux and reflux, ebb and flow, which physical science has observed and recorded in all departments of nature. An alternation such as that of Day and Night, Life and Death, Sleeping and Waking, is a fact so common, so perfectly universal and without exception, that it is easy to comprehend that in it we see one of the absolutely fundamental Laws of the Universe.

Moreover, the Secret Doctrine teaches:

(c) The fundamental identity of all Souls with the Universal Over-Soul, the latter being itself an aspect of the Unknown Root; and the obligatory pilgrimage for every Soul—and spark of the former—through the Cycle of Incarnation (or "Necessity") in accordance with Cyclic and Karmic law, during the whole term. In other words, no purely spiritual Buddhi (Divine Soul) can have an independent (conscious) existence before the spark which issued from the pure Essence of the Universal Sixth Principle—or the OVER-SOUL—has (a) passed through every elemental form of the phenomenal world of that Manvantara, and (b) acquired individuality, first by natural impulse, and then by self-induced and self-devised efforts (checked by its Karma), thus ascending through all the degrees of intelligence, from the lowest to the highest Manas, from mineral and plant, up to the holiest archangel (Dhyani-Buddha).

> H. P. Blavatsky, *An Abridgement of The Secret Doctrine*, Elizabeth Preston and Christmas Humphreys, eds. (Wheaton, Illinois: Theosophical Publishing House, 1967), pp. 10–13.
> Quotation marks and other references to other parts of *The Secret Doctrine* omitted.

I myself can report two occasions on which I have met a Master, both of us being in the physical vehicle. One of Them was the Adept to whom the name of Jupiter was assigned in the book, *The Lives of Alcyone*, who greatly assisted in the writing of portions of Madame Blavatsky's famous work *Isis Unveiled,* when that was being done in Philadelphia and New York. When I was living at Adyar, He was so kind as to request my revered teacher, Swami T. Subba Row, to bring me to call upon Him. Obeying His summons we journeyed to His house, and were most graciously received by Him. After a long conversation of the deepest interest, we had the honour of dining with Him, Brahmin though He be, and spent the night and part of the next day under his roof. In that case it will be admitted that there could be no question of illusion. The other Adept whom I had the privilege of encountering physically was the Master the Comte de St. Germain, called sometimes the Prince Rakoczy. I met Him under quite ordinary circumstances (without any previous appointment, and as though by chance) walking down the Corso in Rome, dressed just as any Italian gentleman might be. He took me up into the gardens on the Pincian Hill, and we sat for more than an hour talking about the Society and its work; or perhaps I should rather say that He spoke and I listened, although when He asked questions I answered.

Other members of the Brotherhood I have seen under varying circumstances. My first encounter with one of them was in a hotel in Cairo; I was on my way out to India with Madame Blavatsky and some others, and we stayed in that city for a time. We all used to gather in Madame Blavatsky's room for work, and I was sitting on the floor, cutting out and arranging for her a quantity of newspaper articles which she wanted. She sat at a table close by; indeed my left arm was actually touching her dress. The door of the room was in full sight, and it certainly did not open; but quite suddenly, without any preparation, there was a man standing almost between me and Madame Blavatsky, within touch of both of us. It gave me a great start, and I jumped up in some confusion; Madame Blavatsky was much amused and said: "If you do not know enough not to be startled at such a trifle as that, you will not get far in this occult work." I was introduced to the visitor, who was not then an Adept, but an Arhat, which is one grade below that state; he has since become the Master Djwal Kul.

Some months after that the Master Morya came to us one day, looking exactly as though in a physical body; He walked through the room where I was in order to communicate with Madame Blavatsky, who was in her bedroom inside. That was the first time I had seen Him plainly and clearly, for I had not then developed my latent senses sufficiently to remember what I saw in the subtle body. I saw the Master Kuthumi under similar conditions on the roof of our Headquarters at Adyar; He was stepping over a balustrade as though He had just materialized from the empty air on the other side of it. I have also many times seen the Master Djwal Kul on that roof in the same way.

C. W. LEADBEATER, *The Masters and the Path*
(Adyar, Madras, India: The Theosophical
Publishing House, 1925, 1965), pp. 8–9.

2. The Full Moon Meditation Groups

Alice Bailey (1880–1949), the founder of a devolution of Theosophy, had a varied and eventful life. Born, like Annie Besant and other of the strong women of occultism, of an upper class English family, she was an ill-adjusted and headstrong child. When she was fifteen, she saw a vision of a man in a turban whom she later believed was her Master. But as a young woman, she was for a time fervently evangelical, working with a mission to preach hellfire sermons to British troops in India during the First World War. Again like Annie Besant, she was briefly and unhappily married to an Anglican clergyman, and came to Theosophy after the emotional ordeal of marital breakup. In Alice Bailey's case, this happened in America, where she had come with her husband. Soon she was working as manager of the vegetarian cafeteria of the Theosophical school at Krotona in Hollywood.

One afternoon as she was walking in the hills surrounding the community, she felt she was being contacted by a Master called "The Tibetan" who wished her to serve as his amanuensis. She produced a long series of books. This development, and her charges that the Theosophical Society was controlled by members of the Esoteric Section, led to her withdrawal with her fiancé, Foster Bailey. In 1923 they established the Arcane School in New York, and out of it have emanated the teachings which mark the distinctive set of groups now under consideration.[7]

It was in the World War II period that the peculiarly eschatological quality these groups acquired first became apparent—especially in Mrs. Bailey's *The Reappearance of the Christ*. We are told that because of the tremendous exigencies of the day, the spiritual yearnings of mankind are raised to such a pitch that the coming of the Christ principle, whether in an individual or a new age of illumination, is being brought closer. The work of meditation groups was to encourage this advent by setting up spiritual currents. This is done by repeating prayerfully the Great Invocation, in conjunction with visualization of the funnelling down of the power of the Hierarchy.

The atmosphere of groups in the Full Moon Meditation tradition is a little different from that of continuing Theosophists. The Full Moon groups have made an impact in certain idealistic upper class circles. There is much talk of the United Nations, and international understanding and cooperation, perhaps epitomized by a recording one member has of Eleanor Roosevelt reciting their Great Invocation. The groups have also acquired a certain tincture of avant-garde art and music. Festivals and meditation group meetings are likely to be enlivened with modern dance performances and futuristic concerts, as well as by Wagner, favored by an older generation of occultists.

I have attended a series of Full Moon Meditation Group meetings in a large home in Los Angeles. The group consisted of some twenty persons, mostly elderly. Inside, a pale blue-green fireplace bore small white statues of the Virgin Mary on either end of the mantle. In the center of the room, a square white column had upon it a living flame surrounded by greens—I thought of old Druidic or Brahman rites. The lady of the house, a tall, statuesque woman, presided over the ceremonies. She opened one meeting by telling of the fact that they met every full moon and at equinoxes and solstices. These are times when special spiritual energies are available from the Hierarchy. We listened to music of Bach, Mahler, and Wagner from four stereo speakers.

The next event was modern dance by a pupil of Ruth St. Denis, a famous teacher of choreography, who had been a member of this group until her recent death. To the music of the "Ave Maria," the dancer interpreted the figure of the Blessed Virgin. Candles held by each member of the group were lit from the central fire in a simple ritual. An elderly lady gave an address. Since it was the full moon of Leo, she talked on its message in simple, rational terms, including the main esoteric concepts. Finally, the meeting concluded, after long preparation, with a slow and solemn recitation of the Great Invocation Alice Bailey received as the most effective means of strengthening the Hierarchy:

> From the point of Light within the Mind of God
> Let light stream forth into the minds of men.
> Let LIGHT descend on Earth.
>
> From the point of Love within the Heart of God
> Let Love stream forth into the hearts of men.
> May CHRIST return to Earth.
>
> From the centre where the Will of God is known
> Let Purpose guide the little wills of men—
> The PURPOSE which the Masters know and serve.
>
> From the centre which we call the race of men

Let the Plan of Love and Light work out
 And may it seal the door where evil dwells.
Let Light and Love and Power
Restore the Plan on Earth.

The great occasion of the Meditation Groups is the annual Wesak Festival, held in late spring in the full moon of Taurus every year. The legend of this occasion, based on a vision of Alice Bailey, tells us that on this day the Buddha, the Christ, and the Masters gather in a certain valley in the Himalayas, and that the union of meditation with theirs is of special power. Typically, all the meditation groups of a wide area will gather together to unite in silence, to hear an address, and to appreciate modern music and dance. The festivals are typically done with great taste and beauty. Attending, along with persons in conventional dress, are some young people with long hair and beads.

There is no central organization of Full Moon Meditation Groups, although the two correspondence schools, the Arcane School and the School of Esoteric Studies, the periodical *The Beacon,* and the informal publicity organization in Ojai, Meditation Groups Inc., serve as unifying forces. Groups vary in nature; some are doubtless rather dilettante, others take seriously the need to study the massive works of "The Tibetan." There is one, The Diamond Foundation, concerned with setting aside a savings account for the use of the Teacher upon his return; several thousand dollars have already been saved.

In this school, we see a movement grown out of Theosophy which has acquired its own flavor. There is a show of modernity and rationality and scientism, together with a new myth blending the eschatological hope of the 1940s kind of liberalism and One World idealism, a continuing covert excitement in the old marvel at revelations of the Masters, plus an affirmation, stronger than in other Theosophy groups, of the communicative power of the new aesthetic. Probably this movement peaked in the early postwar years. It has had some difficulty as well as some success in finding its place in the spiritual climate of the sixties and seventies. But it remains an attractive expression of Theosophy.

Reading Selection: Full Moon Meditation Groups

This is a passage from one of the books published under the name of Alice A. Bailey, but believed to have been given to her by "The Tibetan." The passage summarizes what has come to be the central focus of these groups—spiritual preparation for the return of the Christ principle. The Hierarchy of Masters is striving to prepare mankind for this great event, but the lines of psychic force which can prepare a way for his return need also to be strengthened by human desire, invocation, and mediation. Thoughts have a life of their own; to know how to form them rightly to make vessels for this next step of spiritual evolution is a skill. Training in this task, and the exercise of it, is the work of the meditation groups.

This new invocative work will be the keynote of the coming world religion and will fall into two parts. There will be the invocative work of the masses of the people, everywhere, trained by the spiritually minded people of the world (working in the churches whenever possible under an enlightened clergy) to accept the fact of the approaching spiritual energies, focused through Christ and His spiritual Hierarchy, and trained also to voice their demand for light, liberation and understanding. There will also be the skilled work of invocation as practised by those who have trained their minds through right meditation, who know the potency of formulas, mantrams and invocations and who work consciously. They will increasingly use certain great formulas of words which will later be given to the race, just as the Lord's Prayer was given by the Christ, and as the New Invocation has been given out for use at this time by the Hierarchy.

This new religious science for which prayer, meditation and ritual have prepared humanity, will train its people to present—at stated periods throughout the year—the voiced demand of the people of the world for relationship with God and for a closer spiritual relation to each other. This work, when rightly carried forward, will evoke response from the waiting Hierarchy and from its Head, the Christ. Through this response, the belief of the masses will gradually be changed into the conviction of the knowers. In this way, the mass of men will be transformed and spiritualised, and the two great divine centres of energy or groups—the Hierarchy and Humanity itself—will begin to work in complete at-one-ment and unity. Then the Kingdom of God will indeed and in truth be functioning on earth.

ALICE A. BAILEY, *The Reappearance of the Christ* (New York: Lucis Publishing Company, 1948, 1962), pp. 152–53.

---

3. Anthroposophy

Rudolf Steiner (1861–1925) was born of Austrian Catholic parents. Fascinated by the type of mind which could combine scientific insight with romantic and mystical vision, he early attained some distinction as editor of Goethe's scientific work. A youthful bent for occultism led him into Theosophy. He served as head of the German section of the Theosophical Society from 1902 to 1909.

But Steiner was uneasy with Theosophy's orientalism and its emphasis on marvellous occurrences. He felt that stress should be placed on the scientific study of the spiritual world and man's initiations into it, and he also felt that Christ was an even greater symbol of its reality than any Eastern Master. In 1912 he founded a new group, originally intended as a fellowship within Theosophy, but soon for all practical purposes independent—the Anthroposophical Society (from the Greek *anthropos,* "man," and *sophia,* "wisdom").

Steiner had a charismatic personality, and many stories were told of his clairvoyant and psychic powers. He performed psychic healing on members of the families of many highly placed persons in German society. At the time of the First World War, Steiner was accused (unjustly, it now seems) of having undue influence on the first German Chief of Staff, General von Moltke, through his intimate friendship with Frau von Moltke. Although his real concerns were other than social or political, it can well be imagined that a man of such reputation would have no difficulty gathering a circle about him. The new Anthroposophical Society retained, with some technical differences, Theosophy's view of the spiritual basis of reality, the subtle constitution of man, reincarnation, and the possibility of initiatory experiences which expand consciousness of the spiritual realm. But little was made of belief in hidden Masters and occult communication.

Steiner taught that man had originally shared the spiritual consciousness of the cosmos, its fundamental reality. Matter is real, but is derivative from spirit. The mind of man has two parts, like the Hindu *jiva* and *atman,* one which can know and the other, the Absolute, which is the ultimate that can be known and is within as well as without. Man's present knowledge is only a vestige of primordial cognition. He has, however, a latent capacity for horizonless vision, and there are certain disciplines by which it can be recovered. Steiner did not reduce the process to mere techniques, however; the initiatory openings may come through study, music, art, and the informed use of imagination. The matter can be objectively and usefully understood to some degree, and Steiner saw his work as the organization of a science of initiation. Such categories as the Theosophical "law of seven," which saw levels of mind, stages of cosmic evolution, grades of Masters, planets, etc., as arranged in septets, were important to him.

Partly through the work of a former Evangelical pastor, Friedrich Rittelmeyer (1872–1938), Anthroposophy came to have a definite Christian bias. Jesus Christ is the one avatar, the one fully initiated person in human history, the one who has full supersensory perception. The story of his life, death, and resurrection is interpreted as a mystery drama of initiation.

Steiner and Rittelmeyer formed the Christian Community Church as a worship-centered expression of Anthroposophy. The Society and the Church are not necessarily identical in either membership or governance, but are closely affiliated in spirit.

Meetings of the Anthroposophical Society are mainly of the lecture and study type. Topics include not only matters from the revered works of Rudolf Steiner, but a great variety of other subjects, for that is in keeping with the founder's vast range of concerns. He himself contributed to education; agriculture; architecture; and, at least as to phisophic theory, science and medicine; and the organization of society. He designed the Goetheanum, or headquarters of the Society, in Dornach, Switzerland; he wrote plays and contributed to the theory of organic farming. Anthroposophists are likely to be interested in architecture, art, and music (especially the operas of Richard Wagner), in the education of retarded children, in organic agriculture—in any matter like these which is related to understanding man's spiritual nature and the evolution of spirit through initiatory openings. Anthroposophists have made real contributions in many of these fields.

The worship of the Christian Community Church is basically on the Protestant model, but the clergy are called "priests" and the central act of worship is the Eucharist or Holy Communion. The rite is seen as a contact with Christ, the fully developed man, which opens one to what he was, true man. It is called the Act of the Consecration of Man.

In harmony with its emphasis on education, Anthroposophy has established well-regarded private schools called Waldorf Schools. They have stressed the value of art and drama in creative education, and make use of eurhythmic exercises.

At the present time, Anthroposophy seems to attract a certain number of people of all ages, perhaps due in part to its educational work. Despite the practical emphasis on verbal communication, artists, dancers, and musicians find in it an integrative philosophy which makes what they do more meaningful. There is a rather charming flavor of cultural central Europe about it—one might even say a Weimar Republic style of aesthetic intellectualism and mystical idealism. One meets many persons of Germanic descent. But Anthroposophy has deeply impressed many persons in other cultural areas, such as the distinguished British linguistic philosopher Owen Barfield. Perhaps Anthroposophy could be called a "demythologized Theosophy," for it keeps the metaphysics and adventure of initiation of Theosophy without the elements which personify cosmic mysteries and make them into narratives.

Reading Selection: Anthroposophy

The world of Anthroposophical literature, beginning with the books of Rudolf Steiner himself, is vast and weighty. It is not easy to isolate any few paragraphs which do justice to the whole of the concept. Perhaps these from an article in an Anthroposophical journal suggest the tone, and something of the content, as well as any. We see a typical continual reference to the seminal ideas of Steiner, as well as an exemplification of several of his fundamental principles. Steiner was above all concerned with the unification of the scientific and spiritual world views. He held that matter and spirit were both equally real. To him this was no lip service platitude, but a firm operating axiom to be applied in every sort of investigation and to every decision of life. Spirit meant the idea, consciousness, and unitive factors. Ideas are absolutely real entities, independent of the particular thinker, and constitute a whole real world to be explored by initiatory experiences. This world can be known just as the physical world is known by the scientist. Finally, both worlds can be wholly known together at once with all the factors of their interaction. This is the final goal, manifested in the Christ. But along the way, say Anthroposophists, even an imperfect awareness of these things opens up great new dimensions in the understanding of aesthetics, education, and physical matter, and new possibilities in ·fields like agriculture and healing.

Everything in nature is built upon logical, mathematical, numerical principles and laws which were in existence in the mind of the Creator even before nature existed. The *idea*, the blueprint, the architectural plan of things to come must exist prior to physical manifestation. At best, man can discover the principles according to which nature operates. "To recognize nature means to re-create it in one's mind," said Schelling. These principles belong in the realm of *idea*, not however as abstract thought or speculation but within a realm of reality which is accessible to observation and logic. With this background in mind, a different concept of that which we call "life" arises.

Considering life as a phenomenon in the Goethean sense, we cannot be satisfied to seek the seat of life in matter alone. It is true that matter is necessary to make life manifest, visible, to show things which grow. How often do we hear the question: what is the "substance" which carries life? Is it oxygen, protein, enzymes, ribonucleic acid, ATP, or what? No single substance is life; it is the concerted interaction of many or all substances, organized for "definite purpose and performance," which makes life. No chemist will ever discover "life," for his concern is substance, matter. He learns about the "body" of life. In order to analyze, he has to destroy life and operate with its corpse.

Comes the biologist and physiologist and points out the functional relationship, the directional or organizing factor. One would wish the biologist would grow wings and accept life as an independent agency, force, principle or energy. It is here that the difficulty of the modern scientist lies. He is fascinated by the performance of physical energies—warmth, electricity, magnetism, mechanical energy—which are convertible, one into another, obeying the laws of thermodynamics. He studies the spectrum of light with its different energy displays. He has the electron, the atom, the proton and neutron and many other smaller and smaller particles already known and more particles still to come. He uses the electron microscope to look deeper into the minute structures of the cells—the nuclei, the mitochondria, the helical structure of genetic material, etc., etc. All these are parts of life but not life itself. These are the tools with which life operates.

The manifold differentiations and specializations have brought about the desire for integration, grouping together, in order that one might see the interrelationship. Toward the middle of the present century, science made many strides in the direction of this integration. It even now begins to rediscover the truth of that fundamental concept so important to Goethe—"the whole is more than the sum of its parts." The whole of life, its totality, is more than all the knowledge about the "body" of life, that is, its physical manifestation.

The breakthrough in the conceptual realm was made by Rudolf Steiner. His theory of cognition, his teachings with regard to the etheric, formative forces have shown the path.

EHRENFRIED E. PFEIFFER, "A New Concept of Life: An Alternative to an Atomized World," *Journal for Anthroposophy*, No. 6 (Autumn 1967), published by the Anthroposophical Society in America, New York, N.Y. 10016, pp. 3–4.

4. Rosicrucianism

We have seen that the title Rosicrucian has a long-standing history in the alternative reality tradition. In the seventeenth century, Rosicrucianism became almost synonymous with this tradition. Today, however, the name is chiefly identified in the popular mind with the specific teachings of two organizations, both founded, at least outwardly, in this century, though drawing from the remoter past. A few other small groups also claim the title, and there has been no small acrimony among them as to legitimacy of its use.

The two most substantial groups of Rosicrucians are the Rosicrucian Fellowship, with its international headquarters at Mt. Ecclesia, Oceanside, California, and the Ancient and Mystical Order Rosae Crucis in San Jose, California. The latter is the best-known group. It has engaged in a widespread advertising campaign for a number of years.

The older of the two groups, and the one most influenced by Theosophy, is, however, the Rosicrucian Fellowship, founded in 1907 by Carl Louis van Grasshoff, who used the pen name Max Heindel. Born of a noble family in Germany in 1865, Heindel came to America in 1895 and to Los Angeles in 1903. There he became active in Theosophy, serving as vice-president of the local lodge from 1904 to 1905. Thereafter, he worked as a Theosophical lecturer.

He claimed that while he was in Europe in 1907 a marvellous being, whom he later learned was an elder brother in the occult Rosicrucian Order, appeared to him and offered him help. After several more visits, in which he was tested, Heindel reported he was taken by the brother to a temple of the Rose Cross near the border between Germany and Bohemia. Here he spent about a month receiving personal instruction by the elder brothers. This initiatory experience is considered by the group as its real founding. Heindel wrote what he had learned in his basic book, *Rosicrucian Cosmo-Conception.*[8] By 1910, the book had been published and Heindel had established several Fellowship Centers. Later, it was imparted to him that he was to establish a temple, which he did at Mt. Ecclesia.

The basic doctrine of the Rosicrucian Fellowship is common to Theosophy—world evolution, reincarnation, secret initiation, invisible helpers, and elder brothers. But the atmosphere is all Western, and there is special emphasis on healing and on astrology; the initiatory symbolism of the latter is much elaborated. One who is admitted into the Fellowship must give up tobacco, liquor, and meat.

The few Rosicrucian Fellowship churches have something of an old-fashioned Protestant atmosphere. Over the altar hang curtains, opened only when worship begins, unveiling a rose-covered cross. The service will have the usual hymns and scripture, but the prayer will be more in the New Thought style of sending out "good vibrations" than of intercession. There is generally no minister; members conduct the service themselves. At times there are lecturers from Oceanside. It appears that this group is attracting few younger persons at the present time.

The other Rosicrucian group, the AMORC, as it is usually abbreviated, is far larger. It claims not to be a "religion," but a "worldwide fraternal organization" on the Masonic model which teaches a philosophy and practices designed to enable the individual to use ordinarily latent faculties for the sake of improving his abilities and leading a more satisfying life. The Order has a temple and conducts ceremonies of a lodge type, as do branch lodges on a smaller scale. In its literature, the Order states as its "traditional history" that it is descended from an ancient Egyptian mystery school whose first Master was the Pharoah Akhnaton, and that a great number of the most enlightened minds of history have been counted among its members. In some periods, however, it has been less visible than in others. The present cycle of visible work was begun in 1915 by H. Spencer Lewis (1883–1939), a New York advertising man. His son is now "Imperator" or Chief Executive of the Order.

Its place as a voice in the alternative reality tradition is evident from the fact that the literature of Rosicrucianism speaks of the golden secret, which is that man has two natures, a "duality of self." Besides the physical body, there is a "greater inner self." This secret is the key to the Rosicrucian understanding of the question of death and the development of psychic powers, including the projection of consciousness out of the body. These techniques and the philosophy which goes with them are obtained in lessons sent out from the headquarters in San Jose, which the individual may study at home or with a local lodge.

The headquarters in San Jose, Rosicrucian Park, reflect the magnitude of the activity. Covering an entire city block, it contains not only modern, computerized offices for the extensive mailing activities of the Order, but a fine Egyptological museum and a science museum, reflecting two interests which the Order clearly hopes to unify, and a large temple and auditorium. These have all become a major tourist attraction.

The AMORC is much larger, and more geared to a popular audience, than most other groups in this book. This fact has to some extent shaped the character of its message. The similarity of the structure, ritual, and some of the terminology to Freemasonry has no doubt aided in its acceptance in America, where Masonry is very "establishment." The insistence that AMORC is not a religion has unquestionably helped many who would feel reluctant to reject their traditional church to accept the Order's teaching and membership—and the alternative reality tradition. In part, for this reason, AMORC has played a special role in shaping the culture of modern America.

Reading Selection: Rosicrucianism

The following passage is from an attractive introductory booklet issued to prospective members by the Ancient and Mystical Order Rosae Crucis (AMORC). It makes clear the basic teachings: a dualistic view of mind and body, the possibility of greatly developing the powers of mind, the conviction that wisdom regarding this has been acquired by ancient secret brotherhoods and is now available through the Order. It emphasizes the belief that this particular wisdom—all that the Order is concerned with—is not tied to religion.

You have often had the experience of an *intuitive impression,* a hunch or idea that was most enlightening but seemed to come from nowhere. Do you know that intuition can provide an answer for almost every question, a solution to many predicaments in which you find yourself? Do you know that it can aid you in keeping the affairs of your life in order? Do you further know that this *intuitive knowledge* is part of a universal cosmic intelligence which pervades the entire universe and every cell of your being and that you can command it to serve you— that you can draw upon it as you will? While millions of men and women rely solely upon their brains and the training which is given to them through education, those who know the esoteric wisdom wait for no hunches. They do not rely solely upon their outer minds but are able to draw upon the vast resources they possess and which also exist in the cosmic forces around them.

Psychologists today say that man uses only a fraction of the inherent power with which he is imbued as a human being. The secret brotherhoods have known for centuries how to command and use much more of this power to round out and enjoy an enriched life. Hundreds of the so-called mysteries are understandable and workable laws of the universe to those who master this esoteric (inner) knowledge.

"Why," you may ask, "is not this knowledge generally and widely disseminated to mankind today? Why, if such illuminating truths exist and are available to man, is he deprived of them?" We have shown what occurred in ancient times when the attempt was made to teach man these simple truths. They were often suppressed. Even today, such knowledge cannot be taught to everyone. To those who are sincere in bettering their own lives and advancing humanity, such knowledge becomes a power for good. On the other hand, in the hands of the selfish and the bigoted, the same knowledge might become a factor for misuse and further persecution of the ignorant and the helpless. But today, as we have said, it has survived because of the careful guardianship of the brotherhood mystery schools and societies.

The oldest of these *humanitarian societies,* worldwide in extent and *not a religion,* is the Rosicrucians. It offers you this knowledge, as old as time, for the fullness of life, free of any religious intolerance or political or other prejudices or biases.

> The Mastery of Life (San Jose, California:
> Supreme Grand Lodge of The Ancient and
> Mystical Order Rosae Crucis, 1965), pp. 13–14.

5. Modern Gnosticism

The greatest problem which early Christianity had to face was not persecutors without, but diversity of opinion within. The main challenge to the historical, linear conception of time which, as we have seen, was the most distinctive gift of the Judaeo-Christian tradition to modernity was that collection of schools known as Gnosticism. Gnostics accepted the special meaning of Jesus Christ, but their interpretation of him, and of things in general, was far closer than that of normative Christianity to the alternative reality tradition.

Details of different Gnostic systems varied.[9] But they had in common a world view shaped by Hellenism and Neoplatonism, as well as by esoteric Judaism, Zoroastrianism, and the ancient heritages of Egypt and Mesopotamia. The Gnostic sought, out of the symbol systems of all these strains together with Christianity, to construct a picture in which he could find his identity. His quest was, in the words of one ancient writer, "to seek myself and know who I was, and who and in what manner I now am, that I may again become that which I was." In the midst of the destruction of cultures and the appalling brutality of the Roman world, there were those who needed above all to know who they were. They felt they were isolated individuals with some kind of wholly valuable essence within, lost and strayed into a callous and meaningless world for which they were never made.

Stephan Hoeller, the Los Angeles leader of a modern Gnostic group, states that what is most important about Gnosticism to him is that it presents an "intrapsychic" deity. God in all his complexities is found within the self as well as without. It is perhaps the first religion, at least in the West, which is wholly nontribal and centered upon the discovery of infinity within the psyche of the single individual. Society and history are alike irrelevant to this discovery, which leads out of them as out of realms of evil.

In Gnosticism, then, the soul of the individual was seen as a spark of the divine which had fallen an inexpressible distance from the world of light. Usually a mythological interpretation of the fall is provided, employing spatial metaphors for psychological realities which are actually, according to modern Gnostics, subjective. (The thought of C. G. Jung, who was quite sympathetic to Gnosticism, is much employed.) The spark in man is viewed as alien in this world of time and matter. Like a fish out of his element, it undergoes great suffering in such an uncongenial environment. Jesus Christ is an envoy from the worlds of light, from far above the God of the Old Testament (who was sometimes regarded as a false god, a part of the fallen sphere). Jesus draws to himself those lost fragments of the light who are able to see in him a beacon lit in their true home.

Mythical narrative language is always a necessary part of the expression of ultimate things. Man's problem is that while he incurably wants to know the most that can be known, what things are in their widest dimension, who he was and who he is and who he can become, all his experiences are limited to particulars. We do not experience Pleasure and Pain, but this pleasure and that pain, this excellent meal or that toothache, as C. S. Lewis once pointed out. We can, however, tell stories in such a way that particular joys and pains and events seem to explain what is always true. The Gnostics devised complicated stories of how the lower of the aeons, or transcendent spheres of light, fell through ignorance and desire, and in the end produced this world of space and time in which sparks of light were trapped, and of how the escape could be made through Christ. But the Gnostic was looking for radical reversal, for experience of a wholly other state of consciousness. This state should be immediately available since it is predicated by the ground of one's being, the divine snared within, and not upon historical processes. The Gnostic mood was antihistorical, since the route to salvation via kings, battles, laws, and eventually a Last Day was associated with the enslaving God of the Old Testament still honored by other Christians. For Gnostics, it was rather a matter of a vertical ascent *now* by means of a new and total state of consciousness bestowed by right *gnosis*—knowledge that is not so much factual as total insight, intuitive understanding, called *epignosis*, or recognition. The experience is brought down to an intrapsychic process triggered by certain symbols such as Christ.

This position, although admittedly not very different from the view of Christianity of many Christians, differs from New Testament Christianity. The New Testament holds that the events of Christ's life are true and definitive on both the psychic and historical levels. The myth is also true as an event. The Bible does not regard the scenario of the life of Christ just as an allegory of metaphysical or intrapsychic realities. It is much more oriented toward the total redemption of all the world, matter and spirit alike, at the End. It is much more convinced that the suffering of the cosmos is caused by sin rather than by a finitude imposed upon the divine spark from conditions beyond man's control.

The complex theological issues cannot be discussed here. Basically, Gnosticism appeals to a feeling that the anguish of one's alienated state, and the pathetic suffering of the world, are beyond help under the conditions of the world, or even of space and time. One is then susceptible to teachers who say, "What you have heard is the outer shell, but there is within a deeper, more immediate mystery of why you suffer in this harsh world, and how to escape from it. You are not meant for this world at all; forget it, prepare to return to your eternal home far above in the arena of light."

This appeal, and the elitism it implies, has of course been repeated by any number of groups throughout the ages. All cults, virtually by definition, contain a strong element of it. Madame Blavatsky, particularly in *Isis Unveiled*, drew heavily upon classical Gnosticism. But pure Gnosticism differs from Theosophy in that Gnosticism suggests the entrapment of the light is due to something having gone wrong, a cosmic mistake or fall, beyond our control (so we rightly feel lost), but not beyond the control of aeons or archangels who should have done better. Very basic to Theosophy is the sense of security engendered by a belief, on the other hand, that everything in the cosmos is going according to plan, or is at least subject to inexorable karmic law—there is thus a reason for all that we suffer in the past. Both moods obviously appeal to deep, but different, needs of human subjectivity.

There are those in this age who have made the same Gnostic appeal. "I Am" is, in important respects, a modern Gnostic movement. A few others have explicitly termed themselves Gnostics. One such group is the Order of the Pleroma, founded by an Australian-born Gnostic teacher, Ronald Powell, now residing in London, who calls himself Richard, Duc de Palatine. He had been a Theosophist and priest of the Liberal Catholic Church in Australia. In the early 1950s he went to Europe and, after associating with certain tiny Gnostic sects which have functioned there for some years, ended by establishing his own group, the Pleroma. He also set up a corresponding church of the Liberal Catholic type, the Pre-Nicene Catholic Church. In 1959 he appointed the Hungarian-born Theosophist, Stephan Hoeller, a man of considerable esoteric learning, to begin work in America. The American group has four or five active study centers and some three hundred members, but is presently declining.

The teaching of the Order of the Pleroma is a generalized Gnosticism which does not draw from any one ancient teacher. Apart from the liturgy of the Pre-Nicene Catholic Church, there are only classes which study and discuss such favorite Gnostic texts as the *Gospel of Thomas,* the *Pistis Sophia,* and so forth. Progression is a matter of gradated lessons; initiation is subjective. The Duc de Palatine has had some ideas about making advancement and the organizational structure more orderly, but both remain nebulous. An advanced circle, the Disciplina Arcani, has a pseudo-Masonic ritual based on a round table, but it is not practiced much. The majority of people in the Order of the Pleroma, perhaps because of its Theosophical background, are less interested in expressing existential alienation through the group than in discovering the "true" esoteric teachings of Christianity and in attaining a Neoplatonist sort of mystical realization with the help of Gnostic literature. The Order believes simply that Gnosticism is the true Christian faith, and that so-called orthodox Christianity is erroneous. The real point of Christianity, then, is the initiation of the individual into the light which is his true home. The suffering, death, and resurrection of Christ is an allegory of the initiatory process, and not efficacious in itself.

The ecclesiastical wing of the movement, the Pre-Nicene Catholic Church, offers baptism, the mass, and all other Catholic initiations and sacraments. Typical of many "old Catholic" churches, it is a tiny body rich in episcopal titles, claims of apostolic succession, and lavish liturgy. Its clerics use vestments and ceremonies characteristic of the Roman Catholic or Anglican mass, but the liturgy is dilated with Gnostic terminology. A prayer toward the beginning starts

Give ear unto us, O Indwelling One, while we sing Thy praises, Thou Mystery before all Uncontainables and Impassables, Who did shine forth in Thy Mystery, in order that the Mystery that is from the beginning should be completed in us...

Mr. Hoeller has now separated his organization in Los Angeles from the Duc de Palatine's. The crisis which led to this split began when de Palatine started talking of settling in southern California. According to Hoeller, de Palatine had been moving more and more toward a personal interpretation of Gnosticism based on his own mystical experiences; Hoeller wants more of a study group. He calls his new group the Sophia Gnostic Center. Mr. Hoeller has the happy capacity to view his activity with a sense of perspective and humor.

The influence of Theosophy in the emergence of this group's neo-Gnosticism is evident. The Duc de Palatine in his own writing frequently quotes Madame Blavatsky, usually in agreement, occasionally in disagreement. Especially congenial, of course, is her conviction that undistorted Christianity is identical with the "ancient wisdom" which in turn is fairly Gnostic—the drama of the soul as the principle of light warring against matter as darkness. For de Palatine the deepest Gnostic symbol is Christ's extension on the "cross of matter." De Palatine even talks of the soul's return as a love affair between the true heavenly soul (feminine) and the (masculine) soul gone forth, as on a knightly mission, to learn—an heroic image more Neoplatonist or Theosophical than Gnostic.

At any rate, these teachers, like Steiner and others, reacted against the orientalism of Theosophy. For them, a Western emphasis on active rite, keen intellectual knowledge, and unambiguous affirmation of the eternal soul finding its path back to the light down many reincarnations and aeons is preferable to yogic psychosomatic exercises and alleged life- and self-negation.

Reading Selection: Modern Gnosticism

The following passage was written especially for this book by Stephen Hoeller, leader of the Sophia Gnostic Center in Los Angeles.

AN OUTLINE OF GNOSTICISM*

Gnosticism may first of all be defined simply as *mystical religion.* By this we do not mean that occult phenomena and psychism ought to take the place of traditional religious practices, or that purely negative conceptions of Divinity, vague reasoning, or a distaste for practical action should constitute the essence of religious life. None of these things are the essence of mystical religion but its aberrations.

Gnosticism in the above noted sense is as old as humanity itself. Gnosis means knowledge, as distinguished from mere belief, or blind faith based on hearsay. The Gnostics of all ages and faiths have asserted that man is capable of first-hand knowledge regarding the essential nature of things human and divine, and that the attainment of such direct, immediate and absolute knowledge is the greatest hope and promise of our earthly existence. Statements advancing this proposition can be found in all religions and religious philosophies, from the Upanishads to the wisdom of ancient Egypt, and from the Gathas of

---

*As taught in such modern Gnostic movements as the Gnostic Society, The Brotherhood of the Pleroma, The Pre-Nicene Catholic Church, The Church of the Gnosis, and others.

Zarathustra to the mystery-cults of Greece and Rome. In a more restricted sense the Gnostic movement of the first Christian Centuries includes the teachings of Basilides (c. 130 A.D.), Valentinus (c. 150 A.D.), Marcion, Ptolemaeus, Cerinthus, Menander, Saturninus, Bardesanes, but there exists much justification for including Apollonius of Tyana, Simon Magus, Clement of Alexandria, and the church father Origen into the illustrious company of the Gnostic teachers. Many students feel that St. Paul the Apostle could be justly included in this company, for his Gnostic orientation is evident in many of his epistles, perhaps most clearly in First Corinthians 2:7, where he says: "But we speak the wisdom of God in a mystery, the hidden wisdom [Gnosis] which none of the rulers of this aion knew." Some of the most important points of Gnostic teaching are as follows:

At the root-base of all consciousness there is a transcendental field, named Pleroma or fullness, from which emerge more limited fields of consciousness in series, each with properties revealing the original Principle. This fullness may perhaps be envisioned as identical with the basis of psychic energy resident within the Collective Unconscious discovered by C. G. Jung, and the objective and purpose of the efforts of the Gnostic is to establish an effective, conscious contact with this ultimate Source of all Power and Life, which resides constantly at the very back of our consciousness, and is therefore always available. This unobstructed contact can be established only when the dominion of the rulers (demiurgoi, archons) is broken, that is, when man is no longer subject to the attachments and fascinations of the lower worlds of sense perceptions, emotions, and analytical reason, but having transcended the latter, has put on the "vesture of light" and thus has accomplished what modern analytical psychology calls total integration, and the mystics of the first Christian centuries called "the divine Gnosis."

This process of integration, or growth, in the Gnosis is attained by the double method of (1) esoteric sacramental ritualism, and (2) the allegorical interpretation of the biblical scriptures through the proper recognition of their spiritual and psychological symbolism. It is interesting to note that the two remnants of this double method are still to be found in the exoteric orientation of the Catholic and Protestant churches, which are still the exponents respectively of sacramentalism and of an interest in the Bible. Thus in a certain sense Gnosticism supplies the missing link between Catholicism and Protestantism by explaining the sacramental rituals not as mere magic performed in memory of historical events, but as the externalization of internal psychic alchemy, and on the other hand by regarding the Bible not as history but as mythology of the most sublime and valuable kind. To the Gnostic myth is truer than history, for it depicts the eternally recurring story of man's soul, its vicissitudes and its ultimate triumph over the external world.

The Gnostic believes that Divinity is resident in every man, and that the mission of great teachers, such as Christ, is to facilitate the emergence of the innate Divinity of all humans. Most Gnostics believe in some form of reembodiment and they hold that although life in the body on earth must of necessity appear as a limitation and a calamity to the soul, it is a self-imposed limitation, a calamity voluntarily entered into for a definite purpose, namely the overcoming of the world and the transforming of all creatures and things into the essence of light. In order to properly explain the nature and purpose of man's life on earth the modern Gnostics distinguish between the *lesser self* (Personality) and the *true self* (Divine Soul) of man. The former perishes after every earth life while the latter endures. In the Gnostic system we find the statement that the temporal personality survives the death of the body, but not indefinitely. After the passage of some time, the emotions and intellect of man, which survived the passage of his body, also undergo a form of death, and then the true self or soul begins to form a new personality for the purpose of a new incarnation. The Gnostic is aware of and studies the manifold environmental forces and influences which are involved in the formation of his personality and in the shaping of his earthly destiny. Hence at least a rudimentary knowledge of astrology and of some of the other occult arts are considered useful tools for the Gnostic while he still finds himself in incarnation in the physical universe.

Essentially, however, Gnosticism ancient and modern is *mystical* as well as *psychological religion,* i.e., a view of the religious effort wherein God, the Commandments, the Angelic and Demonic powers, and just about every aspect of religious doctrine are considered to be interior to man. No wonder that such great students of psychology as the late Dr. C. G. Jung have given abundant evidence of their interest in and admiration for Gnosticism. Indeed to all well-informed modern Gnostics, Jung must appear as one of the major apostles of their ancient faith in contemporary guise.

The great student of Gnosticism, G.R.S. Mead, wrote, "The Gnostic strives for the knowledge of God, the science of realities, the Gnosis of the things that are; wisdom is his goal, the holy things of life his study." To this most eloquent and true statement we may add that unlike the believer, who remains content with secondhand knowledge derived from the testimony of others, the Gnostic fervently desires to become a knower of the ultimate realities of authentic being. He follows no one, save the eternal light within his own heart; he trusts no other Savior except the saving power resident within his soul. Thus, in the words of the Gospel of Phillip, the Gnostic becomes not only a Christian, but a Christ.

Stephan A. Hoeller

6. The "I Am" Movement

No doubt inspired by the talk of the Masters of the Theosophists, between 1900 and 1940 particularly, a number of persons claimed contact with Masters and with ancient and esoteric orders offering a message to the world. The last and most dramatic important movement of this type is "I Am." Few religious activities have had such a meteoric rise and fall as "I Am." At its apex in the late thirties, it must have represented the greatest popular diffusion Theosophical concepts ever attained. Its leaders, the Ballard family, could fill the largest auditoriums in the largest American cities with fervent followers. Now the movement, while still in existence, is little known save by those whose memories reach back to the tumultuous days of the Great Depression and the Second World War.

The founder was Guy Ballard (1878–1939). Born in Kansas, Ballard had long been interested in occultism, had practiced Spiritualism in Chicago in the twenties, and had studied teachings of the Theosophical sort in libraries in Los Angeles. By profession he was engaged in mining exploration and promotion. In 1930 while he was working near Mt. Shasta in northern California, he had his initiatory contact with the hidden world.

Deep in the woods, Ballard reports in his first book, *Unveiled Mysteries*,[10] he encountered a beautiful, godlike figure who gave him a marvellous drink and introduced himself as the Master Saint-Germain. Using Ballard as example and messenger, the adept first of all wanted to restore to mankind the truths of reincarnation. He showed Ballard many of his former lives, which he had shared with his wife Edna (Lotus) and their son Donald, in fabulous ancient civilizations. In the course of these tours, the Master painstakingly imparted information about karma, the inner reality of the divine (the "Mighty 'I Am' Presence"), occult world history, and the creative power of thought. The writing is very smooth and simple. One cannot but admire the effectiveness with which Ballard presented in a truly popular and American manner the basic teaching and sense of wonder which underlies Theosophy. The author employed fast-paced interspersing of fantastic events with philosophical discourse phrased in homespun and highly visual language.

Apart from the general Theosophical world view, the "I Am" teachings have certain distinctive characteristics, all of which no doubt contributed, along with the readability of the books, to its remarkable spread. One trait is the American setting and nationalistic overtones. The Masters are found not in faraway Egypt or Tibet, but also in the then-romantic American West—Mt. Shasta, the Grand Tetons, and Yellowstone. The Masters become known to Wyoming ranchers, Colorado miners, and Arizona prospectors. Moreover, it is said that humanity began in America, and that this is the seventh and last cycle of history, under the Lord of the Seventh Ray, Saint-Germain. As the history of this epoch began in America, so will it end there. This nation will be the vessel of light to bring the world into new and paradisal times. While there were and are rightist overtones to the movement's attitude toward America, in large part it can be seen simply as a thorough indigenization of the Theosophical experience.

The "I Am" movement makes rich use of color. The rays of the Masters, the spiritual characteristics of people are all given vivid color adjectives. "I Am" bookshops and centers are gaudy with color diagrams and lights. Ballard's writing is packed with color words. Fascinated by mines and gold, Ballard loved to depict the Masters' retreats as underground, reminiscent of the halls of fairy tale dwarves. One leader in the movement has said that color is really all there is; everything is energy and electrons, and energy comes to us as color. Sound—talking—is also energy, but is largely destructive, and has done much to get mankind into the trouble which surrounds him. That color can overcome it is much invoked by "I Am" students.

The three Ballards travelled in the thirties as "Accredited Messengers" of the Masters lecturing about these revelations. Sometimes further messages from the Ascended Masters were produced in public or private, especially from Saint-Germain or the Master Jesus. The basic teaching is that the "Mighty 'I Am' Presence" is both God and immediately available. With typical concreteness, it is said that one's "individualized" Presence is a pure reservoir of energy stationed over the head. Power can be drawn from it at will. Mediatory between the "I Am" and men are a host of Ascended Masters, such as Saint-Germain and Jesus. At one time all were human beings who, through purifying their lives, became able to transcend the physical world.

Ascension is the goal of human life. The secret is attaining equilibrium in the "causal body" (a Theosophical term), the karma-made aura about a person which reflects his deeds and desires. Ordinarily the aura is both dark and light, and when its darkness reaches a point where the person can no longer be of much service, or make much progress, he dies physically to begin another life. But if, through purification of diet and thought, the causal body becomes fully luminous, like an inflated balloon it lets go of the earth. The person ascends to join the Ascended Masters and share their unconditioned state of joy and free service. Properly, ascension comes without death, unexpectedly, instantly as the causal body brims over with light. However, in 1938 a dispensation was given that persons who had devoted themselves so much to the movement that they had not given all they might to personal purification could upon normal death ascend from the after-death state without reincarnation.

A very important part of "I Am" is the matter of "decrees." A decree is the use of concentrated psychic power, created by thought, colored light, and chanting, to disperse evil influences, and black magicians, to discarnate "entities" of evil intent and "enemies of America." Just as it is really thought and word that lead to destruction, so can they help to counteract it. Karma cannot be destroyed, but it can be changed. I have been told that "I Am" stopped the Watts riots of 1965. At the time the trouble broke out, 700 young people of "I Am" happened to be gathered at Mt. Shasta for a conclave, and they focused powerful decrees against it. Records of past karmic debts can be done away by the "violet consuming fire" which is like the grace of the New Testament. It liberates persons from the toils of what has gone before.

From 1937 to 1940, we are now told, "I Am" worked publicly in order to cast a broad net to filter out, through testing, a small but serious group. The decline in numbers began with the death of Guy Ballard on December 29, 1939. Despite the claim of Edna Ballard that he had become an Ascended Master, the fact that physical death rather than evident ascension had taken place was too much for many believers. The following year a sensational trial of the leaders of the movement for obtaining money under fraudulent pretenses cast further discredit upon it, even though the indictment was later voided by the Supreme Court.

The movement looked upon the falling away as a time of trial. Those who remained became secretive and withdrawn. The decree rituals are not open to nonmembers. Under Edna Ballard's leadership the movement stressed more and more the puritanism implicit in the original writings. Members who are "one hundred percenters" are to give up tobacco, alcohol, meat, and sex. They do not keep pets either. An antisexual bias is evident in much of the literature. It is expected that students will sublimate sexual drives into service of the Masters, and it is indicated that ascension can come only to those who have given up all sexual activity, even for procreation.

"I Am" is still alive today. It has temples, reading rooms, and radio programs in a number of cities. It was directed by Edna Ballard until her death in 1971. Mt. Shasta is a major center.

In the summer of 1970 I visited Mt. Shasta and talked with a pleasant lady who had been a member of "I Am" for many years. She lived on the spotless grounds of the Saint-Germain Foundation. In an amphitheatre on these grounds every summer "I Am" stages a pageant of the life of the "Beloved Master Jesus." The crucifixion is left out of this version, for the ascension is what is believed to be important. Focusing on the crufixion, I was told, only encourages the "sinister forces." "I Am" also owns two hotels in the vicinity of the village of Mt. Shasta, where youth and adult conclaves are held every summer. Services are held every evening in a sanctuary in the village. The pageant is done by the young people, but Mrs. Ballard came each year to direct it.

The lady at Mt. Shasta told me that the present generation is the last in which the "sinister forces" will be present. A new age is coming when, as on Venus, vibrations will be too high and too pure for evil. Unready persons will then have to reincarnate on another planet able to take their lower wavelength. Earth will be very evolved, and many will ascend. In the present situation, Ascended Masters can help; they come and go in this world devoted to service. In the past, Saint-Germain had been Samuel, Joseph, Columbus, Roger Bacon, Francis Bacon, as well as the eighteenth century magus. He appeared in a vision to Washington as the revolutionary general prayed at Valley Forge. America has a special destiny as a center of the light, and "I Am" members do much "work for America."

The story of relations between "I Am" and the community of Mt. Shasta is rather interesting. When "I Am" began to establish work at their sacred mountain in the forties, there was considerable local antagonism. "I Am" was accused of weird and fantastic practices, and slander followed its members. In 1948 Mrs. Ballard was a special guest of the Mt. Shasta Chamber of Commerce. She explained the "I Am" activities, stressing the work for a better world and saying their beliefs were based on the Bible.

Full acceptance did not come until 1955, however, when the general public was first invited to attend the pageant of the life of Christ. Three thousand came and were awed. The play culminated in an ascension of Christ by means of an elevator cleverly concealed in a pine tree. Then Mrs. Ballard solemnly bore an American flag to the device and had it wafted aloft as a symbol of the ascension of America as a nation. The next day seventeen local business concerns purchased a full-page ad in the *Mt. Shasta Herald* thanking the "I Am" movement for the invitation to the pageant and warmly praising the group. The pageant is now held every summer to the mutual benefit of the religion and the tourism-based economy of the town.

Fundamentally, however, "I Am" seems a faith of the Gnostic type, calling believers on the basis of a special revelation away from the chains of matter and history directly into the realms of light.

7. The Liberal Catholic Church

The interior of the typical Liberal Catholic Church looks very much like that of a Roman Catholic or high Anglican church quite untouched by any recent liturgical reforms. The altar will be against the back wall of the sanctuary, ornamented with six candlesticks, cross, and frontal. The only unusual item is a picture of Jesus directly over the cross on the altar. The celebration of high mass in the Liberal Catholic Church too reminds the visitor of an ornate, traditional Roman Catholic or Anglo-Catholic rite. Numerous clergy and acolytes in resplendent copes and chasubles and surplices, swinging censers which cloud the church with fragrant incense, enter in procession. Moving with the slowness of ancient ritual, they approach the altar chanting and genuflecting.

The words of the rite are in English, generally reminiscent of the Episcopal or Roman Catholic rite, but with certain variations, some in the direction of Gnostic interpretations of Christianity. The confession does not suggest that "we are miserable sinners," but rather that "often we forget the glory of our heritage and wander from the path which leads to righteousness." After the consecration of the elements of bread and wine for the Communion, all stand to sing "O Come, All Ye Faithful."

It is in the sermon that the traditional Christian may be most surprised, however. He may hear of an impersonal Absolute beyond the conceptualized personal God, of the appearance of Masters and the deceased in etheric bodies, of "esoteric" interpretations of Christianity in which the festivals of the Christian year and events in the life of Christ are symbols of occult realities far older and more far-reaching than the short span since the first century A.D.

The Liberal Catholic Church is a body founded by Theosophists; many of its members are also Theosophists. While priding itself on allowing complete freedom of belief, it generally interprets Christianity along Theosophical lines. It was founded by James Ingall Wedgewood in London in 1916. Wedgewood was a former Anglican priest who had left Anglicanism to become a Theosophist. But the real intellectual leader of the new ecclesiastical expression of Theosophy was another former

Anglican priest, C. W. Leadbeater. His book, *The Science of the Sacraments,* is the standard Liberal Catholic theological work.

Why did a Theosophist like Leadbeater, who had for so long repudiated ritualism and distinctively Christian concepts, suddenly and enthusiastically support this seemingly unlikely new movement? Leadbeater was a man of remarkable psychic vision who, at least according to his descriptions of them, saw many things beyond ordinary visibility—Masters, angels, devas, auras, the colored shapes assumed by various thoughts and moods and emotions above the person's head, and lines of psychic force. One Sunday he happened to attend mass in an obscure Sicilian Catholic Church, and was amazed to observe powerful waves of prayerful feeling rolling from the peasant congregation to the altar, and splendid light descending from above onto the priest and altar and consecrated bread and wine. The experience suggested a new view of the rite. It combined word, gesture, and thought to funnel and focus the transcendent energies which the Masters know and serve to make them accessible to man. A basic premise of Theosophy was the existence of such invisible mental energy; here was a way it could be tapped. To do so through a rite modeled on the mass did not, in Leadbeater's view, require acceptance of the orthodox concept of the uniqueness of Christ. The Liberal Catholic liturgy could be seen as a Western counterpart to the Brahman sacrifices of India, which can be interpreted Theosophically.

The Liberal Catholic Church, then, is an institution designed to put into operation these forces, and to teach the esoteric interpretation of Christianity—within freedom—in the context of its Catholic rather than Protestant tradition. That is to say, it puts nonverbal ceremonial as well as verbal communication at its center.

The most fundamental idea is that of "Thought-forms." Leadbeater and Annie Besant wrote a book of that title with paintings illustrating what Leadbeater saw around the forms of persons in various spiritual states; these can be modified by ritual, prayer, and sacrament. Thought and form create a single whole and enhance each other. The ritual builds up a geometric form which contains power, as do the vestments, gestures, and meditations. Even the incense is full of elves, delightful beings entrapped in it, who help to distribute its grace, and angels come to bathe in the light radiating from the Host.

It is a quasi-instrumentalist concept of worship and the sacraments, suggesting an arranged creation and impartation of grace. But the notion of the relation of matter and thought, and of the power of thought, is certainly different from that of either ordinary materialism or ordinary Christianity.

Unfortunately, like Theosophy itself, Liberal Catholicism has suffered from personality problems and divisions. At the present time, in the

U.S. there are three Liberal Catholic denominations: The Liberal Catholic Church, with only a few members headed by the Most Rev. Edward M. Matthews of Miranda, California (according to a court ruling he has legal claim to the original U.S. Charter for the Liberal Catholic Church); the International Liberal Catholic Church, related to groups in Canada and Holland with some 3,000 members in North America (one-third of them in St. Thomas Liberal Catholic Church in New York); and the United Liberal Catholic Church, related to Liberal Catholics in Great Britain, Australia, and elsewhere, and also closest to Theosophy, with some 1500 U.S. members (10,000 worldwide). In all branches there is a very high ratio of clergy to laity; many parishes seem to be largely priests and deacons and their families. Many clergy have private altars in their homes and say mass alone daily, for the work of creating good psychic forces, while strengthened by the presence of a congregation, is not dependent upon their presence.

It does not appear that the Liberal Catholic Church is growing in numbers or influence today. But there is in its basic work of creating out of the mass a psychic cathedral of powerful invisible forces an enduring charm and beauty.

Reading Selection: The Liberal Catholic Church

The passage given below from C. W. Leadbeater's Science of the Sacraments *concerning the meaning of the consecration of the Host, or round flat wafer of bread, in the Roman Catholic and Liberal Catholic mass illustrates the nature of his beliefs, and those generally of the Liberal Catholic Church, about this sacrament. To him, the celebration of the mass is really the creation of a psychic structure, by thought and act, through which certain supernal spiritual forces can flow. Reflecting the Theosophical concept of God, these spiritual forces are essentially impersonal (unlike the Roman Catholic view) though splendid, and one can "plug into" them in a rather objective way, though of course a deep sense of morality and reverence is important.*

To understand the true relation between the physical matter of the Host and its counterparts requires the sight of other and higher dimensions of space. So in a sense we are only describing a diagram when we say that the Angel of the Presence brushes aside a bundle of wires or lines running up from the wafer to the Deity, but there is no other way of making the process thinkable to those who cannot see in the inner worlds. If we try to analyse the thing we shall find it rather complicated, because every atom has always its connection with the Deity. Truly the divine life is everywhere, as I have already said, but through the act of consecration, a special manifestation of it flashes out in the matter of the Host, welling up from the very heart of the Christ, so that it becomes in that moment a veritable epiphany of Him. It is then that the Host glows with unearthly radiance, as befits the most precious gift of God to man.

It was this glow which first brought to my notice the possibility of studying clairvoyantly the hidden side of the eucharistic Service. It may perhaps help the reader to realize the actuality and the material nature of the phenomenon if I reproduce here an account (written soon afterwards) of the first occasion on which I had the opportunity of observing it.

> My attention was first called to this matter by watching the effect produced by the celebration of the Mass in a Roman Catholic church in a little village in Sicily. Those who know that most beautiful of islands will understand that one does not meet with the Roman Catholic Church there in its most intellectual form, and neither the Priest nor the people could be described as especially highly developed; yet the quite ordinary celebration of the Mass was a magnificent display of the application of occult force.

> At the moment of consecration the Host glowed with the most dazzling brightness; it became in fact a veritable sun to the eye of the clairvoyant, and as the Priest lifted it above the heads of the people I noticed that two distinct varieties of spiritual force poured forth from it, which might perhaps be taken as roughly corresponding to the light of the sun and the streamers of his corona. The first (let us call it Force A) rayed out impartially in all directions upon the people in the church; indeed, it penetrated the walls of the church as though they were not there, and influenced a considerable section of the surrounding country.

> The Rt. Rev. C. W. LEADBEATER, *The Science of the Sacraments* (Adyar, Madras, India: Theosophical Publishing House, 1929), pp. 232–34. Quotation in the last two paragraphs originally from C. W. LEADBEATER, *The Hidden Side of Things*, Vol. I, pp. 232–34.

Notes

1 Helena Petrovna Blavatsky: *Isis Unveiled: A Master-Key to the Mysteries of Ancient and Modern Science and Theology* (New York: T.W. Bouton, 1877). Since republished several times by others. Unlike later Theosophy, this book shows little influence of Eastern thought, not even generally affirming

physical reincarnation, but retaining successive planes in the world of spirit akin to those of A. J. Davis.

2 The phenomenon of the letters is presented in A. P. Sinnett, *The Occult World* (London: Theosophical Publishing House, reprinted 1969). Many of the letters are published in A. T. Barker, ed., *The Mahatma Letters to A. P. Sinnett* (London: Rider and Co., 1933).

3 For the controversy see Chapter Two, note 21. In this connection, it must be remembered that Madame Blavatsky was a magus, that is to say, a "shaman in civilization." William Howells has this to say about the shaman (and much the same could be said about many spiritualist mediums):

> The shamans know, of course, that their tricks are impositions, but at the same time everyone who has studied them agrees that they really believe in their power to deal with spirits. Here is a point, about the end justifying the means, which is germane to this and to all conscious augmenting of religious illusion. The shaman's main purport is an honest one and he believes in it, and does not consider it incongruous if his powers give him the right to hoodwink his followers in minor technical matters.

The Heathens: Primitive Man and his Religions (New York: American Museum of Natural History, published by arrangement with Doubleday & Company, Inc., 1962), pp. 132–33.

H.P.B. undoubtedly did believe in the Masters, and that she was receiving dictation from them as she went into the various states of altered consciousness which came so easily to her and in which she did so much of her writing. But it may not have always been clear to others that, as she herself recognized, letters ostensibly by a Master's own hand could actually be written by a *chela* or disciple in that hand. How H.P.B. reconciled in her own mind—whichever that was—the many things done by the many personalities who appeared to use her is a mystery. See Mary K. Neff, *Personal Memoirs of H. P. Blavatsky* (Wheaton, Illinois: Theosophical Publishing House, 1937, 1967), pp. 151–53.

4 *The Secret Doctrine* begins with a commentary on a cosmogonic poem called "The Stanzas of Dzyan," which H.P.B. says was originally written in a very ancient language called Senzar, and preserved by Masters in central Asian caves. Nonetheless, various scholars have detected familiar motifs in the poem. René Guénon, *Le théosophisme: histoire d'un pseudo-religion* (Paris: Éditions Traditionnelles, 1965), p. 97. says the Dzyan seems to be based on fragments of the Tibetan Kanjur and Tanjur published in 1836 as the twentieth volume of the *Asiatic Researches* of Alexandre Csoma de Körös, the distinguished pioneer Orientalist, in Calcutta. But the renowned scholar of Jewish mysticism, Gersham Scholem, in *Major Trends in Jewish Mysticism* (New York: Schocken Books, Inc., 1961), Note 2 to Lecture VI, p. 398, expresses the opinion that the mysterious *Book Dzyan* owes much to a Jewish Zoharic Kabbalistic writing, the *Sifra Di-Tseniutha*. A Latin translation of this medieval work appears in Knorr von Rosenroth's *Kabbala Denudata* (1677–84), from which H.P.B. drew heavily.

To some Dzyan suggests the Sanskrit *dhyana* (meditation; cf. Chinese *Ch'an*, Japanese *Zen*, which are transliterations); but to Scholem it suggests Di-Tsen.

[5] The influence of Edward Bulwer-Lytton (Lord Lytton; 1803–73), *Zanoni* (Boston: Little, Brown, and Co., 1932), and other of his novels as well, on H.P.B., A. P. Sinnett, and others for the concept of the Masters should be appreciated. This romantic tale of a mysterious Italian gentleman of indefinitely great wealth and age, yet continuing youth, who resided for some years in the interior of India, who was equally at ease with all languages, who talked of occult initiations and of the lore of the Chaldeans, Magi, Platonists, and the like, and who turned out to be a survivor of the Rosicrucian fraternity, is mentioned by H.P.B. Sinnett even castigates Lytton for "having learned so much as he certainly did, [being] content to use up his information merely as an ornament of fiction." The jibe is not entirely pointless for it is well known that Lytton did take magic and occultism seriously and was much influenced by Eliphas Levi. In any case, Lytton's books so powerfully affected the imagination of certain persons of his day, in reviving the ancient and Eastern figure of the magus, that it became part of that small class of fiction which creates fervent and invincible belief in the veracity of its world! In the novel, Zanoni, disciple of the Rosicrucian Mejnour, gave up the occult for the sake of human love when a choice was necessary—quite the opposite of the choice of H.P.B. and others of the leading early Theosophists! See, on Lytton and H.P.B., Sten Bodvar Liljegren, *Bulwer-Lytton's Novels and Isis Unveiled* (Cambridge: Harvard University Press, 1957).

[6] "A.E." (George Russell), *Voices of the Stones* (London: The Macmillan Company, Publishers, 1925), p. 21. Reprinted by kind permission of Mr. Diarmuid Russell.

[7] The fullest independent summary of the life and teaching of Alice Bailey is found in J. Stillson Judah, *The History and Philosophy of the Metaphysical Movements in America* (Philadelphia: Westminster Press, 1967), pp. 119–33.

[8] Max Heindel, *Rosicrucian Cosmo-Conception* (Oceanside, Calif.: Rosicrucian Fellowship, 1937).

[9] See Hans Jonas, *The Gnostic Religion* (Boston: Beacon Press, Inc., 1958, 1963); Robert M. Grant, *Gnosticism and Early Christianity* (New York: Harper & Row, Publishers, 1966); and, for Gnostic texts, R.M. Grant, *Gnosticism* (New York: Harper & Row, Publishers, 1961).

[10] *Unveiled Mysteries* was written under the pen name Godfré Ray King (Chicago: The Saint-Germain Press, 1934).

four

the descent of the mighty ones:
spiritualism and ufo cults

Spiritualists are those for whom the most meaningful religious experience is communication with the spirits of the departed—spirits either of loved ones, or of great and noble figures on "the other side." UFO (Unidentified Flying Objects) cults are centered around the "flying saucers" which have been staples of journalism and discussion since 1947. Invariably, it is believed in the cults that many, at least, of these objects bear envoys from a superior and benevolent civilization on another world who have come to warn and aid mankind in his folly.

What do these two have in common? First, as with many other cult groups, they have a conviction that against the backdrop of an ultimately monistic and impersonal universe range powerful and generally invisible friends superior to man and to what we would consider natural. But among Spiritualists and UFO people, these mighty ones do not have the *récherché* atmosphere of the Theosophical masters with their overtones of the cryptic past and the exotic Orient.

Rather, save in the case of the Aetherius Society which has obviously been influenced by Theosophy, Spiritualism and the UFO groups fundamentally reflect a new and direct discovery of symbols of mediation in the fabric of American life. The wise ones come as American Indians, Spirit Doctors, departed relatives, or from a futuristic technology. Both types of groups employ the same manner of communication: vision and marvellous journeys, trance speaking and writing, seance circles, and telepathy. The close interaction between Spiritualism and UFO cults is not surprising, for one finds there is much exchange of persons between them.

At a meeting of a UFO group, Understanding, Inc., which I attended in 1968, the speaker was an individual who claimed to be Chief Standing Horse, a full-blooded American Indian, despite his blue eyes and pale features. He was a "contactee" whose story related trips to Mars, Venus, Orean, and Clarion (the last two being planets unknown to science but described by several UFO groups).

The story had elements in common with many shamanistic and UFO accounts. He originally made contact with "saucerian" friends through three mysterious men who called on him in Oklahoma during a Spiritualist convention. Aboard the ship to which they took him, he met a beautiful initiatory female. One spaceship on which he rode was shaped like a giant Indian arrow. He displayed a strange piece of metal as evidence of his story. His forte was a very folksy humor and sentimentality which oddly changed the milieu of saucerism from pseudoscience to an atmosphere more akin to that of certain southern churches. It turned out, in fact, that the Chief is pastor of a Spiritualist church. (One is reminded of the Indian Guide theme so prominent in Spiritualism.) He ended by saying that he has subsequently made spiritualist contact with some of the other-worldly friends he met in his marvellous journeys. His wife reported also that departed persons from earth have been located on the paradisical planet Orean, along with the beautiful initiatory lady and other acquaintances from his space voyage.

In the writings of Spiritualism and UFO cults alike, the Ultimate will be spoken of in such rather abstract terms as "Infinite Intelligence," "Great Oversoul of All," "Great Guiding Force," and so forth. But the spirit intermediaries, and space brothers, will be addressed in terms of intimate, though respectful, fellowship: "Help us, O Angel Loved Ones . . ." "thrice blessed are these Saviors of a whole planetary race."

Companionship with these intermediaries has typically a particularism, delightful naïveté, and casualness toward rational structure which, together with the shamanistic overtones in technique, makes the phenomena best approached through folk religion categories. Indeed, it could perhaps be argued that Spiritualism is an original religious creation from what may be the closest approach there has been to a genuine folk culture in America—the frontier. (The UFO cults would then be a typical folk revitalization movement, akin to Cargo Cults elsewhere, of this tradition.) Of course, there is in Spiritualism an absence of long folk tradition and an almost absurd lack of significant scale in comparison to the popular religion, for example, of Bolivia or Brazil.

Yet there are interesting parallels. The folk religion of Latin American peasants is local and particular. Devotion is not to a saint in general, but to his manifestation in a particular shrine, and vows to the saint are finite, explicit, and on behalf of specific favors. God becomes virtually a *deus otiosus,* a vague and impersonal absolute behind the colorful and particular cultus of the saints, their glittering shrines, festivals, and processions. In Bolivia, the Virgin of Copacabana is popularly thought to be different from the Virgin of Cotoca; people make a particular commitment to an individual saintly patron.

But in a broader sense, they are all the same. There is no real difference in function, related to the historical characteristics of each, between the Blessed Virgin, the Saint Benedict, or the Saint Anthony of Latin American folk piety. Gibbon remarked once that for the common people all the religions of the Hellenistic world were equally true. Perhaps this has always been the case with the "common people," insofar as their religion is folk religion. Within the confines of this system, change means only change in form—a new patron, a new shrine, a new but equivalent devotional practice. Change is not propelled by rational construction or by historical process, but by new hierophany; it may be called "innovation by miracle."

It is no doubt understandable that in Latin America, especially in Brazil, Spiritualism and UFO enthusiasms have had great modern success. But in the same way, Spiritualism in America evokes a world of individual helpers and particularized miracle. Despite the fact that a large number of American Spiritualists are of Roman Catholic background, the frontier Protestantism which lies behind it has precluded the building of great pilgrimage shrines for its supernormal allies.

· But the helpers are there. In a Spiritualist church in Indiana, I saw the woman minister and her assistants (also mostly women; like other forms of folk religion, Spiritualism has strong matriarchal overtones) go about the congregation telling every person present individually of the guardianship of his particular "spirit band." I had with me a sage "Spirit Doctor" and certain deceased relatives.

Life histories in the religion are constructed of marvellous events. A Spiritualist minister received, he told me, his call as a child with a series of seizures during which strange untoward voices spoke through him. His parents were deeply concerned, but finally an elderly Spiritualist minister recognized them as spirit voices. When the subject realized this, the voices resolved themselves into four aides on the "other side," who have ever since been this medium's "controls." This happened on a farm in Illinois in this century; it might have been the call of a paleolithic shaman.

Communication with intermediaries is mainly by subjective means, although one may be initiated into contact with them by an event which seems concrete and objective. It is like the shaman's initiatory experience, followed by his relatively quiet and steady communication with the spirit band he has subdued. But though the initiatory event was private, the public manifestation of the sacred will display its fruits—regular communication with the other world in trance.

·The UFO cult, unless it is itself also Spritualist, has less emphasis on the production of phenomena in the meeting. There will, in fact, perhaps be no formal worship, only a lecture style account by the contactee of his experience. The UFO circle may represent modernization in the sense that the reinterpretation of the Spiritualist tenet in the terminology of "technological myth" has led to an ostensibly more secular organization. But the group certainly lives in the aura of UFOs as bearers of mystery and transcendence. Accounts of sightings are eagerly exchanged. Many persons believe themselves to be in telepathic communication with the saucer's occupants. They receive not only messages of world importance, but also guidance from extraterrestrial friends in personal problems.

In some cases, individual contactees have delivered trance messages from UFOs in a manner virtually indentical to the trance-preaching of Spiritualism. Another device has been the "circle," in which each individual in a small group adds something to a message the group believes it is collectively receiving from another world. Basically, however, UFOism is even more centered than Spiritualism upon the charismatic, shamanistic individual. Its greatest events, such as the Giant Rock Space Convention, are focused upon them and are principally opportunities for these contactees to tell their story.

The several UFO contactee movements form a distinctive clique of their own. Though they are rather remote from the externalia of the "hip" generation or the sensitivity awareness enthusiasts, they do not live in the world of the older Spiritualists either. For them, lectures, books, verbal communication, and conceptual thought are still normative, yet UFO cults could only have come after science and technology had crossed the mental horizon decisively. The power of myth has not been lost in non-verbal immediacy. The power of the present world has not given way to the attractiveness of the past as the locus of mythical reality. The UFO religious movement, like science fiction as a genre, peaked about 1960. This moment seems to coincide with the final stages of uncritical popular acceptance of science and technology as the primary bearers of meaning in the secular world, and of the whole acceptance of mythical scenarios in the religious before the later reversal in favor of social orientation or nonconceptual sensory and mystical immediacy. The present UFO movements are a cultic perpetuation of that point through their amalgamation of technological and mythical visions among their now aging members.

C. G. Jung, in his important treatment of the psychic meaning of the phenomenon written about 1960, *Flying Saucers: A Modern Myth of Things Seen in the Sky*, calls attention to the appearance in the cultic type of literature of "technological angels" who come carried by these vehicles. He wrote:

We have here a golden opportunity of seeing how a legend is formed, and how in a difficult and dark time for humanity a miraculous tale grows up of an attempted intervention by extra-terrestial "heavenly" powers— and this at the very time when human fantasy is seriously considering the possibility of space travel and of visiting or even invading other planets.[1]

Jung did not emphasize the character of the contemporary myth-forming so much as the archetypal nature of the UFO form itself—the disc-shaped object in the sky. He felt that it typified the mandala, the circular symbol of psychic wholeness. In a characteristic way, he illustrated from the dreams of modern persons, from art ancient and modern, and from myth, the recurrence of this symbol. Some saucer enthusiasts have also ransacked ancient literature to produce previous cases of celestial disc apparitions. However, they also generally stress that the present contacts are connected with the "New Age," and hence are of a different and eschatological nature.

Despite the fact that certain ancient parallels, like Ezekiel's wheels and the *vimana* of the Mahabharata, may occur, we should stress the paradox of continuing religious content and new symbol. This is what is implied by Jung's saying they are "*technological* angels." Virtually all the other new religions, however futuristic they may claim to be, keep a metaphysical frame of reference, or make contact with quasispiritual beings, like the Theosophical Hierarchy. These contacts could have been talked of thousands of years ago as well as today. But the precise form of revelation which animates the saucer movements could have only emerged in the context of modern astronomical and technological awareness. It is a religious by-product of science, not to mention science fiction. These groups are of no less interest than the Cargo Cults, for like them they represent an almost entire transference to modern vehicles of a traditional religious scenario and cast. It is the ancient story of angelic and savior beings from an (or the) other world who communicate with elect persons and transfer marvellous powers and esoteric knowledge, and thereafter usher in a paradisical age. But in the UFO cults the myth and cast are as modern as the flight of Apollo spacecraft, though not secular.

1. The Spiritualist Church

This section will not attempt to sort out the denominational history of Spiritualism. This has been done, at least sufficiently to indicate the fluidity of the situation and the kind of issues and personality clashes that have caused division.[2] The basic points of contention have been controversy over the introduction of reincarnation and other Theosophical principles, and whether or not Spiritualists are Christian. Andrew Jackson Davis, the major Spiritualist thinker, accepted neither reincarnation nor Christianity, but his spiritual progeny have found themselves pulled by the Christian environment and the Theosophical domination of the intellectual life of the occult world.

But excessive attention could be given the denominational forms of Spiritualism. If, of the three forms of religious expression, the social may be given first consideration in Spiritualism, it is not because the organization of Spiritualist churches or denominations is important, but because of their actual social structure as gatherings around an initiated, charismatic leader.

· Forms have a strange symbolic value for Spiritualists, but there seems to be a marked dichotomy between theory and practice. Perhaps because they are unequivocally in the nineteenth century tradition, Spiritualists generally have a highly elaborate constitution both on the local and denominational levels, and are constantly tinkering with it. They are careful to incorporate as a religious body. Of course, to some extent this protects them from laws against fortune-telling. Yet at the same time, there is a sense of unreality about the formal structure. Most groups are very small, probably the majority of attenders are not members, and attendance is often quite fluid and overlapping. Spiritualist churches appear and disappear, and change names and denominations, with remarkable alacrity. Denominations are little more than paper organizations issuing certificates of ordination, manuals, and periodicals. In recent years this process of flux and fragmentation seems to have accelerated. The reason is, of course, that in reality Spiritualist churches are merely the followings of particular mediums, who even buy and sell church buildings. Each gathers his or her own congregation. If the medium retires or moves away, the church is not likely to continue under the same name, and perhaps not under the same denominational affiliation with the National Spiritualist Association, the Universal Church of the Master, or some other of the score or more groups.

Training of Spiritualist ministers is spotty. Some denominations offer schooling in connection with summer camps, or by correspondence, but standards are rarely rigidly enforced. Of course, these features of loose organization, personality-centered churches, and little training are "bad" only if the pattern of the major Christian denominations is taken as a standard. But this may be like comparing the amoeba and the whale. Spiritualism may represent a different, and in some ways more persistent, type of religious experience which of its own nature does not require the same orientation to denominational social expression or ministerial initiation by verbal education.

Doubtless because it has the oldest continuing tradition of all the groups we are examining, the Spiritualist church may strike the visitor as having a conservative if not "dated" atmosphere. Something in it remains of the 1850s. Yet beside the old Americana is a sense of doing a daring thing which puts its practitioners at odds with their background. The ethos is lower-middle class theological liberalism. The typical Spiritualist church offers a strange combination of pietistic hymns and decor and very broad doctrine; there is no hell, truth is in all religions, man is judged by his deeds, the "New Thought" concept of the value of thinking positive, creative thoughts. It offers an excellent example of the history of religions theorem that cultic form in religion usually changes much more slowly than verbal expression.

· But rather than continue with general discussion, perhaps it would be more interesting to describe a typical Spiritualist church. In 1970 I visited one in a run-down, inner-city section of Los Angeles. This church was at the moment a branch of the United Church of the Master. Characteristically it was in the process of revising its constitution to set itself up as the flagship of a new denomination, to be called United Christ Church. In an inordinate number of cases, Spiritualist churches I have visited have been in this process. (The United Church of the Master, as a denomination, had a meteoric rise a few years previously, at least on the West Coast. It took over most of what had been the once-promising Spiritualist Episcopal Church, but it seems now to have fragmented. When I attempted to visit the UCM's general headquarters in San Jose in 1971, the building had been turned into a seamstress shop.)

The typical Spiritualist church is designed like a traditional Protestant church, with pulpit, altar holding open Bible, and stained glass windows, but with a perhaps garish maximum of such accoutrements as flowers, candles, cloth altar hangings, and sentimental pictures of the Master. There is an odd resemblence in taste to the cluttered Victorian parlor. This was true of the church I visited. It was a store-front building, and had the conventional altar and portrait of Jesus. But the difference lay in the fact that behind the altar were the crudely painted symbols of the major religions of the world.

The service opened with hymns, led by a short, stocky lady minister. She was of quite advanced years, but obviously strong, determined, and keen-witted, a typical Spiritualist priestess-matriarch who guides a band of children of all ages both in this world and that of spirit, and who makes up for what she lacks in formal education with the ageless psychic intuition of the village wise-woman. The hymns were of a sentimental type, such as "Blessed Assurance," and "In the Garden."

The congregation was mixed; there were blacks, whites, and Mexican-Americans, and young and old, but the leadership was mostly white. All were clearly lower-middle class, dressed in neat, simple clothes. None, not even the young people, showed other than docile external conformity to the norms of the respectable, industrious workingman; there was no long hair or "hip" dress. If there was rebellion, it was clearly spiritual, for this was no working class Catholic parish or evangelical temple.

The principal minister was a youngish, handsome man with close-cropped black hair and a short-sleeved gray clerical shirt. The elderly lady minister took a seat in the sanctuary and smiled benignly; the young man was obviously her protegé. He spoke an invocation and a word of welcome. He said that the church draws from the scriptures of all faiths. The lesson that morning was read from the *Aquarian Gospel of Jesus Christ*. This book, written by Levi H. Dowling allegedly through "tuning in" to the "akashic records" which Theosophists and others believe carry a permanent imprint of all past events in the atmosphere, contains supposed events in the life of Christ not found in the ordinary New Testament, including a journey to India. This book is very frequently read as scripture in Spiritualist and other cult churches. The passage I heard described Jesus talking in Benares with brahmans.[3]

The reading was followed by a short, simple, attractive sermon on knowing God everywhere. After another hymn, announcements were given: a Tuesday evening message-only service, a Thursday evening healing service. The announcements were typical. Spiritualists like a week-night service at which they can concentrate on what to them is most exciting—receiving messages from the spirit world. Healing by prayer and laying on of hands is also important in most Spiritualist churches; it is part of the atmosphere of warm, comforting psychic force and charismatic power the faith produces. The new denomination, United Christ Church, was then discussed. Over two hundred ministers, it was said, had expressed interest in it. Emphasis was placed on the fact that the new denomination would be run by ministers only; there would be no lay boards. In this connection, of course, it must be kept in mind that few Spiritualist ministers are full-time professionals and that many members of the congregation in any church have mediumistic gifts, are accounted ministers, and bear impressive ordination certificates.

Next came the part to which everyone was obviously looking forward, the spirit messages. Typically, the minister-medium takes a seat facing the congregation, and goes into light trance, often with a few jerking, spasmodic motions. Then, with the help of one of his "controls," who will speak through him in altered voice, he will give a general message and deliver individual messages to members of the congregation. Individuals are told about the future of their health, family relations, travel, and job. Pastoral advice and encouragement is intermixed with the message, and assurance given of spirit guardianship.

In many cases, other mediums or ministers in the congregation—those who have taken "medium development classes"—get up to give either individual or general messages. In this case, one was an elderly black gentleman who told, among other things, of his taking an out-of-the-body trip to Viet Nam where he saw his son.

Then the young minister gave a remarkable account of a trip he had taken the past week—allegedly in the body—by Air Force jet to Washington, where he had been asked to give a seance and service for the President and his family in the White House. This fantastic narration was given with perfect calm and control, convincing manner, and great elaboration of detail.

Most Spiritualist churches do not vary greatly from this pattern. A few decades ago more use was made of devices such as the trumpet through which the spirit spoke, production of ectoplasm in which the spirit takes shape, and the like. These performances may still be seen at Spiritualist camps such as Lily Dale in New York and Chesterfield in Indiana. "Zenor," leader of the Agasha temple in Los Angeles, reminds one a little of Mesmer in that he passes around a metal rod supposedly charged with healing force which everyone may hold for healing vibrations. His principal "control" is an ancient Egyptian priest named Agasha. He also receives messages from deceased loved ones for members of the congregation, who come forward to have them whispered in their ears.

At the First United Spiritualist Church in Gardena, California, reservations must be made for the Tuesday and Thursday night seances, for they are very popular and the number is limited to twenty. These persons sit in a circle in a darkened room. After going into trance, the minister delivers messages from four spirits. They fall into a typical pattern: a temperamental Hindu philosopher, heavy and ponderous; Harry, a hoarse-voiced man; two American Indians, one a serious guide, the other full of folk humor. The Hindu and Harry answer metaphysical questions, the others bring messages from spirits of loved ones and tell details of the furnishings of one's house and of one's personal life, sometimes quite accurately.

· The doctrine of Spiritualism, as summarized in the *Spiritualist Manual* of the National Spiritualist Association, affirms belief in "Infinite Intelligence," nature as its expression, individual continuity after death, communication with the "so-called dead" proven by Spiritualism, and moral responsibility.[4] The tone is perhaps what is of most interest. The language tends to be abstract, and omits any reference to Christ or the authority of the Christian scriptures. It would be possible to affirm these principles, as did Andrew Jackson Davis, and reject the name Christian, though many Spiritualists will state that Spiritualism is taught in the Bible. Belief in the "planes" proposed by Davis, based on Swedenborg, is widespread. The reference to scientific proof of communication with the departed indicates that Spiritualism, like UFOism, can perhaps be seen under the guise of "technological myth"; a shamanism rationalized and justified by modern psychical research.

Most important, though, is the experience of mental expansion towards infinity and ultimate transformation through the phenomena of communication. Spiritualist experience suggests an "unobstructed universe." Mind—spirit—overcomes the conditionedness of space, time, and body. The hierophany of mediumistic miracle suggests a cosmos less drab and confining and hopeless than it seems. Spiritualism provides a church for people, like the young minister who related the marvellous journey to Washington, of uncircumscribed mind. Its mentalist orientation suggests, finally, that one can construct one's self, life history, and world from that which emerges out of psychic phenomena and the images and personalities from the unconscious. This audacious proposition, radically dangerous or liberating as one wishes, is really the premise of the whole alternative reality and cult tradition.

Reading Selection: Spiritualism

The following passages from a Spiritualist textbook illustrate the religion's mentalist tone, and the high value given the ideas of progress and education.

Invisible communicators have often made the point in their explanations of the Etheric that the after-life is mental, but then they sometimes add slyly, "But so is your world!" This is profoundly true. The only difference between the earth plane and the higher spheres is *vibrational frequency of consciousness*. This difference, of course, is of very great importance, and is very real to those experiencing it.

The lower planes or spheres of the Etheric World are relatively low in vibration and tend to harmonize easily with the consciousness of earth. As one ascends in the hierarchy or graded levels of the spheres the vibrations become progressively higher, and a more refined consciousness is required for attunement.

B. J. FITZGERALD, *A New Text of Spiritual Philosophy and Religion* (Los Angeles: De Vorss & Co., 1954), p. 38.

The reader inevitably asks the question at this point, just what are the dwellers in the Etheric doing?...Just as our earthly life centers largely about the physical body and its insistent needs, so does spiritual life center about the growth of mind and soul. Life in the spheres is basically *educative* and devoted to the unfoldment and elevation of consciousness...It may surprise some to know that in the Etheric are wonderful schools, conservatories of music, academies of the arts, of all beauties and refinements. There are marvellous libraries and books, truly heavenly music.

Most strugglers in the vales of earth fail to obtain adequate expression in realms of creativeness, beauty and culture. The harsh struggle to maintain the body does not permit sustained cultural activity. In the Etheric the situation is much changed.

FITZGERALD, A *New Text of Spiritual Philosophy and Religion*, pp. 46–47.

2. Giant Rock Space Convention

A discussion of the UFO movements should properly open with the Giant Rock conventions, for these annual meetings have between 1954 and 1970 brought together the saucer community. The organizer and master of ceremonies is George Van Tassell, proprietor of the small Giant Rock airport near Yucca Valley, California, on the Mojave Desert some three hours drive east of Los Angeles. A large, balding, plain-spoken man with a background in aeronautics, Mr. Van Tassell is a natural leader. He has been associated with flying saucers for some time. In 1952 he published a book, *I Rode in a Flying Saucer*,[5] containing an account of his initiatory experience with UFOs. He was sleeping on the desert with his wife. A ship landed nearby in the middle of the night. His wife remained asleep, but Mr. Van Tassell went aboard and talked with the crew.

He believes that the Giant Rock area is a "natural cone of receptivity" for saucers, and that they are constantly over the region and send messages that he can receive telepathically. Bryant and Helen Reeve describe vividly in 1957 his going into a light trance after hymn singing amid a circle of family and friends until an "energy beam" from a UFO entered his mind. (Notice the spiritualist milieu.) It is, he says, not a soft voice but strong words or thoughts which appear suddenly and crowd out all other ideas; he converses with the space beings in a normal tone of voice.[6]

Although these space communications are held by invitation only and have lessened lately, Mr. Van Tassell has held simple religious services every Friday evening. He also reports that he has met the UFO people physically—they have come to call on him—for there are some who are incognito in our world and visit UFO believers.

More recently Mr. Van Tassell has emphasized religious and scientific work. He is the leader of a "Ministry of Universal Wisdom, Inc." through which he publishes a paper, *Proceedings of the College of Universal Wisdom* offering religious comment and news of his activities. Most of its space is now devoted to his "Integratron," a large electrical device in a round domed building and a local landmark. He hopes through it to develop antigravity and time travel and to restore youth to aging cells. The ideas for it were given from outer space.

I attended the fifteenth Space Convention at Giant Rock on September 28, 1968. The meetings lasted two days and consisted largely of a series of open-air talks by contactees and others. There is something of the atmosphere of an old-fashioned camp meeting, complete with signs following, for quite often it is reported saucers appear overhead to sanction the proceedings. A high platform for a rostrum is set up against a huge boulder some four stories high. In front are chairs for the several hundred listeners, many protected from the blazing sun by umbrellas. Participants arrive by car, motorcycle, and plane. Many spend the night at the site in trailers and tents. The group was mixed—there were young people in "hip" dress, cowboys, and elderly ladies of the most conventional sort. Some fifteen stalls surrounded the arena offering the wares of occultist and UFO groups.

The first speaker I heard was Frank Stranges, an evangelist who has moved heavily into the UFO field with books and lectures and movies. He has lately tended to emphasize the this-worldly possibilities in UFO phenomena. His address considered that UFOs may have been developed toward the end of the war by Germans and are now being launched from secret Nazi bases in South America. They would thus approach a demonic rather than angelic role.

The second speaker was Orfeo Angelucci, an American of Italian descent who has attracted attention for the purity of the religious motifs which emerge in his story. Jung devoted some ten pages of an essay to Angelucci.[7] A slight, pleasant, and intensely sincere man, Angelucci told his story fluently, as one who has recited it many times.

He told how, beginning on the night of May 23, 1952, he had met with a marvellous man and woman from another world who had come by saucer. On a couple of later occasions he rode their splendid vehicle, ringing with the music of the spheres, to their paradisical world. They had promised help to suffering mankind, and had designated him an evangelist of this experience. Angelucci's experience ended in his mystical marriage to the spacewoman named Lyra. The religious character of the

experiences is shown in such expressions as, upon meeting the marvellous visitors, he felt an exaltation "as though momentarily I had transcended mortality and was somehow related to these superior beings." It was as though he had "felt another world, or something akin to a whole universe."

This story speaks for itself in regard to psychology of religion as well as any of William James's narrations, or any account of shamanistic or mystical initiation. It may be pointed out that Mr. Angelucci's education was limited, but that he had previously dabbled in occult science, and that his vocation was aeronautical mechanics. We see a far-reaching merger of technological and religious themes, the one the vehicle of the other.

3. Understanding, Inc.

The contactee tradition was initiated by George Adamski and continued by other early claimants of flying saucer rides, such as Truman Bethurum.[8] We cannot give space here to their accounts for they did not crystalize into groups. Another early experience which did, however, was that of Daniel Fry. A group which has long met monthly in Inglewood, a suburb of Los Angeles, is Understanding International, Inc. This organization, which has its headquarters in Oregon, was founded by Mr. Fry, who is still its president.

Mr. Fry was an employee of the White Sands Proving Ground near Las Cruces, New Mexico, in 1950. On July 4 of that year he missed a bus going into town for the holiday and took a solitary walk on the desert in the evening. He was met by a UFO in which he was given a ride to New York and back in half an hour. In the course of the journey he was given messages from Alan, his invisible mentor. These included homilies on true science, the importance of understanding, and information that the saucer people are the remnant of a past supercivilization on earth which destroyed itself through annihilating wars. Only three shiploads of persons managed to escape death or biological degeneration through radiation by flying to Mars. Now they return to warn their earth kin.[9] (It is interesting to note that a number of contactees presume the saucer people to be not alien but separated and highly perfected earthmen, or at least some sort of mysterious kin.)

Understanding Unit 15, the Inglewood group, meets monthly to hear speakers, largely contactees, discuss saucer topics. Most of the prominent contactees appear regularly. There is no particular religious practice connected with the meeting, although interestingly the New Age Prayer derived from the Alice Bailey writings is used as an invocation.

On November 23, 1968, the tenth anniversary of the local group, the speaker was Daniel Fry himself. A stocky, rich-voiced, articulate man, he gave the image of the science entrepreneur rather than the religionist. He did not discuss his initiatory experience, but rather talked knowingly of Washington and universities and UFO and rocket research, indicating that saucer enthusiasts were only ahead of the times. He showed a movie on the history of flight. Then, moving into scientific eschatology, he projected a human future—now enjoyed by the saucer people—in which man, freed from the face of planets, will live generation after generation on great self-sustaining ships in space, swinging as whim directs them from one world to another. The meeting ended as Mr. Fry and five or six other contactees, conservatively dressed and standing with their wives, had their picture taken before a tenth anniversary cake.

Understanding, Inc. does not have sessions in which contact is attempted. It is presently the only UFO group (excluding Aetherius and Giant Rock) in the Los Angeles area which has regular meetings. But several years ago, when there were perhaps half a dozen members, some meetings included telepathic contact such as that practiced by Van Tassell on the desert.

Reading Selection: Understanding, Inc.

Here are the contents of a mailing announcing the program of a coming meeting of a branch of Understanding, Inc. Most articles in the organization's periodical deal with world peace, inspirational topics, and relatively unsensational reports from newspapers of UFO sightings. But UFO contacts and telepathic communication with beings from other worlds are probably what kindles greatest enthusiasm among members. Notice how, typically, the communications in this broadsheet pull together favorite themes of esotericism, such as the great pyramid, piety toward the Creator, and a feeling of wonder that such ordinary people as those in the organization are made privy to secrets unknown to the wise of our world.

THE INGLEWOOD UNIT OF UNDERSTANDING
PRESENTS
"VOICE FROM OTHER PLANETS"

This coming Saturday, March 22, 1969 at 8:00 P.M., the Inglewood Unit 15 of Understanding will present another program of special tape recordings of "VOICES FROM OTHER PLANETS"....

On this occasion four tapes will be played, all narrated by Beings from other planets. These are:

1. *"INTERPLANETARY SPACECRAFT."* The message on this tape tells of the different types, sizes, shapes, and speed of the spacecraft used in interplanetary travel. Mention will also be made of two most unusual spacecraft used only on rare occasions and then only under circumstances of the utmost importance.

2. *"A GALACTIC TOUR."* This tape takes us on a journey far removed from our solar system and out into that area of space known as our Galaxy. Several of the brightest stars are visited: Alpha Centauri, Beta Centauri, Aldebaran, Betelgeuse and Procyon where the wonders of our Creator's handiwork and the cultures and technologies of his people are touched upon. Most astounding.

3. *"THE GREAT PYRAMID."* The message on this tape takes us back into the far distant past and tells when, why, and how our great Pyramid was constructed. Furthermore, it unveils in part the mystery of the great Pyramid.

4. *"MASAR."* The message on this type deals with the planet Mars. It tells of many facets of Martian life, education and cultural developments.

PLAN NOW to come and bring your entire family and friends to hear the voices of these Beings and their messages for, truly, this is "THE PROGRAM UNIQUE portraying events and revealing information that may affect the lives of all people, even YOU."

The public is cordially invited. Tape recorders too. Admission is by donation.

4. Amalgamated Flying Saucer Clubs of America

Gabriel Green is one of the most attractive figures of the saucer world. He is head of the Amalgamated Flying Saucer Clubs of America. Not a major contactee himself, Mr. Green has through his periodicals, conventions, lectures, saucerian paraphernalia, wide friendships, and integrative reflections served as a focal point. In 1960 he ran for president, but withdrew finally in favor of John F. Kennedy. In 1962 he ran for U.S. Senator in the Democratic primary on an ultraliberal antibomb platform.

These political efforts seem to have been the results of promptings from saucer contacts, although this was not mentioned in the campaign literature. The contacts, he says, were from the planet Clarion. They first reached him through the mediumship of other saucer enthusiasts, or even by telephone. Then the extraterrestrial persons appeared at his home, keeping appointments made by these contacts. One, named Rentan, was only four feet tall, but otherwise they were indistinguishable from earthly humans by sight. The stage of meeting these visitors physically, he says, seems to pass with all contactees. It is a kind of initiation or preliminary in the adventure. After rapport has been achieved by such gross means, telepathy takes over.

Mr. Green lives in the pleasant Los Feliz district of Los Angeles, which is also the headquarters of the AFSCA. His activities seem now not to have the fervor of several years ago, when he was running for high office and mass rallies and great conventions were held. (These are all recorded in the fascinating back files of his magazines.) But Mr. Green still busies himself with editing, lecturing, and selling pins, books, bumper stickers ("Flying Saucers are Real—the Air Force Doesn't Exist"), and other curiosities. When I called on him, I found him a still youngish and modest man. He is confident without show of learning. Although he does not claim to know everything, he has heard all the stock reactions and arguments to his point of view, and knows how to handle them on their own level.

He said that he first organized UFO work in 1956 as the Los Angeles Interplanetary Study Group, which sponsored contactee speakers. When their messages were presented on tape, music was often played beforehand on the same tape to set a mood. On one of the first occasions, the music continued even after the tape was turned off—this wonder was only one of many signs. However, he has not been sponsoring contactee meetings for some time. This work has now been taken over by Understanding, Inc. Several years ago the area had eight or ten such groups; now there is only one. Mr. Green conceded that as the subject of UFOs becomes more popular on the newsstands, the intense contactee movement seems to be declining.

This is partly, he said, because some contactees seem to confuse their own message with absolute truth, and see all others negatively. Others either before or after the contact experience do not exhibit the best ethical behavior, and one or two may be too interested in making money. But Mr. Green was convinced that nearly all of them had had a genuine contact, and are sincerely dedicated to spreading its message.

Concerning the inconsistencies of contactee information and the naïveté of many reporters of such experiences, Mr. Green made several lucid comments. If messages contain inconsistent data, it may be that the extraterrestrials deliberately include inaccurate matter for our sakes, to make us do independent thinking and analysis and not become dependent on them like children. Persons who receive messages are usually the obscure of this world, often with limited education. This is because people established in the academic or financial or political worlds find contact too threatening and are too quick to reject a call. Moreover, a new generation, starting with new leaders brought up to accept contacts, must be developed. Finally, the ability to receive contacts requires certain psychic and telepathic gifts. As is well known from psychical research generally, this ability does not necessarily accord with intellectual or moral stature. We may note that the same sort of explanations are apparent in other religious groups as they explain their revelations.

Mr. Green said, "The Saucer People say, 'Let's take the babes, people who don't know anything, not those who have degrees.'" Hence the saucer movement is like a training group. But most contactees become too dogmatic. People begin worshipping them, and react against them when their frailties are revealed.

Mr. Green said that the extraterrestrials contact by telepathy more than by face-to-face meetings. There have been perhaps a hundred face-to-face meetings, and only a few major ones. But many telepathic communications have been received. In a group, often one person will have such a message, then others will get ideas, and after some trial and development will also be able to receive. After ten or twelve years in the movement, he developed telepathy. It started when Daniel Fry was with him. He began operating a Ouija Board which he drew himself. Mr. Green tried it and things began coming through. Then he wondered, why bother with the board? Messages began coming directly, mainly in answer to mentally posed questions. Now, when he is talking with someone, or alone, guidance to problems and questions come regularly by ideas appearing in his head. Quite a few other people deliver into tape recorders, a few use Ouija Boards or automatic writing. But he insisted this does not have much in common with Spiritualism. Saucer communication is concerned with world problems rather than contacting departed loved ones—though once contacted the saucer people will give help in personal matters too if necessary to further the cause. But before this is available, one has to get into the movement and learn enough to be of use.

Mr. Green pointed out that most of the contactees bring essentially the same message of reform from the saucer people. The extraterrestrials see us as savages, but they are trying to help us within the limits of respect for our freedom to develop sufficiently to enter their universe. A basic necessity, and one very important to him, is economic reform. In the space economy, money is not used. We must, he said, change to a non-money economy based on responsibility and sincerity in producer and consumer before we can adequately progress. The non-money economy, which he can explain in some detail, is a totally new concept, neither capitalism nor socialism. The basic reason the extraterrestrials are here is to get us to make these reforms and become nondestructive before we can associate with them. We must have the space economy and a world government so they can contact a single head, and we can send representatives to the galactic parliament.

Mr. Green seemed a little disappointed by the slowness of developments. He had expected something climactic, a positive showing of the extraterrestrials, before now. It must come soon, or the crest will pass; the people who have been trained as contactees are getting old. There was a note of discouragement. But then he said he expected definite evidence to come to light in the near future. The U.S., and especially southern California, is a center. Most contactees are in this area, which is meaningful. But while the UFOs must intervene directly, they will not until we are sufficiently organized and prepared.

The AFSCA periodicals have, therefore, emphasized economic reform and world unity from the beginning. In this respect they have, like the saucer movement in general, moved close to New Age type of language, breathing an expansive eschatological expectation. Issues for the past several years have contained the extended communications of Bob Renaud, a young man in Washington, Massachusetts, who has received saucer transmissions on his shortwave radio. After hearing from an attractive initiatory female, Lin-Erri, he received voluminous information on the social and economic and even recreational life of the space worlds. Needless to say, it is much in contrast to the greed, violence, and dogmatism of earth.

Recently, Mr. Renaud has also begun to be caught up in the cosmic battle aspect of the phenomenon. He has been visited by mysterious "men in black," an increasing complaint among persons involved in saucers. They have tried to threaten him and to bomb his car, and one pressed an ominous ring against his forehead. The implication is that just as spiritual ascent opens the saint to demonic attack, so involvement in the affairs of the cosmic helpers may open earthmen to their antagonists, whoever they may be.

Reading Selection: Amalgamated Flying Saucer Clubs of America

The following paragraphs are from a one-page informational flyer issued by the Amalgamated Flying Saucer Clubs of America. They were written by Gabriel Green. We can here see clearly his combination of utopian social idealism and open acceptance of the claims of UFO contactees.

The appearance of Flying Saucers in our skies is fast becoming common knowledge, but it is not as well known that hundreds of people have not only seen them, but have actually ridden in these craft and personally met their occupants. These "contactees" discovered that the pilots and other crew members of these interplanetary spaceships were *not* grotesque beings, but were, instead, highly intelligent, friendly men and women from civilizations evolved far in advance of our own.

To the Earth people they contacted, the Space People told of their advanced sciences and of their relatively Utopian way of life. To our planet, in the throes of social and political upheaval and teetering on the brink of self-annihilation by nuclear warfare, they had come, they said, to show us the way out of our crisis and the solutions to our problems. It is this information and knowledge that the Amalgamated Flying Saucer Clubs of America, a nonprofit organization, has endeavored to bring to public attention since its inception in January 1959, and which is published in our magazine *Flying Saucers International*.

The scientific and technical knowledge to be gained from the Space People is a wealth of beneficial information which could transform this world from its present chaotic state into a utopian-like society, far beyond today's most optimistic concepts. Some of the many amazing benefits of the knowledge already received from the Space People, or promised by them if we will welcome them in a friendly manner, are: elimination of disease, poverty, and smog; solving of the problem of automation and unemployment; a way to finance all public works projects and aid to other countries without taxation; an extended life span; a greater measure of personal freedom, economic security, and abundance; and for many living today, personal journeys to other planets beyond the stars.

With the aid of our Space Brothers, the Flying Saucer movement is rapidly growing into a dynamic worldwide social reform movement, dedicated to the mental, physical, spiritual, and economic emancipation of man. This new Space Age ideology to champion the dignity and rights of man, to free him from economic bondage, and to liberate him from the confines of regimentation, limitation, and want, will render impotent those antiquated, totalitarian philosophies based upon force and coercion. This will create a true Brotherhood of Man on Earth through the application of the philosophy of love, through service to others.

GABRIEL GREEN, "A Letter from AFSCA's
President," in Amalgamated Flying Saucer Clubs
of America mailing, undated, early 1960s.

5. The Aetherius Society

If most of the movements and contactees discussed so far are broadly and sanguinely eschatological, at least at first, the Aetherius Society represents the apocalyptic wing of the movement. Perhaps significantly, it has by far the tightest cultic organization, and the most explicitly religious structure. To present it in a few paragraphs is a difficult task, for its writings are oceanic and its concepts and undertakings elaborate. It has moved away from a grounding in saucer phenomena to direct psychic communication with etheric beings and to "metaphysics," although its inception is certainly tied to saucer stimuli and it originally made much of observations by members.

The Aetherius movement began with revelations received by George King in London, England, in 1954. Mr. King, who had long studied and practiced occultism and yoga and allegedly goes easily into samadhic trance, was and is the focal point of the society. An audible voice told him, "Prepare yourself, you are to become the voice of Interplanetary Parliament." Early the next year he was named by a Master Aetherius of Venus the "Primary Terrestrial Mental Channel." Thereafter Mr. King began delivering, in trance, wisdom and instruction from Aetherius and such Masters as Jesus and a Chinese saint, Goo-Ling. These Masters appear to be identical to the "Great White Lodge" of Theosophy, but saucers were regarded as the bearers of these beings or of their emissaries, as well as of "magnetic" or spiritual power which was to be appropriated. Thus at certain times, called "Spiritual Pushes," a large ship in orbit around earth sends out particular power, and special services are held to direct it. Originally something of a sensation in England, Mr. King spoke out of trance in a dramatic manner on television and radio. A small but dedicated group gathered around him in London to carry out the cosmic instructions. Mr. King has since moved to Los Angeles.

One of the first and most interesting endeavors of the Society was Operation Starlight, to give it its typically military title. Under instructions from Aetherius, members went first to Holdstone Down in England where they saw Master Jesus revealed in cosmic light. Then between July 23, 1958, and February 25, 1959, nine mountains in England were designated "Holy Mountains" and "New Age Power Centers" by the Cosmic Masters through George King. Subsequently other mountains throughout the world, including four in America, were similarly charged. These are favorite places of pilgrimage by members.

A recent project has been Operation Karmalight, successfully concluded on February 24, 1969, and it is in it that the apocalyptic tendencies have come into full view. A basic belief is that evil karma has gained sway on earth through the greed of men. The work of the Society is to assist the cosmic Masters to counteract it through wisdom and insight. A slight action at the right time and place can move a large mass. The counteracting efforts include the sufferings of the Society itself, especially those of Mr. King, whose periodic ill health is seen in this light.

For example, a "Psychic Center" is held to exist in the Pacific Ocean just off the California coast. Here somehow is the focal point of the world's bad karma. The Society has purchased a yacht, and has worked on transferring power from the nearest charged mountain, Mt. San Antonio just northeast of Los Angeles, to this center by machines of "identical substance." This project is called Operation Bluewater.

The greatest secret, however, and the crux of Operation Karmalight, was the revelation of the Three Saviors. The present moment is a time of tremendous crisis. Earth is ready to enter the New Age, the Aquarian Age, but the weight of evil karma, especially that engendered by the recent wars, has instead given rein to certain "Black Magicians" who are striving to enslave man. They are constituted on the "lower astral plane" and are of truly demonical power. In the past they gave body to such men as Nero and Hitler; now their power is all the greater. They can weave ghastly mental illusions as well as employ hideous bacteriological and atomic warfare, and a few can wield "devic forces." Mankind unaided could not hope to withstand them, and they would shortly render earth a literal hell.

But the Cosmic Brotherhood has warred against them on earth's behalf, even if the aid of man through the Aetherius Society was needed. The Masters sent several "Special Power Transmissions" in recent years to rescue mankind from crises. One on October 22, 1962, prevented the Cuba crisis from breaking into war. Other more arcane emergencies occurred on February 6, 1962, November 24, 1963, and November 19, 1964. The greatest event was on July 8, 1964. This day, called the Cosmic Initiation of Earth, was the day three great adepts, adopting "gross bodies" in a way comparable to a man becoming an animal, descended to earth to prosecute the war against the "Black Magicians." The Cosmic Initiation of Earth has glorious connotations, and July 8 is now the greatest Holy Day of the Society.

All depended on the labors of the three Adepts in this crisis. They are called the "Three Brilliant Lights" and their heroism is greatly lauded. It was with extreme sacrifice they entered this realm of deep danger. Jesus himself in one transmission acknowledged their action to be greater than his earlier saving action on earth.

They took up positions on Mt. Shasta, over Peru, and over the Atlantic. The newsletter described the action month by month. The tone was extremely tense. They warred with spiritual power and with electronic equipment of fantastic delicacy. They attacked enemy submarines and fortress strongholds, all presumably on the astral plane. All praise and blessing was given them, and it was emphasized the war was not over; they could lose. The Society had to support them with meditation, services, and its exercises of spiritual technology. The war appears to have a cosmic side; there are occasional hints of an intergalactic conflict climaxing between March 29, 1966 and March 24, 1967 in a "Battle of Gotha" which involved fifty-five sorties into "the hells." There are also allusions to a galactic source of evil called The Android.

Emphasis in this cult is placed on decision. The theme is continually that "this is the hour." The New Age may come only through strenuous combat, and fantastic times of trial will attend its birth. It is man who allows evil, and he must cooperate in its eradication, even though the Saviors do what he cannot. The world is finally awaiting the next great Avatar to Earth, but he can only come when karma is moving toward good balance.[10]

A circular issued early in 1969 announced that Operation Karmalight had been successfully concluded on February 24, 1969. The Adepts had brought a "Prince of Light from the Spiritual Hierarchy—the Lord Babaji" into direct battle with the dark power, and it was vanquished. Celebrations were called for. A lecture at the Society reviewing the progress of Operation Karmalight on April 12, 1969, expressed the spirit of the Society. On the one hand, there was a tight board-of-directors presentation of its chronology, replete with graphs. On the other was a strange joy of apocalyptic deliverance. The speaker told of how tense the atmosphere at headquarters was in the last weeks of the battle. All on the "inside" had training in "psychic warfare." But finally Satan was "transmuted" and "put back on the path of reincarnation" by the Master Babaji.

I had a feeling that I was witnessing a mythologizing of the modern experience in the conclusion of Operation Karmalight. The story was that up to now Satan, the "Black Magician," and his cohorts in the "Lower Astral Realm" have controlled most of mankind's actions. Now this power is shattered and broken, and there is a vacuum of force into which light can be poured. For a month after the February 24 the energy trans-mitters of the Society put force into the hole, it was said, but now it is up to mankind. The astral and karmic forces are churning, and millions could turn into the way of evolution. The dark pressure is off, but where we go from here is up to us. One lady at the meeting said, "They have been putting the pressure on us, now we can on them." Cannot the "Lower Astral Realm" stand for the unconscious, and "casting light into it" after its central power is broken—though lieutenants of Satan are said still to be around, able to cause wars and other trouble—speak of the experience of "mankind come of age"?

The Aetherius Society is headquartered in an attractive rambling stucco building in the heart of Hollywood. One enters through a commodious bookstore full of the group's periodicals going back as far as the early fifties, books of George King, and tapes of transmission. One or two members are usually in attendance. About ten live on the grounds and are always on call for special operations. (I understand that in London about 300 members live within a block or two of the Society, to be called upon for concentrated prayer at any time. Senior personnel are continually moving back and forth between the two cities on missions.)

George King himself lives in semiseclusion in a small apartment on the Los Angeles grounds. He is greatly venerated by the faithful. One member said, "He is the most warm, compassionate person I've ever known." The tapes containing his transmissions from the Cosmic Masters are carefully put into "the safest vault in England" for preservation for posterity, which presumably will appreciate their significance. The most important, of course, find their way into the many books published under King's name. Healing ministrations are available at the Headquarters. Lately, George King has been giving general lectures which present a basically Theosophical view of such matters as life after death and the Masters.

To the right of the bookstore is a simple but tasteful hall with a seating capacity of perhaps fifty. The strains of sacred music in stereo comes from a speaker, and incense is in the air. The ornamentation suggests the strange syncretism of the group. Over the rostrum is a conventional colored picture of Jesus, on the front of the rostrum the Sanskrit letters for Om, to its right on the wall a quote from Saint Goo-Ling. Around the wall are pictures of members of the Society in the mountains and at sea on Operations Sunbeam, Bluewater, and Starlight.

I attended the 11 A.M. Sunday morning service on July 7, 1968. About thirty worshippers were present. A little to my surprise, all were very conservatively dressed, and a good proportion were neat elderly persons. The service included such oriental practices as reciting the mantram, "Om mani padme hum" and meditation, reading lengthy dictations from the Masters including Jesus, delivered through George King, and old-fashioned Protestant items such as a sermon and the singing of evangelical hymns. There was a typical excited fervor combined with a military precision. The Aetherius Society, despite a rather more relaxed and "churchly" atmosphere in the worship service, sees itself as an army engaged in an apocalyptic battle at the end of the age, all unknown to the mass of bemused people of the world, whose salvation is now being wrought by spiritual struggle outside their comprehension.

Reading Selection: The Aetherius Society

These lines are from a broadsheet issued by the Aetherius Society announcing services in connection with one of the most important events in their calendar, the seasons called Spiritual Pushes. These irregular occasions are times when, it is said, energy from a certain UFO greatly enhances the spiritual power of the actions of earthlings. This mailing was issued while Operation Karmalight was in progress. Information about such events as this is given by the Masters through George King to members. In it one observes the virtually military sense of authority and precision which characterizes the pronouncements of the Aetherius Society. One notes also that Gotha, the Three Adepts, and the cosmic battle they are waging has become a simple day-by-day reality, and charges daily life with a tense excitement and importance.

As you read this, the Third Satellite, which is virtually a floating Spiritual Temple, will be in orbit of this Earth. This time is known as a "Spiritual Push", when all unselfish actions on behalf of others are enhanced 3000 times by the energies sent to you by the glorious Masters from this Satellite.

This Satellite will definitely leave terrestrial orbit on December 1, 1968, at 4:00 P.M. Pacific Standard Time.

As you know, many times in the past, the Three Adepts (Who are Interplanetary Intelligences living on Earth in terrestrial bodies) have come to the rescue of all people on Earth by manipulating energies from the Third Satellite on your behalf. Unfortunately, the Three Adepts, operating as They are, on an assignment directly under the Supreme Law of Karma, called OPERATION KARMALIGHT, are not allowed—by the Divine Law of Karma—to manipulate the energies from Satellite No. 3 for you at this time. But, and we should all thank God for it, there are on Earth, at the moment, two other Intelligences from a World known as "Gotha", which is millions of miles outside of this Solar System. These two Intelligences will send out great Holy power to every man, woman and child on Earth over the weekend of the 23th and 24th of November, providing that we play our part in this vital operation. It is with this in mind that The Aetherius Society has arranged the following Services....

We realize that the notice is short, but this cannot be helped as our President has just been informed by the Masters from Gotha that They are able to perform this Spiritual Service on behalf of mankind.

Even though this is short notice for most of you, we make a concerted appeal for your cooperation at this important time as it will benefit—in one way or another—the whole of the human race.

If you cannot attend all these Services, then please come to as many as you can. If through other commitments, you are only able to attend one or two of them, that will be better than not attending at all.

Mankind needs your help and this is a practical—not theoretical—but practical and sure way to help, not only mankind, but yourselves as well.

AII SERVICES ARE OPEN TO MEMBERS AND NON-MEMBERS ALIKE.

BROADSHEET, The Aetherius Society, Los Angeles
Headquarters, 1968.

Notes

[1] Carl G. Jung, *Flying Saucers: A Modern Myth of Things Seen in the Sky* (New York: Harcourt Brace Jovanovitch, Inc. [Signet Books], 1969), p. 27.

[2] See Charles S. Braden, *These Also Believe: A Study of Modern American Cults and Minority Religious Movements* (New York: The Macmillan Company, Publishers, 1949), pp. 319–57; and J. Stillson Judah, *The History and Philosophy of the Metaphysical Movement in America* (Philadelphia: Westminster Press, 1967), pp. 50–91, for summaries to date of publication of these books.

[3] Edgar T. Goodspeed, *Modern Apocrypha* (Boston: Beacon Press, Inc., 1956) gives a useful account of the story of this and other modern "scriptures" used by Spiritualists and esotericists.

[4] The major points of the "Declaration of Principles" adopted by the National Spiritualist Association, 1899 and 1909, are as follows:

1. We believe in Infinite Intelligence.
2. We believe that the phenomena of Nature, both physical and spiritual, are the expression of Infinite Intelligence.
3. We affirm that a correct understanding of such expression and living in accordance therewith constitute true religion.
4. We affirm that the existence and personal identity of the individual continue after the change called death.

5. We affirm that communication with the so-called dead is a fact, scientifically proven by the phenomena of Spiritualism.

6. We believe that the highest morality is contained in the Golden Rule, "Whatsoever ye would that others should do unto you, do ye also unto them."

7. We affirm the moral responsibility of the individual, and that he makes his own happiness or unhappiness as he obeys or disobeys Nature's physical and spiritual laws.

8. We affirm that the doorway to reformation is never closed against any human soul, here or hereafter.

Spiritualist Manual (Washington, D.C.: National Spiritualist Association, 1944), pp. 22–23.

5 George Van Tassell, *I Rode in a Flying Saucer* (Los Angeles: New Age Publishing Co., 1952).

6 Bryant and Helen Reeves, *Flying Saucer Pilgrimage* (Amherst, Wisconsin: Amherst Press, 1957), pp. 95–98. This book, although far from scholarly, is a fascinating introduction to the major contactees and their activities.

7 Jung, *Flying Saucers,* pp. 119–26. See also Orfeo Angelucci's own book, *The Secret of the Saucers* (Amherst, Wisconsin: Amherst Press, 1955).

8 See George Adamski and Desmond Leslie, *Flying Saucers Have Landed* (New York: British Book Center, 1953); George Adamski, *Inside the Flying Saucers* (New York: Abelard-Schuman, Ltd., 1955); Truman Betherum, *Aboard a Flying Saucer* (Los Angeles: DeVorss & Company, 1954). For a summary of the Fry and Betherum experiences, see Gavin Gibbons, *On Board the Flying Saucers* (New York: Paperback Library, 1967).

9 Daniel Fry, *The White Sands Incident* (Los Angeles: New Age Publishing Co., 1964, and Louisville: Best Books, 1966); and his *Alan's Message to Men of Earth* (Los Angeles: New Age Publishing Co., 1965).

10 See George King, *The Day the Gods Came,* and *The Three Saviors Are Here!* (both Los Angeles: Aetherius Society, 1967); and Newsletter, *The Aetherius Society,* passim.

five

the crystal within:
initiatory groups

In certain Australian tribes, it is believed that the shaman has had his internal organs removed as a part of his excruciating and regenerating initiatory ordeal, and that they have been replaced by organs of crystal or quartz. The ordinary person has only soft, corruptible viscera, but the shaman is transformed; he holds within himself the hard, geometric, quasi-eternal luster of miraculous crystal. These deep-concealed splendors give the initiated shaman vision, awareness, and knowledge of the mysterious currents which run in the worlds of spirit and destiny.

Comparably, the goal of occultists and initiates today is a new self of crystalline lucidity, permanence, and luminosity. The groups they belong to believe it is possible for man to have states as different from his present condition as rock is from flesh, and much better able to withstand the vicissitudes of the world. They believe these states can be attained by employing laws and forces in nature and psychology which are hidden from the uninitiated mind, and therefore may be called *occult*. Actually these laws and forces are not mysterious, but knowable and almost mathematically precise, working as normally and predictibly as gravitation. It is not so much by fervor that one attains the goal, but by knowledge, technical skill, and persistence. The goal, however, is more than knowledge. It is the shaman's goal: crystal, lucid vision, mobility on all levels of being, power and invincibility.

Michael H. Murphy, Director of the Esalen Institute, has said we need a Western *sadhana*. In India, a *sadhana* is a spiritual path, in the sense of a concrete and specific program for the use of meditation techniques, physical activities, and ritual under the direction of a master. If one practices the *sadhana* he has undertaken faithfully, whether it be yoga, devotion to a particular god, or Buddhist contemplation, it should lead to radical but predictible changes in the individual's mental and spiritual state. All cultures except our own, says Mr. Murphy, have within them traditional *sadhanas* for those who wish them: the way of the shaman, the holy man, the adept, or even of the householder who, as many do in some societies, embarks upon a carefully plotted spiritual regimen with an interior goal in mind. But the emphasis in Western religion upon freedom, God's sovereign grace, and the primary importance of ethical obligation to others has resulted in a corresponding disparagement of calculated individual spiritual attainment. That is why our culture as a whole lacks this element which older cultures have. It is easy to disparage these paths and those who undertake them as "selfish." But Mr. Murphy believes that the neurotic materialism of our culture is due to a lack of real personal spiritual goals and a failure to release the potential in man which such paths unlock.

Of course there has been no shortage of attempts to present *sadhanas* to the West. Western psychoanalytic procedures, and even more some newer techniques emerging out of the humanistic psychology movement, are rightly considered by Mr. Murphy to be steps toward the development of a *sadhana* deeply rooted in the nature of the Western psyche. They are, however, outside the scope of the present survey. Other groups, to be considered later, present *sadhanas* imported intact from the East with the contention that there is no real reason why westerners cannot utilize them. The Theosophical and Neo-Pagan groups represent in part attempts to recover *sadhanas* believed buried in the Western tradition, but half-forgotten. However, in practice they are more ritual or educational than initiatory "mystery schools."

The occult groups now under consideration are in a special class because they represent modern Western endeavors to articulate a precise *sadhana*, and their major concern is to initiate people into it and lead them through its convolutions. They may owe some debts to the remote past or to the East, but they are not mere reconstructions of the ways of a magus of antiquity. Rather, they all have behind them a Western and modern individual of the magus type. The magi who founded them have walked the hard streets of our modern European and American cities; they have travelled in automobiles and spoken on telephones, even if in their hearts they were shamans or wizards. They are people like Paul Francis Case of the Adytum Temple, or L. Ron Hubbard of Scientology, or G. Gurdjieff. Enigmatic, independent men in the midst of our steel and concrete, they have baffled or infuriated many, but have drawn followers with a promise of making them new men, with powers far beyond those of others.

1. Gurdjieff Groups

An excellent example of the modern, Western magus is Georges Ivanovitch Gurdjieff (1872–1949). He has probably influenced Western cults and esotericism more than any other modern figure except Madame Blavatsky. Gurdjieff was born in the Caucasus region of Russia of Russian, Greek, and Armenian ancestry. His early life is even more obscure than that of Madame Blavatsky, but like her he claimed to have travelled widely in central Asia and there to have met representatives of a Hidden Brotherhood (probably Sufi) which preserved an occult tradition. The teaching concerned opening up higher levels of consciousness than that attained by the average person; the vehicle was to be what were called "Fourth Way Schools," which were not for the fakir, or yogi, or monk, but for the person in the midst of ordinary life.

Gurdjieff's theories became widely known through his greatest disciple, P. D. Ouspensky (1878–1947), who met him in Moscow in 1915 and later came with him to western Europe. Ouspensky had the mind of a philosopher, however, and it may be questionable whether his classroom lecture tone fully represents the master. Gurdjieff was a magus, and his own approach had about it the lightness, the puzzlement, and the indirectness of his kind. At his famous "Institute for the Harmonious Development of Man" in Fontainebleau, France, his disciples found stringent manual labor alternated with lavish banquets and classes in Eastern dance (of which he was a master) interpreted by dialogue worthy of a Zen *roshi*. His writings, such as *All and Everything*, are not metaphysical exposition, but fantastic allegorical satire striving to awaken man to the futility of trying to improve his unhappy condition simply by changing his external environment without changing himself.

Gurdjieff was a small, dark man, with a cleft chin and a huge Nietzschean moustache. He was perhaps nondescript save for the marvellous piercing black eyes which impressed all who met him. His manner ranged from radiant expansiveness to mysterious remoteness, but seemed never unintentional. Of him Olga de Hartmann wrote:

> Mr. Gurdjieff was an unknown person, a mystery. Nobody knew about his teaching, nobody knew his origin or why he appeared in Moscow and St. Petersburg. But whoever came in contact with him wished to follow him...He was a magus, and he presented a new way to the world...[1]

Everyone who writes about Gurdjieff and his teaching seems compelled to give prominence to the recitation of how he came to meet the great man, how his life was transfixed and transformed by the meeting. No one particularly writes about Gurdjieff who has not had this experience; no one who had it and can write refrains.

Thomas de Hartmann, one of his most faithful disciples, tells of his first meeting with Gurdjieff during the First World War. De Hartmann was an aristocrat, an officer, and a promising composer. But Gurdjieff had required that they meet in a disreputable Petrograd cafe at which de Hartmann did not want to be seen. Gurdjieff and a companion appeared in Caucasian black coats, bushy moustaches and dirty cuffs. Then de Hartmann noticed Gurdjieff's eyes:

> By this time I realized that the eyes of Mr. Gurdjieff were of unusual depth and penetration. The word "beautiful" would hardly be appropriate, but I will say that until that moment I had never seen such eyes nor felt such a look.[2]

They said little, but after leaving, de Hartmann reports he was long silent, and that after the meeting

> my life became a sort of fairy tale. From early childhood I had read fairy tales and their meaning stayed with me always. To go forward, and never forget the real aim, to overcome obstacles, to hope for help from unknown sources if one's aspiration were a true one. . . . The wish to be with Mr. Gurdjieff now became the only reality.[3]

Another devoted disciple, P. D. Ouspensky, also first met Gurdjieff in a cafe during the World War I through a friend. He describes the impression this way:

> I remember this meeting very well. We arrived at a small cafe in a noisy though not central street. I saw a man of an oriental type, no longer young, with a black moustache and piercing eyes, who astonished me first of all because he seemed to be disguised and completely out of keeping with the place and its atmosphere. . . . [He] in a black overcoat with a velvet collar and a black bowler hat, produced the strange, unexpected, and almost alarming impression of a man poorly disguised, the sight of whom embarrasses you because you see he is not what he pretends to be and yet you have to speak and behave as though you did not see it.[4]

Yet such is the trickster quality of the magus. Soon enough de Hartmann, Ouspensky, and many others were caught up in his web. All else became for them unreal, and what was real were the discussions they had with Gurdjieff about awakening higher planes of consciousness, and the calisthenic exercises Gurdjieff taught them which expressed the teaching. When the Russian Revolution came shortly after these meeting, a small band accompanied Gurdjieff in exile, first to Tiflis, then to Constantinople for about a year, then to Berlin. Finally in 1922 the emigré group arrived in Fontainebleau.

There Gurdjieff and his group bought a manor, the Château du Prieuré, where it was at last possible to establish the Institute on a proper scale. The life at the Institute was demanding, particularly when one considers the aristocratic background of many of its members. Married persons could belong; otherwise it was virtually monastic. Residents at the Prieuré included Russians, Frenchmen, Britishers, and the New Zealand novelist Katherine Mansfield, who died there. A bell at six woke everyone, breakfast was coffee and bread, and members went straight to work. Save for a simple lunch, outside work continued until darkness. Then they would dress for the evening meal, which on occasion would be a banquet in the grand style. After supper, at eight o'clock, Gurdjieff would sometimes speak, and the "Sacred Gymnastics" would take place. In his management of the center, Gurdjieff would very often play the role of a cruel and unreasonable despot; he would order a project begun, and then abandoned, or shout harshly at people for stupidity, or demand work be done at top speed. At other times he would explain the reasons for these episodes.

In 1923 the entourage presented their "Sacred Gymnastics" with music arranged by de Hartmann in Paris, and in 1924 in America. These events sparked widespread interest in what Gurdjieff was doing. After his return from America, Gurdjieff suffered an automobile accident from which he was slow to recover. However, this gave him time to write. He began *Meetings With Remarkable Men* and *All and Everything*, his two books.

Gurdjieff felt that pupils should remain with him only for a limited period of time, and then go back into the world. Some could not break the spell of his fascination, and failed to go; upon them he made more and more intolerable demands. Finally, by the early thirties, very few were left, and in 1933 the Prieuré was sold. Gurdjieff continued to travel, and groups based on his principles were organized by former students of the Prieuré around the world. Gurdjieff died in 1949.

There are today groups studying the teachings of Gurdjieff in the major cities of Europe and America, some under the leadership of persons from his succession. They maintain as did Gurdjieff that man is not now living at his full potential, but is asleep. To evolve to greater awareness requires work. In a real sense this sleeping state is "against nature," for the organism can function as it is and does not need to evolve. Yet there is a capacity for more if one can set his will to it. Certain little-known laws can help. The universe is made of vibrations, and one can jump from one level to another. These jumps can be induced by the experiences of Gurdjieff's music, dance, and labor.

Gurdjieff groups try to continue this program of active improvement. The groups feel there should be alteration between public and private work. Some are now very quiet and even secretive. A former student of mine once invited me to attend a meeting of a Los Angeles group, of which he was a dedicated member, but apologetically had to tell me the day before the meeting that he would have to rescind the invitation since the group felt it would be unwise to have visitors. Usually, he said, an inquirer should first read a book like Gurdjieff's *All and Everything*. If he emerges from that task aflame with enthusiasm, he may be considered a serious candidate. Meetings consist mainly of living room discussions, but from time to time the group devotes weekends to the practice of labor and calesthenics in the Gurdjieff manner. Members tend to be upper class professional people; musicians are especially attracted to the movement, perhaps because of the influence of de Hartmann, and because of the great use of musical metaphors.

There is no central organization in Gurdjieff groups, but the name and tradition is potent. Teachers and groups, some independent and some in a succession going back to the Fontainebleau school, spring up continually. In one group, members were asked to practice daily yoga-type exercises, maintain awareness of themselves as a center of consciousness, and try to experience a variety of kinds of temperament by deliberately experimenting with walking and talking like an opposite personality type. At some meetings, costumes would be used. On other occasions the individual would be asked to stand nude alone in front of a mirror for fifteen minutes a day. A diary of one's high and low points, omissions, and experiences would be kept. The purpose of all these activities is to make the individual much more aware of himself, and to attain the experience of opposites and hence of wholeness on one level. From this platform one can climb to higher consciousness in the midst of life.

Undoubtedly the most serious and important group in America is The Gurdjieff Foundation of New York under Lord Pentland, which keeps in touch with the major Gurdjieff groups abroad. Founded in 1953, the New York Foundation owns a building on 63rd Street containing meeting rooms, dance studio, library, workshops, and music room. Some 500 people are involved in activities such as a class for academic studies of initiatory traditions and music, dance, and work projects which are intended, in the Gurdjieff tradition, to create a combined mental-emotional-physical experience leading to progress in coordinating one's thinking, emotional, and moving centers, thus leading to an awakening from sleep. A comparable Gurdjieff Foundation was started in San Francisco in 1955. Gurdjieff put considerable emphasis, as we have seen, on the importance of group experience for his kind of teaching, and on its applicability to life in the modern world. The Foundations try to preserve these emphases, as do the other Gurdjieff groups.

Reading Selection: Gurdjieff

Gurdjieff intended All and Everything *to be the name of a series of three books. The first is generally called* All and Everything, *with the subtitle,* An Objectively Impartial Criticism of the Life of Man, *or* Beelzebub's Tales to his Grandson. *The second book is* Meetings with Remarkable Men. *The third never appeared. Parleying to fantastic extremes of complexity, wit, and subtlety the oriental gift for veiling philosophic acumen in fancy and parable, in the first book Gurdjieff describes with whimsical satire the follies of human life in the form of an account by a visitor, Beelzebub, from another planet. The book was published only after his death, for although Gurdjieff first wrote it in the late twenties, the author preferred to keep it in manuscript form for reading aloud to his followers. His intent was to bring the hearer, or reader, gently and with laughter to the hard conclusion that nothing man does on the level of changing his environment—the horizontal level, as it were—can improve his state of inner dissatisfaction. Only changing the level of his consciousness can do this. In a note at the end of the book, "From the Author," Gurdjieff hints at his solution.*

The expression which has reached us from ancient times, "the first liberation of man," refers to just this possibility of crossing from the stream which is predestined to disappear into the nether regions into the stream which empties itself into the vast spaces of the boundless ocean.

To cross into the other stream is not so easy—merely to wish and you cross. For this, it is first of all necessary consciously to crystallize in yourself data for engendering in your common presences a constant unquenchable impulse of desire for such a crossing, and then, afterwards, a long corresponding preparation.

For this crossing it is necessary first of all to renounce all that seems to you "blessings"—but which are, in reality, automatically and slavishly acquired habits—present in this stream of life.

In other words, it is necessary to become dead to what has become for you your ordinary life.

It is just this death that is spoken of in all religions.

It is defined in the saying which has reached us from remote antiquity, "Without death no resurrection," that is to say, "If you do not die you will not be resurrected."

The death referred to is not the death of the body, since for such a death there is no need of resurrection.

For if there is a soul, and moreover, an immortal soul, it can dispense with a resurrection of the body.

Nor is the necessity of resurrection our appearance before the awful Judgment of the Lord God, as we have been taught by the Fathers of the Church.

No! Even Jesus Christ and all the other prophets sent from Above spoke of the death which might occur even during life, that is to say, of the death of that "Tyrant" from whom proceeds our slavery in this life and solely form the liberation from which depends the first chief liberation of man.

G. GURDJIEFF, *All and Everything* (New York: Harcourt Brace Jovanovitch, Inc., 1950), pp. 1232–33.

2. The Prosperos

The "orthodox" Gurdjieff groups are only the core of the founder's influence; there are other "Fourth Way Schools." An example is The Prosperos. While basically inspired by Gurdjieff's concept of a "Fourth Way School," The Prosperos has developed its own variations on his *sadhana,* and has as its founder and leader a man who is a modern magus in his own right, Thane Walker. As is typical of the magus, no one knows the tale of his life or his age, but all agree he is an unbelievably magnetic personality, not warm so much as awe-inspiring and dynamic. Those close to him say that, like Gurdjieff, he can play any role, but is always consciously in control of a situation, and by his presence can govern the interaction of people in a group from an observer's position. He never "lets down," but is always the magus, whether as teacher, "devil's advocate," or father figure to the band of young enthusiasts around him. He is always a presence and a catalyst.

Thane, as he is always called, was born in Nodaway County, Missouri, probably in the 1890s. No one knows his age, unless he does, but he enjoys telling funny stories about his hometown. He has been married twice, and has been teaching for some forty-five years. He has been all over the world. He claims to have been one of the first psychologists in America, to have been put in a Nazi concentration camp for writing an article entitled "I Saw Hitler Make Black Magic," to have been a Marine Corps officer, and to have entertained American troops in Japan during the Occupation and all over the Pacific. Hawaii was home to him for some years and has a special place in his heart.

Mr. Walker also claims to have been a pupil of Gurdjieff, and to have modeled himself as a teacher on Gurdjieff more than on anyone else. He follows Gurdjieff's idea of teacher-student relationship; he wants to disorient the student, which he does through stories and making unreasonable demands. But he feels that more scientific methods of therapy are demanded today than Gurdjieff's music and exercises. He has drawn from the New Thought literature, Freud, Jung, and other modern schools of psychology, and from the occult and astrological traditions.

The Prosperos, named after the magician in Shakespeare's *The Tempest*, was chartered in Florida in 1956. The Founders were Mr. Walker and a Phez Kahlil. The headquarters were subsequently moved about the country with extraordinary frequency.

The Prosperos emphasizes verbal instruction. In the words of a periodical,

> In ancient times, The Prosperos would have been called a "Mystery School" and the Master of the School a "Teacher King." The popular phrase in our era is a "School of the Fourth Way" and Thane is simply called, "Teacher."
>
> The awesome lineage which is the heritage of The Prosperos has always been transmitted through one key-method: the oral tradition—the "ear-whispered word."[5]

There is no precise public statement of teaching. It is something which has to be experienced in classes, activities, and living together, although some of the classes have mimeographed texts. But a fairly accurate picture of the doctrine can be deduced from lectures and material which is available. Basically, a monistic idealism is assumed.

To The Prosperos, there is only the One Mind. Reality can be experienced only by seeing from its perspective, but most people are generally forgetful of the true self and allow their vision to be clouded by the senses and the memory. This is the immemorial teaching of the mystics, but their ways of overcoming it have generally been those which Gurdjieff, Ouspensky, and The Prosperos would term the first three ways: the fakir through the will, the yogi through the intellect, and the monk through the emotions. The "Fourth Way" both transcends these and is available to the person in the world. The Prosperos calls this method for identifying the individual with the One "Translation."

In Translation classes, the student is taught that God is simply the capacity to create and govern thoughts, that is, consciousness. But the thoughts of the Absolute mind, the "Reality Self," are not the same as the way they come out in the "beliefs" of the finite "human-equation mind." Straightening out this disequilibrium is the function of "conversation in heaven," (rather surprisingly, Walker uses much Bible allegory) or applied ontology, which enables one to see his situation as God, the Reality Self, not as he sees it from his partial, finite perspective. The Translation process has five steps: (1) Statement of Being (What are the facts about reality?); (2) Uncovering the Lie or Error (What do the senses claim?); (3) Argument (I'm going to test these claims.); (4) Summing up Results; and (5) Establishing the Absolute, the only point from which Truth can be demonstrated (seeing things as God sees them).

The delusions of the memory are also attacked. Consciousness, as Prospero, is all reason, and he must through the aid of Ariel, the transcendent superconsciousness (Reality), control Caliban, the unconscious, who is all memory. Subduing memories and liberating one's true self from them is called "Releasing the Hidden Splendor."

The Prosperos experience happens through lectures, closed classes in "Translation," "Releasing the Hidden Splendor," and other topics, and in intensive sessions. In his classes, Walker creates many kinds of experiences.

Perhaps the most significant part of the Prosperos experience, however, derives from the nature of the group. Most members are now in California and number perhaps 3000. They tend to be young, successful, employed in business or entertainment, liberal, expansive in life style. They talk strongly against orthodoxy in anything. They are optimistic, oriented toward change, enjoy talking about the future, the need for new attitudes toward sexual morals, and for creating a "transcendent society." Some members live with Thane in the headquarters building or in a co-op. They say that young people of the "hip" type are "proto-mutants," the first of a new kind of man with a new way of relating to the earth, and that The Prosperos is trying to help them find a way to do it.

The Prosperos has an inner circle called the High Watch, made up of those who have completed three classes ("Translation," "Releasing the Hidden Splendor," and "Crown Mysteries"), submitted two theses, and delivered an oral dissertation. The Trustees are elected by the membership of the High Watch at the annual Prosperos Assembly. Nonetheless, it is evident that Walker, the "Dean," is the real center of cohesion for the group; he is magus and father to the many young people around him. He has trained one personal student, a lady; the future fate of The Prosperos will no doubt depend on her ability to catch the Dean's charisma.

Reading Selection: The Prosperos

The psychological world view of most of the initiatory groups of modern origin shares with Freudians the fundamental assumption that it is the unconscious mind, as storage bin of past memories and hurts and servile reactions, which is the enemy of psychic freedom. At the same time, they share with the humanistic psychologists, such as Maslow, the conviction that man, freed from the unconscious mind, can attain a state of ecstatic "being," a pure undeprived consciousness of union with the universe and mental sovereignty over it. They feel that this is man's truly natural state. Finally, and without regard for any inconsistency, they believe with the Jungians that the myth-like images which the imagination can draw out of the depths of the mind provide powerful tools for defeating the unconscious mind and allowing the self to soar free into present being-consciousness. Here, expounding their favorite myth, that of Shakespeare's The Tempest, *a writer from The Prosperos portrays the process beautifully.*

Discovering that he has the ability of magic, Prospero casts his eerie spells on all who enter the "island" to which he has been exiled. Through the exercise of his mind, he can interpret, project, rationalize, imagine and see all life as he wishes and to suit has fancy; but only within the "island" of his own comprehension. He recognizes his dual mentality; the conscious mind (Prospero, the magician) and the unconscious mind (Caliban), the unreliable, lying, diabolical monster who would destroy Prospero's magic abilities. Prospero discovers another facet of his mentality, the supra-conscious Ariel, the intuitive, altruistic, understanding agent, ready to aid Prospero when called upon.

As the play unfolds, it appears that Prospero has considerable control over Ariel, who does his bidding on the promise that Ariel will be set free of slavery when the goal is accomplished. Caliban, on the other hand, seems cooperative and bows in submission, only to turn upon his master in sly, sullen deceitfulness. Both servants respond only when *called upon* and *commanded* by their master. Man, functioning from the state of persona, realizes he is lost in his separateness. The negative qualities, misbeliefs, misinterpretations, evil appearances, lusts and sense testimony of the carnel nature are ever at war with the pure comprehension of truth and the altruistic nature. As man realizes that he can control his whole nature only by recognition of the whole, he begins to take command of the good life and sees this reward as an achievement rather than a gift. In the play, Prospero finds himself caught up in the action, and thus out of control, he stands to one side, observing. However, when in control, he sits upon a throne, high above the action.

HOWARD HORTON, "The Tempest: The Story
of You," Mentation, III, 1, p. 12.

3. Scientology

Few of the organizations we are dealing with have attracted as much recent enthusiasm or controversy as Scientology. It has been accused of many things. Its members, on the other hand, with joyful, contagious fervor claim that Scientology can give "total freedom." Those who have reached the state of "Clear" make statements like:

> There is no name to describe the way I feel. At last I am cause. I am Clear—I can do anything I want to do. I feel like a child with a new life—everything is so wonderful and beautiful.
>
> Clear is Clear!
>
> It's unlike anything I could have imagined. The colors, the clarity, the brightness of everything is beyond belief. Everything is so new, I feel new born. I am filled with the wonder of everything.[6]

An organization which can produce, by any means, such moving statements as these must have something remarkable in its life—and some remarkable personality behind it. On first impression, one may wonder just where to look for the marvel. The usual pictures of the founder, L. Ron Hubbard, which hang in every Scientology building, do not suggest at first glance what the man is—a contemporary magus and master in a class with the hypnotic-eyed Blavatsky or Gurdjieff, if not greater. The face is fairly ordinary save for tiny, sharp eyes embedded in kindly crinkles. But from out of the mind behind those intense blue eyes has grown an initiatory procedure of fantastic complexity and effectiveness, a technique which challenges orthodox psychology, and a worldwide organization. Those few Scientologists who have had the privilege of meeting "Ron" himself on his converted cattle boat describe the experience in ecstatic terms.

The churches and centers of Scientology have about them something of the atmosphere of a regimental office in the modern bureaucratic army, with its abbreviations, neologisms, routing charts, chain of command, its air of intricate and mystifying efficiency. Behind much of this is the stream of tapes, books, bulletins, and directives which come from L. Ron Hubbard, founder and spiritual leader of Scientology. The experience of Scientology seems essentially two-pronged. On the one hand, there is the sense of enthusiasm, confidence, and camaraderie which derives from being part of an aggressive, close organization, together with the feel of modernity and certainty which technical language and organizational polish communicate. On the other hand, the product is not a new brand of soap or the services of a government department, but an experience described in language which reminds one of the shaman's flight, and a philosophy in which dimensions, indeed universes, rise and fall with the shifting of consciousness.

These sides are represented respectively in the outer and inner life of Mr. Hubbard. He was born March 13, 1911 in Tilden, Nebraska. His father was an officer in the Navy. Hubbard grew up on his grandfather's Montana ranch, though he accompanied his father on tours of duty in the Far East. He graduated from high school in Washington, D.C., then studied at George Washington University, leaving in the early thirties. He participated in three ethnological expeditions to Central America, and did some pioneer flying. His main vocation, however, came to be film writing and science fiction; he had published in *Astounding Science Fiction* by 1938. He was remarkably prolific. Certain of his stories suggest in embryo that imaginative and futuristic idealism which is expressed in developed Scientology. There is the idea that living men can be trapped in a writer's fantasy, or the idea that the whole cosmos may be the fantasy of a single organism living in it. In later Scientological thought, we find that all sense of individual alienation, and all universes, stem from turbulence in theta or thought, which in its pure form, as "static," is without motion or dimension and the ground of the universes. Keen perception can dissolve these enslaving veils; only that which is not directly observed tends to persist.

The life of L. Ron Hubbard already displays several motifs of the magus archetype: an out-of-the-ordinary childhood, wide travel, and a spirit-is-all and power-of-imagination world view. He appeared to fulfill the same pattern during the war years. Hubbard was a Naval officer. He has said it is a matter of medical record that he was twice officially pronounced dead during that time—the shaman's initiation. He was once dead for eight minutes during an operation, and during this time he received a vital message to impart.[7]

After the war, Hubbard returned to fiction writing. By the end of the forties, however, he had taken up with another intense concern. In 1950 L. Ron Hubbard published his most famous book, *Dianetics*. It was an immediate sensation, rating articles in the mass media and much discussion. The ideas of this book are the basis of Scientology.

Hubbard taught that there are two parts to the mind, the analytic and the reactive. They correspond roughly but not exactly to the psychoanalytic conscious and unconscious. Experiences of shock cause "engrams" or sensory impressions of the event to be recorded in the reactive mind. These records produce mental and psychosomatic troubles until they are dislodged. Dianetics effected dislodgment of engrams by "dianetic reverie"—a patient would talk until the engrams were released through reenactment of the event. Many engrams, it seems, were produced in the womb, often by attempted abortion. When the process was completed, the patient would be what was called "Clear." (The present use of this term in Scientology connotes a higher state of spiritual development than the Dianetic "Clear.")

Hubbard established a Hubbard Dianetic Research Foundation in Elizabeth, New Jersey. Differences involving the direction of research in the organization centering around the matter of past lives and the immortal spiritual nature of man, together with legal problems, led him to move the Foundation to Los Angeles, to Witchita, and finally to Phoenix. There Scientology was founded in 1952 as the Hubbard Association of Scientologists. Scientology was different from Dianetics in at least two important respects: the concept of the thetan and the use of the E-meter. The thetan is the individual consciousness, which Hubbard said has the capacity to separate from the body and mind, and to create MEST—matter, energy, space, and time. To be Clear is to understand more fully how one is a spiritual being or a thetan, and thereby to gain control over one's mind and physical environment.

The E-meter, the indicator used in liberating the thetan, has been used frequently—though not exclusively—as a "confessional aid" since the early fifties. It is an electrical device which measures the resistence of an object to electric current. In processing, the procedures undergone in becoming Clear, the E-meter is employed to indicate areas of reaction, that is, of tension, in a person's response to verbal and other stimuli so that he can explore that area of resistance. The "preclear" holds one can attached to the dial of the machine in each hand as he is asked questions by the "auditor," with concentration, of course, on dealing with troublesome areas. The response is measured on the dial. The electric charge is very slight, but in Scientological experience this measurement is related to uncovering areas of emotional stress and marking one's elimination of them so that he can "go Clear" and find "total freedom."

In 1954, Hubbard established the Founding Church of Scientology in Washington, D.C. Since then, the symbolism of the movement has become increasingly ecclesiastical, though participation in this side of it is optional. Ministers of the Church of Scientology frequently wear clerical collars and pectoral crosses, there are informal Sunday services and a liturgical manual for occasional offices such as weddings and funerals.

In 1959 Hubbard moved to England, where he started the Hubbard College of Scientology at Saint Hill, in Sussex. Since 1964 he has lived aboard his ship on the Mediterranean, surrounded by an elite body called the Sea Org. Scientology has been through many parliamentary and legal battles in Britain, the United States, and Australia, and is not yet clear of them. But there is reason to believe that, as Scientology matures and more and more successes speak for themselves, its public image will become favorable.

As indicated by the concept of the thetan, Scientology has a highly dualistic idea of the relation of soul and body typical of the ultimately monistic alternative reality tradition. The origin of MEST (matter, energy, space, and time: the phenomenal world) lies in the thetan, that is, the consciousness. Mind, ideas, considerations are prior to MEST. As Hubbard says, "Reality is agreement." One who discovers the thetan lives this experientially. Hubbard teaches that for anything to persist it must shield a lie, for when the eye of truth (that is, the mind which has clarity toward the "static" or unmodulated reality) looks at anything in the MEST world, it undergoes "vanishment."

The next stage in Scientology after becoming Clear is to become an "Operating Thetan," or OT. The OT is independent of time and place and all the toils of MEST. "Out of the body" experiences are common among them, to judge from accounts of OTs. One says:

> To be stably exterior to my body as I am now is the fulfillment of one of my oldest and most favorite dreams. I can extend myself at will, permeating the substance of the physical universe. I can sense, touch, taste, and see things without using my body. I can really know. . . .

Another:

> There were times when my auditing room seemed to dissolve and I found myself being and perceiving in a completely different location. Once I found myself on a beach. I could see and hear the waves of the ocean and smell the salty spray. Another time I visited a castle and was intrigued to find that it was electrically lighted. I continue to have such experiences at quiet times when I am not distracted by the demands of life.
>
> I know who I am in or out of a body. . . .[8]

Such experiences certainly suggest the perpetuation of shamanistic motifs and the alternative reality tradition. So does the intensely initiatory character of Scientology. Its whole reason for being is to pass candidates through its "tech"—the grades, self-discoveries, and breakthroughs which culminate in such states of consciousness as these. The monetary cost is not slight; few individuals are likely to reach Clear without the expenditure of about a thousand dollars, and there are the OT stages beyond Clear. Money is refunded to those who are dissatisfied, however, and the whole process is supposed to be at once challenging and delightful, like a game. "If it's not fun, it's not Scientology," is a common saying. With its certified staff, its magus, and its strongly in-group feeling, Scientology is not unlike an ancient wisdom school with a totally twentieth century vocabulary and environment.

In October 1970 I attended a "Clear Night," a weekly event at the "Celebrity Center" of Scientology in Los Angeles. The Celebrity Center has the atmosphere of a small night club, complete with uniformed doorman, hinting at an entry into a world of glamor which some of those attracted to Scientology have perhaps never known. Inside there was an auditorium and, against one wall, a nonalcoholic bar. The atmosphere was very friendly, warm, and outgoing. It was evident that the world of Scientology was, for those in it, happy, secure, and virtually a family. There was no admission charge, but attractive girls behind desks by the door made sure they got the names and addressses of non-Scientologists who came to Clear Night. They would be made members of the "I Want to Go Clear Club" and would receive weekly mailings thereafter.

The program began with banjo and guitar music of professional quality. Then a high-ranking member of the Sea Org—an older, balding man with a winning smile—announced amid wild cheers that Ron had just released a new grade: Class VII OT, the highest so far, in which the thetan becomes even more free of the body, mind, and MEST. He indicated it is precise, "closely audited," yet he could only describe its effects with ecstatic "wows," "gollies," and pauses. He also said seventy-five new auditors would be hired at good pay. Then an official just back from Ron's ship told about a new "power processing" route which will give auditors especially the effectiveness they need to help their preclears.

The dual role of Ron, the Founder, as chief teacher and charismatic initiator through the "tech" was vividly apparent. The veneration of Scientologists for this man, who so adeptly combines efficiency, paternalism, and a hieratic remoteness, is evident; and he has begun speaking of himself in virtually messianic terms, talking of his wearing "the boots of responsibility for this universe."

Clear Night proceeded with the remarkable testimonies of those who had just made Clear or one of the OT grades. One young lady who had become Clear mentioned the popular song, "Someone Else is Singing

my Song," and said, "Now I know what my song is." A man who had achieved OT III commented that he no longer had stage fright. Most impressively, a legal secretary who had achieved OT VII, the highest mark to date, said that as one goes through the grades it's like a big thetan hand was reaching down to help. She said that now she is in a MEST body, but is really independent of it; she is really in a thetan universe, looking in and controlling the MEST one. She read from a Buddhist scripture and from an article about the coming Buddha Maitreya. This suggested to me an interesting eschatological interpretation of the thetan experience. She said the thetan is like Maitreya—in the world, but no longer reactive to it. This would mean that like a bodhisattva, the thetan is free of karma but remains in the world out of compassion, and is able to operate solely on that level. Typified by this attractive statement, recent Scientological literature has used far more sympatheticaly than before the art and scriptures of Buddhism and other Eastern religions, with which it obviously has much in common metaphysically despite totally different (and, Scientologists would say, much more effective) terminology and techniques.

Like most successful new and initiatory religions, Scientology is a meritocracy in which appointment to office comes down from higher levels in the organization. Attention is always paid to maintaining integrity of teaching and example among officers and members. The interests of the Church of Scientology are rapidly broadening, however. Recently it has developed an impressive work in the rehabilitation of prisoners and institutionalized drug users. Scientology continues Ron Hubbard's old feud with professional psychiatry in a new activist and respectable form. A Scientology minister, the Rev. Kenneth J. Whitman, was in 1970 president of the Citizens Commission of Human Rights, Inc., a group organized to defend the legal rights of mental patients which has won the support of some leading psychiatrists and lawyers.

Scientology has also recently given considerable attention to the spiritual needs of artists, musicians, and theatrical people. The Celebrity Center in Los Angeles, and similar centers in other cities, houses not only Clear Nights, but amateur and professional drama and music performances. There are studios available for painting and sculpture, and continual art shows. At any time of day, the attractive building is full of young people happy and busy with creativity. The freedom in creativity of the artist is said to be a part of the total freedom Scientology releases, and the power of its artists the first fruits of what it will bring the world.

Most of the people in Scientology are young adults. Since, for many people, it involves a heavy commitment both of time and money, it may immediately become the most important thing in life; social life

and intellectual life revolve around it. But unlike traditional psychotherapy, Scientology also provides a vital, sustaining, creative "family"
during the time of this commitment and after. When one considers that,
in investing in Scientology, one is acquiring almost a total life—friends,
entertainment, and avocation—the very high cost, whether one agrees
philosophically with Scientology or not, is seen in a new perspective.
Of course, many persons who take auditing do so only as a part-time
matter and without this degree of life reorientation. On the other hand,
some, after Clear, enter professional work for Scientology, partly to pay
for their own further auditing, partly no doubt because the organization
has become very central to them, and because producing results and
conviction in others is reinforcing to their own experience.

Scientology can quickly amount to an entire and real cosmos, as it
should according to its own metaphysics. For an increasing number
of persons, this is the way it is. Yet, as the OT VII who spoke of Maitreya
shows, it is possible to be an advanced Scientologist and not be un-
sophisticated or a one-track "true believer," For many the experience is
powerful and liberating, the commitment light and easy.

Reading Selection: Scientology

*The literature of Scientology, most of it from L. Ron Hubbard's hand,
is vast. The following passage, however, sums up some of its basic
assumptions, and appropriately culminates in a breathtaking suggestion
of the Scientological goal. The idealistic and monistic philosophy is
evident; the flat and technical diction is typical of the original sources,
in contrast to the ecstatic testimonies of Clears.*

Scientology as a science is composed of many axioms (self-evident
truths, as in geometry). There are some fifty-eight of these axioms in
addition to the two hundred more axioms of Dianetics which preceded
the Scientology axioms.

The first axiom of Scientology is:

Axiom 1. Life is basically a static. (Definition: A life static has no
mass, no motion, no wave-length, no location in space or in time. It has
the ability to postulate and to perceive.)

Definition: In Scientology, the word "postulate" means to cause a thinkingness or consideration. It is a specially applied word and is defined
as causative thinkingness.

*Axiom 2. The static is capable of considerations, postulates and
opinions.*

Axiom 3. Space, energy, objects, form and time are the result of considerations made and/or agreed upon or not by the static, and are perceived solely because the static considers that it can perceive them.

Axiom 4. Space is a viewpoint of dimension. (Space is caused by looking out from a point. The only actuality of space is the agreed upon consideration that one perceives through something, and this we call space.)

Axiom 5. Energy consists of postulated particles in space. (One considers that energy exists and that he can perceive energy. One also considers that energy behaves according to certain agreed upon laws. These assumptions or considerations are the totality of energy.)

Axiom 6. Objects consist of grouped particles and solids.

Axiom 7. Time is basically a postulate that space and particles will persist. (The rate of their persistence is what we measure with clocks and the motion of heavenly bodies.)

Axiom 8. The apparency of time is the change of position of particles in space.

Axiom 9. Change is the primary manifestation of time.

Axiom 10. The highest purpose in the universe is the creation of an effect....

It is as though one had entered into an honorable bargain with fellow beings to hold these things in common. Once this is done, or once such a "contract" or agreement exists, one has the fundamentals of a universe. Specialized considerations based on the above make one or another kind of universe.

[Hubbard then says that there are three classes of universes: the agreed upon or physical universe, one's own universe, and the other person's universe, in which an individual may become entrapped, as for example, a son in his father's.]

We must, however, assume, because it is so evident, that an individual only gets into traps and circumstances he intends to get into. Certain it is that, having gotten into such a position, he may be unwilling to remain in it, but a trap is always preceded by one's own choice of entrance. We must assume a very wide freedom of choice on the part of a thetan, since it is almost impossible to conceive how a thetan could get himself trapped even though he consented to it. By actual demonstration a thetan goes through walls, barriers, vanishes space, appears anywhere at will and does other remarkable things. It must be, then, that an individual can be trapped only when he considers that he is trapped. In view of the fact that the totality of existence is based upon his own considerations, we find that the limitations he has must have been invited by himself, otherwise they could not be eradicated by the individual under processing, since the only one who is present with the pre-clear is the Auditor, and past associates of the preclear, while not present, do desensitize, under auditing, in the preclear's mind. Therefore it must have been the preclear who kept them there. The preclear by processing can resolve all of his difficulties without going and finding other persons or consulting other universes. Thus the totality of entrapment, aberration, even injury, torture, insanity and other distasteful items are basically considerations a thetan is making and holding right now in present time. This must be the case since time itself is a postulate or considera-tion on his own part.

L. RON HUBBARD, *Scientology:*
The Fundamentals of Thought. Copyright ©
1956 by L. Ron Hubbard. (Edinburgh:
The Publications Organization Worldwide,
1968), pp. 75–80.

4. Abilitism

A movement like Scientology, which has made such a powerful impact on a certain segment of the population for two decades, and which has required such strong commitment, is bound to produce schisms, imita-tions, and reactions. There have been several such movements. Typical of them is Abilitism, whose founder, Charles Berner (1929–   ), spent some ten years in Scientology. Then, probably under the influence of the new ideas being percolated by the humanistic psychologists and sensitivity trainers, he broke with Hubbard to create a group oriented toward a more flexible, open, and love-centered kind of release. He felt that Scientology was too directed toward power, whereas the real human goal in enlightenment is perfecting the ability to love and communicate totally with all other persons. His techniques were borrowed from Scientology in some specifics, but are redirected toward this end.

The history of Abilitism is short; it was founded in 1965. But since then H. Charles Berner, his wife Ava, and associates have established a major center at Lucerne Valley, California, with a "seminary," and centers in several cities.

The basic assumptions of Berner's Abilitism are (1) that each person is a conscious spiritual entity without prior source, that is, each person is God in the sense of being uncaused, and has an absolute being in and of himself; (2) that there are other people; and so (3) each person is individually and separately God. The problem then is communication. Each person, as God, is perfect already, but there are difficulties in his *relating* with the perfection of the God in others. These are attributable to *thoughts* which we put out as barriers owing to fixed attitudes into which we have locked ourselves, such as "I am my body." Like Scientology, Abilitism holds matter, energy, space, and time to be the product of considerations, or thoughts about matter. They may be due to the subconscious (the Scientological "reactive mind") which is the storage bin of uncompleted communications. The goal is to live free of these impediments by living just in the consciousness without the thoughts which impede the direct *understanding* people can have together. This state is *enlightenment*. In its pure state, it is an absolute, direct, clear, permanent, simple experience—as absolute as the Buddha's enlightenment, but different in that it involves other people. Abilitism offers several exercises to help achieve this state.

The basic one is the relating exercise. It combines silent meditation with articulation of the meditation. Two persons sit facing each other. One asks the other a question which has been given to him on a piece of paper by the director. The question might be something like, "Tell me how you want to be loved." "Tell me who you are." "Tell me what a thought is." For the next five minutes, the person who is asked the question meditates on it and expresses verbally what he thinks and feels, while the first person listens intently but remains completely silent, unless he repeats the question. The roles are repeated alternately for forty-five minutes. The effect is a peculiar and profound sense of openness simultaneously to one's own spiritual depths and the equally rich reality of another person's depths.

Abilitism also offers Intensives, lasting three or more days, intended to produce a direct breakthrough to enlightenment. Goals include complete mastery over MEST so that they are not barriers to communication. The relating exercise is employed eighteen hours a day, with breaks for lectures, work, recreation, and meals. The questions employed, such as "Tell me what life is," are especially designed for the goal. Other Intensives deal with other problems such as marriage, attitudes toward the body, and so forth.

Abilitism is a new faith, but it shows every sign of becoming another very modern entity in the age-old alternative reality tradition. Its founding, its mentalist world view, its goal, all suggest the tradition, although its techniques and emphasis on communication with others are a new and welcome addition. As with Scientology and The Prosperos, its membership tends to be young adults. The organization is enthusiastic and rather aggressive about reaching people; contacts will be telephoned several times. Plans are afoot to extend to all major cities of the United States in the very near future.

Reading Selection: Abilitism

This passage from a basic set of lectures on the teachings of Abilitism by Charles Berner suggests not only certain important ideas, but also something of his manner. The fresh, colloquial, but lucid style derives from Mr. Berner's essentially oral orientation. One can picture him, probably dressed in a sweater, seated in the midst of a room full of listeners, mostly young. He is master of the situation; words like these are what come out:

We have you and the other person; all right, now there are two things that go wrong in interpersonal relationships. We discussed earlier how you are an all-knowing entity. In other words, you are God. That is your true nature, and the other person is an all-knowing entity, he is God. All right, so if you are all-knowing and he is all-knowing, what can go wrong? Well, there is a difference between knowing and understanding. Knowing is something that you do by yourself. You just know. But understanding involves another. You understand someone else. The point is that knowing and understanding are two different phenomena. Knowingness, which is what you have, you just know; you can know a lot of things. You can know what you are, you can know all about Life. But when it comes to receiving a communication of a thought from another person to you or from you, in getting your thought over to him so that *he* knows what you've been thinking, that is understanding each other. Understanding the other person is a separate phenomenon from knowingness. Knowingness is just you. Understanding involves another. Now once you get these two ideas separated, the thing resolves very quickly.

You know everything. He knows everything, but you and he don't understand everything because the only thing there is to understand is the other person and what he is up to and unless he has communicated it to you, you don't have it. You could make the mistake of confusing the two. This is what originally went wrong.

H. CHARLES BERNER, *The Ultimate Formula of Life* (Lucerne Valley, California: Causation Press, 1968), p. 47.

5. Builders of the Adytum

The Builders of the Adytum is a small but interesting group which is representative of those who, without going the way of Witchcraft or Neo-Paganism, seek to focus their spiritual life upon the Hermetic and Kabbalistic tradition. Rather than starting anew, with new terminology, like the Gurdjieff and Scientological groups, the BOTA, as it is commonly called, has remained conservative in language and symbol. Its temple is brilliant with beautiful luminous paintings of the Tarot cards around the walls, and the altar is rich with the black and white pillars of Solomon and the Kabbalistic Tree. But this group is in the tradition of the modern return of the magus.

Its real founder was Paul Foster Case (1884–1954). When young, Case had been a magician especially interested in playing cards. At sixteen, he was asked by someone where playing cards came from. Not knowing, he began research. His investigations led him to the Tarot, and thence to the Kabbalah and Hermeticism. About 1910, he was initiated into the Order of the Golden Dawn in New York. This was the famous esoteric and magical society which, based in London, at one time numbered among its members such writers as W. B. Yeats, Algernon Blackwood, Arthur Machen, A. E. Waite, and the notorious Aleister Crowley, who was expelled. Six months after his initiation, the U.S. head of the Order died. Case succeeded him. But his youth and the fact that he had published (before his initiation) two articles on the Tarot allegedly revealing secrets of the Order led to dissension, and Case resigned. In 1920 he founded the Builders of the Adytum (a Greek word meaning inner temple or sanctuary) in New York. He believed that he had been led in this, as he was in his studies, by a "Master of Wisdom," like the Theosophical masters, who spoke to him in a gentle, reasonable voice, instructing or guiding him to particular pages of books. In 1933 he moved the BOTA to Los Angeles. The other branches, except for one in New Zealand, are defunct, but the Los Angeles temple, called the Temple of Tarot and Holy Qabalah, and the correspondence course work seem to be flourishing as never before.

This growth is due to the effectiveness of Case's successor, Ann Davies, a dynamic and charismatic person who is virtually a magus in her own right. Ann Davies met Case in 1943. Before that, she says, she had been through atheism, agnosticism, Buddhist mysticism, and yoga. But upon meeting Case there was an "immediate recognition" that this was her spiritual master. She worked closely with him until his death in 1954, and then succeeded him.

There is the feeling that Ann Davies actually has much more charisma, if less scholarship, than Paul Foster Case. Although slightly lame, she is a colorful and prepossessing woman. With long black hair, flashingly engaging eyes, and sweeping spectacular gowns, she is indeed the mistress of her temple, and in the midst of its rituals suggests some priestess of antiquity. The literature describes her mystical experiences, and much publicity is given to the remarkable healing of a tumor in her dog, Tzaddi, after prayer.

Instruction in the temple uses as its points of reference the Kabbalistic Tree—the sephiroth emerging from the Ein Soph or Eternal Mystery—and the Tarot as symbolic representations of the cosmos interpreted by the Kabbalah. Ann Davies's sermons, however, are anything but pedantic —there are anecdotes, digressions, and warm affirmative sequences more reminiscent of New Thought than occultism. The world view is basically Hermetic or Neoplatonist: Cosmic Consciousness is the root of all; the world of concepts and form emanates from it; through knowledge and initiation one can make the Great Return; the Kabbalah and Tarot are a tight, highly integrated, analytic symbol system spelling this out and offering a road for the Return.

What is perhaps most distinctive about the Builders of the Adytum is the use of ritual. Although the basic structure of the service is more Protestant than Catholic or Jewish, it does involve a degree of communal work—chanting, singing, raising hands, even swinging lamps. Much is made of the importance of ritual. Ann Davies says that the world itself is the ritual of God, down to the atoms and electrons. All of life is ritual; without it one would have no evolution because there would be no reorganization. Consciousness in everything is the creator, but it works through ritual. Reincarnation is affirmed.

The service begins with a dramatic entry by Ann Davies, and a high-minded affirmation with responses by the choir. Then, after announcements, is the sermon. There are prayers, scripture, music, and silent meditation, all rather Gnostic in tone but phrased in such a way as not to be offensive to the average liberal Christian. The service ends with healing affirmations for the sick in mind or body typical of the New Thought churches in style, though somewhat enriched by Ann Davies's occult imagination.

The Builders of the Adytum basically draw from the same class as the older generation of New Thought and "metaphysical" bodies. The majority seems to be middle-aged or above, there are more women than men, and all are quite conventional in dress. Despite the importance of the Kabbalah, few if any are of Jewish background. Recently a few young people in "mod" attire have started attending occasionally, probably on the basis of the very important role of the Tarot cards and occultism in their spiritual culture. Ann Davies seems proud of their interest, commenting that once a group of "hippies" had visited the temple and, when the lights were off and the giant Tarot cards around the walls were glowing with their radiant colors, related that it was better than a drug "trip." But admittedly the style of the temple, with its symbols of continuity with liberal Protestantism in the worship and its emphasis on verbal communication in the classes and correspondence courses, is not at one with the preferred style of the spiritual quest of the younger generation. It will be interesting to observe whether their intense interest in the subject matter will be able to overcome the "generation gap" in style.

Reading Selection: Builders of the Adytum

The following passage by Ann Davies appeared in an issue of the Adytum News-Notes, *a periodical of the Builders of Adytum. It was written, we are told, in response to many requests. Here Ann Davies in her direct, vivacious, and far-reaching manner, tells about an initiatory experience of her own, and also reveals something of the difference between the Western and Eastern mystical traditions.*

At age 27, having spent several years in concentrated occult study and research, coupled with strenuous self-analysis, I realized that I was now well prepared to undertake *formal* meditation. I had already developed considerable facility in watching my thoughts, emotions and actions from the vantage point of the observer, though I had no teacher (so I thought!). I had carefully mapped my course that I might be protected from falling into the traps of, or being snared by, self-delusion or illusion.

I was going to settle for nothing but REALITY... *whatever that Reality might be!* IS THERE A GOD? I had to know the answer to this question as desperately as a drowning man gasps for air.

I had a light lunch on the date I set for my first formal meditation. I then cleansed the apartment thoroughly, holding in mind that this was a symbolic cleansing of my environment. At dinnertime instead of eating, I took a bath, concentrating on washing away (symbolically) all patterns of false knowledge. I spent the next two hours analyzing the Quest that had brought me thus far. Realizing that this, my first formal meditation, was just a beginning, I reminded myself that I would probably have to meditate daily for years...or a lifetime...in order to receive an answer to my question...if there *was* an answer!

I donned a loose robe, turned off all the light except for the night light in the hallway, and sat down in a comfortable chair. I started to breathe deeply, rhythmically, slowly. I instructed myself to let go of all tensions as the deep, rhythmic breathing continued. I then placed my full and concentrated attention about a foot above my head as I literally hurled my question upward to that point.

...*IS THERE A GOD?*

IS THERE A GOD? The quivering, all-consuming question! Every fibre of my being...every inbreath...every outbreath...everything meaningful...my entire past... my entire future...all this energy, and more was gathered together by my mind and heart into the question of questions! Unwaveringly I held my question as the one and only point of concentrated attention. Nothing was permitted to impinge or disrupt. No other thought was permitted to intrude. NOTHING ELSE MATTERED!

The vibration continued up, and when it reached my meditative point I became Beginningless-Endless Consciousness. Never a time I was not. I was pure Consciousness with nothing to be conscious of...except I AM. Neither birth nor death...neither Person nor persons. Never a time I could not BE, because WAS and WILL BE were eternally I AM. I was Cosmic Consciousness. I was Samadhi. I was Foreverness. Ecstatic but serene.

Did I receive an answer to my meditative question? The answer is, of course, "Yes!" I achieved Samadhi at my first formal meditation. That which Eastern Swamis and Gurus yearn for through a life time of disciplines. That which Eastern Occultism considers the GOAL! But I knew better! I knew that this was just a beginning. I knew that Cosmic Consciousness could even be a trap. An invitation to rest in the Ultimate, thereby giving up further evolution in the delusion that the Ultimate had been attained. I therefore *BEGAN* my researches into Consciousness at the point where others have mistakenly thought they had achieved the final liberation.

I was out to discover *WHY* evolution existed with all its pain, separateness, etc. I was out to discover how individualism occurred and what was its destiny. I was out to prove or disprove Reincarnation, Personal survival, etc.

Now that I knew *GOD IS*, I had Eternity in which to research the rest of the Mysteries.

ANN DAVIES, "My Mystical Universe, Part XII,"
Adytum News-Notes, (1967), pp. 1–3.

6. The Church of Light

The Church of Light is a body whose main focus is astrology. This ancient art has always been a substantial part of the occult tradition, although it has generally been an adjunct intellectual sport or tool of the wise whose major concern is expansion of consciousness. Yet it is not unrelated, for its symbols can also be taken as symbols of the Return. Its study can be a means of attaining tranquillity and balance of consciousness, as well as a means of utilizing the powers of the psyche or cosmos in the quest. In the case of the Church of Light, the astrological part of the alternative reality tradition has been made the key to the whole although it teaches other related aspects of it, such as Tarot, and affirms its basic impersonal monism and soul-body dualism.

The founder was Elbert Benjamine (1882–1951), who wrote under the name C. C. Zain. In the last years of the nineteenth century he devoted himself to occult studies, developing his psychic abilities, and in the year 1900, he said he contacted an arcane order called The Brotherhood of Light. This order, it is said, separated itself from the Egyptian priesthood in 2440 B.C. From then on it survived as the custodian of the Religion of the Stars. The Greek philosophers Thales, Pythagoras, Plato, and others were initiated into it, and it has preserved learning even in the darkest times. In some periods its membership has for the most part been on the "Inner Plane," but it has also had its representatives, if not its highest leadership, in the physical world. Benjamine studied for nine years under its tutelage, and then in 1909 took a mysterious journey during which he was inducted as a member of a council of three which manages its affairs in this world. He was also given instructions to prepare a course of study, a complete system of occult learning, so that the Religion of the Stars could be made more available in the coming Aquarian Age. In 1915 Benjamine came to Los Angeles where he began teaching and working on the instruction, which was finally completed in 1934. The instruction is comprised of 210 lessons, published in twenty-two substantial books.

The replication of the magus archetype in this life story is evident, and is borne out by the descriptions of his character in the group's literature. He was a man of warm, emotional kindness, yet "few people ever saw him as he really was"; he had to protect himself against those who wished to attract his attention for selfish reasons; his method of teaching could be enigmatic, for he would not solve people's problems for them; and he had sometimes to work on a cosmic scale.

In 1932, the Church of Light was founded. At times it suffered adversity, although recently, owing to the general upsurge of interest in astrology, it has prospered mightily. In addition to the Church in

Los Angeles, it has contact persons and in some cases study groups in many cities around the world.

The Church of Light's official statements of principles tend not to mention astrology, but to talk of the evolution of the soul, from man to angel or spirit. In a manner reminiscent of A. J. Davis, reincarnation is denied, but it is held that the soul passes through higher and higher levels in the transmundane cosmos. The compatibility of the teachings with science, and the fact they are not to be received just upon authority, is stressed. Spokesmen seem particularly avid to repudiate orthodoxy. Yet it is clear that members are most interested in the Church's astrological teachings. Its bookstore sells largely astrological books, its symbolism is primarily astrological, and at least half of Benjamine's twenty-two lesson books treat astrology. It seems that it is the keystone of his occult system, as the Aquarian Age concept is of its timing.

This is explained as being because the law of correspondences, which is central to Neoplatonism and the alternate reality tradition, provides the main dynamic for the soul's evolution and the laws which govern it. Everything in human life has its correspondence to a Zodiacal sign or planet. The stars provide a language by which life can be read. The Tarot, which occupy second place in the Church of Light's symbolism, is another way of saying the same things. Understanding astrology can enable one to employ "mental alchemy," to turn negative influences in one's life to good by mentally strengthening the power of its opposite. If there is too much Mars, Venus is the answer. Astrology provides a sense of the total cosmic and psychic environment in which man can learn to gain this sort of power and to grow. The stars are man's fundamental Bible, or Word of God, for instruction and encouragement.

The Church of Light has fifty degrees of initiation, culminating in the Soul Degree in which one must demonstrate there has been specific realization of higher states of consciousness. The work of the fiftieth degree is imparted secretly to a member when he is ready.

The major exoteric work of the Church of Light is the classes, mostly general instruction in astrology open to the public. Religious services are held only once a month, at three on a Sunday afternoon. They are quite simple. There is an opening and closing ritual of saying the "Church of Light Mantram" with arms upraised, a statement of principles, two or three talks, and a healing meditation. Members are also supposed to do the Mantram daily at noon.

The membership is mostly middle-aged, and consists predominantly of women of middle class background. As many as half are widows, divorced, or single. All, even the young people, seem very conventional in dress and manner. The Church makes it known that they encourage only serious students, those interested in spiritual development, not just fortune-telling or fads.

Reading Selection: The Church of Light

The following few paragraphs are from the lesson series written by C. C. Zain, and reflect his sober tone and continuing efforts to build bridges between the ancient science of astrology and the modern world.

The Stellarian religion is called The Religion of the Stars because astrology affords the best possible road-map for guidance to the most effective and highest type of life. It not only gives the most reliable instructions as to what he should do to live his religion, but it also instructs him how best he can do the things which his religion indicates he should do.

If astrology and other inner-plane conditions are so important in religion, and if knowledge of them when applied will increase the individual's success, happiness, spirituality and freedom from illness 100%, why do so many academic intellects refuse to consider or investigate them?

With time, distance and gravitation on the inner plane having properties so radically different than they have on earth, should we expect inner-plane weather to operate according to the same laws weather operates on earth? Einstein's Special Theory of Relativity carried to its logical conclusion indicates that inner-plane weather affects the individual, not merely according to his inner constitution, but through certain time-space relationships. These time-space relationships that indicate the inner-plane weather affecting the individual are measured by progressed aspects.

Just how the inner-plane weather affects an individual, however, is not dependent upon any theory. For even as time, distance and gravitation properties on the inner plane have been determined experimentally by university scientists, so have the properties of inner-plane weather, and how it works to affect individuals, groups, cities, nations and world affairs been determined experimentally through statistical studies carried out in the process of astrological research.

C. C. ZAIN (Elbert Benjamine), *Astrology is Religion's Road Map* (Los Angeles: The Church of Light, 1949), pp. 229–31.

Notes

1 Thomas de Hartmann, *Our Life with Mr. Gurdjieff* (New York: Cooper Square Publishers, Inc., 1964), p. xiii.

2 de Hartmann, *Our Life with Mr. Gurdjieff*, p. 5.

3 de Hartmann, *Our Life with Mr. Gurdjieff*, p. 6.

4 P. D. Ouspensky, *In Search of the Miraculous* (New York: Harcourt Brace Jovanovitch, Inc., 1949), p. 7.

5 *The Prosperos Newsletter* 10, 10 (March 1970), p. 5.

6 Advanced Organization of the Church of Scientology of California, *Advanced Success Stories*, 1970. Single sheet publication.

7 Biographical data is largely based on "L. Ron Hubbard," *Scientology: The Field Staff Magazine*, I, No. 1 (© 1968), p. 7.

8 Advanced Organization, *Advanced Success Stories*.

SIX

the edenic bower:
neo-paganism

In Pasadena, California, on the second floor of an old Victorian house, there is an Egyptian temple. Around the walls of the room are bright life-size paintings of some of the oldest known gods of mankind, gods thought long dead but now alive again—Isis, Osiris, hawk-headed Horus, wise ibis-headed Thoth, Hathor, Sekhmet. Around the center of the room is a magic circle, and in the middle of it an altar on which rests an ankh and other implements of ritual magic. A black mirror is set against one wall. In it the ancient gods of the Nile are called up visibly. They are not dead, this group, the Church of the Eternal Source, believes, though it is long since they have been worshipped. What they represent is still real in our minds (in the same sense as the Jungian archetypes), and in the Mind beyond our minds. They can be called back. As one Neo-Pagan put it, "The ancient gods are not dead, but they think we are."

The diverse people in tiny groups who make up Neo-Paganism in America have in common that they believe something in man died with the death of the ancient gods. They are not, many of them, virulently anti-Christian; some even consider themselves Christians as well as affirmers of something else. But besides our conventional American world, they have another homeland too. One of the devotees of ancient Egypt said, "The Egypt of the pharoahs and the gods is like a state, a country, to which we belong." They may be patrons of ancient Egyptian or Greek religion, or Druidism, or Wicca (Witchcraft), ceremonial magic, or even Satanism. They are partisans of some Western religious tradition other than Judaism or Christianity.

The "other country" is a land of a different feeling for the relation of man to nature, to his passions, to his imagination. If they are polytheistic, it is in terms of Paul Tillich's statement that polytheism is not a matter of quantity but of quality. It is a way of affirming as religiously valid the subtle, shimmering changes of color, mood, and force in nature and the psyche. One is not subordinate to another, but they are different, and nature and man (the two are deeply continuous) are cooperations of different forces within a pluralistic universe.

At the Egyptian temple, I was told that the real meaning of ancient Egyptian religion is that the gods represent many paths to the goal of the central religious experience which defies words and images. The gods represent the different desires and goals of life (one prays to a god of wisdom for wisdom, to a god of love for love). All of them can be brought, not into an absolute unity, but into a balanced pattern, like Jung's mandalas, which represent totality. The members of this group strongly rejected any suggestion that their view of the cosmos was one of pluralistic chaos; they instead brought out quaternary diagrams of the relationships of the Egyptian gods showing their interaction with the four seasons, directions, and so forth. They also indicated that they always represented the balancing of male and female. These two principles are coequal in Egypt. If the masculine may seem to have a slight edge (the primacy of the sun and of pharaoh), that is because the feminine, Isis, is by nature more reticent and concealed, but is no less powerful. I did not feel that the Egyptian temple group was an exception to the theorem that the new religions are monistic; the mandalic symbols of totality suggested the monistic mind at work.

The unifying theme among the diverse traditions represented in this chapter is the ecology of man's relation to nature and to the various parts of himself. As Neo-Pagans understand it, the Judaeo-Christian tradition teaches that the human intellectual will is to have domination over the world, and over the unruly lesser parts of the human psyche, just as it, in turn, is to be subordinate to the One God and his will. The Neo-Pagans hold that, on the contrary, man must find a niche in the world, neither high nor low, where he cooperates with nature and its deep forces on a basis of reverence and exchange. Of the parts of man, the imagination should be first among equals, for man's true glory is not in what he commands, but in what he sees. What wonders he sees of nature and of himself he leaves untouched, save to glorify and celebrate them.

What Neo-Pagans seek is a new cosmic religion oriented to the tides not of history but of nature—the four directions, the seasons, the path of the sun—and of the timeless configurations of the psyche. They seek not that morality which comes of imposing the will on the reluctant flesh,

nor the mystical trance which is the fruit of asceticism, but the expansiveness of spirit which comes of allowing nature and rite to lower the
gates confining the civilized imagination. For them, this is the spirit
called up by the names "pagan" and "polytheism." These words do not
suggest for them, as they still do for others, images of unbridled orgies
and grotesque idols reeking with the blood of sacrifice. Rather they
suggest a romantic, living, and changing world continuous with human
fancy and feeling instead of one dead and subdued; a religion of atmosphere instead of faith; a cosmos, in a word, constructed by the imagination (considered the surest guide to what is in the heart of things)
instead of by the analytic intellect or bare faith, which seeks only the
outer husks.

When respected and indeed deliberately heightened, imagination is
a faculty not only of fantasy but also of tremendous power. It can make
the emotions feel the gods within things, and the eyes see them, and
divine forces go out into the world to sow love, or prophesy, or fear.
Evocation, calling up the gods from within the self, is true magic.
Magical evocation is propelled by unleashing the forces touched by
one's childhood wonder at sunsets, fairy tales, and dreams, forces too
much pent up in the modern adult. These are the powers called
"anagogic" by Jung, a great favorite of almost all the cults in the modern
alternative reality tradition.

These Neo-Pagan groups have in common a particular emphasis on
the second of the three forms of religious expression, the "practical"—
rite, gesture, ceremonial act. It is through corporate "work" that the
magical cosmos is evoked; it is "made" by ritual actions that demarcate
and celebrate it, and by acts done as if it were present.

The essence of each group discussed in this book, like each of the
great world religions, is best approached through one of the three
Wachian forms of expression, even though all three are found in every
group. In Theosophy it is verbal expression which gives the easiest
avenue for initial understanding. In the case of some of the Oriental
groups, it is the sociological function they have in the youth culture.
With most of the Neo-Pagan groups, it certainly is the second, cultus and
ritual. The teaching is often pale in comparison with the fascination with
the rites, both for members and observers. Despite the necessity of a
group for the performance of the rites, the composition and persistence
of particular groups is highly unstable—even by cult standards.

By looking at the rites, it is possible to grasp what is being done. A
secondary world is created in a special time and place, one far different
from the outside world—though it may be, as with all sacred times and
places, intended to manifest the hidden archetypes and realities behind
the outer shadows. A magic circle is drawn, the sacred is separated from

the profane. Within the circle the implements of ceremonial magic—wand, sword, cup, and pentacle—reign with power. Or an old Druidic festival is celebrated with flowers and dance. By these gestures a world is perceived in which anagogy and wonder write their own history. When this is seen, one may ask about the other forms of expression:—*what* people are doing this, and *how* they explain themselves.

These groups pride themselves on being in the Western tradition. Much is made of differences between Eastern and Western psychology. It is said that yogic and meditation techniques of the East are not suitable for the average westerner. Rather, the methods involving imagination and magical operations are a truly Western method of achieving the same ultimate goal, and are the methods most people in the West should be using.

The Neo-Pagan groups have a close relationship with the occult and initiatory groups. Whether they call themselves witches, or magicians, or something else, the Kabbalah, Tarot cards, astrology, and the Gurdjieffian idea of opening up a new level of consciousness comprise the intellectual framework. The main difference is that the Neo-Pagan groups may use formal rite, often quite elaborate, in place of more purely psychological or intellectual exercise, and recently have become more and more concerned with man's relationship with nature, and with the exfoliation of mythologies. But they also treasure the Western alternative reality tradition. They typically hold that the Kabbalah, magic, and the rest of it originated in ancient Egypt (though the Kabbalah was later superficially Hebraicized) in the "ancient mystery schools." Egypt and its progeny thus make up an eternally valid realm of the spirit, not less capable of reality and power today than ever.

The roots of modern Neo-Paganism lie in romanticism. The romantic's exaltation of feeling and imagination as ways to move out of the prison-house of William Blake's "number, weight, and measure" has obvious affinity with the magician's more systematic use of the same forces. A key figure in the application of romantic feeling to magic was the French exseminarian Alphonse Louis Constant (1810–75), who wrote under the name Eliphas Levi. While remaining a Roman Catholic, Constant claimed also to be an occult initiate. He wrote books, elegant in style and daring in speculation but often suspect as to scholarship, on the history and theory of the Kabbalah and magic. He pressed home the concept of the supremacy of imagination, the eye of the soul by which the magician gains power over the primal matter—inert until awakened by its life-bearing touch—and hence is able to do what he will. Another well-known French occultist, and the founder of an order, was Gerard Encausse (1865–1916), who wrote under the name Papus.

In Britain, certain Masons realized that this world was rightly theirs as well, though the average lodge was scarcely concerned with real magic. In 1888 a group of Master Masons organized the Order of the Golden Dawn, by far the most famous of the many esoteric groups which sprang up in the late nineteenth century. A number of well-known names are connected with it, or the Stella Matutina (a reformed and more Christian version), including writers like W. B. Yeats, Algernon Blackwood, Arthur Machen, and Charles Williams. The Golden Dawn's principle leader was S. L. MacGregor Mathers (1854–1917), brother-in-law of the philosopher Henri Bergson. Mathers claimed occult contact with three Secret Chiefs in Paris who belonged to a mysterious inner order guiding the Work. The Golden Dawn offered a series of degrees of initiation. Each had its own rituals. To attain each degree, the candidate had to prove he had acquired competence in magical works, such as invocation, evocation, crystal-reading, making symbolic talismans, and astrology. An "Egyptian mass" invoking Isis was performed in Mathers's home, which was appointed like an Egyptian temple. Mathers translated and edited the works of Abramelin the Mage (1362–1460?), which offer a clarity and practicality rare among the grimoires.[1] The Order's institutional life was never smooth, and came to an end after the First World War. But it shaped the thinking of a number of persons who have since been very influential in occult and magical circles.

The most important Figure influenced by its activities was Aleister Crowley (1875–1947), notorious magician and writer of a number of books on magic, or "magick" as he insisted on spelling it. His personality has fascinated biographers and imitators.[2] Flamboyant, a gifted poet, given to exaggeration, heroin addict, and widely travelled, he played the role of magus with rather too much self-dramatization. Yet he made the idea of "magick" an exciting game and motif for a style of life in which his motto, "Do what you will shall be the whole of the Law," was the theme (meaning, of course, "Let magic give you the power to do what you will"). Recently his books have been enjoying a revival. Expelled from the Golden Dawn, Crowley founded his own order, A. A. (*Argentinum Astrum*). In 1912 he became head in Britain of a German group called O.T.O. (*Ordo Templarum Orientalis*) founded in 1895 by Karl Kellner. This group, which still survives in German and Crowleyite wings, practiced sex magic and used some Eastern as well as Western terms.

The Neo-Pagan movement breaks down into two broad categories: the magical groups, deeply influenced by the model of the Order of the Golden Dawn, the O.T.O., and Crowley; and the nature-orientated groups. The former are the more antiquarian; they love to discuss editions of old grimoires, and the complicated histories of groups and lineages. They delight in precise and fussy ritualism, though the object is the evocation of an intense emotional power which can, it is said, produce levitation and the apparition of gods and demons.

The nature-oriented groups are more purely romantic; they prefer woodsy settings to incense and altars; they dance and plant trees. They are deeply influenced by Robert Graves, especially his *White Goddess*. And they are less concerned with evocation than celebration of the goddesses they know are already there. The mood is spontaneous rather than precise, though the rite may be as beautiful and complex as a country dance.

Somewhere in between these groups lies Witchcraft. Allegedly it is the ancient pre-Christian religion of Britain, for its partisans follow the theory of Margaret Murray. Gerald Gardner, the proprietor of a Witchcraft museum on the Isle of Man and author of apologetics for "Wicca" as a religion is a favorite.[3] Today there is much talk about Witchcraft, but I have not found as much as one would suppose of sociological substance behind the cloud of rumor fanned by sensational journalism—at least in America. Many people use herb-magic and oil-magic and the like which have many origins, including Creole voodoo. People write books and newspaper columns and run shops as "witches." Especially in the youth subculture, some experiment with rites said to be Witchcraft.

There are many "occult" shops which encourage experimentation by providing the necessary wares. Commonly, Witchcraft practice will begin with candle-magic. Burning candles of special color, shape, and aroma, together with simple chants, to achieve magically desired ends, can be done alone. A girl might, after a quarrel with her boyfriend, in her despair decide to burn a candle to try to get him back. If (as is perhaps likely to happen in any case) he does call her a day or two later to make up, the girl may be convinced of the power of Witchcraft, and buy more candles, herbs, books of charms, and other paraphernalia. Then, as she enters deeper and deeper into this world, she may make contact with other persons of the same interests and be invited to work with them in a "coven," and gain the greater power which a group brings to each person in it. Many tales are told of the power of such groups to bless and curse.

Besides this kind of campus and commercial Witchcraft, some forty or fifty small groups in America endeavor to practice "Wicca" as a serious religion. Wicca is an intense but diverse faith, in some ways more a mood than a doctrine, even though highly social and ritual for many. It is hard to generalize about it. Basically, though, religious practitioners hold a vision of a world dominated by the great Mother Goddess, and her consort the Horned God. They are personified respectively by the high priestess and high priest of the coven. Rituals to purify members, call down the power of these deities, and work spells for good are usually held at least every full moon, and are deeply attuned to moon, seasons, and nature.

American Wicca is divided into several different traditions, which have mainly to do with the style of the ritual. "Gardnerian" covens, in the lineage of those founded by Gerald Gardner, generally employ highly energetic chanting and dancing in the nude. "Traditional" covens used clothed and slower paced rites supposed to be derived directly from the "Old Religion" through an underground transmission; homey implements, bones, herbs, and stones take the place of the elegant equipment of the mage as aids to the transformation of consciousness and the evocation of the Old Ones, the gods of Wicca. On the other hand, "Alexandrian" Witchcraft augments the Wicca heritage with the familiar Kabbalist-occultist line of astrology, ceremonial magic, and cognate lore.

In all of this, it is significant that some religionists, and some independent writers and psychics, now want to call themselves witches is worthy of comment. The word has a tortured heritage among us. To select it as an identity is to those a particular stance over against the great Witchcraft persecutions, Christianity fairy tales, and modern alienation.

Satanism is also a special case. Satanists too are fewer in number than publicity would suggest. But there are those in America who consider themselves worshippers of Satan, and they are easier to find than true "old religion" witches. Satanism's apparatus is like that of ceremonial magic—though with its own symbols and rites—and its beliefs have contact with nature orientation. Satan is held by some Satanists to be not the "enemy" but the life-force, the libido, so to speak, and so cannot be other than a good to be affirmed. But there is a special psychological convolution in the mind of the Satanist which sets him apart, or rather by which he sets himself apart. His "good" must be precisely that which commonly represents what is most evil. In a peculiar manner he binds himself to the world of the majority culture as Neo-Pagans do not. Strictly, his use of a Judaeo-Christian name for his "deity" perhaps excludes him from the category Neo-Pagan.

In practice, however, Satanists inhabit the same spiritual underground as the others; people in all the groups in this chapter tend to know each other, and some move from one orientation to another, and borrow techniques from one another—though I hasten to add that those who are not Satanists regard Satanism as rather silly, and are careful never to identify themselves with it or its usages. Satanism must be distinguished from modern Witchcraft and ceremonial magic.

The Neo-Pagans experiment with different ways of creating through action, through performed gestures of rite and festival, or imagination, a secondary world which in time becomes, as it is meant to, the participant's primary world. They seek to restore a proper balance between masculine and feminine symbolization of the sacred. They seek to recover a sense of wonder and respect as religious feelings towards nature in all its moods and toward the human body and psyche. Thus they want to find a new totality, perhaps in reaction to a schizophrenic culture. They look for it in a new cosmic religion that vehemently rejects the religious value of history, while it radically affirms the religious value of raising the level of consciousness through stimulation of the imagination by ritually creating a suggestive and sacred milieu.

1. Feraferia

A sprinkling of groups around the country are attempting to revive specific religious long believed dead, or to create new religions in the ancient spirit. The British Druids who perform rites from time to time at Stonehenge are fairly well known. In 1963 the Reformed Druids of North America was founded at Carleton College in Minnesota. At first it was mainly a joke. Undergraduates could avoid the compulsory chapel attendance requirement if they expressed a religious preference other than Protestant Christianity and practiced it. But the movement spread to several other campuses, and it is said that even after the chapel attendance regulation was repealed the following year, the Druidic rites continued, for some had found the ancient ceremonies in oak groves, celebrating the passing seasons—Beltane, Samhain, and so forth—to be more meaningful than they had at first supposed.

An even more serious movement of the Neo-Pagan type is Feraferia, now centered in Pasadena, California.[4] Although Feraferia has only twenty-two initiates and about 100 members, it merits careful study for several reasons. It represents the expressions of the role of leader, history, teaching, rite, and sociology characteristic of Neo-Paganism. Significantly, Feraferia emphasizes rite, and uses a highly mythic language in its verbal expression. Typically, the social group is highly unstable, save for a tiny core. But the ritual expression is the glory of the group; it has shown a remarkable ability to create a sacred cosmos in and out of which individuals may move.

The founder of Feraferia is Frederick M. Adams. Mr. Adams incorporated Feraferia on August 2, 1967, but this action was only the culmination of a long string of preparatory events. Mr. Adams, now in his forties, was raised in the Altadena area north of Los Angeles. As a youth he spent great amounts of time exploring the mountains in the region and getting to know nature intimately. In his college years, he studied Greek and Celtic folklore, and read the works of Jung, Carl

Kerenyi, Mircea Eliade, Robert Graves, J. J. Bachofen, and Henry Bailey Stevens.[5] All of these writers, and others of the same type, influenced him profoundly.

Mr. Adams states that in the spring of 1956, while walking across the campus of Los Angeles City College (where he had been studying fine arts and anthropology), a sudden illuminative experience struck him. He was seized by a sense of the "mysterium tremendum" in feminine form. He suddenly realized that "the feminine is a priori." The experience was not quite visual, yet it was a real confrontation with a presence outside himself. He was dazed, and walked about confusedly for some minutes, muttering "This is it. . . . She is it." The reading and meditating he had been doing in an inchoate, unresolved way all fell into place. From then on Mr. Adams devoted himself wholly—apart from the necessities of life—to the service of the feminine sacred.

He first tried this vocation between 1957 and 1959 by living in a multifamily commune in the Sierra Madre with a group interested in the same ideals. Seasonal festivals were held in an outdoor temple to the "Maiden Goddess of Wildness." In the name is foreshadowed two major themes of Feraferia, the pedomorphic or child-form representation of the goddess, and the equation of wilderness with sacred ground. As Feraferia does today in festivals, the group practiced nudism. A publication called *Hesperian Life* was issued, celebrating the concept of a return to a paradisical horticultural society. Stevens, a major guide to this group, believed the garden of the Hesperides was a mythical representation of that ideal. The communal group made some use of psychedelic drugs (then legal), recording all their experiences in a journal. After 1959 Mr. Adams withdrew from the community to write and travel. He visited the principal sites of Paganism in Europe and made contact with Neo-Pagan groups in Britain.

The name Feraferia ("nature celebration") came to the founder in 1967 as an intuition. By similar inspiration he received the group's symbol, the "stang," a trident with sun and crescent moon superimposed. The banner was unfurled for the first time on the vernal equinox of 1967 at a great "love-in" in the Los Angeles Elysian Park. The concept of Feraferia was now virtually complete.

Feraferia holds that religious life should be a part of sensitive interaction with nature and one's own erotic awareness. Any mysticism, or dualism, or false monism which divorces the real from the natural, or the particular, or the erotic is wrong, for man with earth, sky, and sea are one huge biome, or living organism. One is whole only insofar as he recognizes this unity and lives to celebrate it. The symbol of the whole earth biome is Kore, the divine maiden of the Greeks.

The feminine is for Mr. Adams and Feraferia a more fundamental archetype for the whole than the masculine, though paradoxically they are also equal. The nature of the masculine is to penetrate, separate, and analyze; that of the feminine is to include, to underlie, to unite. Therefore without impairing the essence of either, the feminine—the Kore—is the mythical, living, personal name for the unity of all things. Much is said of the harm man has done to himself and to nature by the exaltation of the masculine archetype, good in itself, to a supreme place.

Kore is all aspects of the feminine, for they are all one in supplying the ground of union. Kore is alike mother and daughter, Demeter and Persephone. She is reborn every year and goes every year through all stages of femininity. The Feraferia calendar, based on Robert Graves's "Tree Calendar," is a celebration of her progress—her birth with the divine lord Kouros in early spring, her emergence from childhood, her nuptials, her retiring beneath the earth in winter.

However, the supreme archetypal form of Kore, Frederick Adams maintains, is not the "Great Mother" but the pubescent maiden, for the heart of nature is not merely nourishing and life-bearing, but also erotic, flirtatious, arousing passion.

> To inform the dawning Eco-Psychic Age of Aquarius, wherein celebration will determine subsistence, a long repressed image of divinity is reemerging: the Merry Maiden, Madimi, Rima, Alice in Wonderland, Princess Ozma, Julia, Lolita, Candy, Zazie of the Metro, Brigette, Barbarella, and Wendy—a grotesque and incongruous assembly at first sight—are all early harbingers of the Heavenly Nymphet. She alone may negotiate free interaction between the other three anthropomorphic divinities of the Holy Family. These are the Great Mother, Who dominated the Old and New Stone Ages; the Great Father, Who initiated the Early Patriarchal Era; and the Son, Who crystalized the megalopolitan mentality of the Late Patriarchal Era. It is the Dainty Daughter of the Silver Crescent Who will transmute the saturate works of Father and Son to wholeness in the Maternal Ground of Existence, without sacrificing the valid achievements of masculine articulation. And She accomplishes this without a crippling imposition of parental or heroic authority images. How delightful to behold Her tease and tickle Father and Son into respectably natural, Life-affirming pagan Gods again.
>
> The character of the KORE SOTEIRA, or Holy Maiden Savioress, is hard to delineate precisely because it portends the para-rational and permits incommensurables to interfuse without violence at last. The Antic Covenant of the Magic Maiden is radically permissive.[6]

A visitor to Frederick Adams's home is made immediately aware that this is no ordinary suburban house. The front porch is full of signs and symbols from out of the past—wreaths, crossed sticks, painted stones. In the backyard trees have been planted and given names. There is a henge—a circle of forked sticks oriented to the pole star and the rising sun. The group has a larger henge in the mountains to the north. Within the house are shrines to sun and moon, and a shrine room whose floor is a large wheel on which the passing days and seasons and motions of the planets are marked with stones. Here, the important news is not what comes in the paper, but what nature is doing.

Permissive polytheism is quite consistent with the cultus of the Magic Maiden. Its whole mood favors an openness to the coequal spirituality of each particular of time and place. The now voluminous writings of Frederick Adams in his monthly periodical, *Korythalia,* frequently evoke this feeling. He disparages one-pointedness, whether of heroism or of asceticism or intellectualism. Celebrate rather the unique beauty of each season, weather, tree, mountain, and mood—under the aegis of the imagination this sensitivity is best expressed by polytheism.

A glance at a Feraferia rite makes this evident. Consider the spring seasonal festival, Beltane.[7] At the beginning, nude male and female participants form separate files and face the gates of henge. The leader, holding a torch, faces west and chants:

> Moon Door, Moon Door, Door of Alder, bound with Willow, open now, revealing night, and fiery stars, and silver moon, and demiurgic dark.

Then, facing east:

> Sun Door, Sun Door, Oaken Door, bedecked with holly, open now, revealing day, and azure airs, and golden sun, and archetypal light.

The participants then one by one enter the circle of unhewn tree-trunks, with the care one shows toward a sacred place. They make a slow circle clockwise within it, and gather at the east end. The upright there is made an altar. Incense is lit on it. All raise arms in invocation, and the leader calls:

> Antheides and the Great Fays of the East, Dawn, and Spring, join us now in the Faerie Ring between Worlds. Through the portal between Moon and Sun, return into your Earth Abodes from the far Faerieland of Stars.

Other prayers and invocations are offered, such as:

> Oh Holy Maiden of the kindling quick of merging mist and mazing echo: The Innocent Bounty of the trees bares your Faerie Flesh and

Wildness, Wonder, Magic, Mirth, and Love.... Your beauty seals our
bridal with all Life. The dance of your green pulse unfolds all bodies
from earth's fragrant form. Evoe Kore!"

Within the ring the group structure dissolves somewhat. Members
sing, dance, or meditate individually. About half an hour later they
re-form to leave. They circle clockwise again, embrace mildly, and leave.
The gates of the Other World are once more solemnly closed.

Another popular rite is a tree planting ceremony, which can be performed any time.

The rites of initiation into Feraferia are designed to give the novice
an experience of identification with nature and with Kore. The rite takes
place at the henge. First, the gods and goddesses of the twenty-two
biomes of earth and the astronomical bodies are called to the vicinity of
the circle. They are then invoked to its center, where they combine to
form mystically the body—as it were, the physiological system—of the
Magic Maiden. The initiate then seeks to associate the parts of his own
body—his airs, fibers, blood, etc.—with the corresponding part of the
ecosystem of nature through the mesocosmic image of Kore's body. He
uses sounds and words which capture the energy of each part. There is
then ecstatic dancing; one may, if moved to, take a pledge to Kore.

The purpose of Feraferia clearly is to recover an ecstatic vision of
wholeness and unity which uttterly respects the reality of the particular.
It brings together not only man and nature, but man and each seasonal
and geographical particular of nature, and also man and each style of
his own consciousness—masculine and feminine, analytic and dream,
vision and fantasy. Feraferia art, often quite beautiful, is generally
surrealistic, reflecting the sacred worlds of dream and fantasy.

The membership of Feraferia is mostly middle-aged. Typically, Feraferians are people who have been involved in movements like pacifism,
ecology, and utopianism. In Feraferia they seem to find adequate religious
expression of what has long been their real spiritual concerns. Contrary
to what one might expect, Feraferia is not just a product of the "hippie"
culture—its roots go back before it, and it has outlasted its peak. But
parallels and mutual influence with the larger spiritual quest of the
sixties exist.

The vision of Feraferia is predominantly Frederick Adams's and most
of the writing, devising of rituals, and art has been his. The group
has little structure except as a circle around a charismatic leader. It
probably as yet has no potential to survive him as a sociological entity.
The problem inherent in the leadership role of such a visionary is well
portrayed—the group could scarcely exist without him, yet there are
those who feel his domination stifles the Neo-Pagan creativity of others,

and that his vision is so personal and intricate that it does not communicate itself easily. Some have been through Feraferia and have left to explore other forms of Neo-Paganism. Yet one could argue that strong personal leadership is necessary in something as potentially multiform and individualistic as Neo-Paganism. The role of the symbol-maker is always thankless and ambivalent. Only time can tell whether he is in anticipatory touch with emerging changes in the collective psyche.

Feraferia sees itself as a precursor of a future culture in which the feminine archetype in Magic Maiden form will recover religious centrality, and in which mankind will recover a sense of ecological reverence. The new culture will be in part something new—Feraferians prefer to talk less of return to the past than of "transformation."

Some aspects of ancient paganism they do not wish to emulate. The new Magic Maiden personification of the feminine sacred will not desire the cruel sacrifices or somber dedication of the older loving/devouring Mother. The concept of the primal horticultural paradise is recognized to be something of a valuable myth. There is talk among some Feraferians of the establishment of a paradisal community which would probably be horticultural, vegetarian, and in all ways—work, play, celebration—live close to nature and its shifting moods, preserving trees, wildness, and all things intact. Feraferians believe that now society must move in something like this direction, or perish. They see themselves as the advance guard of a future culture very different from the present. Their real task is to aid this evolution through providing symbols and stimulation.

Reading Selection: Feraferia

To appreciate fully the spirit of Feraferia, one must have some experience of participation in its life. Next best is reading the monthly magazine, Korythalia. *This magazine is not simply a chronicle of meetings and events—it is an immersion in another world. There are ecstatic comments on books, mountains, music, and pagan theology, mostly written by Frederick Adams. For every month there is a lunar calendar, providing for each day a wide series of correspondences, ranging from stages of dress or undress of Ishtar to types of terrain which fit the mood of the day. Here is a passage on polytheism, one more systematic than much of Adams' writing:*

There are five modalities of polytheistic manifestation:

A. The great Pantheistic-Panerotic Goddess, the Lady Breath of Wildness, the Queen Tree of Stars and All Worlds. One of Her condensed vowel names is AWIYA. Ultimately She allows every unique being to share Her ontological priority.

B. Her two children, the Divine Lovers, who establish the passionate polarity of creation. They are KORE and KOUROS, acknowledging the precedence of KORE. As Maiden Savioress, she enshrines the essence of childlike delicacy, lyrical sacredness, romantic and spritely spirituality. She guarantees transcendence for every unique Presence. Finally, she is the true Muse of the dawning Faerie Age of Aquarius.

C. The seven Gods and Goddesses of the major World Biomes, or Archetypal Landscapes, who link with Sun, Moon, and the five visible Planets through the days of the Sacred Week.

D. Indwelling tutelary Spirits of specific Nature regions, features, forms, and forces. With the help of pagan Celebrants, these may quicken Holy Earth into fully conscious LAND-SKY-LOVE-BODIES.

E. Freely roving Faerie Bands of Ancestral Spirits promoting the growth potencies of the Biosphere while awaiting reincarnation.

The natural fountainhead of human endeavor is not reasonable utility but extravagant mythopoeia. The myths and dreams of Paradise, common to all peoples, predict future actualities for this Planet. Trans-cultural images of the glowing orchard of innocent love constellate from the Collective Unconscious an evolutionary FIAT of Cosmos. Feraferia will found Sanctuaries in accordance with the universal specifications of Paradise...These Sanctuaries are intended to replace trash heap cities as normative environs for human community. From these centers, men, women, and children will find their true pagan vocation in seasonal celebration and service to the surrounding Wilderness region, and thus help generate Faerieland.

> FREDERICK C. ADAMS, "Oracles of the
> Faerie Faith," *Korythalia* I, 6 (1970) p. 2.

———————————◆———————————

2. Church of All Worlds

In 1961 a noted science fiction writer, Robert A. Heinlein, published a novel, *Stranger in a Strange Land.* It is about an earthman, Valentine Michael Smith, who, due to a mishap of interplanetary exploration, was born on Mars and raised by Martians. The principal purpose of a Martian's life is to "grok," to intuit the "fullness" of something completely from within.

When Smith was brought to Earth, he seemed at first out of place. He did not understand elementary things, yet the deep things of character and Earth's wisdom he could accurately intuit in a moment. He moves about Earth at once guileless and wise. There gathers around him a small circle of sympathetic young people. They much preferred Martian to Earth attitudes. Their outlook is best hinted at in the Martian greeting, "Thou art God." However, Smith did "grok" that one earthly experience is more beautiful in principle than anything on Mars—coequal love between the sexes. But he wondered why it seemed to create such problems and inhibitions for earthlings.

Eventually Smith created a religion, the "Church of All Worlds," for his companions. It took the form of paradisical communities called "Nests," in which the best of both planets was brought together. In the Nests they could learn Martian, and be initiated into the lore and psychic skill of that planet. They also joyfully practiced sexual love within the family of the Nest.

This book was one of the bibles of the youth of the sixties, for in a real sense they felt they were Martians on Earth. Childlike and mystical, lovers of beauty and harmony and magic, impatient of materialistic values and moral codes, they too seemed not to fit, almost to have dropped from another world. Many, like Smith's friends, were seeking with eager desperation an alternative life style, other modes of relationship between man and nature, and different ways of understanding the relationship of consciousness and cosmos.

In 1961 Tim Zell and Lance Christie, both students at Westminster College in Missouri, met and began discussing matters like these. Out of these discussions the Church of All Worlds was born. While by no means primarily concerned with Heinlein's novel, they found much in its critique of our society of interest, and elected to make some use of its colorful terminology. Tim Zell is now Primate of the Church of All Worlds, and publishes a magazine called *Green Egg*, which is issued eight times a year. He lives in St. Louis, where he works as a social psychologist. Lance Christie, in the same field, lives in Los Angeles. Under the stimuli of personal contacts and the publication, branches or Nests of the Church of All Worlds have appeared in these and several other cities.

Membership, now at around 700, is predominantly young adults of college background, the median age being about thirty. There is a membership application form, upon which the applicant states, among other things of a similar nature, that "I seek to learn ways which may help me toward Self-Actualization," and that

I hereby dedicate myself to a way of life which is non-destructive, peaceful, creative, joyous, alive, non-violent, loving, life-affirming, free, responsible, ecstatic, aware, nonhypocritical, gentle, courageous, honest, tolerant, humanistic, nonauthoritarian, benevolent, moral, growth-oriented, and ecologically sane.

As in the novelistic Church of All Worlds, there are nine circles of advancement for members named after the nine planets. The requirements include study, writing, sensitivity and encounter group experience, and active participation in the life of the church. A published bibliography gives some idea of the range of interests: The Vision; Community and Education; Ethics; Pagan Religion; Ecology; Human Ecology; Theology of Monism and Emergent Evolution; Psychology of Developing Potential; Sexuality; Comparative Religions.

The Nests of the Church of All Worlds meet in an informal yet purposive manner. Often there are long and lively discussions. From time to time, feeling that multimedia, multisensory participatory experience can be of more importance than cognitive ideas and verbalism in attaining the sort of awareness they are seeking, they try other things. It may be a sensitivity or encounter experiment; it may be the enactment of a Pagan ritual which bears a sense of human involvement in the drama of nature and the cosmic cycles. The Nests thus far do not attempt full communal life.

The Church of All Worlds understands itself as part of the Neo-Pagan movement. Its members, both intellectually and sensually oriented, take this first of all to mean that man must discover himself as part, not sovereign, of a world biological unity, within which men must find an ecological slot, cooperating rather than competing with his own kind, as do all successful species. In view of current sober predictions of catastrophic disaster for mankind and the earth within a century if exploitation of resources continues at the present rate, and in view of the obvious fact that this juggernaut to apocalyptic doom—a world without fuel, hungry, and yet doubtless warring over what scraps remain—will not be halted without a swift and radical alteration of goals, attitudes, and life style, the importance of these discussions is obvious.

The language of ancient Paganism, like that of *Stranger in a Strange Land*, is taken metaphorically, but the issues are real. Recent discussion in the Nests has, partly under the influence of Teilhard de Chardin, moved in the direction of considering the whole biosphere of Earth as a single living organism. As the Mother of all within itself, it may be regarded as feminine—the Goddess—and the evolution of consciousness is reaching a point at which it can become aware of itself as such. Then the true nature of the cancer-like self-destruction of the tissues of the organism by certain malignant "cells" within it can be grasped by its unitary mind.

It is to this kind of thinking that this unusual but lively meeting of old Pagan world view, the provocative images of some modern novels and bio-philosophic reflection, and a group of vigorous, socially experimental young adults, has come. The fundamental point of religious focus for them is the greeting phrase, "Thou art God." This phrase is the basis of the ethics implicit in the Church of All Worlds experience. It suggests, they feel, an entire ethical system not found in any other religion, summarized in the concept of "total responsibility through total existential freedom." There is no external authority to whom one can appeal and upon whom one can shift blame. We are each God, so each have God's responsibility. Whether the world ravages itself to death, or the lovely goddess comes to consciousness on this planet, is up to us. This is the mirror the Church of All Worlds wishes to hold up to the present generation.

Reading Selection: Church of All Worlds

As described in Heinlein's Stranger in a Strange Land, *the Nests of the Church of All Worlds are as much communes as religious bodies in the conventional sense. Most members take off their clothes upon entering. There are occasional lectures, initiations, and entertainment—sometimes with miraculous happenings—but for the most part people merely make love, talk, and study Martian, which must be learned before one can make real progress. A huge brass bowl is by the door; those with money put it in, those who need money take out what they need. The usual greeting is "Thou art God." The actual Church of All Worlds, of course, does not strictly emulate that described in* Stranger, *but it does share the central conviction that the Nests of the Chuch are not so much places for religious "services" as models for a new style of life based on radical pantheism. Here Jill, one of the principals in the novel, talks about the Church:*

"Let's say it's not a religion. It *is* a church, in every legal and moral sense. But we're not trying to bring people to God; that's a contradiction, you can't say it in Martian. We're not trying to get people to have faith, what we offer is not faith but truth—truth they can check. Truth for here-and-now, truth as matter of fact as an ironing board and as useful as bread...so practical that it can make war and hunger and violence and hate as unnecessary as...well, as clothes in the Nest. But they have to learn Martian. That's the hitch—finding enough people honest enough to believe what they see, willing to work hard—it *is* hard—to learn the language it must be taught in. This truth can't be stated in English any more than Beethoven's Fifth can be." She smiled. "But Mike never hurries. He screens thousands...finds a few...and some trickle into the Nest and he trains them further. Someday Mike will have us so thoroughly trained that we can start other nests, then it can snowball. But there's no hurry. None of us is really trained."

ROBERT A. HEINLEIN, *Stranger in a Strange Land*
(New York: Berkley Publishing Corp., 1969),
p. 330.
Reprinted by permission of
G. P. Putnam's Sons from *Stranger in a Strange
Land* by ROBERT A. HEINLEIN. Copyright ©
1961 by Robert A. Heinlein.

---

3. Ceremonial Magic

In the spring of 1970 I was privileged to attend a meeting of a number of the leading ceremonial magicians, Satanists, and witches in the Los Angeles area. The meeting was held in an apartment in Hollywood, dark save for red and black lamps. Against one wall was a slowly spinning hypnotic disc. In the gloom about twenty people sat talking in low, vibrant voices; conversing on magic amid such an atmosphere was part of the self-image which shaped the life of each.

Yet it was also a question of image which had brought them together. It was shortly after the Tate murder case, the movie *Rosemary's Baby,* and certain sensational magazine articles about the occult. These people were concerned for the public relations image of their craft. However, it was not easy to arrive at any common plan of action, though the discussion was fascinating to an outsider. Witches, magicians, and Satanists did not wish to be identified with one another. More important, there were two kinds of attitudes toward public relations (both often apparent in the same person). First was a feeling of wanting the public to understand that they were kind, harmless folk who had their own religion, an ancient one with much to be said for it, and that the popular notion that they were people who perform vile rites and work evil was base calumny worthy of the witch hunt days. Secondly there was a feeling of rejoicing in being known as a great wizard, or even Satanist, and loving the glamor of dark mystery and strange arcane rites which clusters around them. The legend which goes before the mighty sorcerer is, in fact, a part of his technique for attaining the real purpose of magic, some argued, the opening up of new levels of consciousness. It is like Gurdjieff's enigmas, or Crowley's exaggeration; it shakes loose the ordinary footings of the mind.

This led to a second discussion on what really happens in invocation. The central act of ceremonial magic is the calling up of a god, generally one of the pagan gods of Egypt, Babylon, or Greece, or one of the "demons" of vaguely Alexandrian or Hebrew derivation mentioned in the old grimoires. Those present who were involved with ceremonial magic debated what actually occurs. Some said that they truly see a figure, however vague and shadowy, appear in the magic triangle at the heart of the rite. Others argued, with some sophistication, that the real invocation is an evocation. It is a calling up of the veiled wisdom and splendor of the unconscious; the intense emotion and suggestive setting of the rite enable gods to surface. As one put it, "I don't know whether the god is objectively outside myself or is a part of myself, but it doesn't matter because in any case he teaches me things I didn't know before."

The meaning of this remark was made clearer to me several months later. In the fall of 1970, campuses in the Los Angeles area were blanketed with a flyer which read:

THE O ∴ T ∴ A ∴ PRESENTS AN OPEN CLASS IN THE ART OF...MAGICK

... THE 'GREAT WORK' OF THE HERMETIC PHILOSOPHERS, THE SECRETS OF SOLOMON, AGRIPPA, CROWLEY—THE AUTHENTIC TECHNIQUES AND ANCIENT RITUALS THAT OPENED THE FORBIDDEN DOOR TO IMMORTALITY!

MAGICK is not to be confused with witchcraft (wicca) and has nothing whatsoever to do with satanism. However, real MAGICK is not for the timid soul or the prude. The student of MAGICK is concerned with *eternal* truths and values.

Operations in certain spheres require courage and total personal commitment. You do not have to be a recondite occult scholar to learn THE ART. In fact, the less misinformation you have assimilated the better... The Magickal student's greatest asset is his or her *imagination*...

At the bottom of the sheet phone numbers were given. I telephoned, visited a couple of the introductory sessions, and enjoyed several long conversations with the leader of the OTA. He turned out to be one of the magicians I had met at the previous meeting, although the OTA in its present form is a new body. The founder is a free-lance writer who has been in the practice of magic for some twenty years, and has a marvellous collection of the requisite books and equipment.

The meetings were held in private homes, but the atmosphere was unmistakable. An ornate cloth was laid over a square altar on one side, and on it lay the traditional four implements—sword, wand, cup, and pentacle. A collection of the principal books was evident behind the altar: Regardie's edition of the rituals of the Golden Dawn, Mathers's translation of Abramelin the Mage, the Goetia, the Legemeton, Barrett's *Magus*, and the like. The senior brothers of the Order were clad in long, hooded, monkish robes.

It was explained to inquirers it would not be possible for those not initiated actually to see or participate in a real magical operation. But they could learn the history and meaning of the work.

A student presented a talk on history. It was given out, rightly or wrongly, that this tradition originated in ancient Egypt in the priestly "mystery schools," was encapsulated in the Kabbalah, and is in fact the source of much of Eastern yoga, Buddhism, and so forth. It has been perpetuated in the Western esoteric tradition running down through the Golden Dawn and (in part) Crowley to the present Order.

Of greater interest was the informal discussion of the actual practice of magical operations by a group like this. As stated, they center around the evocation of a "demon"—really a pagan god, like Apollo or Astarte. As in Neoplatonic theurgy, they are invoked in a "receiver," an individual of the same sex as the deity. The group does not claim the powers of "high magic" visibly and externally to manifest the deity. The "receiver" has about the same function as a Spiritualist medium, although this term is not used. There can be either a "contact" or a "possession" evocation, depending on whether the presence of the Other is merely felt, as a force of tremendous emotional weight, or totally occupies the subject.

The presence is called up through manipulation of the implements with strong, massive gestures, and above all uttering the Words of Command for that deity in the old grimoires. The air is one of robes, fervor, incense, and the altar surrounded by the magic circle. Admittedly, on occasions the evocation fails, and may be repeated over and over. When it comes, though, the feeling is unmistakable. The "receiver" shakes and becomes transformed with the visage of the god. Then, the deity must be dismissed, or serious psychic effects will follow.

The rite is, the OTA founder stated, in a sense an evocation of madness as the world understands it. Yet it also gives wisdom and an assurance of immortality, a feeling of anagogic wonder, a knowledge of the power of will to create a world. One also hears of the conjuration of the power of visible levitation and lesser magic.

Even though ceremonial magicians will use one of the grimoires as a guide, the details of the rite may vary from one magician to another, for the purpose is to produce an effect which is basically psychological, and different practitioners may find different procedures best suited to the individual personality. Yet there are three basic steps.

First, the magician purifies himself by fasting, continence, and breaking the ordinary pattern of his life, as preparation for producing the altered state of consciousness to be evoked in the ritual. He takes elaborate steps to prepare the implements. He may perform quiet routine rites to the four directions or to consecrate the tools.

Second, he robes himself and stands in the circle, behind the altar, and holds the wand and sword. Smoke from incense and burning herbs swirls around him. He begins an incantation to call up the spirit he has determined to summon. If there is a receiver, he or she stands beside him; other members of the circle present are at hand. He speaks in a tone of command, uttering the words in a rhythmic, hypnotic voice, over and over, at a more and more rapid pace, until he is in a virtual frenzy. Thus his inner energies are raised to a fever pitch. As one magician put it, he is deliberately inducing a "temporary insanity." In this atmosphere, surrounded by the fumes of the burning herbs and the intense engagement of psychic fervor, the spirit is believed to appear—the "receiver" shakes and "becomes" the god, or the shape of a form is seen in the dark smoke over the triangle. To increase the frenzy, there may be other inducements such as vigorous controlling and threatening gestures of sword and wand, sacrifice, sexual excitement.

Third, after the invocation or evocation, it is necessary to dismiss the spirit. This is believed just as important as summoning it, for a spirit who remains after the rite can cause no small amount of harm.[8]

Behind an operation like this there is the shaking ecstasy of the ancient shaman. Most of the members of the group I visited were young and, one felt, impressionable. They were of college background, part of that rootless and searching intelligentsia which is assuming more and more the features of a distinct class in modern America, and which populates so many new cults. At best, they are expressing that fundamental belief in the supremacy of thought and imagination which seems to flow self-evidently through their culture. Yet there is also a new birth of symbolism and the power of total atmosphere.

In the world of Oriental import religions, the trend seems to favor a growth of interest in Tibetan Buddhism, with its elaborate rituals centering on evocation of the *Yidam* or patronal deity. On the side of the Western tradition, ceremonial magic, also centered on making a ritual cosmos and calling up a god in the middle of it, is making headway. Perhaps, in the next decades, Lamaism and magic will be what Zen and other kinds of meditation were in the last. The implications of this "new wave," if it really takes hold, are manifold and will probably be much discussed. They would have to include a shift from inner- to outer-directed mentalism, a new assault on the battered world view of Western science and a new affirmation of the power of imaginative and emotional energy. They represent a growing confidence (or one might argue desperation) on the part of the spiritual counter-culture. Not content to create a place of inward calm, it now strives to reach out and construct its own universe, replete with gods or demons, and new laws, in which the man of caged feelings can find a spacious home.

Perhaps the newness of the new wave can be questioned. So far, it has not yet reached the proportions of the same sort of thing in England when the Golden Dawn was in its heyday, or the Germany of the Weimar Republic. In both cases magic and occultism were rife, and there was a vogue for "nature" and central Asia. Both subcultures were widely heralded as "pagan" and antirational. But the alternative reality tradition has never the same effect in each outcropping because the setting is different. Comparisons with other times and places can be illuminating, but are never decisive for interpretation. In some ways the present vogue, which does not share the mood of romantic reactionism characteristic of the earlier periods, has a greater potential for genuine cultural creativity.

Reading Selection: Ceremonial Magic

The spirit of ceremonial magic, and witchcraft insofar as it employs comparable rites, is best ascertained from observing the practical directions which a modern magician would follow. Some lines from a consecration ritual for a ceremonial dagger are given here. The dagger is intended for employment in other rituals, and not for any other use. Notice the Kabbalistic stress on the emergence of light, and thus of the miniature "cosmos" of the ritual setting and action, out of the darkness of the Divine Ground. The performance of a rite is like a repetition of this creation by emanation, and so a redoing of it in order to direct the powers of creation to a particular end. Notice also the emphasis on the four directions and the four elements; these are symbolized over and over again by colors, zodiacal signs, implements, offered substances, etc. The number four (the square), the four directions, and the four elements, all suggest cosmic religion—the religion of the nonhistorical integration of man through ritual.

The importance of consecrating Magical Implements cannot be over-emphasized...The Ceremony of Consecration for the Dagger (used in the Pentagram and Hexagram Rituals, etc.) is very simple but must be done carefully, reverently and with the very highest motives.

When we Consecrate a Magical Implement, we invoke the highest forces and imbue our Implement with those forces and powers. This means that we become channels through which the various forces called upon flow. Thus, the flow through us into the Magical Implement. Remember this: IN ALL CEREMONIAL MAGIC, WE ARE AT ALL TIMES A CHANNEL FOR THE FORCES AS WELL AS A DIRECTOR OF THE POWERS. There, the condition of the channel is of utmost importance. Your state of physical and mental health, sincerity and motive, determine the success or failure of your efforts.

PREPARATION

Always bathe completely before any Ceremony of Magic. Don a clean white robe. Enter your Sanctum with bare feet; you are treading upon sacred ground.

If you have a private Sanctum for your worship and work, so much the better. If not, then you should try to set aside a corner of a room and keep that corner inviolate. Such a corner can be concealed by a folding screen or room-divider.

This ceremony should be performed when the Moon is in the Sign of Aquarius.

Your Altar should be a double cube, 36 × 18 × 18 inches. It should be painted black to symbolize that "out of the darkness (ignorance) came the Light (Wisdom and Knowledge)"....

On your Altar place a Red Rose, a Vigil Light (small candle) in a ruby red glass, a Paten on which is placed Salt and cubes of Bread, a Triangle surmounted by a Cross, a Cup of Water.... At the Southeast corner of the Altar place a small stand covered with a piece of yellow silk. On this stand place a Censer with a small amount of powdered incense ready to light.... In a tiny glass dish (a small crystal salt dish will do) place a little oil. (Any of Air Oils will do.) Also, on this stand, place a small square of red silk or a bag made of red silk. Your Dagger will be kept in this bag or wrapped in the square of red silk when it is not being used. On top of this red silk place the Dagger which is to be Consecrated.

Fill the Cup with Water, light the Lamp and ignite the Incense. You are now ready to perform the Ritual of Consecration for the Dagger.

CEREMONY OF CONSECRATION

Stand at the West of your Altar and face East, raise both hands to a 45 degree angle, fingers pointing East and say:

"Holy art Thou, Lord of the Universe.
Holy art Thou, whom Nature hath not Formed.
Holy art Thou, the Vast and the Mighty One.
Lord of the Light and of the Darkness."

Drop your arms and walk to the East of the Altar, pick up the Rose, face the East and with the Rose make a cross in the Air toward the East, draw a circle around the Cross and vibrate the Divine Name, "Yeheshua." Holding the Rose walk to the North of the Altar, face North, again draw the Cross and the Circle in the Air but this time vibrate the Angel's Name, "Cambriel"...

Walk to the North of the Altar, then to the West and pick up the Cup of Lustral Water. Walk to the South of the Altar then to the East. Face the East, dip the thumb and forefinger into the Water, sprinkle three times to the East and say: "So, first the Priest who governeth the works of Fire must sprinkle with the Lustrous Water of the loud-resounding Sea." Walk to the North of the Altar, face North, dip Thumb and forefinger into the Water, while sprinkling toward the North three times, say: "I purify by Water."...

[In this manner the four directions are purified by the four elements before the actual imbuing of the dagger with power.]

"AIMA," *Consecration Ritual for Ceremonial Dagger* (Los Angeles: Hermetic Science Center, 1965), pp. 1–2.

4. Satanism

One of the participants in the discussion about the public image of Witchcraft and magic was a leader of a Satanist group called The Brotherhood of the Ram. This individual was also the proprietor of a night club. The club had one wall covered with satanic symbols— inverted cross, inverted star with the two points up, ram's head—and was obviously the scene of after-hours rituals. I have seen an example of the "pact" which adherents of this group had to sign, and seal with their own blood—a pledge to renounce all other devotion, and adore Satan alone, to renounce "chrism baptism" and follow the way of joy and pleasure with Satan now and forever.

With the recession of the power of Christian rite and symbol in our culture, the traditional Satanic act of worship, the "black mass," appears to be declining in popularity.[9] What meaning is there in parodying Christian worship for a generation which has scarcely experienced its power? It is being replaced by more informal scenarios, ranging from gruesome animal sacrifices to recitations of poems of Baudelaire to evocations of Satan in the manner of the ceremonial magicians. In the group which I mentioned, the room contained items which the leader was able to bring home from his work in a pathology laboratory. These included the traditional "Hand of Glory," a human head with the top of the skull neatly taken off, as well as an alleged ancient mummy. Expression in worship consisted of florid invocations to Satan, some in Latin, initiation of new members by their signing a pact and sealing it with blood, and a rite of exchange of psychic energy between a girl and the mummy. Many Satanic rites include liberal use of drugs and orgy.

Interpretations of the meaning of Satan vary from "traditionalist" views of him as the antagonist of the Christian God to modern views of him as a symbol of the "life-force," creative evolution, or the affirmation of innocent pleasure. Proponents of the first see Satan more or less as the Miltonic Lucifer, a proud but heroic rebel with whom they identify. He is, contrary to lies told about him by the churches, able to reward his followers with an eternity of carnal pleasure, and with opportunity for revenge, around his dark throne.

A more sophisticated view is characteristic of the well-known Church of Satan founded in San Francisco by Anton LaVey in 1966 on Walpurgisnacht, the eve of Mayday when, in Germany, witches were believed to fly about and celebrate. On that macabre eve LaVey shaved his head and proclaimed himself priest of the new faith. With a background as animal trainer, criminologist, and ceremonial magician, he founded the Church of Satan, he says, because he felt the ordinary churches were twisting and distorting the nature of man, making it impossible for him to find true joy. He speaks of a doctrine of divine nonintervention. If there is a God, he is unable to intervene in human events. Spirituality, therefore, has no place on earth and its practice can only be self-deceptive, leading to the futility of a life based on a false premise. If man is to worship anything, it ought to be his own natural desires, which are what is closest to him and control him. Satan is a symbol of the material world and this carnal nature of man. LaVey believes it

is necessary for man to indulge himself, so long as he does :
hurts another who does not want to be hurt. To him Sa
a counterbalancing force. God is remote and unconcerne
but Satan embodies the life, joy, pleasure, and particularity intimate and
important to man.

The rituals of the group include a "black mass" with the body of a
nude woman as the altar. They also include a rite of communal cursing
in which members ventilate resentment and anger. In performances
virtually approaching psychodrama Satanists act out means of coping
with people and circumstances threatening to them.

The Church of Satan is the only Satanist organization which operates
publicly and attracts educated and "respectable" people. The bulk of
the membership (LaVey claims some 7,000 members and sympathizers)
is young, but, like many Satanist organizations, appeals less to the
obviously alienated than to those who are intellectual and analytic and
superficially "straight."

The need to identify oneself as a Satanist is a complex and devious
thing. It indicates, certainly, a powerful inner rebellion. It usually com-
ports with a strong power drive or, alternatively, a desire to be a "slave."
It often represents sadistic-masochistic traits, either mild or in some
cases of pathological intensity. However, Mr. LaVey's church indicates
it is capable of a different style. The future of Satanism will probably
depend on the extent to which frankly hedonistic people feel a need
for a religious rationale for their way of life, and one which inevitably
has overtones of sensational rebellion.

Reading Selection: Satanism

*Undoubtedly the most readable and systematic modern exposition of
Satanism as a way of thought and life is Anton Szandor LaVey's The
Satanic Bible. It also, no doubt, is the most moderate and sane, for
while LaVey offers much bombastic invective against conventional
religion and morality, obviously designed to titillate or shock, he is careful to avoid committing the Satanist to an exploitative or sadistic attitude
toward man or beast. The Satanic religious mystique is what distinguishes it from the hedonism of a fundamentally normal salesman on a
convention trip. There is no talk of orgy and sacrifice as rites, or of blood
or vengeance.*

Love is one of the most intense emotions felt by man; another is hate.
Forcing yourself to feel indiscriminate love is very unnatural. If you try
to love everyone you only lessen your feelings for those who deserve

your love. Repressed hatred can lead to many physical and emotional ailments. By learning to release your hatred towards those who deserve it, you cleanse yourself of these malignant emotions and need not take your pent-up hatred out on your loved ones...

Every pharisaical religionist claims to love his enemies, even though when wronged he consoles himself by thinking, "God will punish them." Instead of admitting to themselves that they are capable of hating their foes and treating them in the manner they deserve, they say: "There, but for the grace of God, go I," and "pray" for them. Why should we humiliate and lower ourselves by drawing such inaccurate comparisons?

Satanism has been thought of as being synonymous with cruelty and brutality. This is so only because people are afraid to face the truth—and the truth is that human beings are not all benign or all loving. Just because the Satanist admits he is capable of both love *and* hate, he is considered hateful. On the contrary, because he is able to give vent to his hatred through ritualized expression, he is far *more* capable of love—the deepest kind of love. By honestly recognizing and admitting to both the hate and the love he feels, there is no confusing one emotion with the other. Without being able to experience one of these emotions, you cannot *fully* experience the other.

Anton Szandor LaVey, *The Satanic Bible*
(New York: Avon Books, 1969), pp. 64–65.
© Anton Szandor LaVey, 1969.

Notes

[1] The historical and ritual documents of the Golden Dawn have been published by the former secretary of Aleister Crowley, Israel Regardie, as *The Golden Dawn* (2nd ed.) (St. Paul, Minnesota: Llewellyn Publications, 1970).

[2] The best biography is J. Symonds, *The Great Beast* (New York: Roy Publishers, Inc., 1952). See also Symonds's *The Magic of Aleister Crowley* (London: Muller, 1958), and J. Symonds and K. Grant, eds., *The Confessions of Aleister Crowley* (New York: Hill and Wang, Inc., 1970). The latter is his autobiography, or "autohagiography," as he liked to call it.

[3] See Gerald Gardner, *Witchcraft Today* (New York: Citadel Press, 1970).

[4] I am indebted to research done on Feraferia by a former student of mine, Mr. Dale S. Beldin. Most of the material on Feraferia has appeared in an article, Robert S. Ellwood, "Notes on a Neo-Pagan Religious Group in America" University of Chicago Press, *History of Religions*, XI, No. 1 (August 1971), 125–39. More extensive treatment of some aspects of it will be found in this article.

5 Henry Bailey Stevens, *The Recovery of Culture* (New York: Harper & Row, Publishers, 1953) is not as well known as the works of the other writers cited. But this book has had a deep influence on nature utopians like Frederick Adams. Stevens, an ardent vegetarian, argues that man was first a tender of trees, that there was a horticultural era before the "fall" into hunting and the subsequent sacrifice-linked agricultural period. This early horticultural paradise is symbolized in myth by such names as Hesperides, Avalon, etc.

6 Frederick C. Adams, "The Kore," p. 1. © Feraferia, Inc. 1969.

7 The Feraferian seasonal cycle is generally derived from the Celtic, although otherwise the group has been moving more and more in a Greek direction. The nine seasons represented by the nine pillars in the henge are: (1) *Ostara–East*. The birth of the divine male/female pair, Kouros and Kore; (2) *Beltane–Southeast*. The emergence of the Divine Maiden and the Kouros from childhood; pubescence and engagement. (3) *Midsummer–South*. The embrace of Kore and Kouros in the spirit of ripening love; marriage and coitus. (4) *Lugnasad–Southwest*. The congression in love of Kore and Kouros, revealing the Kore as a whole. (5) *Harvest Home–West*. Homecoming; Kore blossoms in the earth landscape; reaping the Harvest. (6) *Samhain–Northwest*. The Kore becomes sleepy and prepares to retire; the end of the harvest. (7) *Repose–The Center*. The Kore retreats beneath the earth, where all cosmic energy gathers, hidden from sight. The entire universe in a state of rest. (8) *Yule–North*. All life forces are gathered beneath the earth, converging inside the body of Kore. The life forces of the universe are thus impregnated in her body. (9) *Oimlec–Northeast*. The end of gestation; another divine Kore/Kouros pair is ready for birth. The seeds beneath the earth crack and begin to grope for the surface.

8 For the outline of the three stages of a magical operation, I am indebted to the article "The Roots of Ritual Magic," in *Man, Myth, and Magic*, No. 11, pp. 297–300.

9 For this and other of the data and interpretations in this discussion of Satanism, I am indebted to Arthur Lyons, *The Second Coming: Satanism in America* (New York: Dodd, Mead & Co., 1970).

seven

the ganges flows west:
hindu movements in america

The official Holy Land for most Americans is Palestine, a tiny, rocky, coastal strip of land at the eastern end of the Mediterranean. Here a few shepherd tribes exchanged contentiousness over wells and flocks for the rugged justice of a divine law. Burned by its righteousness, glowering prophets did not shrink from confronting kings, and later one, on a dry hillock, bloodied the wood of the symbol which has since haunted rampant and virile Europe.

But another holy land also worries the consciousness of the West. This land is also possessed by religion, but a land could scarcely be more different from Palestine. This land is not small and bare, but vast and lush with broad holy rivers, deep jungle noisy with parrots, and northern mountains gleaming white as the dawn of the day of creation. Here patriarchs and prophets tenaciously holding to God's law are replaced by sensuous and surrealistic gods and goddesses as brilliant and dreamlike and bizarre as tropical flowers. Indirectly, through recalling forgotten reveries, or through the seductiveness of half-closed eyes, or the charm of impudent languor, they pull the devotee into the flowery pastures of divine delights or the gory arena of spiritual strife.

Here palaces and temples raise towers so strange as to seem almost botanical. Matted-haired masters of the soul remain bent unmoving in red dawn and sunset. Shaven priests mutter in an old and sacred tongue before the holy flame. Here the rough equity of the law does not run, and here there have been human beings by birth so impure they could not emerge in the light of day, and others clad in peacock plumes and the shifting, colored gleam of jewels. This is India, whose

215

very name and diversity suggests a wonder and imagination worthy of God.

I first visited a "native" Hindu temple on the island of Fiji. It was by the side of a dusty road, and the oppressive, humid air and vegetation suggested southern India. First, upon entering the open-air precincts, I saw a great lingam, the vaguely phallic pillar which is the most common devotional symbol of Shiva. The emblem of this god, the Absolute from which all cosmic energies, creative and destructive alike, derive, was surrounded by open grillwork. Offering pans of colored rice placed in front of the lingam attracted innumerable birds, who flew in through the grill to peck at it. An image of Shiva's animal "vehicle," Nandi the bull, faced the shrine. Behind the bull stood Ganesha, the elephant-headed god, remover of worldly or spiritual obstacles, who is Shiva's son. The base of his open-air statue was piled with rotting fruit.

A little behind the lingam stood a temple building. When I initially visited the temple, I did not approach this structure, for a priest, naked above the waist, was assisting several sari-clad ladies in worshop. Later, when I returned, I gazed into the dark sanctuary to meet the oval white ghostly eyes of a black figure. A single lamp flamed beside him. This was Krishna, the marvellous child, the divine lover, the hero, he whose every glance and word and breath has impenetrable mystery. The eyes in that gloom were incredibly numinous; they have followed me since. On walls between the entrance and the image were crude paintings of the milkmaids who, consumed with inseparable passions of human and divine love, followed Krishna about on moonlight nights as he played his flute and danced and sported with them. On these dank, foul-smelling walls they ran decorously in full billowing skirts. About the grassy yard of the temples wandered children, domestic animals, and squadrons of birds.

The Hinduism of this temple complex is not the form in which it has been generally presented by its Western advocates. Yet this is the Hinduism of India's vast peasant culture which underlies the rest. Like all such cultures it has its deep wisdom and soaring mythical images, as well as its provinciality. Without taking this Hinduism into account, one cannot really understand the message of the "export versions" of Hinduism.

During my visit, I was struck by the sense of continuity between the temple and the riotous, rotting organic life around it. This was no spotless American church, dead but for cut flowers, doors and windows shut tight against all incursions of nonhuman life. Although made by human hands, Hindu temples seem to grow out of the soil like prodigious plants. The human society and temples of India seem like growths stretching away from nature yet unsevered from its veins. They are products of some unfathomable biological interaction between man's seething mental and physical drives and the primordial tropical energy of nature. It is to the *biological* flavor of Hinduism that one returns for understanding. Hinduism presses the potential of biology far beyond where others might set up dualisms of man and nature or mind and body.

Hindu society is not a contractual state, but a great organism. By means of the caste system, every individual finds his place through the biological process of birth and contributes to the whole like a cell of the body. The lingam suggests assimilation of the divine life-force to the sexual—a force creative and destructive, like God, and bearing the closest organic equivalents to eternity, the genetic molecules.

The fantastic numinous Hindu gods, dwelling in the dark cave-like interior of the temple (called the *garbha* or "womb"), are uncanny just because they are forms half-remembered, surfacings from the subtle deeps where mind grapples with such biological demigods as parents, sex, food, and shadowy recollections of the womb and the magically omnipotent infant. Yoga requires a skillful and persistent combined engineering of physiological and psychological forces. It says these two are ultimately one. It suggests the goal, *samadhi*, blissful unconditioned awareness, is the epitome or ultimate objective of the unceasing biological process. It is a total unveiling of that consciousness and perception which life seems to want, free of the limitations life ordinarily imposes. This attainment is, for Hinduism, the real transcendence. To Hinduism, the meaningful dualism is not of man and nature, or of mind and body, but of the infinite or unconditioned and the finite or conditioned. Mind, the unconscious, human society, and nature are all part of a biological continuum, all on one side of the dualism, because they are all alike conditioned; only the breakthrough which sees them all at once and so makes the many one moves to the other side. It is no blasphemy that birds and gods share the same offerings; it symbolizes they are alike in the circle of conception and consumption.

It is doubtless India's willingness explore and exploit the full magic of mankind's psychosomatic nature that has appealed to many Westerners. In the spiritual paths of India, there is, of course, place for self-denial, but no small psychological difference lies between the asceticism of respectful cooperation with the body and deliberate sexual sublimation, and the asceticism of warfare between the spirit and the flesh. Even more important, perhaps, the tales of fabulous lore and holy men of wondrous powers allow a new sanctification of the romantic faculties of marvel in days of minimalized belief—no wonder of India is greater than that of the splendid divine presence within. For some who have made the *Journey to the East* of Hermann Hesse's novel (often physically never leaving the West), it is the quest for the Distant which unlocks the Past, the sunrise East of ultimate origins—for the secret of lost identity, for the barely remembered splendor of the childhood world. The secret of this quest for the individual is to find the unity of mind, fantasy, and body; its myth is the shaman-like flight to a faraway and extraordinary land.

Consciously at least, the fundamental attraction of Hinduism for many westerners has been the hope it holds up for the experience of radical nondualism. Nondualism or Advaita is the message of Vedanta, the most important school of Hindu philosophy in recent centuries. Of course, most Hindus are not consciously so much Vedantists as "dualists" who worship one or another of the gods as personal and "other." Some quite sophisticated theistic philosophies have grown out of this tradition, whether of the "modified nondualistic" or radically dualistic type, to interpret that sense of difference from God which moves man to worship God. The Krishna Consciousness movement has come out of one of those theistic traditions which sees Krishna as the single supreme God with whom man can exchange love. But despite this, one senses that there is a level on which Vedanta best explains much of Hindu culture, and that it is the quest for access to the nondualistic experience which activates most of the West's spiritual interest in India.

The realization of the unity of spirit and biology, of the splendid presence within, suggests leaving behind all the ambiguity of history, the nonintegrated personality, and the nonintegrated cosmos. India implies to westerners that this experience is not dependent on time or place or creed, or need be despaired of, but can be attained anywhere, any time, with right help and right procedure, for it is the way things really are. There is only Brahman, the universal Absolute, who is the pure undifferentiated reality inside everything, to whom the world is just a drama or game. Probably many have come to Hindu groups, believing that if they could really comprehend and make real within such passages as this from one of the ancient Upanishads, they would know all that really needs to be known, and all would be well.

> O Brahman Supreme!
> Formless art thou, and yet
> (Though the reason none knows)
> Thou bringest forth many forms;
> Thou bringest them forth, and then
> Withdrawest them to thyself.
> Fill us with thoughts of thee!
>
> Thou art the fire,
> Thou art the sun,
> Thou art the air,
> Thou art the moon,
> Thou art the starry firmament,

Thou art Brahman Supreme:
Thou art the waters—thou
The creator of all!

Thou art woman, thou art man,
Thou art the youth, thou art the maiden,
Thou art the old man tottering with his staff;
Thou facest everywhere.

Thou art the dark butterfly,
Thou art the green parrot with red eyes,
Thou art the thunder cloud, the seasons, the seas
Without beginning art thou,
Beyond time, beyond space.
Thou art he from whom sprang
The three worlds.

One thou art, one only.
Born from many wombs,
Thou hast become many:
Unto thee all return.
Thou, Lord God, bestowest all blessings,
Thou the Light, thou the Adorable One.
Whoever finds thee
Finds infinite peace.[1]

The several sides of Hinduism have immigrated to the United States
in different waves. The first and most influential, of course, has been
philosophic. If one accepts the not unreasonable presupposition that
there was some Hindu and Buddhist impact on Neoplatonism, then the
whole alternative reality tradition in the West has never been without
some savor of India. This Upanishadic strain of thought was rediscovered
through direct access to the sources in modern translations such as those
of Ram Mohan Roy in the early 19th century. Ralph Waldo Emerson
was deeply affected by this kind of thought, as was Schopenhauer in
Germany. The centrality of this teaching was affirmed by the first Hindu
religious organization (excluding Theosophy) established in the West,
the Vedanta Society.

Next to arrive were yoga groups, as though to supply means for
attaining concretely the promises of Vedanta. Lastly, in the Krishna
Consciousness group has come *bhakti*, devotional Hinduism. It is strongly
opposed to the nondualistic interpretation of Hinduism, worshipping
Krishna as a personal God other than man or the cosmos.

There are other aspects of Hinduism too. The careful, precise rituals
of the Brahmans and the pious householder, so different in tone from
the emotional waves of bhaktic fervor, have found less favor, although
many Vedantists practice some of them, and there is a "Vedic Temple"
in New York and California. The caste system is little more than an
embarrassment. On the other hand, karma yoga, the ideal of liberation

through selfless action in the world made so famous and related specifically to the nonviolence of Mohandas Gandhi, has lastingly changed Western politics and manifested itself in such men as Martin Luther King. If this gift of Hinduism has produced no particular cult group, that is because its influence has been far too broad for such expression.

1. The Ramakrishna Mission and Vedanta Societies

The first and most influential Hindu groups in the West, the centers affiliated with the Ramakrishna Order of India, draws from the spirituality of a modern saint, Ramakrishna (1836–86), who knew virtually nothing of Western learning, and who never travelled outside northern India. Yet had the movement drawn from any other person, it would have been less deep, for Ramakrishna as much as any man summed up within himself the breadth of Hinduism: Vedanta and devotion to the gods, priesthood, yoga, and tantric sexual sublimation. He expressed the peculiarly Hindu fashion of broad mindedness by trying the devotionalism of several other religions, including Islam and Christianity, and finding in them the same spiritual essence he knew in Hinduism.

Ramakrishna was born in a country village in Bengal of Brahman parents. In the manner of Indian holy men, marvellous tales are told of his infancy and childhood. As a young man, he went with his brother to Calcutta where they were to serve as priests in the temple of a rich widow of low caste. The temple was to Kali, the great mother, consort of Shiva, who represents the phenomenal world which both masks and reveals God. Probably no Hindu deity is less calculated to win the understanding of the West than Kali, for she represents Time and the loving and devouring Mother at once; two of her four hands hold gifts and blessing, two hold terrible devices, a bloody sword and a severed head. But some say that to understand entirely this deity is to understand the full meaning of the harsh world and the joy that lies beyond its changes.

So it was that the gentle Ramakrishna loved her with deep passion, calling her "Mother." He would take no action without first referring it to her. When he married a child bride, as arranged by his family, he insisted on calling her "Mother," identifying her with Kali, and once placed her on an altar as a living idol and worshipped her the night through. But he was also initiated into Vedanta, and it is said that in the practice of nondualistic meditation he accomplished in a night what for others would take years. When he took up experimentally the practice of Krishna devotion, he (as is customary) spiritually identified himself with the milkmaids who followed the winsome Lord around, consumed with love, and we hear that Ramakrishna's dress and mincing step in this period were so authentically feminine not even the market women could tell the difference. In the same "total immersion" mood, he practiced what he understood to be Muslim and Christian piety.

This was Ramakrishna: entirely consumed with spirituality, childlike, sometimes impetuously demanding of his followers, possessed of a subjective virtuosity able to comprehend and participate in any path to God.

He summarized marvellously the rich, interior spirituality of India, and pioneered in showing its relevance to the paths of the other faiths. But such a man obviously calls for a St. Paul if his image and message is to endure. Such an apostle was found in the person of Swami Vivekananda (1863–1902). Through him Ramakrishna became the preeminent window into Hinduism from the West. Vivekananda had been a modern Indian educated in the Western scientific tradition. But, dissatisfied with naturalism and scepticism, he sought out the famous Ramakrishna, just before Ramakrisha's death. He was transformed and became Ramakrishna's leading disciple. After the master's passing, Vivekananda's powerful personality, great oratorical gifts, and organizational ability made the movement into something new: an international fraternity based on Hindu principles, dedicated to service as well as mysticism.

It was in 1893 that Vivekananda came into his own. He had heard about a World Parliament of Religions to be held in Chicago, and was determined to attend. In those days, at the height of the colonial era, to presume to bring a message from Asia to the West was an unimaginably more audacious enterprise than today. The now well-walked trail had scarcely been disturbed since antiquity. Vivekananda, not even knowing the time of the now-otherwise-forgotten Congress, arrived in America months too early. Robbed and cheated in his innocence, he ran out of money, went on to Boston, and was reduced to begging. But he met influential friends. When he finally addressed the Congress in his turban and dramatic orange and crimson habit, his striking personality and verbal fluency overwhelmed everyone; he won a raptuous following. He was popular, indeed a social lion, wherever he went; he was a favorite especially among women.

Upon the heels of this success, the Vedanta Society of New York was founded by Vivekananda in 1896 to perpetuate his teaching and work. In its early years, Vedanta was most influential in the highest ranks of society, attracting as it always has prominant, creative, and "interesting" people, such as Sarah Bernhardt, Nicolas Tesla, Paul Carus, and Ella

Wheeler Wilcox. Some unlikely westerners—including a former lady socialist and a former newspaperman—became swamis of the new movement. More recent ornaments of the Society have been the prominent novelists Aldous Huxley and Christopher Isherwood.

Leaving the American work in charge of Western and Indian leaders, Vivekananda went to Europe and finally triumphally returned to his homeland in 1897. He founded the admirable Ramakrishna Order to further the saint's work. In India, seeing the need there for social service work, the Society has labored among India's teeming poor. Believing the West's poverty was spiritual, Vivekananda established the Ramakrishna Mission as a vehicle for the Order's activities and sent swamis or trained teachers and spiritual masters of the Order to the "Vedanta Centers" which had appeared in the wake of his Western travels. All too soon, in 1902, Vivekandanda died.

The Ramakrishna Mission of the Ramakrishna Order in India is the real structure of the Vedanta Centers. Each American and European center is governed by a local board of trustees, but is given spiritual leadership by a swami of the Order sent to America; in this lies what relationship they have. There is no general American Vedanta Society. Some centers are not even called Vedanta Societies, such as the Ramakrishna-Vivekananda Center of New York. There are other groups in this country, not affiliated with the Ramakrishna Mission, which also call themselves Vedanta Societies.

In some ways, Ramakrishna Mission Societies remain expressions of the turn-of-the-century upper class enthusiasm for the East upon which it so readily capitalized. Content with the belief that it enshrines the "perenniel philosophy," the Mission and its societies have not sought to adjust very conspicuously to changing spiritual vogues and moods. Possibly for this very reason, though, membership is growing steadily and has a fair proportion of young people.

The Vedanta temple will usually be set in beautiful, formally landscaped grounds. Within, a simple altar will have resting on it a picture of Ramakrishna. Probably there will also be a tasteful image of a Hindu deity such as the dancing Shiva, as well as Christian images, but they will not be blatant enough to offend those who might be attracted to Hindu philosophy but put off by "idolatry."

On entering the Temple before a lecture meeting, there will be a striking quality of meditative silence. The seats will be arranged rather as in a Protestant church, but the atmosphere is somehow neither the reverent hush of the Episcopal church, nor the intense mindfulness of the Zen hall. It is rather an inward, calm peace, still and full. Many persons, with heads bowed, will be apparently in deep meditation; often meditators can be seen in the temple throughout the week as well.

The swami enters in his orange robes. A choir may present a hymn. The swami will perhaps open with the ancient Upanishadic chant: "From the unreal lead us to the real, from darkness lead us to light, from death lead us to immortality." There may be scripture, prayer, silence, announcements, and an address. Sometimes, at the close, Indian music is played, suggesting in the midst of the high-mindedness some hint of the romance of India.

Typically, Vedanta temples offer weeknight classes in the Upanishads and the *Bhagavad Gita*. The Swamis also spend much time giving private spiritual instruction to students. No particular technique is advocated. The Vedanta Societies are less concerned with hatha or physical yoga, taught in so many places, than with the impartation of the nondualist philosophy, and teaching a balanced spiritual life in which the four paths of devotion, work, discrimination, and meditation are practiced harmoniously.

The traditional Hindu ritualistic worship is also a part of the Ramakrishna tradition. It may be directed toward Ramakrishna himself, as a God-realized saint and (some believe) avatar of Vishnu, or toward his consort Sri Sarada Devi, or some other Hindu deity may be one's "Chosen Ideal." To do the worship properly, one must first receive *diksha*, or initiation by receiving a mantram. Ritual worship is offered daily in all the shrines and temples of the Vedanta Society of Southern California from 12 P.M. to 1 P.M. All monastics and many householders of the Society who find this form of discipline helpful participate. The worship combines elements of Vedic, bhaktic, and tantric ritual, as do most Hindu rituals nowadays. An *arati* or vesper service is offered daily also.

Almost all members of the Society have some kind of shrine in their home where they meditate daily. If they do not undertake a complete pattern of daily ritual worship, they at least offer incense and flowers to the deity.

On certain days a special worship or *puja* is held. There is then a long ritual worship, followed by *homa* (fire offering) and eating of *prasad* or food offered during the worship by everyone. At the Hollywood Temple this is done on Sri Ramakrishna's birthday, Sri Sarada Devi's birthday, Swami Vivekananda's birthday, Swami Brahmananda's birthday, Kali puja, Shiva ratri (Indian festivals of these deities), and Christmas day. Twice a month there is a Ram Nam, a song service to the god Rama.

In southern California the Vedanta Society maintains religious houses. There are convents and monasteries in conjunction with the temples in Hollywood and Santa Barbara, and a monastery on 300 acres of hilly grassland in Trabuco Canyon, Orange County. Here a handful of monks lead a life of work, study, and some three hours of worship and meditation daily.

In all these activities, the basic message is "three fundamental truths": That man's real nature is divine; that the aim of man's life on earth is to unfold and manifest this Godhead, eternally existent in man, but hidden; that truth is universal. These three principles are the tests for all action and belief. The good is what aids in unfolding the divine within; man is one with every creature, for all are also the divine. That truth is universal means that all religion, all gods, are manifestations of the universal impersonal Being and the path to that Godhead. It is ignorance, not seeing clearly, which causes us to be lost from him in the many and the separate, and which causes us to worship him under personalized and conceptualized forms. All this worship can also be accepted, for it is movement away from the toils of ego.

Reading Selection: The Vedanta Society

This selection is from a very interesting book offering statements by westerners who have been attracted to Vedanta. The writer here is the well-known novelist Christopher Isherwood.

Vedanta is non-dualistic. Psychologically, this was of the greatest importance to me; because of my fear and hatred of God as the father-figure. I don't think I could ever have swallowed what *began* with dualism. Vedanta began by telling me that I was the Atman, and that the Atman was Brahman; the Godhead was my own real nature, and the real nature of all that I experienced as the external, surrounding universe. Having taught me this, it could go on to explain that this one immanent and transcendent Godhead may project all sorts of divine forms and incarnations which are, as the Gita says, its "million faces." To the eyes of this world, the One appears as many. Thus explained, dualism no longer seemed repulsive to me; for I could now think of the gods as mirrors in which man could dimly see what would otherwise be quite invisible to him, the splendour of his own immortal image. By looking deeply and single-mindedly into these mirrors, you could come gradually to know your own real nature; and, when that nature, that Atman, was fully known and entered into, the mirror-gods would no longer be necessary, since the beholder would be absolutely united with his reflection. This approach to dualism via non-dualism appealed so strongly to my temperament that I soon found myself taking part enthusiastically in the cult of Sri Ramakrishna, and even going into Christian churches I happened to be passing, to kneel for a while before the altar. Obviously, I had been longing to do this for years. I was a frustrated devotee.

Christopher Isherwood, in *What Vedanta Means to Me*, ed. JOHN YALE (London: Rider and Co., 1961), pp. 43–44. © The Vedanta Society of Southern California.

2. The Self-Realization Fellowship

Over twenty years after Vivekananda's pioneering penetration of America as a spiritual envoy from India, another representative of that land, called Paramahansa Yogananda, repeated the journey. He too made his first impact in Boston, at a congress of liberal religionists (in his case, the International Congress of Religious Liberals in 1920, held under the auspices of the Unitarian Church), but soon was headquartered in Los Angeles which was to become the nucleus for more than 150 Self-Realization Fellowship Centers on four continents. In contrast to Vivekananda's meteoric career, Yogananda (1893–1952) remained in America over thirty years, the first Hindu master to teach in the West for such an extended period of time. A vivid and winning personality combined with his willingness to use American publicity methods to promote what he believed was something America greatly needed, and the experienced value of his teachings for many people, made an indelible mark on the course of American spirituality.

He was a yogi rather than an intellectual Vedantist, and brought with him the fundamental teaching of traditional yoga philosophy, based on the ancient Yoga Sutras of Patanjali (approximately 100 B.C.), that we, underneath all apparent limitation and frustration, are an eternal divine soul. We have drives for love, joy, and power because we have a capacity for our true inheritance, infinite and divine love, joy, and power. But because of ignorance, limitation of sight, we misdirect it toward outer things in the material world. As a yogi, Yogananda brought with him not only this teaching, but techniques for doing something about it. Through yoga one can redirect one's life-energy (*prana*) from outward things towards the opening of the centers (*chakras*) which give the spiritual sight necessary for realization of one's true nature.

The man who more than anyone else has made this teaching available to the West was born Mukunda Lal Ghosh near Calcutta. He has given us a fascinating account of his life in the well-known *Autobiography of a Yogi,* a book widely distributed by the Self-Realization Fellowship. Yogananda was a Bengali; many of the Hindu missioners to the West have been of that quick, intelligent, poetic race. His father was a prosperous and devout railway official.

There are accounts that as a child Yogananda was endowed with remarkable psychic powers. There is an impression from his autobiography that as he grew up, he increasingly sensed an unusual spiritual drive which had to be realized. With a young man's warm enthusiasm, he was fascinated by the holy men of India. He visited one after another, observing their powers and ways of life. One could produce perfumes out of the air; another made tigers as gentle as house cats. In themselves, however, these abilities were not what the future teacher of the West, burning with a potential for divine cosmic consciousness yet to be unleashed, would settle for.

For all his spiritual seeking, Yogananda, as a youth and throughout his life, does not appear a stiflingly sober-sided pietist or an unapproachable paragon of godliness. In this is the real strength which he brought to his unique mission. He was less like the rocklike virtue of the notoriously conservative and cross-grained conventional *sadhu,* and more like the strength of a bubbling, ever-fresh stream winning its course with liquid flexibility and persistence. He was clearly charming, popular with friends, endowed with intelligence and a light, almost romantic spirit, though his love was for the divine end of all loves. Rich, sensuous poetic language came naturally to him as he communicated his spiritual experiences and the vision of the cosmos they imparted to him. Compared to the impoverished world of many westerners, his was one of fabulous wonder and beauty, the cosmos as it is opened to the eye of *samadhi.* It is also a world where seeming miracles, psychic feats, and phenomenal control of the physical body and even of life and death, are expected.

Yogananda's search for a master was fulfilled when he was initiated by Swami Yukteswar, a disciple of the family guru. Both in turn were said to be of the spiritual lineage of Swami Babaji, a master who had lived many centuries in the Himalayas and would remain in the body till the end of this age of the world. Swami Babaji is the highest patron of the Self-Realization Fellowship.

Upon coming to America in 1920, Paramahansa Yogananda ("Paramahansa" is the title of a Master Yogi, "Yogananda" is his name in religion) lectured, wrote devotional books, and founded the Self-Realization Fellowship as a vehicle for his teaching mission. In addition to the basic philosophy of the Yoga Sutras, he taught a specific technique, *kriya yoga.* It is a means for withdrawal of the life-energy from the outer concerns to the opening of the spiritual centers. The brain is an electric powerhouse for the body. Current goes from it down the spinal column. By right "magnetization" of this current, through techniques of *pranayama* or life-energy control, meditating on the cosmic syllable "Aum," and yogic exercise, one can open the centers and attain bliss. By the same token, one fantastically accelerates the speed of human evolution in his own case. Even conscious control of death is offered.

This half-metaphorical use of the vocabulary of modern, Western science to interpret to Western audiences the ancient wisdom of *kundalini yoga* is characteristic of the teaching skill of the yoga master in the West. A very basic point of his message is that yoga's philosophy and methods are scientific and entirely reinforced by the discoveries of Western science. Individual discovery and use of them can be empirical and experiential, like a laboratory experiment, and does not need to depend on scriptural or ecclesiastical authority, though in developing them sometimes trust is needed in the greater knowledge of his guru.

Nontheless, the Self-Realization Fellowship teaches that the yoga philosophy and methods, accessible as they are to empirical and scientific verification, underline all the great religions and scriptures. They are the essence, core, and substance of every religion. All the words and myths and symbols of the others can be seen as inevitably garbled expressions of man's intuitive sense of the truth of the goals of yoga and the stages by which it is attained. Patanjali's famous "Eight Steps" of Raja Yoga are: *yama* or negative rules for moral conduct, *niyama* or positive rules for living, *asanas* or postures, *pranayama* or control of the life-energy, *pratyahara* or "interiorization" of the mind and energy, *dharana* or concentration, *dhyana* or meditation, and *samadhi* or union and cosmic consciousness. Thus the Ten Commandments can be understood not as arbitrary laws but as articulations of *yama* or the preliminary moral stance necessary for further spiritual growth. Yoga teaching can help us to understand "hard sayings" of the Gospels, such as "If thine eye offend thee, pluck it out." This means not literal self-mutilation, but withdrawal of life-energy from the outer senses to the inner (*pratyahara*). Yogananda was convinced that Jesus and Paul and other spiritual masters of all times and places were yoga masters, with much the same message as his, though the message frequently needed to be accommodated to varying conditions of preparation, and was not always presented in its fullness. But it is the reality about man and his destiny which has given rise to all religions.

The westerner with an attachment to Christianity or science, or both, could be assured that he could find nothing at odds with either in the message from the East. Even though it seems that today neither science nor Christianity have the prestige of some years ago, Yogananda's teaching is persuasive for many Americans. His Fellowship, his "Churches of All Religions," his classes and printed teachings have been greatly successful. His books sell well, and SRF lecturers easily fill large auditoriums in cities around the country.

The last remarkable event of Yogananda's life was the incorruptibility of his physical body for twenty days after his death, until the cover was placed on the casket for the last time. This was something of a sensation at the time, receiving nationwide attention in newspapers and magazines.

The Self-Realization Fellowship consists of laity and Renunciants. The latter have generally completed the introductory series of fifty-some lessons and begun the practice of kriya yoga, meditate at least two hours a day, and live a monastic life. The present head of the Fellowship is a nun whose religious name is Daya Mata, a Sanskrit name meaning "Mother of Compassion," chosen by the Paramahansa himself. The governing board, over which Daya Mata presides, consists of eight persons who have been members at least twenty years.

The Fellowship has branches all over the world, including India where, as the Yogoda Satsang, it is fairly extensive. In the United States nine of its forty-four centers are in California. A prominant landmark in west Los Angeles is the SRF "Lake Shrine," a beautifully landscaped park with such diverse attractions as lotus towers, a Dutch windmill, a houseboat, and some of the ashes of Mahatma Gandhi whom Yogananda had initiated into Kriya Yoga and whom he greatly admired. To the south, a seaside retreat is found at Encinitas.

Although the organization is controlled by persons whose experience goes back to the days of Yogananda himself, attenders and worshippers at SRF include old-timers, middle-aged seekers, and many young people, some in very "mod" dress. The Sunday morning worship or "lecture" is held in a chapel where many come to meditate through the week. The belief that what is taught and experienced here is the reality which underlies all religion is evidenced in the visible combination of cross and lotus, pictures of Yogananda and images of saints. The meeting begins with chants rather than hymns. The address, on a topic such as "How to Play Well Your Part in Life," "Filling the Mind with God," "Your Superconscious Power of Success," is presented by a personable westerner wearing an ochre robe. His tone, and the whole atmosphere, will be one of tranquillity. During the week, most centers offer further lectures and yoga classes.

I recently attended an SRF service in a small, crowded chapel. Persons of all ages were present, though the group tended toward middleage. The young people there seemed very serious. On the altar were six equal-sized pictures of Masters, including Jesus and Yogananda, but a large colored picture of Yogananada was set to the side and toward the front, with flowers before it as well as on the altar. Certain small SRF customs, striking to the visitor, establish the atmosphere. Members may greet each other with the Indian *namaste* (bow with palms pressed together) rather than a Western handshake. Yogananda is often just referred to reverently as "Master." As they enter many stand before the pictures with folded hands a moment before sitting down.

Soft music played before the service. The minister, an American, began with an invocation of God as Father, Mother, and Friend, and of the saints and sages of all religions, and of "our guru." The closing blessing contained the same formula.

The service is drawn from many sources in a friendly and "low-key" style. Music consisted of Indian chants such as "Hymn to Brahma" accompanied by a harmonium. The last verse of the "Battle Hymn of the Republic" closes all services. Announcements, concerning conferences, classes, and the Sunday School, were rather lengthy. The address itself was a blending of scriptures (Genesis, the New Testament, the *Bhagavad Gita*, and the writings of Yogananda), chants, silent meditation, and words by the minister who used Vedantic and Christian language interchangeably. It should be emphasized that this syncretism is deliberate and wholly in accord with the premises of SRF. The "popular" level of some aspects of its public activity is quite in accord with the spirit of Yogananda, who (like Jesus) was not concerned with intellectuals only, but with bringing his message in appropriate vesture to all sorts of people.

Yogananda has become an image—a remarkable, deep, sweet, poetic, ecstatic man enraptured of cosmic life—who has changed the map of American religious life. The image of the yogi has affected other movements. Others from India have built on it, but Yogananda started it in our day. Let him add a few words.

When you find that your soul, your heart, every wisp of inspiration, every speck of the vast blue sky and its shining star-blossoms, the mountains, the earth, the whippoorwill, and the bluebells are all tied together with one cord of rhythm, one cord of joy, one cord of unity, one cord of Spirit, then you shall know that all are but waves in His cosmic sea.[2]

Reading Selection: The Self-Realization Fellowship

In this passage taken from his autobiography, Yogananda describes his first great experience of yogic cosmic consciousness. The mystical experience occurred when he was still a young man living and studying with his guru or master, Swami Yukteswar.

My body became immovably rooted; breath was drawn out of my lungs as if by some huge magnet. Soul and mind instantly lost their physical bondage, and streamed out like a fluid piercing light from my every pore. The flesh was as though dead, yet in my intense awareness I knew that never before had I been fully alive. My sense of identity was no longer narrowly confined to a body, but embraced the circumambient atoms. People on distant streets seemed to be moving gently over my own remote periphery. The roots of plants and trees appeared through a dim transparency of the soil; I discerned the inward flow of their sap.

The whole vicinity lay bare before me. My ordinary frontal vision was now changed to a vast spherical sight, simultaneously all-perceptive. Through the back of my head I saw men strolling far down Rai Ghat Road, and noticed also a white cow who was leisurely approaching. When she reached the space in front of the open ashram gate, I observed her with my two physical eyes. As she passed by, behind the brick wall, I saw her clearly still.

All objects within my panoramic gaze trembled and vibrated like quick motion pictures. My body, Master's, the pillared courtyard, the furniture and floor, the trees and sunshine, occasionally became violently agitated, until all melted into a luminescent sea; even as sugar crystals, thrown into a glass of water, dissolve after being shaken. The unifying light alternated with materializations of form, the metamorphoses revealing the law of cause and effect in creation.

An oceanic joy broke upon calm endless shores of my soul. The Spirit of God, I realized, is exhaustless Bliss; His body is countless tissues of light. A swelling glory within me began to envelop towns, continents, the earth, solar and stellar systems, tenuous nebulae, and floating universes. The entire cosmos, gently luminous, like a city seen afar at night, glimmered within the infinitude of my being. The sharply etched global outlines faded somewhat at the farthest edges; there I could see a mellow radiance, ever-undiminished. It was indescribably subtle; the planetary pictures were formed of a grosser light.

The divine dispersion of rays poured from an Eternal Source, blazing into galaxies, transfigured with ineffable auras. Again and again I saw the creative beams condense into constellations, then resolve into sheets of transparent flame. By rhythmic reversion, sextillion worlds passed into diaphanous luster; fire became firmament.

I cognized the center of the empyrean as a point of intuitive perception in my heart. Irradiating splendor issued from my nucleus to every part of the universal structure. Blissful *amrita*, the nectar of immortality, pulsed through me with a quicksilverlike fluidity. The creative voice of God I heard resounding as *Aum*,* the vibration of the Cosmic Motor.

---

*"In the beginning was the Word, and the Word was with God, and the Word was God." John 1:1. [Note in original.]

Suddenly the breath returned to my lungs. With a disappointment almost unbearable, I realized that my infinite immensity was lost. Once more I was limited to the humiliating cage of a body, not easily accommodative to the Spirit. Like a prodigal child, I had run away from my macrocosmic home and imprisoned myself in a narrow microcosm.

My guru was standing motionless before me; I started to drop at his holy feet in gratitude for the experience in cosmic consciousness which I had long passionately sought. He held me upright, and spoke calmly, unpretentiously.

"You must not get overdrunk with ecstasy. Much work yet remains for you in the world. Come; let us sweep the balcony floor; then we shall walk by the Ganges."

PARAMAHANSA YOGANANDA, *Autobiography of a Yogi* (Los Angeles: Self-Realization Fellowship), pp. 149–51. Copyright © 1946, Paramahansa Yogananda.

3. The Maharishi Mahesh Yogi's Transcendental Meditation Movement

My first formal encounter with Transcendental Meditation was a lecture given by the Maharishi himself. It was in the fall of 1967, he was at the peak of his popularity, and the auditorium was filled with eager young people anxious to find out what had attracted the Beatles to this guru from exotic India. So far as spectacle was concerned, they were not disappointed. The master, with his tiger skin pallet, his long gray hair and beard, roses twirling in his hands, his twinkly eyes and bubbling giggle, was obviously a figure with the other-worldly charisma of temple incense and Himalayan ashrams.

Subsequent lectures I have heard on Transcendental Meditation ("TM") have been by westerners instructed as teachers by the Maharishi. They have included Jerry Jarvis, founder of the Students International Meditation Society, and others. They have all been as crisp and clean-cut and as sophisticatedly soft-sell as aerospace engineers. Eschewing religious overtones and oriental jargon, they present TM as a rational, streamlined means of acquiring greater happiness and efficiency. Meditation does not, they say, involve ascetic withdrawal, but makes it possible to enjoy life.

I later spent an evening with a campus group of TM practitioners. The meeting was held in a typically nondescript and disorganized student apartment. Part of the evening was spent in an attempt to show some films of Maharishi's triumph at Harvard. There was one snafu after another: the film broke, the projector failed, and finally much of the picture was unseen. But the group endured all of this with considerable equanimity. The experience of their group meditation was, for me, a deep one. A peculiar peace fell over the darkened room in which ten or twelve people were centered into silence. Even through closed eyes, one could somehow sense the presence of the others, as though each were a supporting and upholding pillar.

The basic teaching of TM is that it is possible fully to enjoy life by getting to the ground of joy through meditation. It is continually emphasized that transcendental meditation is a *natural* process. Unlike methods based on asceticism, yoga, and concentration, it never involves procedures which go against the normal functioning of the organism. Maybe after years of effort and association, one can condition oneself to experience a bliss-trance upon the stimuli of certain yogic actions, we are told, but this is essentially a reversal of what is natural.

TM employs the natural desire of the self to quest for expansion, joy, and ecstasy by seeking the subtlest level below biological, mechanical, chemical, molecular, atomic, and subatomic material reality—to the ground of being itself, which is of course the same as Brahman in Vedanta thought. The Maharishi's teaching is quite deliberately a popularized Vedanta. Thoughts in the mind are like bubbles rising up from great depths; we are ordinarily aware only of their surface manifestation. But by following thoughts back, or by exploring beneath phenomenal reality, we can move toward contact with original, unruffled consciousness. Too often we deal with problems just on their own level. We cannot solve the problem of darkness by rearranging darkness, but only by bringing light.

The natural tendency of the mind is to seek a field of greater happiness, and this is what it will do naturally once the distractions of thought, speech, and action have been stopped by withdrawal from them. This is meditation. It is not meditation *about* anything, or setting a mood, or giving oneself an emotional charge. It is stopping all subjective or external stimuli which keep the mind on the periphery, thereby releasing it to do what comes naturally to it, to go to its own center, the still point of greatest joy.

While reaching this point is not an end in itself apart from the enjoyment of life, it is said that it greatly enhances that joy. The movement presents much evidence from physiological experiments to the effect that the fifteen to twenty minutes of meditation twice daily by practitioners gives them deeper rest than deep sleep, reducing metabolism and oxygen consumption while the mind is fully awake. This is said to be a unique "fourth state" of consciousness. Physically and mentally refreshing, it energizes a person to use a vastly wider range of mental powers, and therefore become more creative, as well as happier.[3]

The movement was begun by the Maharishi Mahesh Yogi in 1959 as the Spiritual Regeneration Movement. Its founder, like so many founders of Western Hindu movements, had a college education. In this case, it was in physics. But he turned to seek realization instead, and studied for fourteen years as a close disciple of Swami Brahmananda Saraswati. It was under the guidance of this master, leader of one of the venerable monasteries founded by the great Shankara, that he came to realize that the true Vedic and Vedanta teaching pointed to the great simplicity and availability of the ultimate spiritual ground. It was also that Swami who encouraged his personable disciple to bring this treasure to the West, as well as to the peoples of India, from whom it had so long been concealed.

This determination led to tours of the West beginning in 1959, which in the sixties led to remarkable success. Most publicized, of course, was the adherence of the Beatles to the Maharishi in the middle of the decade. They spent some months at his training center in Rishikesh, before leaving him in disappointment. The publicity era, which included also pictures of the master riding in chauffered limousines, and an abortive and ill-advised speaking-concert tour with a famous rock group, produced an inevitable reaction as the bubble burst. Rumors spread alleging commercialism and hunger for fame behind the façade of pop spirituality. Doubtless these were for the most part unjustified. Naïveté rather than crasser motives were mostly responsible for the Hindu sage's mistakes in his meteoric Western adventure.

The movement is still growing, steadily if less spectacularly, and is probably on a firmer basis. The Maharishi, after announcing in 1968 that a ten-year period of public activity had ended, no longer speaks much to general audiences, but concerns himself with training instructors at his center in Rishikesh, now moved to Italy. The number of persons who have taken advanced training is increasing, and their zeal is impressive. Even though there is less media coverage, the activity claims some three to four hundred thousand meditators worldwide, and growth in the number of initiators.

The movement has several wings, of which the most important are the Students International Meditation Society (SIMS), and the adult Spiritual Regeneration Movement. Of these, SIMS appears to be the most vigorous. Its program for initiating individuals into the practice of meditation is well honed. General lectures are presented in a series of two, the first dealing with general philosophy—the need, the psychology, the evidence. The second, presumably attended only by those seriously attracted by the first, gives more details on the process of meditation itself and initiation into it.

The Maharishi retains a rough, westernized approximation of the ancient guru's initiation of disciples. It is individual, requires a token sacrifice, and a personal impartation. Those who wish to be initiated must be off "non-prescribed drugs" for fifteen days. They must bring to the initiatory meeting twelve fresh flowers, some fresh fruit, a clean white handkerchief, and a contribution of money, ranging from $35 for students to $120 for an adult couple. It is said the money requirement can be waived in case of inability to pay, and is the only expected support for the work of the movement. The initiate should not have eaten for several hours before the initiation. The initiator gives the student his mantram and instructs him how to use it properly. The initiator also performs a ceremony of thanksgiving and purification, in which the articles the new meditator brought are used as well as rice and water.

In any case, the initiate meets individually with a teacher, who instructs him in meditation and gives him his personal mantram, or sound, which he says "internally" to help him go into meditation. The mantram is to be kept secret, never to be said aloud, and is in harmony with the vibrations of the personality. Only initiators, who have been taught the principles of assigning mantras by the Maharishi in three-month training sessions, and initiated into this power, may impart them.

After receiving his mantra, the initiate practices meditation and meets daily with a small group to discuss his experiences for the next three days. He returns ten days later for checking, and once a month for as long as he wishes. The procedure from the first lecture to the final checking is called the "seven steps to bliss." There are books he can buy and read, and advanced classes he can take, and he may even become an initiator himself. But there is no great pressure in these directions; it depends on the bent of the individual meditator.

The Meditation Movement's adherents are attractive people with shining eyes and soft voices. They believe they know the most direct cure for the ills of the world, and the Maharishi has said that if only 10 percent of the world's population were to start meditating, the spiritual effect would be so great as to end war and strife.

Reading Selection: The Maharishi Mahesh Yogi's Transcendental Meditation Movement

This passage from a Spiritual Regeneration Movement booklet describes in simple words the basic principle of why meditation works.

Children are unpredictable and difficult to control, yet any child's reaction, if you hold out a piece of candy to him, is easy to forecast. Water is not easy to confine, yet it, too, behaves predictably in certain circumstances: it will always run down hill; it will always find its own level, if permitted to.

By the same token, the mind, left to its own devices will always prefer to seek a field of greater happiness. Given the choice between an ugly and a beautiful sight, the eye will invariably be drawn to the beautiful. As between a harsh sound and a pleasing one, the ear will seek out the more charming.

It is not necessary to drag the attention toward attractive objects; to learn to prefer lovely and happy things requires no arduous instruction. The mind will automatically focus on them to the exclusion of other things, if given the opportunity.

The transcendental field, being true bliss, represents perfect happiness. It is the ultimate in "attractiveness." Were it made aware of this, the mind would seek out such a field with no need for any pointing and directing. It would automatically be drawn to it in increasing degree as the mind's consciousness and awareness of this contact developed and took hold.

The only thing that is needed, then, to take advantage of this natural inclination is a vehicle of some sort which will conduct the mind's attention surely and swiftly to the source it seeks, establish contact with it, and return the attention once again to the gross level from which it started.

To act as such a vehicle, Maharishi has chosen the medium of sound. The vibrations created by a sound or its mental image inexorably seek the source which gives rise to the thought, traversing the same path we have been describing, to reach eventually the thought's very genesis, which is none other than the absolute field. In the course of the journey the vibrations become progressively more refined and, by the same token, more powerful.

The attention, directed inward, is thus borne toward the field it is most naturally inclined to seek. It arrives eventually at the final threshold and transcends it, crossing the boundary line between the subtlest field of relative existence and the eternal, absolute ocean of pure Being.

M. B. JACKSON, *Transcendental Meditation as Taught by Maharishi Mahesh Yogi* (Los Angeles: Spiritual Regeneration Movement Foundation of America, 1967), pp. 14–15.

4. International Sivananda Yoga Society

Somewhere in the back of the mind of anyone who is at all attracted to the spirituality of India there lies a vision of deep Himalayan caves, or refuges in jungle forests, populated by scantily-clad recluses. Entranced and in strange postures, they are masters of yoga. Knowing secrets of combining the chemistry of diet and breath and the biophysics of posture with the subtler sciences of the psyche, they are able to attain both superb health and mental liberation.

Doubtless many stories of great yogis are fanciful, but one great modern master who is not fictional is Swami Sivananda, even though Mircea Eliade used him as a character in one of his fantastic tales.[4] Trained as a medical doctor, Swami Sivananda (1887–1963), after a successful career, renounced professional life to become a yogi. His worldly abilities were not lost, however, and Sivananda was innovative in establishing modern institutions centering around yoga—the Sivananda Ashrams, the Divine Life Society, the Sivananda Free Hospital, and the Vedanta Forest University. He wrote many books, and in 1953 convened a World Parliament of Religions. All of these activities centered in Rishikesh, traditionally a city of sages in the Himalayan foothills. Here those sick both in body and soul gathered around the sage, who lived in simple dignity and who used his knowledge both of medicine and yoga to heal and teach.

One of his leading disciples was Swami Vishnu-Devananda (born 1927). A young, extroverted exponent of the ancient science, he came to America shortly before the death of his master. He became the first yoga teacher to get a pilot's license. Flying about in his private plane, he has established yoga centers in some twenty-five communities, and two large yoga camps, one in Quebec and another in the Bahamas. The headquarters are in Montreal. Also interested in advancing yoga philosophy as a means to a better world, Vishnu-Devananda started a movement called T.W.O., True World Order, on the grounds of the yogic sense of harmony, mutual understanding, vegetarianism, health, and sublimation of violence.

Swami Vishnu-Devananda has emphasized the practice of *hatha yoga,* the physical yoga of breathing and postures, as his specialty. He has written a useful illustrated book on the subject. Other masters have worked primarily on other aspects of the field, such as *raja yoga,* the yoga of deep meditation which leads to liberation, or the yogic techniques for raising the *kundalini,* the "serpent power" coiled at the base of the spine, which opens the psychic and spiritual centers along the spinal column.

Indeed, the word *yoga* has sometimes been used so broadly as to include virtually any aspect of Hinduism regarded as a means of liberation. There is talk of *bhakti yoga,* the practice of devotion; *karma yoga,* the path advocated in part of the *Bhagavad Gita* of doing one's duty in the world; *mantra yoga,* or the recitation of verbal formulas; and so forth. These do not, in themselves, involve the physical and meditational techniques commonly associated with the word at all. Perhaps it is clearer to use the term *marga* or path for these, and to restrict yoga to practices involving intense concentration, psychosomatic exercises, and a definite course of development followed under a teacher or guru.

There is a definite tradition of yoga in this narrower sense based on the famous Yoga Sutras of Patanjali (around the first century B.C.). Here the purpose of the discipline is to give the spirit independence of the conditioned existence of space and time and the body. This is done through gaining control of the whole system—body, emotions, and mind —by the highest levels of mind, so that the spirit can be allowed to shine forth as sovereign in its own house. It is for this reason, and not just for the sake of physical health, that one makes the physical and emotional systems into a finely tuned instrument, clean, supple, and amenable to the higher will. To attain the true end of yoga, these exercises are accompanied by meditations designed to stop the riotous activity of the stream of consciousness mind. Although theoretically hatha yoga comes before raja (meditative) yoga, most Western practitioners find that both go very well together. The literature and instructions of the Sivananda Yoga Center certainly encourage a Vedanta philosophical interpretation of the meaning of the experience. Vedanta is undoubtedly favored by most modern Hindu yoga teachers. For them, the "spirit" isolated, put in control, and thereby liberated through the process is not merely the individual spirit, but is the outcropping in that person of Brahman, the universal mind and ground of being, the one real existent, realization of whom within oneself is the end of all ends.

Most Western yoga classes do not require any highly Hindu religious practice, but claim to present a technique anyone can receive on any level he wishes—as a physical exercise only, or as an aid to meditation, or as a total way of life. Of course, some of the postures do derive from devotional attitudes, or from the *mudras* or traditional gestures of certain gods, and some breathing and other exercises do not make much sense except in light of the esoteric teaching about the *kundalini,* psychic centers, and so forth. But the benefits of yoga are appreciated by a much wider audience than would be prepared to accept its religious background. I once visited a couple of yoga classes at a Roman Catholic college with several priests and nuns among its members.[5]

A group like the Sivananda Yoga Center, however, does function as something of an outpost of Hinduism. It attracts spiritual seekers, and between the library of Hindu books, the atmosphere of incense and Hindu art, and the contagious atmosphere of enthusiasm over Indian food and visiting charismatic Indian swamis in colorful robes, one feels that the message of yoga as a complete way of life—and thought—is transmitted to many, and for them Yoga-Vedanta values become central standards of judgment.

Reading Selection: International Sivananda Yoga Society

These paragraphs are from an information sheet put out by the Sivananda Yoga Society. They summarize the yoga philosophy as understood by the Society and show how it interacts with the yogic concern for diet, health, and the body.

Yoga is a way of complete life. There are a number of different subdivisions in Yoga, but only *one* Yoga, with all paths leading to the same goal. Some teachers advise students to follow one path, and ignore the others. We feel that following a synthesis of all Yoga techniques is best suited for rapid progress. There are five requisites for this Yogic life: (1) proper exercise, (2) proper breathing, (3) proper diet, (4) relaxation, and (5) positive thinking and meditation. Regular day and evening classes are given here, and lectures in the philosophy are held Sundays at 7:30 P.M.

In this modern, mechanized world, our physical bodies are not given the necessary exercise to keep them in a state of health, and only in a healthy body can there be a healthy mind. In this healthy body one should have much flexibility, be a healthy mind. Unfortunately, most Americans have never even experienced the feeling of a relaxed, healthy body, let alone that in accord with a powerful, peaceful mind. In this healthy body, one should have much flexibility, as well as properly functioning glands and organs. Through Yoga exercises the whole body is restored to its natural health and vigor. For people who lead busy lives, you will find that time spent in practicing Yoga will more than make up for itself in peace of mind, relief from tension, and improved health.

To derive energy from the food we eat we must combine it with oxygen, so proper breathing is essential. Mind and thought are intimately connected with breath and relaxation. Proper breathing techniques aid one in achieving emotional control, physical health and inner calmness. Yoga breathing exercises (pranayama) are not dangerous, if learned from a competant teacher, but should never be attempted without proper guidance or from a book. Yoga techniques teach one to give the body and mind maximum relaxation and rejuvenation in a short period of time.

Food is an important limb in Yoga. The building blocks of our body and mind are the foods we eat. A vegetarian diet is advocated for physical, moral and spiritual reasons. Regular lectures are given explaining the advantages, enjoyments and practical hints to following such a diet.

Thought is the most powerful force on earth. Through meditation and focusing the mind, one is able to tap the hidden powers within and apply them to his daily life. To be truly content and have direction in life, we must have a goal and a philosophy. Vedanta philosophy shows man's relation to the universe and helps him answer the age old question "Who am I?" There is no dogmatism in Yoga Vedanta. Students may accept what they believe and experience to be true, and leave the rest. Some people who practice Yoga have little interest in the philosophy. However, they are undoubtedly interested in reaping peace of mind, relief from tension, and improved health.

> Sivananda Yoga Society, "About the Sivananda
> Yoga Society and Yoga Philosophy," undated
> (about 1969).

5. The International Society for Krishna Consciousness

Probably one of the most conspicuous of all new religious groups today is the Krishna Consciousness Society. This fellowship, with its core of totally dedicated, full-time devotees, is committed to a strict, conservative but ecstatic interpretation of a school of Hinduism. These devotees, mostly young, wearing yellow robes, their heads shaved except for a topknot in back, are common sights as they dance and sing "Hare Krishna" on the streets of many large American cities. Clearly transported by rapture, they sing the sacred words over and over, accompanied by hand cymbals, drums, and viols. Their hands rise in adoration, their bodies writhe in sensuous rapture. This exotic scene enlivens the workaday business of major downtown streets, college campuses, and the shopping centers of conservative suburbs. Passersby will be given a small card with the address of the local Krishnaite center and an invitation to attend a great "spiritual feast" the coming Sunday afternoon, with dancing, singing, puppet show, talk, and vegetarian food.

Anyone who accepted the invitation would find that the experience on the streets was only a mild foretaste of the exoticism in store for him. In the temple, he might wonder if he were in the right country, though with an open mind he will enjoy a fascinating, beautiful, and unforgettable afternoon. He will find himself in a room clouded with incense and full of a great number of the saffron-robed dancers. At one end will be a wide altar bedecked with images of Krishna the sweet divine lover as an infant, or playing his flute, or with Radha his fresh-faced consort. Pictures bespangle the walls displaying Krishna and the milkmaids in idyllic pastimes, disporting themselves in perfumed, oriental gardens amidst peacocks, paradisal rivers, and blossoming trees under the full moon of an evening of love an aeon long. Other images and paintings suggest the somberer side of the things of God. The famous three faces from the Jagannath temple, part of the Krishna cultus, look like nightmarish primitive masks. Other illustrations show Krishna in earlier, more agressive incarnations—he may be lion-headed, ripping the entrails out of demons in scenes splattered with blood and gore.

In time, after the song and dancing has risen to an ecstatic climax, the offerings begin. Devotees gracefully swing lamps and censers and offer food before the principal images. Following this, an address is given by a young, sincere devotee. A meal, full of strange spicy and sweet vegetarian dishes, is served on paper plates, perhaps eaten with the fingers, Indian-style.

At the back of the room is a large throne-like chair, probably gold and velvet. A photo of a bald, long-faced man with wreaths of flowers around his neck, and the vertical marks of a Vishnu devotee on his forehead, rests in the empty chair. This is His Divine Grace A.C. Bhaktivedanta Swami Prabhupada, the "Spiritual Master" of the Society.

All of the Indian religious movements have behind them a powerful charismatic leader. Like most of the others, Swami Bhaktivedanta (born Abhay Charan De in 1896) was a Bengali of prominant and wealthy family, and received a Western education at the University of Calcutta. He studied under a leading Vishnuite swami as a youth, and was told by that master upon his death to spread Krishna consciousness to the English-speaking world. However, De spent thirty years in business before embarking upon this work in 1965 at the age of seventy. Stories are told of his arrival in America, virtually penniless, with nothing but zeal for his mission.

Bhaktivedanta did not come with precisely the same message or atti-tude as other swami envoys, and, in any case, his delay seems to have been no mistake, for his new gospel was clearly right for the sixties. The story is told by his followers that when he arrived in New York, and began working among the "hippies" and derelicts of the Bowery, he was taken to a reception with a group of other, established swamis, who told him that if he wished to be successful in America, he should wear Western clothes, eat meat, and stress the tolerant all-paths-lead-to-truth interpretation of Hinduism. But he went back to the Bowery. And he continued his work of training an order of Krishnaite devotees who follow four rules of conduct strictly: no eating of meat, fish, or eggs; no illicit sex; no intoxicants; and no gambling. They submit their lives in full obedience to the Spiritual Master, and are eager to proclaim that Krishna is the Supreme Lord, fully personal as well as impersonal, and that Vedantists and other impersonalists misrepresent Hinduism.

With this "hard line" Hinduism, Bhaktivedanta has established centers as flourishing as those of the older groups. The movement is based on the Chaitanya Krishnaite sect, which makes central the life and teachings of Chaitanya Mahaprabhu (1486–1533). Chaitanya is believed by his followers to be an incarnation of Radha and Krishna. Appearing as a devotee he exemplified a "fundamentalist" Krishnaism which exalts Krishna as the personal and supreme Lord, and teaches that devotional ecstasy is the surest way to burn away ignorance and karma, and to attain to supernal bliss. Although the great majority of ordinary Hindus are doubtless bhaktic devotionalists of one of the great deities, Chaitanya Krishnaism differs from other Vishnuite groups which hold Vishnu is the high god, and Krishna merely one incarnation of him. It differs from Vedantic Hinduism—hitherto most represented in the West—which holds all personal gods are but secondary manifestations or accommodations of the impersonal One.

The Krishna Consciousness Society maintains that the Vedas, *Bhagavad Gita,* and canonical lives of Krishna are literally and historically true. Krishna is the supreme personal Lord; he lives in a paradisal world. The souls of all individuals are eternal, and, though intended to love Krishna, are trapped in a series of material bodies owing to ignorance and sensory illusion. By love for Krishna the soul overcomes this identification with the temporary body and lives outside of karma. The devotee's acts are pure and no longer bring retribution. Devotionalism is higher to the Krishnaites than yogic or Vedantic meditation, or moralistic karma yoga, and definitely better than the much-criticized way of impersonalistic philosophy.

A bare doctrinal statement, however, does not reveal the transcendent beauty of Krishnaite devotion and belief. Its core is the accounts of Krishna's life on earth 5000 years ago. The secret meaning of its joyful dances and devotions is participation in the bliss of the milkmaids who loved him then. When Krishna was born in an infant's body in Vrindavan, he brought with him his eternal paradisical world, with all its jewel-like flowers, peacocks, and celestial devotees. For a short time, heaven dwelt before man's eyes in the midst of earth. As an infant, Krishna was as charming and exasperating as God, or the spiritual quest. As God sends earthquake and flood, so Krishna performed pranks like eating clay. But when his foster mother looked into his mouth to see if the clay was there, she saw instead the entire universe. On another occasion when she tried to tie him up, she found to her puzzlement that however much rope she uncoiled, there was never quite enough. In such charming ways, the *Srimad Bhagavatam* (life of Krishna) shows in the infant Krishna, and later in Krishna the mysterious lover whose flute-song in the moonlight draws the milkmaids from their homes to follow his revels, the incomprehensibility and seductive power of God.

To live for intoxication with this mystery, and to hope for rebirth on one of Krishna's paradisical worlds, is sufficient for devotees of the order. Like other alternative reality traditions, ancient and modern, the International Society for Krishna Consciousness is divided into an inner and outer circle. The inner circle leads in effect a monastic life, even though some members may be married. It is the monastic devotees, for the most part considered ministers or seminarians (following a two and one-half year curriculum), who wear the saffron robes and are most conspicuous. Some idea of their life can be gathered from the daily schedule:

3:45 A.M.	— rise, shower, and dress
4:30	— chant
5:45	— read about Krishna
8:30	— communal breakfast
9:00	— temple cleaning
10:00	— work; some to street chanting, some to incense factory, etc.
2:00 P.M.	— afternoon meal
3:00	— afternoon work
6:00	— second shower
7:00	— evening worship ceremony; chanting, dance, offering
10:00	— sleep

The details of the life are closely regulated by the Spiritual Master. He insists that each devotee take two showers daily, and take a cup of warm milk before retiring; these customs are scrupulously followed. There is to be no courtship or dating among devotees, but couples selected by the Spiritual Master may marry when that will advance the cause of Krishna. As in every other area of life, living above personal karma and desire in the freedom of Krishna's love is the important thing. But these arrangements have borne fruit, and it is striking to see tiny children living in the Krishnaite temples, taking part in the chanting and other communal activities. The most extensive Krishnaite commune is a farm in Texas where devotees live an idyllic rural, communal, devotional, and vegetarian life.

A series of initiations imparted by Swami Bhaktivedanta mark the movement by devotees from one stage to another. There are several hundred in the United States, and about 100 American devotees now in India, not so much to learn as to teach, for the Society is expanding its orthodoxy there. As for lay adherents, there are four grades of membership, depending on extent of financial support. But anyone who attends a temple service at least once a month is counted among the several thousand laity; the relationship is really informal and subjective. Many are friendly but perhaps unconvinced kin of devotees.

The group seems to be securely based economically. The Los Angeles branch recently purchased a large former Methodist church, which has become world headquarters, as well as home for its sixty members. The New York temple is even larger, and new temples are opened every year. Sources of income include the assets of those joining, the profits of the incense factory (now the second-biggest U.S. producer), and donations. At the feast every Sunday afternoon, one notices that while ordinary visitors usually contribute a dollar, the families of members may put in a five or ten dollar bill. Some members have outside jobs. The movement has attracted support from wealthy persons in India who have suddenly realized that it has brought worldwide attention to religious concepts precious to them.

The Krishnaite group seems, above all, a family. Although there may be some marriages, they are clearly secondary to the cohesion of the whole Krishnaite family. Most activities are done together; a member senses himself and his companions as a highly distinct body from the outside world. Swami Bhaktivedanta is like a father, and all others his children. The creation of a family, with play, child-like joy, communality, and a highly structured life with few individual decisions, is evident. Most members, like so many young people in our society, clearly want and need a new family, with ways in it for the perpetuation of happy, or wistful, childhood. A large number of persons in the community had previously been in drugs, the "hippie" life, and very chaotic moral and personal life styles. Many also had tried other Eastern religious movements, but found them less satisfactory.

It could be argued that no group breaks more thoroughly with more American values—religious, social, dietary, material—than Krishna Consciousness. But nothing is more disarming than the innocence, kindness, and inner joy of devotees. There is, of course, a "true believer" conviction, but it is not offensive unless one is unable to abide a few persons dancing and singing on the streets. The challenge is deeper than confrontation, and—in its love for a new (to us) image of a personal God—different from either social revolution or the impersonalist alternative reality tradition. Rather, here we see Krishna, the marvellous eternal, omnipotent, and wise child, whose delights never end.

Reading Selection: International Society for Krishna Consciousness

This passage, from one of the shorter of Swami Bhaktivedanta's many books, treats the central phenomenon of Krishna Consciousness, the great mantra. The word Hare *is a vocative form of the word for the energies of God.* Krishna *and* Rama *are both names of the supreme Lord.* Rama *belongs to an earlier divine descent from that of the marvellous Krishna. As Rama he was a heroic prince, and his deeds are described in the epic* Ramayana. *But in the mantra, all these showings of divinity are united in one attribution of praise.*

The transcendental vibration established by the chanting of HARE KRSNA, HARE KRSNA, KRSNA KRSNA, HARE HARE/HARE RĀMA, HARE RĀMA, RĀMA RĀMA, HARE HARE is the sublime method for reviving our transcendental consciousness. As living spiritual souls, we are all originally Krsna conscious entities, but due to our association with matter from time immemorial, our consciousness is now adulterated by the material atmosphere. The material atmosphere, in which we are now living, is called *māyā*, or illusion. *Māyā* means that which is not. And what is this illusion? The illusion is that we are all trying to be lords of material nature, while actually we are under the grip of her stringent laws. When a servant artificially tries to imitate the all-powerful master, it is called illusion. We are trying to exploit the resources of material nature, but actually we are becoming more and more entangled in her complexities. Therefore, although we are engaged in a hard struggle to conquer nature, we are ever more dependent on her. This illusory struggle against material nature can be stopped at once by revival of our eternal Krsna consciousness.

Hare Krsna, Hare Krsna, Krsna Krsna, Hare Hare is the transcendental process for reviving this original pure consciousness. By chanting this transcendental vibration, we can cleanse away all misgivings within; our hearts. The basic principle of all such misgivings is the false consciousness that I am the lord of all I survey.

Krsna consciousness is not an artificial imposition on the mind. This consciousness is the original natural energy of the living entity. When we hear the transcendental vibration, this consciousness is revived. This simplest method of meditation is recommended for this age. By practical experience also, one can perceive that by chanting this *mahāmantra,* or the Great Chanting for Deliverance, one can at once feel a transcendental ecstasy coming through from the spiritual stratum. In the material concept of life we are busy in the matter of sense gratification as if we were in the lower animal stage. A little elevated from this status of sense gratification, one is engaged in mental speculation for the purpose of getting out of the material clutches. A little elevated from this speculative status, when one is intelligent enough, one tries to find out the supreme cause of all causes—within and without. And when one is factually on the plane of spiritual understanding, surpassing the stages of sense, mind and intelligence, he is then on the transcendental plane. This chanting of the Hare Kṛṣṇa *mantra* is enacted from the spiritual platform, and thus this sound vibration surpasses all lower strata of consciousness—namely sensual, mental and intellectual. There is no need, therefore, to understand the language of the *mantra,* nor is there any need for mental speculation nor any intellectual adjustment for chanting this *mahamantra.* It is automatic, from the spiritual platform, and as such, anyone can take part in vibrating this transcendental sound without any previous qualification. In a more advanced stage, of course, one is not expected to commit offenses on grounds of spiritual understanding.

A. C. BHAKTIVEDANTA SWAMI, *Kṛṣṇa Consciousness: The Topmost Yoga System* (Boston: Iskcon Press, 1970), pp. 32–33.

---

6. The Satya Sai Baba Movement

The Satya Sai Baba is a new American religious movement whose founder and teacher has never been to the United States. But in these days of jets and intercontinental telephone, that matters little. Devotees from around the world can fly to India in a few hours, or exchange verbal communication instantaneously.

Not that such physical contact would be entirely necessary in this case, for the center of attention, a smiling and winning holy man in the south of India, is believed to be an *avatar,* a divine incarnation, of Krishna, and of Shiva and his *shakti* or consort. He is a wonder-worker to whom distance and natural law mean little. He embodies the same spontaneous, unassuming, effortless marvel and power as the child Krishna. There are other signs of his presence also—total aversion to meat and the slaughter of animals; childlike whimsy, humor, and charm; and almost pranksterish gaity mingled with deep insight and appeals to righteousness.

All of this seems to be brought together in a living man in India. A prominant lawyer says that Sai Baba cured him of Parkinson's disease with a wave of his hand. Sai Baba continually produces small objects, like rings, pictures of himself, statues of the gods, or prayer beads from out of the air to hand to visitors and devotees as talismans. He materializes out of his body an aromatic gray ash, called *vibhuti*. His followers treasure it as a token of the holy man, and as beneficial for healing and benediction. By now the saint must have distributed tons of the substance. Most remarkable of all, once a year on a festival of Shiva, Sai Baba produces from his mouth one or two small, oblong, stone *linga*—the symbol of Shiva.

Sai Baba was born on November 23, 1926 in a small village, Puttaparthi, in south India, and he has the flamboyance, religious fervor, and lithe grace of that region. As might be expected, stories are told of marvels at his birth. Musical instruments played of their own accord; a harmless cobra appeared under his bed. Even as a child, he could foretell the future and produce flowers and candy just by waving his hands. He also went through strange moods and seizures. He would be quiet, he would writhe like a terrifying deity; he would sing or proclaim that he saw gods passing across the sky. He was god-intoxicated, and no one knew what to make of him.

Then, on May 23, 1940, at the age of thirteen, the fey period—so like the shamanistic initiatory psychopathology—ended as the boy announced, "I am Sai Baba." That was the name in religion of a notable saint who had died in 1918. The new Sai Baba took the title and began to show signs of being a reincarnation of the old holy man. He materialized pictures and displayed knowledge and mannerisms of the former Sai Baba. Yet Sai Baba had lived in a part of India culturally and geographically remote from the tiny southern village where the young boy was brought up; it is not likely that anyone would have even heard of him in the new Sai Baba's obscure village.

In any case, from 1940 Sai Baba left school and all traces of ordinary life. He began his legendary miracles and his life amid his disciples and devotees as teacher and healer. The most famous of all the events occurred in 1963, the same year he declared himself an incarnation of Shiva and his *shakti* or consort as well as of Krishna. He suffered a stroke and four heart attacks, refused medical help, and then miraculously cured himself before an audience of 5,000 in his prayer hall.

In India, Sai Baba's work is no small-scale affair. His village has become a great pilgrimage center. Some 50,000 pour into it annually for festivals. His movement has built schools, dispensaries, and centers all over India. Sai Baba has attracted attention in the highest educational and intellectual circles, and counts leading public figures among his followers.

Even so, this is only prelude, according to Satya Sai Baba. His believers say that he is an avatar or "descent" of God, rather than just a holy man who by his asceticism and piety has become "God-realized," for the following reasons: there was no obvious period of preparation in his life, and an infinite power seems to flow effortlessly through him. Satya Sai Baba seems altogether of a different order from the "ordinary" enlightened man of holy India to his followers. But Sai Baba himself says that he is only the second of a series of three avatars. The first was the former Sai Baba, the second is himself; he will live to be ninety-eight. Then, eight years after his death, he will be reborn as the third avatar, Prema Sai Baba, who will complete the work and will fully manifest God in himself to the world.

So far he has not won the attention outside India that he has in his own country. Sai Baba and his mystique is a very Hindu kind of phenomenon, well understood and accepted by his compatriots, but more baffling perhaps than anything else to those in less fervent lands. Although he has gone to west Africa (where his triumphal tour was mainly among the Hindu population), he has not come to the West, despite many promises and postponed dates. For this reason, he has not emulated Vivekananada or Yogananda or Bhaktivedanta's successes.

But an informal and devoted movement centered around acceptance of Sai Baba's claims, and interest in his phenomena, is growing. In America, its effective leader is called Indra Devi. She is a white-haired lady of Russian birth who owns a yoga retreat on a ranch at Tecate, California, on the Mexican border, and a Sai Baba center in a large house on Sunset Boulevard in Los Angeles. The wife of a German doctor, Indra Devi has the grace and nobility of a European lady of the old school, together with a wispy, almost transparent purity, the result of much fasting and yoga. She lived for many years in India, and generally wears Indian clothes.

At the time of his revelation at thirteen, Sai Baba said "Worship me every Thursday," and that is the main day for activities at the several Sai Baba centers in the West. Usually there will be yoga classes, discussion, and *bhajan* or the chanting of devotional hymns to altars which include pictures of the saint. Books and magazines are available.

It is in hearing the conversation of Sai Baba enthusiasts, however, that the real spirit of the movement becomes evident. Many have been to India, and others are eager to go. Those who have been there tell story after story of the avatar's powers. They wear rings and show pictures materialized by him, and tell of remarkable healings, or prophecies, or ways in which inexplicable rescues from accidents seemed to involve the presence of relics, or even visions, of the saint. It is as though they were caught up in a different world, a world of grace and miracle different from ordinary America. And even more is expected of the future. The liberal press in India has, however, attempted to debunk the Sai Baba phenomena.

The religious teachings of Sai Baba are perhaps less remarkable than his miracles. In India he talks of reestablishing the authority of the Vedas and sounds, in Hindu terms, rather conservative. But he does not seem to feel that Vedantic orthodoxy need be expected of non-Hindus attracted to him. He emphasizes the values of vegetarianism and purity of diet and action characteristic of the Vishnuite tradition. He talks of the central function of the avatar, the restitution of *dharma* or divine law, but in fairly general terms. At his best he rises to the simplicity of the true mystic as he speaks of the love of God rather than of the world, which can never satisfy man's deepest yearnings.

Sai Baba is a vivid personality. He wears brilliant red robes, his dark smiling face looks oddly like a composite of every human race, his long black hair (which, it is said, no scissors can cut) wreathes around his head. In seeing films of him walking through rows of his devotees, healing, distributing *vibhuti*, teaching, one is struck by the thought that the scene suddenly makes the New Testament seem contemporary. He is the holy, charismatic, miraculous personality, walking the dusty roads of a peasant society full of sick and poverty-stricken yet eagerly believing people. We see this in the midst of the twentieth century, recorded on film. We will probably hear more of Satya Sai Baba.

Reading Selection: The Satya Sai Baba Movement

The passage below is by an American writer who devoted considerable time to investigating Sai Baba and his movement. He left Baba impressed with the strange and inexplicable physical and spiritual works he had seen wrought, but uncommitted as to interpretation of it. Here he describes his first meeting with Baba. The phenomenon described is typical of that recorded by countless persons who have been in his presence.

The writer heard of Baba during his first stay in India and through a friend, an Indian novelist, had arranged to meet him.

Baba, in his early forties, was slightly over five feet tall. He wore a bright orange silk dress that hung loosely down to his chunky bare feet; but the first thing one noticed was his Afro-electric hair standing straight out from all parts of his head like a black, kinky halo five or six inches wide. His coloring was the soft beige of a Brahmin. He spoke gently and with great sweetness to each of the seven people in the room, but did not reveal anything about anyone's past or future. He confined his remarks to platitudes about God, love, and devotion. Then, just before Baba ended the audience, he materialized a ruby ring, which he gave to the novelist, and a handful of ashes, which he gave to a woman in the group. Baba was talking to someone else on the other side of the room when suddenly he had stopped in the middle of a sentence and turned to the woman.

"I will cure your appendicitis," he said, as he materialized ashes. "Take this in water three days."

She had suffered an attack of appendicitis the night before and was in great pain. No one had mentioned her attack.

She followed his instructions and three days later, when the pain had completely disappeared, she had two reputable doctors in another town examine her thoroughly. Neither of them could find any trace of appendicitis.

7. Hindu Afterword

The movements we have discussed are not the only Hindu movements and leaders to find some following in the West. The great modern saint Sri Ramana Maharshi, who taught a sort of existentialist Vedanta based on asking in meditation the question, "Who am I?" has attracted interest. Richard Alpert, formerly associated with Timothy Leary in the promotion of LSD, has now given it up in favor of a yogic *sadhana* ("You stay high without ever having to come down") given him by a guru in the Himalayas, and is now Baba Ramdass. He is a very popular figure on college campuses. His headquarters is a commune called Lama in New Mexico. Still more strands in the American Hindu web could be cited.

What they all have in common is a central charismatic figure who seems, in a manner little encountered in the West, to personify a certain spiritual path—both means and goal. It is this immanental divine—not in pantheistic theory, but in persons—which makes India endlessly intringuing, for all its practical squalor, to God-seekers. Slowly, however, the dependence upon teachers able to accommodate and syncretize has lessened in the West, as a thirst in some for the wholeness of Indian culture has grown.

If Christianity, with its concern for justification by faith, for worldly vocation, and for social ethics is partly a religion for those not religious, Hinduism is a religion for the naturally religious. It is for those who take sheer delight in religion's color, festivities, and devotional fervor, in pleasing gorgeous gods, in dreaming of the most opulent heavens conceived by man, in the grim romance of asceticism, and in the deep waters of meditation. It is for such people that Hinduism does work appreciable changes of consciousness. So long as there are those naturally religious, as well as those naturally secular, Hinduism with its mysterious gods and masters will not be without those in all lands who are fascinated by its transpersonal charm.

Notes

1 Swami Prabhavananda and Frederick Manchester, trans., *The Upanishads: Breath of the Eternal* (New York: The New American Library, Mentor Books, 1961), pp. 123–25. Copyright © 1957 by the Vedanta Society of Southern California.

2 Paramahansa Yogananda, *Metaphysical Meditations.* (Copyright © 1964, Self-Realization Fellowship, 3880 San Rafael Avenue, Los Angeles, California 90065), p. 36.

3 See Charles T. Tart, "A Psychologist's Experience with Transcendental Meditation," *Journal of Transpersonal Psychology,* 2 (1971), 135–40; Robert Keith Wallace, "Physiological Effects of Transcendental Meditation," *Science,* 167 (March 27, 1970), 1751–54; Robert Keith Wallace and Herbert Benson, "The Physiology of Meditation," *Scientific American,* February 1972, pp. 85–90; Anthony Campbell, M.D., *Seven States of Consciousness: A Vision of Possibilities Suggested by the Teaching of Maharishi Mahesh Yogi* (New York: Harper Torchbooks, 1973).

4 Mircea Eliade, "Nights at Serampore," in *Two Tales of the Occult,* trans. William Ames Coates (New York: Herder & Herder, 1970), pp. 3–60.

5 See J.-M. Déchanet, *Christian Yoga* (New York: Harper & Row, Publishers, 1960).

eight

the east in the golden west:
other oriental movements

This chapter offers a discussion of a collection of groups based on non-Hindu sources. Three are Buddhist, three are primarily mystical Muslim in inspiration, one is an unusual oriental version of Christianity. Their geographical origin is even more diverse: Japan, India, Iran, Indonesia, Korea, and Tibet.

But this collection of non-Hindu oriental movements has certain points in common. While they all have charismatic leadership, no one has been able to equal the Hindus (especially the Bengalis) in fascinating Americans by sheer force of personality and in sweeping all before them amid waves of publicity. These non-Hindu movements have been sometimes less centered on one personality. They have flourished mainly by reason of the appeal of the actual technique or philosophy of the movement, and have been propagandized more by convinced westerners in the West than by their Eastern advocates.

It would first be well to examine Buddhism and Islam with a view to understanding what it is in them which has made movements based on their experience appealing to some Americans.

Buddhism can be considered an "export version" of Hinduism in the same sense that Christianity is of Judaism. It encapsulates in the saving experience of a single member of that tradition its universal essence. But both new export religions do not bring with them whole societal and cultic traditions, such as the caste system and Brahman sacrifices in Hinduism. For the Buddha, the essential experience was that of *anatman*, or "no self." This term puts in convenient negative form the basic Upanishadic discovery of the unity of the self with the universal,

251

Brahman. The Buddha discovered during the night of his enlightenment, as he sat under the fig tree vowing not to move from there until he had obtained the object of his quest, that man's sense of being an independent separate self is the product, not of experience of reality, but of anxieties created by blind needs and desires. Man is actually just a collection of elements. In the Buddha's dying words, "All aggregates are transitory." But there is hope, hope keener than the seeming despair of this analysis and sharper than desire. By mindfulness of ego illusion one can live in freedom and unconditionedness, swimming in the tides of the universal. One can be an expression of the universal, as adamantine and joyful and fearless as the Whole.

All Buddhist techniques are ultimately means of "turning on" this kind of consciousness. Anything that can stop for a moment the "monkey mind" and give one even a flash of what is left when the anxiety-desire syndrome is halted is precious. Therefore valuable is the numinous wonder of a cool, dark, incense-laden Buddhist temple, with its other-worldly glittering gold lotuses and inward-gazing image; the deep frenzy of Tibetan visualizing of strange Buddhas and gods; the silence of the Zen meditator cut off from external sensual stimuli; the powerful steady chanting of "Nam Myoho Renge Kyo" by adherents of Nichiren Shoshu.

Most modern Westerners who have been interested in following Buddhist practices have taken up with Mahayana, the Buddhism of China, Tibet, and Japan. This great tradition puts most emphasis not on the historical Buddha but on the universal presence of the "Buddha-nature" in every blade of grass and every grain of sand and every sentient being. The Buddha-nature is really an ontologizing of the Buddha's enlightenment experience. It is the true nature of reality, which he let irradiate his being at that moment. Because the Buddha-nature is present everywhere, it can be realized as a man's true nature at any moment, whenever he loosens his grasp on ego-illusions. To aid in this realization, the universe is seen as continuous with the ground of the mind. The universe is visualized as full of Buddhas and Bodhisattvas (beings in enlightenment-consciousness who operate in this world at the same time), who are, as it were, projections of the ideal or enlightened self. Creation of such figures who have psychological rather than historical or "out there" reality, of course, is an important part of the "esoteric" Buddhism of Tibet and some other places. Chanting, rituals, and yogic psychosomatic exercises are among the techniques used to make the "meditation" Buddhas appear.

This tradition employs the archetypes and images of the mind—the same which appear in myth and dream—as doorways into the state of consciousness in which burdensome selfhood disappears. Another popular tradition, Zen, takes an opposite tack. It teaches that all such conceptualizations only perpetuate the structures of self, and that one must be able to break through all forms and images. One can do this through "sitting quietly doing nothing," or by the psychological tension created by the *sesshin,* or intensive Zen training session. The *sesshin* participant barely eats or sleeps for several days. He practices meditation, and has often painful interviews with the *roshi,* or master, through the long days. Finally, the tension builds up until, like water breaking over a dam, he suddenly is struck by the surprise of *satori,* the awareness of seeing things on the Buddha-nature level.

These are all ways of capturing the secure joy of being in tune with ultimate Oneness. The other major religion which lies behind the groups under consideration in this chapter, Islam, is also profoundly concerned with Oneness, but in a very different way. In Islam psychological and cosmic Oneness mean setting to rights the relationship of two entities, the omnipotent personal God and the individual, through submission of man to God, a submission deepened by the exchange of love.

The fundamental tenet of Islam, proclaimed every day by the muezzin from the minaret of every mosque, is that there is no god but God ("Allah" is "The God" in Arabic) and Muhammad is his Prophet, or Envoy. Islam (which means "submission," submission to the absolute will of God) is a supreme example of the emissary style of religious communication. Muhammad is emphatically human. He was selected by God as his final prophet solely by God's will and not on the basis of any great psychic or mystical recommendations, even though orthodox Muslims almost incidentally talk of him as a paragon of virtue.

Nonetheless, the powerful emphasis on the singleness and omnipotence of God gave rise to currents in Islam capable of making contact with the alternative reality tradition in the West, especially as Islam encountered Hellenism, Zoroastrianism, and India on its fringes. On one hand, the tremendousness of the Muslim God encouraged great concern about the legitimacy of lines of communication between this mighty being and ordinary men. Muslim arguments about true *imams,* prophets, and masters provided some fuel for the speculative flames of Theosophy, and also provided prophesies and models for teachers of new gospels like Baha'u'llah of Baha'i and Meher Baba. On the other hand, the greatness and personality of the Islamic God favored a type of mysticism called Sufism marked by yearning, freedom, ecstasy, and awareness of immediacy expressed exquisitely in its classical literature through the language of love and intoxication.

These two traditions often interacted in the Shi'ite Islam of Iran and neighboring areas. That land was one homeland of Shi'ite eschatologists and Sufi mystics. Shi'ah taught that an infallible human teacher is needed to interpret Islam, and that he should be found in the descendents of Ali, Muhammad's cousin. Ali was brought up by the Prophet, married his daughter Fatimah, and was his constant companion. But after the death of Muhammad there was no peace between the heirs of this lineage, the *imams,* and the politico-religious leaders of two successive dynasties called caliphs who usually held the actual power in the expanding Muslim Empire. Indeed, the first eleven *imams* all died violently; the death of the third, Husain, is mourned annually by Shi'ite Muslims with rites of wailing so fervently emotional as to be reminiscent of the ancient wailing for Tammuz or Osiris, and to have seasonal-soteriological overtones.

Against the background of this dark and tragic scenario of the fate which befell the family of the envoy of God, Shi'ah believes that the twelfth *imam,* who was not murdered but who disappeared, is still living. For sixty-nine years he was in hiding, but communicated to the faithful through four ambassadors; he then went into a great hiding, and sent no ambassadors. But he is the Coming One, the *Imam* for all time, and will reappear when the world is full of evil. One can readily understand that this kind of teaching could blend easily into belief in secret Masters, and charge the air with electric apocalyptic expectation. The flavor of Shi'ah's belief in infallible teachers, true though hidden succession, and new revelation is carried over directly in Baha'i, and has deeply tinctured other mysteries of central Asian background, including Theosophy, for the lands where knowledge of the hidden *Imam* were rife were probably among those through which the young Madame Blavatsky wandered.

The Sufis also believed that a hidden hierarchy of saints ruled the world of Islam. This authority was for them based more on spiritual attainment and occult transmission than physical descent from the Prophet. Sufis in the Shi'ite areas claimed that a special secret knowledge of the inner meaning of Islam was passed from Muhammad through Ali and the *Imams.* This tradition was more mystical than the outer husks of the Koranic law.

The further east from its Arabian homeland Islam moved, by and large, the more mystical in temper it became. The lush, tropical islands of Indonesia, with their graceful, smiling people, are in sharp contrast to Saudi Arabia. Although they are predominantly Muslim, it is an Islam modified by an animistic, Hindu, and Buddhist past. Sufism found fertile ground in the islands' pantheistic milieu. Like Sufis, especially dervishes, everywhere, many Indonesian orders have produced religious ecstasy by shouting loud rhythmic praises of Allah, jumping, and dancing strange circular dances. In Java, some members of Sufi orders even stabbed themselves with iron daggers at the height of the ecstasy. Against this background, one can well understand the emergence of the techniques of Subud.

In general the transmittal of these non-Hindu Eastern teachings to the West has been conditioned by two factors: (1) They have made their distinctive experience independent and absolute. They say, in other words, that the truth of their expression of Buddhism or Islam is more important than Buddhism or Islam itself, and of unconditioned universal validity. This makes them rather heterodox in their homelands, but gives them great universality and makes them able to become part of the alternative reality tradition in the West. (2) An unusual teacher or special set of historical circumstances has made transmittal to the West possible.

Tibet, Meher Baba, and Subud come West in part because something in the troubled Western psyche needs them in the same way it needs the alternative reality tradition. The new gospel of Baha'i does not come to the West to communicate Shi'ite Islam, which on its conscious level is no part of it, but because we also need a new messiah and a vision of world unity, and find this movement so detached from its cultural sources as to convince us of its claim to universality.

1. Western Zen

Zen today is not quite as big a symbol of the spiritual counter-culture as it was in the fifties, before LSD and maharishis and astrology had come forward to share the new milieu with it. Indeed, something in the cold water austerity and hard antisymbolism of Zen was incompatible with the luxuriant surrealist fancy of the sixties. But in an earlier day, when "beatniks" talked philosophy over cheap wine in dreary flats unadorned by psychedelic posters, Zen seemed the chief religious token of a total reversal of Western values. It was the day of Kerouac's *Dharma Bums*, whose heroes wandered the littered American hinterland seeing the crown of ten-wondered Avalokiteshvara in the stars and the laughing cosmic Buddha-nature in the heart of the drabbest railway tramp. There were some who were more than just romantics in the Kerouac style. Some went to Japan to practice; some started serious Zen meditation halls in the United States, often under the supervision of master brought from Japan; some underwent the gruelling spiritual marathon of the *sesshin*.

I once attended a typical Thursday-evening *zazen*, or seated meditation, at an American center of the Rinzai denomination of Zen. The *roshi* or master was from a Japanese monastery, but most of the members of this center were Caucasian. Some were students at nearby universities, usually in Asian studies, who lived a communal life in the center and were intending to become Zen monks or priests. Most were persons in the city who come to "sit" fairly often, and to receive guidance from the *roshi*.

As I crossed the flagstoned courtyard of the center, I was met by a courteous European-accented lady who, rightly taking me for a newcomer, instructed me to enter the hall, bow to the image of the Buddha on the altar, and take a seat on one of the two rows of mats on either side of the hall. This I did, sitting cross-legged with spine erect, and eyes pointed toward the floor three feet in front of me. With some thirty other people, I sat in this manner for half an hour. A proctor, one of the students, walked around the hall with a stick on his shoulder. When he saw someone whose mindfulness seemed to be lagging, or whose posture was poor (often the case with me), he would sound the stick sharply on the floor before him, or if it was a stable and experienced member who requested it, would administer a smart but harmless blow on the shoulder.

At the end of a half hour, everyone silently arose, moved to the courtyard, and snaked around it at a half-running pace hands folded for a minute or two, then returned. There was another half hour of meditation, exercise, and then another.

I was then asked if I would like to have an interview with the *roshi*. I said that I would, and was led to a small anteroom. A low table, with a gong on it, was the only piece of furniture; three or four persons were seated on the floor in *zazen* posture beside the table. Beyond this room was the *roshi* in a private audience hall. When he had finished with an interviewee, he rang a bell. The next in line responded by sounding the gong in the audience hall. He would then enter, kowtow (bow touching the forehead to the floor) to the *roshi* as he entered his room, and kowtow once again just before him.

The small, round Zen master, seated high on a vast cushion, wearing a sashed and starchy-winged gown of old Japan, toying with a Japanese fan, greeted me gravely. He took a note of introduction from me.

"So," he said, eyeing me shrewdly, "You're a professor of religion. Do you believe in God?"

Stumbling around, having no real idea how one expressed such things to a Zen master, I tried to say something about my belief in God as the ground of my being and the universe's.

I was cut short. I felt a surprising sting as the master slapped me on the thigh with his folded fan, and said "Not good! NOW how do you believe in God?"

This time I stumbled even more. "Perhaps in the immediacy of the experience..."

"Not good!" he retorted, slapping me again with the fan. "This is your Zen koan. Meditate on it. NOW how do you believe in God?"

The Zen koan is a puzzle-like conundrum (famous ones are "Where was your face before you were born?" "What is the sound of one hand clapping?") designed to bring the mind up against a stoppage of its rational machination, and move it into the empty and marvellous void of enlightenment. I thought I knew what this one, "NOW how do you believe in God?" meant: How do you rub against God in the immediate NOW? Not in reflection upon study or experience of God two years, or two seconds, ago; not in anticipation of God's future disclosures, but NOW, in the flashing moment before the dimensionless NOW has escaped into memory and reflection and its content become thereby twisted into words and concepts, where is God?

I ruminated upon this for a time after a return to the *zazen* position, in the main hall, and tried to push my mind beyond the verbal boxes into which we put all experiences as soon as we are aware we are having them, or only a split-second later. Then I began, if only dimly, to have some feeling of the potential of Zen enlightenment.

I sensed a timeless euphoria. I was lightly floating, as though I might be a half-inch above the mat. All times except the NOW fell away, like something seen through the wrong end of a telescope. I might have been in that Zen meditation hall two hours, which was actually the case, or two weeks, or two years, or two centuries; it didn't matter and wouldn't have felt much different whichever it was. This was my life, the center of my being. I remembered, as a small child, going out in the back yard, lying under the peony bushes. I imagined that I was floating in the midst of black, empty space, with only stars and planets as companions, and that my house, my family, and my life were only a story I was telling myself.

But soon enough this meditation was over, tea was served, and the *roshi* came out to give an address, translated by a Japanese-American member of the group. (The interpreter is a simple gardener by day, but some in the temple say he is a bodhisattva.) Finally, the evening ended with the chanting, in Japanese, of the Heart Sutra. ("Form is emptiness, and emptiness is form...The wisdom that has gone beyond, and beyond the beyond; O what an awakening, all hail!")

On a later occasion, when I told about this experience in speaking to a church group, a medical doctor said to me afterwards that this experience wasn't necessarily "spiritual." The euphoria and timelessness were probably results of the cutting off the circulation in my legs by the unaccustomed posture; Doubtless this is true, but a Zen master would probably have said, "So what?" If man is a unity of mind and body, set over against the One, what difference does it make how much one part of the unity helps the other to realize the One? The spiritual quest is not a battle of spirit against flesh in the East, but a struggle of each to find the other and thereby the Whole. If an experience of the Ecstasy of the One is induced in part by physiological means, does this make it any less "valid"?

The point of Zen is to induce an experience which stops the activity of the "monkey mind," with its continual bouncing from one thing to another. Anything which throws sand in the mind's gears, which brings the mind up against a blank wall, is to the point. It can be counting breaths (from one to ten), merely maintaining mindfulness of breathing, following thoughts until they dissipate like soap bubbles, reflecting on the koans.

This experience is central to Zen, but, of course, its popularity in America depends on more than that. Zen is also a delight in the strange stories told about the old Zen masters, juicy with whimsy and fierce joy. There is, among many Western Zen enthusiasts, a desire to adopt a culture as well as a faith in their passion for the tea ceremony, the painting and architecture and gardens of Zen. In all of these forms the essence which represents the One in it is reached through taking away all that is superfluous and "unnatural." A bird on a bamboo is represented by a half-dozen strokes of the brush. The whole of Buddhism is capsulized in a *haiku* poem:

> An old pond;
> A frog jumps in:
> The sound of water.

And in the art of swordsmanship as taught by masters steeled in Zen, the adept is supposed to be able to cause his opponent to flee without striking a blow, simply by the poise of his pose and visage.

The Buddhist Society of America, called after World War II the First Zen Institute of America, was founded in New York in 1930 by Shigetsu Sasaki (1882–1945), called Sokei-an. The struggling center made some impression and published a delightful periodical, *Cat's Yawn*,[1] until the *roshi* was imprisoned during the War. He was released in 1943, but died before peace was reestablished with his homeland. His widow, an American, Ruth Fuller Sasaki (1893–1967), continued the work. After the New York Center had been well launched in postwar American culture, she moved permanently to Japan. Her labor toward establishing Western Zen on a firm basis of commitment, scholarship, and discipline was indispensable.

The postwar Zen boom, however, was too explosive to be attributed to one line of transmission. The greatest influence was probably not any Western Zen center, but the writing of D. T. Suzuki (1870–1966). The almost countless books on Buddhism and Zen he authored in English, and also those of his American wife, Beatrice Lane Suzuki, and of those westerners who learned Zen from him—Edward Conze, Hubert Benoit, Christmas Humphreys, Alan Watts—have in very large part been Zen as it has appealed to the West. The intense intellectual interest in Zen in the fifties can be traced directly to Suzuki's lectures in Columbia University early in the decade. The strengths (universality, psychological awareness, freedom) of Zen in the West, and also its weaknesses (limited concern for the actual practice of monastic Zen in the East, impatience with discipline) stem from his and his disciples' predilections.

One counterbalance has now come forward in Philip Kapleau's book, *The Three Pillars of Zen*.[2] For him, Zen is less a romantic or existential or crypto-psychoanalytic experience than a hard monastic discipline, even when experienced by laymen. He stresses, unlike Suzuki and Watts, the techniques of sitting and the ordeal of the *sesshin*, and insists that the true fruits of Zen cannot be attained without them.

Out of all this, there are now ten or twelve serious Zen centers in the United States, with legitimately trained masters, including Kapleau's in Rochester and the Rinzai Center I attended in Los Angeles. The largest is undoubtedly the San Francisco Zen Center, with hundreds of students, many resident, in its four locations in the Bay Area. It operates the already-legendary Zen Mountain Center at Tassajara Hot Springs, in the rugged country east of Big Sur. Almost as hard to reach as *satori*, the Center was once a fashionable hot springs resort. The hills are steep, the forests deep and murmuring, the moon large and bright as in ancient myth.

Zen students come to Tassajara to spend several months combining work and meditation and recreation under the direction of the *roshi*. They eat simple but delicious organic vegetarian food, and sit in front of blank brick walls. The *roshi* asks meditators to count breaths for forty minutes without losing count (not easy!) before doing more. In the meantime, nature and time move at different rates than in the city. The 1969 "Tassajara Calendar, Herbal & Bestiary" records such events as:

February—Canyon Wrens sing
        lots of thrushes
        some lavender Shooting Stars
March 19—planted—Chard, green and red.
        Suzuki Roshi: "When it is hot we are hot Buddhas.
        When it is cold we are cold Buddhas."

Mid-June—a desert dryness
>Scattered on the hills Yucca plants send up phallic green
>stalks from the middle of spiked fortresses, then burst into
>tall candles of pure white flowers blazing in the Sun, glowing
>under the Full Moon.

Reading Selection:　Western Zen

*Of many writings by Westerners who have experienced "the taste of
Zen," perhaps this account of an experience of* kensho, *the breakthrough
to enlightenment, best catches its potentialities.* Dokusan *is the interview
between the* roshi *or master and the student.* Mu, *"nothingness" or the
wondrous void, was the* koan *or riddle-like word to focus meditation
given this lady, an American schoolteacher. The experiences took place
during a* sesshin, *or period of intensive Zen practice.*

The morning of the fifth day I stayed home to take care of the children.
I should mention that neither my husband nor I attended sesshin full
time. We took turns going to the 4 A.M. sitting and went home for almost
all meals. I stayed overnight once, my husband not at all.

A little embarrassed at dokusan that afternoon, I confessed that I had
not done zazen at home because of too many interruptions. I was told
that two people had already reached kensho and that if I exerted myself
to the utmost, I could also get kensho. So that night my husband allowed
me to stay overnight.

With Mu I went to bed, with Mu I arose the sixth day. "Don't get
nervous," Tai-san cautioned, "just concentrate." I listened to these words
of wisdom, but was too tired to meditate. My energies were drained. After
breakfast I lay down to rest, doing Mu in a horizontal position, when
suddenly a glow appeared in front of my eyes as though sunshine were
hitting them directly. I clearly heard sounds I had not heard since I was
a little girl sick in bed: my mother's footsteps and the rustling of her
boxes. Having had so many strange experiences already at this sesshin,
I paid no further heed but continued my concentration on Mu throughout the entire morning's sitting. As I was awaiting dokusan a familiar
aroma tantalized my nostrils; it was the tempting smell of my mother's
cooking. My eyes glanced at a red cushion on a brown table, the same
colors of my grandmother's living-room furniture. A door slammed, a
dog barked, a white cloud sailed through a blue sky—I was reliving my
childhood in makyo, hallucinations.

At noon, with the roshi's permission, my husband told me that he
had achieved kensho. "Now or never!" I told myself. "A pumpkin wife
cannot be married to an enlightened husband!" I vividly recalled the

story of the youth with the knife and incense. "Death or deliverance!" became my watchword.

I inhaled deeply and with each exhalation concentrated with all my might on Mu. I felt as though I were all air and would levitate any second. I "crawled" into the belly of a hideous, hairy spider. "Mu! Mu! Mu!" I groaned, and I became a big, black Mu. An angel, it seemed, touched me ever so softly on the shoulder, and I fell backwards. Suddenly I realized that my husband and Tai-san were standing behind me, but I could not move; my feet were absolutely numb. They practically carried me outside, and I sobbed helplessly. "I was already dead," I said to myself. "Why did they have to bring me back to life?" At dokusan the roshi told me that this was but a foretaste of kensho, it was not yet realization.

Then I took a little walk and suddenly the whole experience of the last few days seemed utterly ridiculous to me. "That stupid roshi," I remember thinking, "he and his Oriental hocus-pocus. He just doesn't know what he's talking about." At dinner, half an hour later, as I was fumbling with my chopsticks, I felt like getting up and handing him a fork. "Here, old boy, let's get used to Western ways." I giggled at my own joke. Throughout the evening chanting I could hardly keep a straight face. After the roshi's final words I wanted to pick up my bag and walk out, never to return, so unreal did it all seem.

In his first lecture the roshi had told us that Mu was like a red-hot ball stuck in the throat which one can neither swallow nor spit out. He was right, so right. As I look back, every word, every move was part of the deliberate plan of this venerable teacher. His name, "White Cloud" [Hakuun], indeed fits him. He is the greatest, whitest cloud I have ever experienced, a real antidote to the dark atomic mushroom.

Now I was in bed, doing zazen again. All night long I alternately breathed Mu and fell into trances. I thought of the monk who had reached kensho in just such a state of fatigue. Eventually I must have dozed off in complete exhaustion. Suddenly the same light angel touched me on the shoulder. Only this time I awoke with a bright "Ha!" and realized I was enlightened. The angel was my kind, tired husband tapping me on the shoulder to waken me to go to sesshin.

A strange power propelled me. I looked at the clock—twenty minutes to four, just in time to make the morning sitting. I arose and calmly dressed. My mind raced as I solved problem after problem. I arrived at the sesshin before four o'clock and accepted an offer of coffee with such a positive "Yes" that I could not believe my own ears. When Tai-san came around with his "sword" I told him not to bother hitting me. At dokusan I rushed into the little cottage my teacher was occupying and hugged and kissed him and shook Tai-san's hand, and let loose with such a torrent of comical verbosity that all three of us laughed with delight. The roshi tested and passed me, and I was officially ushered through the gateless gate.

A lifetime has been compressed into one week. A thousand new sensations are bombarding my senses, a thousand new paths are opening before me. I live my life minute by minute, but only now does a warm love pervade my whole being, because I know that I am not just my little self but a great big miraculous Self. My constant thought is to have everybody share this deep satisfaction.

I can think of no better way to end this account than with the vows I chanted at sesshin every morning:

> All beings, however limitless, I vow to save.
> Fantasy and delusion, however endless, I vow to cut off.
> Dharma teachings, however immeasurable, I vow to master.
> Buddha's Way, however lofty, I vow to attain.

PHILIP KAPLEAU, *The Three Pillars of Zen*
(New York and Tokyo: John Weatherhill, Inc.,
1965), pp. 243–45.

---

2. Esoteric Buddhism in America

In Mahayana Buddhism there flow two great and seemingly contrary currents. One streams toward emphasizing the vastness and depth and richness of cosmic reality, the other toward stressing the amazing ease and availability of salvation. According to both, Buddhist salvation is simply seeing the Buddha-nature which is there all the time, in pure consciousness and in every grain of sand and every blade of grass. The Zen form of the second stream tells us that since the Buddha-nature is simple and indivisible, salvation must be a sudden, unexpected experience beyond all symbols, words, and concepts.

The other current flows strongest in what is called Tantric or Esoteric Buddhism. It is the Buddhism of Tibet, Mongolia, and certain denominations of China and Japan. In this Buddhism the mystery and diversity of the path become a participation in the transcendence of the luminous void. It is a Buddhism of the affirmation of images and the frenzy of evocation, of the use of the structures and archetypes of emotionality and consciousness in a quite sophisticated way as dynamic vehicles to propel the adherent along the path to Totality. What Zen would call hallucinations to be disregarded, Tibet would regard as aspects of the mind and (which is the same thing) of the Buddha-nature, to be controlled, exploited, and integrated in order to make a mind really in charge of itself and therefore able to release itself into the nearness and vastness of the One Mind.

I had a vivid impression of the distinction in mood between these two approaches when, while in Japan, I visited in sequence a famous Zen monastery in Kyoto, and then the main monasteries of two sects grounded in the other tradition: Mt. Hiei monastery of the Tendai sect and Mt. Koya of the Shingon sect. The Zen monastery was very attractive with its little gardens and teahouses and priceless paintings and wonderful simplicity and ease with nature. But there was also something on Mt. Hiei and Mt. Koya I missed in Zen. The two mountaintops were crowned with dark forests, and under the gnarled trees lay one ancient temple building after another. Each summit was virtually a Buddhist panorama suggesting many alternative routes to the experience beyond paths and names—here a temple to Vairocana, the Sun Buddha representing the cosmic essence; there one to Amitabha, the Lord of the Western Paradise; another to Kannon, the bodhisattva who is the so-called "goddess of mercy." The cultus of some of the temples suggested deep metaphysical broodings, others the moving simplicity of folk religion. But the cumulative feeling of the esoteric centers was wild and infinite. They were places high in the mountains, amid real and not contrived forests, deep and mysterious, with roaring streams, swayed by a sharp and cold wind from distant seas and high places. Beside these dark and mystic temples, full of magic and occult rites, Zen for the moment seemed a little tame—some old bachelors just drinking tea and sitting in a garden at the bottom of the mountain in the city, while the weird heights remained above.

Nurtured in the Himalayas, Esoteric Buddhism is intertwined with a lively sense of the spiritual meaning of mountains. Its great centers are atop mountains, and it is into the mountains that its adepts go to battle with spiritual entities and emerge victorious. Clearly, the mountain represents the other world; it is where spiritual reality is much closer to solidification, where divine visions and possessions are easier, psychic powers enhanced, and enlightenment states frequent. The mountain is the *axis mundi*, the center of a world of sacral geography where there is access to the time of myth and the reality beyond time.

In northern Japan I visited the living culture of the Yamabushi or "mountain priests" of the Shugendo tradition of Esoteric Buddhism at Mt. Haguro. The adepts of this order, farmers most of the time, at seasonal festivals storm gaily up the mountain to perform vigorous and sacred rites. In the fall a repeatable initiation is held. At the beginning of autumn they participate in a ritual scenario whose symbols and acts represent conception, life in the womb, and the agony and exuberance of birth. Thereafter, ascetics are confined in a lodge on the top of the mountain for a hundred days to prepare spiritually for the new year's rites. At New Year's, dramatic rites are enacted in the dark and the snow. There is a benediction for the coming year by a giant rabbit, a rabbit dance, lighting a new fire, a tug-of-war, and a race of great flaming sledges. Many of the activities require dividing the order into two competitive sides. In all this, ancient mythological motifs are worked into the customs of an Esoteric Buddhist order. The rabbit represents the god of near-by Mt. Gassan, whose name in turn means "Mountain of the Moon." The competition reflects very old ideas of New Year's as a time of chaos and renewal, of rivalry between old and new, light and darkness. Yet the seasonal rites are also marked by the building of a great fire, the *goma*, whose logs represent the bones of the Buddha's body; making it, doing gestures and chanting mantras over it, extinguishing it, have all deep Buddhist meaning—purification, becoming a bodhisattva in this body.[3]

This may all seem remote from America. But after returning from Japan, while visiting at the Tassajara Zen center I saw a curious notice in some American Buddhist newsletter. It told about an Esoteric Buddhist mountaineering group based in San Francisco, and even included a photo of them in real Yamabushi garb ascending one of the Sierras.

Fascinated, I contacted the leader of the group, Mr. Penchakov-Warwick, and later called at the headquarters. It was in his apartment, which was practically consumed by the paraphernalia of the cultus. The troupe is called Kailas Shugendo, appropriately combining the Tibetan and Japanese redactions of Esoteric Buddhism, for Mt. Kailas is the most sacred peak of Tibet, and Shugendo is the title of the mountain tradition in Japan. Around the walls of the main room in the apartment were brilliantly colored paintings of Buddhas and bodhisattvas in the Tibetan manner. The altar at one end was lavish with candles and silver vessels, and was laden with offerings of fruit and rice. There was a fire-pit in the center of the room.

Nearly every evening, ten or twelve people gather around the fire-pit for the *goma* or fire ritual. The room is heavy with incense; the participants are resplendent in checked black and white, with cloth halters and red pom-poms, men and women alike. Offerings are made at the shrine; the wood for the tiny fire is cut with a ritual sword; sutras and mantras are chanted in the amazingly deep-throated Tibetan manner, or in the high fast Japanese style, growing faster and faster to the accompaniment of bells and clappers, as the intensity of the rite grows. The fire is lit. Finally, sweat of fervor streaming from his face, the master passes his hands rapidly through the fire in swift mudra gestures of identification with invincible bodhisattvas.

The founder of this group and its master or *acharya*, Mr. Penchakov-Warwick, states that his grandfather, a Russian of Kalmuk (central Asian Buddhists of Esoteric Buddhist tradition) connections, visited Japan in the nineteenth century and brought back some Shugendo practices. He left Russia at the time of the revolution. He says that he studied theology at the Sorbonne, and travelled with his grandfather to Tibet. Later, he was himself initiated into several esoteric mountain traditions in Japan, including the thousand-day "confinement" for esoteric work on top of Mt. Ontake. There is no doubt that he is remarkably well informed about the ritual, asceticism, and mysticism of the tradition.

Every weekend the group goes to a mountain to practice, for a brief "confinement," the usages of the mountain saints in their proper environment. They do *hi-watari*, or walking on hot coals, *suigyo*, standing under ice-cold water, and the like, developing the power of endurance required by intense concentration and recitation of mantras. A ten-year training program is envisioned, to be climaxed by an American thousand-day mountaintop confinement.

Kailas Shugendo's combination of the mountain mystique with Buddhism is evident. Adherents say that above 8000 feet one can begin to feel the sacredness of the mountain, and ask if we can recover the feeling for sacred mountains which the Indians and Asiatics had. They already (like the many enthusiasts in all sorts of cult groups for Mt. Shasta) have some idea which American mountains are most sacred.

Other Esoteric Buddhists are firmly based in their true spiritual homeland, Tibet. Jacob Needleman writes of that intriguing "land of lost content":

> Gradually, Tibet is coming into view. Instead of a romantic land haunted by a primitive or perverse mystical spirituality, we see the outlines of something breath-taking: an entire nation defined and ruled by the search for inwardness.[4]

Indeed, Tibet at least symbolizes such a concept of the proper direction both of individual life and of society, for no society has ever been so thoroughly directed toward inwardness, nor attained such successful results in its own terms. The brutal destruction of traditional Tibet by Chinese Communist armies has only added a note of tragic poignancy to this land real yet stranger than myth. It is now locked even more irrevocably into the past than it once was behind the walls of the mightiest mountains in the world.

Nevertheless, just as the destruction of Jerusalem spread Judaism all over the world, so the destruction of the Tibetan homeland has created a Tibetan diaspora, not only of ordinary refugees but also of lamas able to teach the spiritual methods long treasured in the monasteries of the "Land of Snows." In places as far apart as Scotland, New Jersey, and California they have established centers, and students are being initiated.[5] In Tibet, more than Shugendo, initiation by transmission of the spiritual power to perform a particular *sadhana* or spiritual path is very important. Power is passed first of all from master to disciple. But even after initiation a long training, up to twenty years, remains before the full fruits of the path can be attained. It is not just a matter of apprehending fleeting illuminative "insights," but of psychological training and practice which is necessary for visualization of deities and perfection of psychic powers which give one the control over the mind finally to reach the "Diamond State," and know experientially that all is Mind.

It is too early to say just what cultural effect the Tibetan diaspora, and the training of western practitioners in its tradition, will have. Nor will I do more than allude to the presence of that tradition, for I would not presume to present in a few pages a spiritual heritage so rich and yet so alien to most westerners.

We now have in the West nearly all major forms of Buddhism. It is interesting to note that the Buddhism popular in the West in any given period usually says more about the state of the West than of Buddhism. In the early years of the century, the supposedly atheistic rationalism of Theravada philosophy was most celebrated, and was much contrasted with the alleged superstition of Mahayana, not to mention Tibet, considered "debased" forms.

In the fifties, as something of a reaction against science, psychoanalysis, and Western materialism, the Zen of D. T. Suzuki and the "beatniks" was in greatest favor. Then, the psychedelic explosion of the sixties, with its exploration of the strange populations of the unconscious, and its feel for the uncanniness of psychic and mystic states of awareness, made suddenly clear what works like *The Tibetan Book of the Dead* were about. It seemed to many this was the deepest and subtlest Buddhism of all. As I have remarked before, the growing interest in Esoteric Buddhism seems to parallel that in Neo-Paganism and ceremonial magic: both create a transformed state of consciousness by creating a sacred visual and auditory environment through visualization and ritual.

Reading Selection: Esoteric Buddhism

Here is a flyer from the Kailas Shugendo movement in San Francisco, which gives some idea of what it means to practice this esoteric way of power from the mountains of Central Asia and Japan in modern America.

SHUGENDO

KAILAS SHUGENDO is a San Francisco based spiritual community, centered around the practices of the SHU-GEN-DO, or WAY-of-SPIRITUAL POWER. This is a religious way without pretense, a life style based upon belief in BUDDHISM, but incorporating means of practice and purification derived from SHINGON, SHINTO, NYINGMA, and KARGUIT traditions, as well as from the many basic shamanistic practices common to all religions.

It is a way for the people, a way which is called OBASKUDO. This idea was first initiated by EN NO OBASOKU around 700 A.D. in rebellion against the corrupted monastic Buddhism of his time. The Obaskudo practices the Buddhism in the light of wisdom of equality; recognizing that all beings are the Buddha, he does not adhere to the conventional ideas of the priest versus the layman, to the isolationism of the monastic life, or to the ideas concerning monkhood and sexuality. Rather, the Obaskudo, utilizes the Tantric means, encompassing all the elements of life, and weaving them into a meaningful foundation for spiritual practice. Basic to the practice of this tantracism is the development of the relationship between man and woman, where in the context of the sexuality is sought a means to the enlightenment experience itself.

Shugendo encourages the community life in order that people may work more creatively and efficiently towards their ideals, as well as to effect an economic liberation, a basic necessity to all creative individuals in order to obtain the time and means by which to pursue their particular disciplines.

The YAMABUSHI, as practioners of this way are called, follow a very rich ritual life cycle, which involves living alternately in both the working atmosphere of the cities, and in the mountains. Daily ritual activity includes morning and evening GOMA (fire offering), cold water practices, chanting, music, and MANTRA practice throughout the day.

Each weekend the Yamabushi move their center of operation to one of the holy mountains within reach of the Bay Area. Depending upon the particular season, the KOMORI (mountain confinement), might take place on Snow Mountain, in the Sierras, or even on Mt. Tamalpais. During their mountain confinement, they practice the SHUGYO (ritual circumambulation of the mountain), HI-WATARI (FIREWALKING), and many other practices designed to tone the body into a healthful state, a necessity for good spiritual progress, and to give the practitioners the spiritual strength and clarity of mind to deal with the problems of the people and our difficult times.

Shingi-Shugen Honshu

---

3. Nichiren Shoshu of America

The house was a neat, white bungalow in a modest residential neighborhood. It might have been the home of an honest working-class family, or of a young organization man on the way up. But it wasn't; it was the district headquarters of a dynamic Japanese Buddhist denomination which has grown phenomenally in its homeland and is now invading the West. The living room contained, that evening, about seventy-five people, mostly young and mostly Caucasian. They were not dancing or drinking cokes together; they were chanting the profound words of an ancient Eastern formula in the strange language of another time and place: *Nam Myoho Renge Kyo*. It is an affirmation that all needful wisdom is subsumed in the Buddhist Lotus Sutra, and that merely reciting the formula of ascription of praise to this book will put one in harmony with the lines of force radiating from all the resplendent Buddhas mentioned in it, and from the central Being of the universe itself, and can unite the phenomenal world and absolute reality.

I had gone to this weekly district meeting of Nichiren Shoshu with a friend at the invitation of a graduate student in political science who had been converted to it. As we entered the room, the chanting had already begun. The crowd was seated on the floor facing a dark black wooden box of an altar containing a white sheet of paper with Sino-Japanese characters on it radiating out from the center; this is the Gohonzon, visual focus of the cultus. It contains the names of important figures in the Lotus Sutra. The assembly recited, in Japanese, verses from the Lotus Sutra and the chant called the Daimoku: *Nam Myoho Renge Kyo*. The recitation was to the accompaniment of the dry rustle of 108 bead rosaries and drums; the resultant sound was an uncanny low jungle-like roar, suggesting unspeakable power.

The chanting ended in a grand rhythmic crash of voices. Next we heard the seemingly incongruous melodies of American hymns and folk-songs, with English words praising the virtues of chanting and propagating the new faith, such as "I've been doing *shakubuku*," to the tune of "I've Been Working on the Railroad." *Shakubuku*, literally "break and subdue," is the Nichiren Shoshu term for aggressive evangelism.

The giving of testimonials followed. This was perhaps the most significant and impressive part of the meeting. The vivacious members of the group were not merely willing to tell what chanting the Daimoku had done for them, but were irrepressible in their enthusiasm. They not only raised their hands to be called upon by the middle-aged leader, but threw their arms into the air, dozens at a time, and even jumped up and down with eagerness.

When they spoke, they told often long-winded but clearly heartfelt tales of deep personal change and acquisition of power. We heard people who, before starting to chant, had been virtual zombies due to drugs, alcoholism, habitual failure, and sense of meaninglessness. They had no friends, no purpose, no abilities they could believe in. They, when introduced to the simple practice of chanting *Nam Myoho Renge Kyo*, saw remarkable changes occur with the first fall of its mantic syllables from their lips—friends gathered around, grades in school improved markedly, strength arose to give up drugs or drink, marriages were saved, great improvements resulted in employment and material prosperity. The contrasting blacks and brilliant sunlight tones of conversion stories in general were evident; clearly we were dealing with a faith which dealt in that psychology.

Others reported more modest, but no less striking, results. One young man had wanted a new guitar, but there appeared no means by which he could get one. However, he had "chanted for it," and a few days later, through a strange series of coincidences, money came into his hands in the necessary amount. It was even said that if a parking place in a crowded business section of town was needed, chanting would make the place appear!

The leader, a personable American, gave a short lecture. It concerned Buddhist doctrine as interpreted by Nichiren Shoshu, and was saved from tediousness by a quite articulate manner and wholly Western style, despite holding firm to Nichiren Shoshu orthodoxy. He spoke of the ten basic states of life: hellish suffering, the incessant hunger of wandering ghosts, animality, angry titans, human tranquillity, heavenly rapture (the six traditional Buddhist planes where karmic reincarnation is possible), learning, following the path, the aspiration for enlightenment of the bodhisattva, the bliss of Buddhahood (four traditional stages of the spiritual ascent). These are all conditions of the present, he said; they are not afterlife conditions, but here and now. A person may move through all ten several times in one day. They can all be brought into "one thought" through the chanting of the Daimoku. This radical drive toward unification of all realities mundane and spiritual into one unity in the immediate present is characteristic of Nichiren Shoshu.

Finally it was announced, after cheers like college yells, that "The meeting is over, the *shakubuku* begins!" Scores of eager faces poured out to transform the world through the Daimoku. Since we were obviously likely subjects, a knot of young people gathered around my companion and me asking us when we would begin chanting, and no excuses would satisfy them.

Nichiren Shoshu can indeed be persuasive. One student of my acquaintance, sent to do a report on the organization, joined some of its exuberant youthful members in invading university dormitories doing *shakubuku*, and ended up being converted himself! The movement is surrounded by happy smiles, creativity, and almost frenetic energy. In the American headquarters building in Santa Monica, California, or any district headquarters, when chanting is not going on, there is likely to be music practice—a fife and drum corps, popular music, chamber music.

The real impact of Nichiren Shoshu comes into being at the great annual conventions. They draw thousands of participants who fill the largest municipal halls. The convention days are packed with parades, stirring lectures, and memorable music performances. Behind them one rightly envisions brisk executive-type men talking on telephones and meeting planes, countless committee meetings, and the expenditure of considerable funds.

This vigorous extroverted activism scarcely fits the conventional Western (and Eastern) image of Buddhism. Instead of rows of monks in silent inward meditation, and a gentle aetherial tolerance of attitude, here are prepossessive people chanting vigorously and acting vigorously, hardly pausing for any "mindfulness" but that of the active moment, and trying to persuade others that their religion is the only truth. Further, they are convinced that beginning in Japan their faith will win the world, and provide the basis of a "Third Civilization" in which Buddhism and society will be one.

But if this is not a conventional Buddhism, its real founder, Nichiren (1222–82) was not a conventional Buddhist saint. He seems rather a transplanted Old Testament prophet, or a Muhammad. He taught an exclusivist religion of the Lotus Sutra, led a great popular movement, feared not to denounce the faithless in the highest places, and predicted national disaster if the nation failed to repent. Though there have been other Buddhists like him in Japan, and there is something in the Japanese temperament which makes him understandable, Nichiren is really unique, like his movement.

Nichiren was trained in the great Mt. Hiei monastery of the Tendai tradition, an ancient Buddhism deeply dyed with esoteric teaching. But amid the social upheavals of the Middle Ages, when feudal warlords rebelled against the old imperial court in Kyoto and the whole country was convulsed with a search for new social and spiritual values, he found himself asking new questions. More can often be told about a religious movement by the questions it is asking than the answers it gives. The old quasi-esoteric Buddhism of the Heian (Kyoto) period was asking the question, "How can all Buddhist philosophy and all human experience be brought into a grand synthesis?" But Nichiren, and other Buddhist figures of the subsequent Kamakura period, like the Protestant reformers of Europe, were asking more personal and mundane religious questions: "How can I be sure that I am saved?" "How can the events of human history be reconciled with Providence?" In this last particular, Nichiren was much disturbed as a young man by the fact that the imperial loyalists were defeated by the warlord insurgents despite the incantations of innumerable Buddhist priests and abbots on behalf of the imperial forces.

Like all who ask the religious question in terms of "How can I be sure that I am saved?" Nichiren ended with a simple key, a sure, entirely sufficient minimum requirement for salvation beyond which all else is just confusing superfluity. For him, that sure key was the Lotus Sutra, considered the embodiment of all necessary Buddhist truth. This great document, whose images remind one of the New Testament Book of Revelation, envisions millions of Buddha worlds and tells that the historical Buddha is but a manifestation of the eternal Buddha-nature, and that since these mysteries are beyond comprehension, simple devotion is as certain a key to liberation as meditation or philosophy. It is not necessary that one study the Lotus Sutra; to chant the Daimoku is to attune oneself mystically with all that it contains, which is all that is needed. It is advantageous, though, to chant before the Gohonzon since it holds the names, and so the power, of the principle Buddhas and bodhisattvas in the book.

Nichiren taught devotion to the Lotus Sutra with monolithic fanaticism. If the nation did not reject all other forms of Buddhism in favor of the Lotus, it would suffer calamity. If the nation were converted to his Buddhism, it would become the center of a new world civilization. For moderns, Nichiren is the one authority; Nichiren Shoshu teaches that he is the Buddha for the present age. The Lotus Sutra is the one book—only faith is necessary; in this one central focus, everything is unified; all seeming polarities meet. The three Buddha expressions—as essence of the universe, as heavenly lord, and as earthly teacher of saving wisdom—are brought together. Nichiren Shoshu also employs such expressions as *shikishin funi*, "body and mind not two," *esho funi*, "individual and environment not two," *obutsu myogo*, "the state and Buddhism one society," and so forth. This radical simplicity and unity, focusing all down to a single intense point, is the secret of Nichiren: one scripture, one man, one country, one object of worship, one practice, all potentialities realized in one moment which is the present. Nichiren Shoshu was one of two major Buddhist denominations established by immediate disciples of Nichiren. Its head temple, containing allegedly Nichiren's tooth and the original Gohonzon drawn by him as principal relics, is on the slopes of Mt. Fuji.

The radical nature of this tradition was revived in our day by T. Makiguchi, who founded an organization for laymen in 1930 called Soka Gakkai, "Value-creation study society." He and his followers soon joined Nichiren Shoshu. Soka Gakkai was based on an "Essay on Value" Makiguchi had written, in which he had substituted "benefit" for "truth" in the traditional triad of "goodness, truth, and beauty." Not all truth is beneficial to man, but benefit, including material benefit, by definition is. It is, of course, chanting the Daimoku which delivers benefit.

The unsubtle secular pragmatism sets the tone for the appeal of the faith, although it should be recognized that it is consistent with its deepest assumptions. If it says, "Other religions promise good things after you die, but only Nichiren Shoshu can deliver them now," or, "Try chanting just for something you want to see if it works," that is not because Nichiren Shoshu is solely materialistic. It is rather because of its premise that there must be unity between all aspects of being rather than mutual exclusiveness. If chanting brings material benefits, the real message is that this affirms the inseparability of matter and non-matter; chanting should lead deeper into the mysteries of the Buddha-nature that unites them.

Because of his refusal to participate in Shinto, Makiguchi fell out of favor with the militaristic government, and he ended his days in prison in 1944. Soka Gakkai was a tiny, obscure sect with the coming of religious freedom in 1945. But its leadership fell into the hands of J. Toda (1900–58), one of the most remarkable religious administrators of modern times. Under his masterful, hard-driving guidance the faith became undoubtedly the fastest-growing religion in the world in the fifties, increasing from a few thousand to some ten million adherents in Japan by the end of the decade. More than any other faith, it filled the spiritual void left in Japan by the discrediting of traditional forms of Shinto and Buddhism, and by the materialism of the phenomenal economic recovery. To lonely people transplanted to the great industrial cities, it offered participation, activity, and a sense of direction.

Soka Gakkai warred fearlessly and often successfully with the great Marxist-oriented trade unions for the loyalty of the working class. The techniques of *shakubuku* were highly developed. Regarded as an act of mercy, *shakubuku* was often effected with a ruthlessness—business boycotts, midnight phone calls, argumentive interruption of the meetings of other religious groups—which brought Soka Gakkai much criticism, but also many converts. Anyone with real familiarity with modern Japan, however, will realize how much fulfillment has been brought by the new faith to millions of plain people whose lives and past values were shattered by war and social transformation. The progress of Soka Gakkai in Japan was climaxed by the creation of its own political party, the Komeito, now the third strongest in the Diet. While the meteoric growth of the faith seems to have let up somewhat in the sixties and seventies, it is still one of the most important social forces in Japan.

Until 1960, Soka Gakkai (still, in Japan, technically a layman's organization within Nichiren Shoshu) showed little interest in spreading to the West. But so close have been ties between the United States and Japan in the postwar era that it would be hard to keep a movement so powerful in one nation from touching the other. A few Americans stationed in Japan on military service had been converted, mostly by Japanese wives and girlfriends. Many Japanese "war brides" came to America as missionaries of the faith; some Japanese-Americans were converted through home contacts. Thus Soka Gakkai acquired an American foothold.

D. Ikeda, Toda's successor, was eager to spread the faith overseas. He established an organization in America in 1960, but at the time of the first convention in 1963 in Chicago, there were had only 10 chapters. By the time of the sixth convention, in Santa Monica in 1969, it claimed 135 chapters and nearly 200,000 members. (The figure is based on the number of "households" which have accepted a Gohonzon, and so is indefinite and doubtless in excess of the number of actual practitioners.)

Activities center in the American headquarters in Santa Monica, California, under the leadership of the General Director, Masayasu Sadanaga (who has recently changed his name to George Williams). The name Soka Gakkai is not used in this country, presumably because of unfavorable publicity its activities in Japan have received here. Nichiren Shoshu of America is thoroughly organized. The basic unit is the District, which meets several times a week; within it are groups and units of five to ten members under the supervision of experienced individuals for communication purposes. Above the District are regional Chapters and General Chapters. In addition, there are men's and women's divisions, a student bureau, a bureau for control of pilgrimages to Japan, the important Min-on which handles the characteristic music groups, and an active publications department, including the newspaper *World Tribune*. Organizational activism is a key part of the spirit of Nichiren Shoshu. But the faith also has two temples in America, one in Honolulu and one in Etiwanda, California. In these, ceremonies such as formal weddings and consecrations of Gohonzons requiring ministrations of Nichiren Shoshu priests are held.

In addition to group meetings, members carry out daily worship called *gongyo*. This consists of reciting certain chapters of the Lotus Sutra, in Japanese, five times in the morning and three times in the evening, followed by chanting the Daimoku until one feels satisfied. This worship is done in front of the Gohonzon, the mandala made by Nichiren enshrined in a box-like wooden altar. The Gohonzon is owned by Nichiren Shoshu, but upon entering the faith one receives, after payment of a small donation, a lifetime loan of one, which is installed by officers of the District in a brief home ceremony. This is the real initiation into Nichiren Shoshu. Of course, chanting is also done silently throughout the day—wherever one is.

The late sixties were days of fantastic growth for Nichiren Shoshu in America. As the organization entered the seventies, it appeared to be entering a period of retrenchment with emphasis on the education and nurture of really committed members. As in Japan, overaggressive *shakubuku* had in some cases produced a negative image or led to the entry of too many fair weather members. Now, in the addresses of leaders and the evangelism of ordinary members, there is less emphasis on promise of immediate phenomenal benefits from chanting, and more on serious points of Buddhist philosophy as interpreted by Nichiren. Indeed, the lectures of some publicists bristle excessively with abstractions and foreign language terminology. An outsider sometimes feels that entirely unnecessary barriers to communication are being raised.

Nonetheless, Nichiren Shoshu communicates itself in its own way through the impressive testimonials of those who have given it a chance, and in the pure enthusiasm and joy of its crowds, full of fellowship, music, and the euphoria of group chanting. They are as clean-cut as midwestern 4-H kids. Nichiren Shoshu encourages no extreme politics, dress, or life style. While it contains many ex-heads and "hippies," its young people seem able to enjoy bus excursions wearing identical sweaters, county fair style parades, and campfire songs. But if Nichiren Shoshu culture may seem to some to border on the over-organized and the banal, it has given many a home. More than that, it has given many a sparkle. Life, they say, is like a rocket rising and flashing within the infinite lotus depths of the Buddha-nature. Let it glitter as it rises.

Reading Selection: Nichiren Shoshu of America

The following conversion story, typical of those continually published in Nichiren Shoshu periodicals and recited at meetings, shows the kind of radical change in the style and meaning of life the movement strives for and frequently achieves. The picture of a happy, outgoing, active life, full of friends and success and inner power, suggests the image of the ideal Nichiren Shoshu member the organization wants to project. The searching, counter-culture background of the convert points toward the source of much of its recruitment and indicates its close relation to that scene even though Nichiren Shoshu's own style is as radically different as the psychology of deep conversion requires.

Picture a frantic nineteen-year-old girl, constantly running from her environment, moving eight times in one year from her nice middle class home to a swanky college in Arizona and finally ending up in Haight-Ashbury. This was Rochelle Byrd's life three years ago.

Her fantasy world was one of drugs, books, peace movements and finally, depression. Inside, she cried to change, but couldn't. She could not control her life. People would come into her life and then leave just as easily. Of herself, Rochelle says, "They could not tolerate my nature. I was on the verge of losing another circle of friends, when fortune really came my way." Here, of course, she was referring to the Gohonzon and Nammyoho-renge-kyo.

When she met the members, she saw smiling, confident faces of people who really seemed to care. Because of this, she chanted the "weird sounding words," thinking too that she would go on some kind of a faraway trip. She went on a trip all right—lots of them—Los Angeles, Japan—all over. But most of all, she went on a real "happiness" trip, a place she had never been to before.

Now, after two years of practice, she's found the things that she'd always been searching for—a happy family, good job and most of all, a rhythmical daily life.

She still runs a lot—to study meetings, discussion meetings, chorus and dance practices, visiting members, and most of all to the Gohonzon. In Rochelle's words, "It's a beautiful trip and a beautiful life!"

"Waking to Reality—'It's Beautiful,'"
World Tribune, Friday, May 1, 1970, p. 6.

4. The Baha'i Faith

North of Chicago along the coast of Lake Michigan in the suburb of Wilmette is a splendid building which looks almost as though it might have been transplanted from a Persian paradise. Its grounds are gorgeously landscaped, and above its nine sides looms a dome spun of such lacy, light filigree as to seem to be floating above the lakeshore. This is the American temple of the Baha'i Faith, a worldwide religion of Iranian origin which holds that its teacher, Baha'u'llah, is the prophet of God for our age, and that its institutions set the pattern for a new universal world order of liberty and peace.

While some have been drawn to Baha'i because of its imposing temple, many more in large and small communities have been reached through the peculiar tradition known as the Baha'i fireside. Leading members of Baha'i hold weekly discussions in their homes around a cozy blazing fireplace to introduce inquirers to the world of this new religion which claims to give an answer to the tortured spiritual quest of modern man in this day of transition.

I once attended a fireside in the home of a prominant judge. (Baha'i seems especially to appeal to the sort of idealism characteristic of people in law.) The evening opened with an exposition of the life of Baha'u'llah, and then of the Baha'i conception of world order. Special stress was laid on Baha'i's fulfilling the expectations of all religions and of modern secular hope for a new and better age. A general discussion accompanied refreshments. Questions centered around reasons for accepting the authority of Baha'u'llah and the attitude of Baha'i toward various ethical problems people in the group faced: the draft, marriage, and so forth.

The quiet, verbal manner with emphasis on social rather than mystical experience suggests that Baha'i is not a cult as we have defined it; basically it is geared to the emissary style, even if more Muslim than Judaeo-Christian in background. In the West, it has even lost most of the Sufi immediacy it had at the beginning. It actually should not appear in this book, but a survey of new religious movements would seem incomplete without Baha'i. The contrast makes the common characteristics of most of the others more apparent.

It is appropriate and significant that this new prophet for a new age should have appeared in Iran, for that land may be considered the homeland of eschatology, or religious beliefs concerning the future and the end of history. It is thus a homeland of the emissary style; and eschatology is the emissary's greatest tool—work and sacrifice now, eschew ecstasy now, for greater glory in the Lord's Day. There, some 2500 years ago, the mighty prophet Zoroaster taught that man must choose between sides in a great cosmic war between the principles of good and evil, and that at the end of the war—the end of history—a new prophet would appear, and the victorious good God, Ahura Mazda, would end the sentence of the wicked in hell and create a new paradisical heaven and earth. Many scholars believe that the subsequent eschatologies of Judaism, Christianity, Islam, and Hindu and Buddhist teachings about the future avatar of Vishnu and the coming Buddha Maitreya were deeply influenced by Zoroaster's primordial vision of man living not in cosmic, eternal-return time, but on the battlefield of a history in which he is judged and which will end in a glorious divine victory.

When Zoroastrianism gave way to Islam in Iran, the Shi'ite wing of the latter faith which took root there was, as might be expected, more strongly eschatological than the legalistic Sunni school of most other Muslims. Shi'ites looked forward eagerly to the coming of the Mahdi, the twelfth *Imam* or successor of Muhammad who, it was believed, had hidden himself but would appear at the right time as a Messiah surrounded by glorious hosts to raise the dead and deliver final revelations and effect the ultimate victory of righteousness. Yet the Shi'ites also had a cultus of the quasi-redemptive sufferings of Husain, the Christ-like nephew of Muhammad. Moreover, Iran is a homeland of the Sufis, the God-intoxicated Muslim mystics whose ecstatic devotionalism tempers the harshness of Islamic fervor.

All of these historical strands met with the incipient modern world to produce the new Baha'i faith. Its first manifestation was in the figure known as the Bab, or "Gate," born Mirza Ali Muhammad (1819–50). As a young man he became involved with a Sufi sect expecting an immanent divine revelation, and in this atmosphere first declared himself the Bab, then that he was the Mahdi himself in 1844. A great number of his Sufi sect accepted his claims, and with their help a fervent Babist religious movement swept through the land. The Bab taught that resurrection and judgment, heaven and hell, are here now in the new divine manifestation, depending on whether individuals accept or reject it. If one accepts, he lives in a universal love and holy ecstasy no power can destroy. This original ecstatic immediacy was quickly tempered by the incursion of history in the form of suffering. Perhaps out of this came its new futurism. Like most enthusiastic religious revivals, Babism was considered blasphemous and disturbing by the unenthusiastic. It suffered persecution from the backward Persian government of the day. Finally in 1850, the Bab himself was martyred. But among his followers was another God-possessed young man, Baha'u'llah (1817–92).

The death of the Bab did not mark the end of Babism. When in 1852 a deranged member of the sect made an attempt on the life of the Shah, fierce persecution broke out anew. A number of members of the Babist sect were thrown into dungeons, including Baha'u'llah. But, as is so often the case, persecution only strengthened faith. Baha'u'llah became convinced that he was called to regenerate the movement. After four months of imprisonment, Baha'u'llah was exiled and went to Baghdad. Later the Ottoman government moved him to Adrianople, then to Constantinople, and finally to the grim prison city of Acre. Just before leaving Baghdad in 1863, he declared that he was the One whose coming had been announced by the Bab, the Chosen of God. He ended his life in house arrest at Acre, though in the later years restrictions were much relaxed and he lived in some comfort and dignity, visited by high and low. According to Baha'is the Bab and Baha'u'llah are Co-Founders of the Faith, though Baha'u'llah represents a culmination of the revelation.

Baha'u'llah was succeeded as leader by his son, called Abdu'l-Baha, (1844–1921), who wrote extensively and lectured in Europe and America, doing much to extend the new teaching. He did not, however, rank himself with the Bab or Baha'u'llah, but saw himself merely a conservor of their faith.

Upon Abdu'l-Baha's death, he was succeeded by his grandson, called Shoghi Effendi, as Guardian of the Faith. Both could add nothing, but were "infallible" interpreters of its meaning. Upon Shoghi Effendi's passing in 1957, this authority passed to the cabinet-like body called the Hands of the Cause of God, and in 1963 to the International House of Justice, now constituted as the supreme governing body and prototype of a world government. It sits in Haifa, Israel.

One God and one world: this is the essence of the Baha'i vision. With this goes the concept of progressive revelation. The founders of all major faiths, Krishna, Buddha, Zoroaster, Moses, Jesus, Muhammad, and now Baha'u'llah, are all manifestations and messengers of God. But they have each spoken the message needed by a particular time and place, and so should not be followed exclusively after their day has passed. The great message of the present founder, Baha'u'llah, is the oneness of mankind. Like all great religious teachers, he was concerned with love and devotion toward God, and with the deep matters of suffering and death and man's ultimate destiny. But he was especially concerned with making the unity of mankind and its practical structures—a world tribunal; equality of all races, nationalities, and sexes; universal peace; universal education; a world calendar; a universal auxiliary language— part of religious faith and vision. The attainment of practical unity was made the object of that most powerful of human drives, the religious. *This* is the day when the unity of mankind can be attained because of universalizing culture and communication. It is desperately needed. It is God's desire and so is the burden of his true prophet for our time. Perhaps a couple millennia or so in the future, the next prophet will come with a new message beyond our present comprehension.

The Baha'i concept of the history of religion is essentially one of continuing revelation through great men. One is reminded of Carlyle's view of history as the strokes of heroes. Baha'i seems to presume that all of a religion, except the life and words of the founder, is deterioration. Perhaps this accounts for the very great zeal to preserve uncorrupted the sayings of Baha'u'llah.

Baha'i sees itself as a new vision of the meaning of history, and a light of hope in mankind's present dark and stormy and often desperate passage from one age to another—the efficacious plan for the next and far better era is already here. Just as Christianity retained some incidentals and externals of Judaism, so Baha'i has retained some externals of its womb-faith, Islam. There are daily prayers and a month-long fast reminiscent of the Muslim Ramadan. It could be argued that Baha'i's basic concepts—radical monotheism, prophet and scripture-centeredness, sus-

picion of priesthood and soteriology and rite—all suggest a perhaps unconscious carry-over of Islamic assumptions about the very nature of
true religion. Indeed, for a long time Baha'i was considered a Muslim
sect. But some Baha'is are willing to allow the providential nature of
this—and rightly point out that these Islamic biases also correspond with
the biases of many present-day European and American religious liberals,
those who have left "Puritan" theology, but not an ingrained "Protestant
ethic" and a negative reaction to anything suggestive of medieval
Catholicism.

Concerning life after death, Baha'is like to talk about this present life
as comparable to the life in the womb, and death as a rebirth, a prelude
to infinite further growth. Heaven and hell are not places but states of
consciousness.

Baha'i life for the believer centers around the local Baha'i community.
It does not have the usual Sunday worship, although temples like the one
in Wilmette have a Sunday lecture. But in addition to the firesides
there is a monthly feast. It is "monthly" according to the Baha'i calendar
of nineteen months of nineteen days each (plus four or five intercalary
days). The nineteen-day feast, for Baha'is only, consists of three parts:
devotional, business, and social. The devotional part will be simple
prayers and readings from the Baha'i writings. The governing body of
a Baha'i community is the Spiritual Assembly, consisting of nine persons
selected by secret ballot without nominations. Throughout the year there
are nine festivals, mostly based on Baha'i history, when Baha'is stay
away from work or school if possible, and the spring nineteen-day fast
when they take no food or drink from dawn to dusk.

Moral and religious discipline is not taken lightly in Baha'i circles.
The local Spiritual Assembly must give consent to marriage of members,
and regardless of the age of bride and groom, they must also obtain the
consent of all four parents if living. Drinking and narcotics are not
allowed. Many people who might otherwise be attracted by the idealism
of Baha'i are put off by its prohibition of participation in demonstrations
and even partisan politics. The local Spiritual Assembly may reprimand
erring members, though the member may appeal to national and world
assemblies. The life style often suggests "deferred reward" and "inner
asceticism," work rather than ecstasy now to produce a good society
later. In his suffering and verbal-legal teachings, Baha'u'llah seems a
model of these values, even though some of his devotional writing tends
toward Sufi mysticism.

The enthusiasm of committed Baha'is who have been seized by its
vision of a new revelation and new world order is splendid. Some become
"Baha'i pioneers," who move, at their own expense, to new places where
the Faith is not yet planted to sow its seeds. It has now spread to some

280 countries and major territories. Presently it seems to be growing most rapidly in the underdeveloped world. Its mission appeals to those for whom work and sacrifice as spiritual values correspond to current historical experience. For them, Baha'i is a vehicle of modernization.

But Baha'i is also making headway in the West. In the U.S., Baha'i membership doubled from 25,000 to 50,000 between 1970 and 1971. Many of the new adherents of Baha'i are young people retaining idealism but disillusioned with the "instant" realization offered by cult mysticism and revolutionary ideology alike. Baha'i is not strictly a cult, since it retains a personal God, a legal and emissary as well as exemplary concept of the prophet, and a social as well as mystical experience orientation in spiritual life.

Reading Selection: Baha'i

The following passage from a classic introduction to the Baha'i faith by an early Western convert sums up well some of the Faith's most important characteristics—love for God and the wide world, continual happy references to the words of Baha'u'llah and Abdu'l-Baha, insistence that while on the one hand it is important to recognize and nourish the good in all religions, on the other it is now a day when new envoys from God have come who must be heard.

When asked on one occasion: "What is a Baha'i?" Abdu'l-Baha replied: "To be a Baha'i simply means to love all the world; to love humanity and try to serve it; to work for universal peace and universal brotherhood." On another occasion He defined a Baha'i as "one endowed with all the perfections of man in activity." In one of His London talks He said that a man may be a Baha'i even if He has never heard the name of Baha'u'llah. He added: "The man who lives the life according to the teachings of Baha'u'llah is already a Baha'i. On the other hand, a man may call himself a Baha'i for fifty years, and if he does not live the life he is not a Baha'i. An ugly man may call himself handsome, but he deceives no one, and a black man may call himself white, yet he deceives no one, not even himself."

One who does not know God's Messengers, however, is like a plant growing in the shade. Although it knows not the sun, it is, nevertheless, absolutely dependent on it. The great Prophets are spiritual suns, and Baha'u'llah is the sun of this "day" in which we live. The suns of former days have warmed and vivified the world, and had those suns not shone, the earth would now be cold and dead, but it is the sunshine of today that alone can ripen the fruits which the suns of former days have kissed into life.

J. E. ESSLEMONT, *Baha'u'llah and the New Era* (Wilmette, Illinois: Baha'i Publishing Trust, revised edition, 1970), pp. 83–84. Original edition published 1923.

5. The Lovers of Meher Baba

Those who recall the enthusiasms of the thirties and those familiar with the religious counter-culture of the sixties will remember posters, newspaper pictures, pins, and rings bearing the photograph of a smiling, avuncular man in Indian dress. No untidy holy man, his black hair is short and neatly combed back in the Western manner, and he is clean-shaven save for a great bushy moustache which makes his broad, brilliant smile as warm as the sun. This is Meher Baba, a son of India and in some ways the most enigmatic of all the figures we have discussed. For he has made the greatest claim of all, saying, "I am God personified," and has seemingly done the least to demonstrate the claim as the world would judge proof. Yet with only quixotic efforts toward organization, continually "letting down" those who trusted him most, he has convinced thousands that his enigmatic charm and unpredictibility is indeed the fascination and inscrutibility of God focused into the world.

This man was born Merwan S. Irani in 1894 in Poona, India. His background reflects a religious universalism. Of Persian lineage, his parents were Parsees or Zoroastrians. But his milieu was, of course, Hindu, and he was much influenced by Sufi mystics. He was educated at a Christian high school.

Clearly his chief concept was the cult of holy men so central to Sufism and one strand of Hinduism. According to this tradition, there are always a certain number of true holy men or "Perfect Masters" alive in the world. Beside what they have, the vagaries of religious belief and practice are unimportant. The essential thing is to find them—or be found by them—love and serve them, and emulate them. In them is all grace and love.

Meher Baba's contact with such persons began when he was nineteen. He sought an aged Muslim woman, Hazrat Babajan, who was famous as a saint. She kissed his forehead, and thereby suddenly made him God-realized and conscious of himself as an avatar or personification of God. He then went through an ordeal virtually like a shamanistic initiation. For three days he lay as though dead, and for a long time he wandered in an ecstasy of infinite bliss but dissociated from his surroundings. Gradually he readjusted, but he was never again able to live a "normal" life. He contacted the Hindu master Sai Baba (the same whom Satya Sai Baba claims to reincarnate), and worked for three years under an advanced disciple of his, Upasni Maharaj. All of these were what Meher Baba called "Perfect Masters." He said that there are at all times five Perfect Masters in the world who sustain it in occult ways. He was recognized by all of them as an avatar (a Hindu term meaning divine "descent" or incarnation), greater than a God-realized master, because the avatar is a showing or self-revelation of God Himself from the other side. Past avatars have been such figures as Krishna, Jesus, Buddha, and other religious founders, and occur about every 700 years.

In 1921 Meher Baba established his first ashram and gathered about him disciples, called *mandali*. Their life was never easy nor secure. Baba's work included the establishment of many orphanages, hospitals, schools, and shelters for the poor. But under Baba's direction, the works seemed erratic. He would order a flourishing and worthwhile philanthropy terminated for no evident reason. He would lead his disciples on trips and turn them around before they reached the announced destination. In all of this, Baba seemed to be either unstable or as mysterious as God.

Baba believed that he must identify with both the highest and lowest of society. In India and his journeys to the West, he was lionized by government officials and movie stars. But he also devoted what some might have considered an inordinate amount of time to searching out the many deranged, God-possessed holy men of India he called *masts*. These strange people, bizarre in utterance, often catatonic, living in filth in dumps, public toilets, and railway stations, he embraced and cleaned and sometimes brought lovingly to his ashram. And in his travels, Meher Baba would visit the sites of past avatars and Perfect Masters, including Jesus and St. Francis, to perform mysterious actions alone there. His Eastern and Western followers believe that he still knows and affects everything that is going on in the world.

Meher Baba is most noted for his silence. From 1925 until his physical death on January 31, 1969, he spoke nothing. Although he wrote considerably and gave lectures with the help of an alphabet board, the silence of the personification of God in the midst of a world so given to continual communication through so many media no doubt bore a deep message. Baba said that he would break his silence by speaking the One Word which would spiritualize the world, manifest his true nature, and open a new age of love.[6] Although on several occasions he promised to break his silence, and set dates, the time was always postponed. Understandably, these seeming failures to fulfill expectations, like Baba's other erratic words and actions, led many to fall away. His death caused some to feel he had not lived up to his promise to speak the One Word. But his devotees point to several veiled predictions he made earlier that he would suffer disease and humiliation before he spoke the "Word of Words" and was glorified. While the previous impression was that the prophecies indicated events that would happen before he "dropped the body," his followers now tell that on the day of his death he wrote, "Today is my crucifixion." They say that only now is the meaning of his humiliation—the taunts of the scoffers—really clear. They remain loyal to him in the expectation that in due time he will vindicate himself. In all of this Baba's lovers, convinced by his radiance and the strange psychic effect he had on them, believe there is enigmatically divine meaning behind his seeming capriciousness and defeat.

Meher Baba's writings and lectures place him definitely within the Sufi tradition, though he is most in the line of those Indian poets like Kabir and Nanak who have dwelt with great creativity on the borderline of Hinduism and Islam, combining Islamic monotheism with a Vedantic sense of divine nondualism and immanence, and Sufi-bhakti fervent devotionalism with its ideal of the fool for the love of God. Baha'i, Subud, and the Meher Baba movement are the three religions in the West most affected by that attractive Muslim mystical current called Sufism.

Meher Baba's formal teachings, most fully expounded in his book *God Speaks,* use mainly Sufi language and quotations from Sufi masters, together with some Vedanta terminology. The basic concept is that God "loses" himself in creation, and then "finds" himself by exterior evolution through stone, metal, vegetation, worms, birds, animals, and man to develop complete consciousness. Then for man there are seven interior states of "involution" or spiritual realization wherein what man understands as full consciousness is lost to be replaced by divine awareness. Those on the seventh plane of this ascent are the Perfect Masters whose consciousness is entirely God's. The avatar may, however, for reasons of divine policy, appear a Master on any of the higher planes. Meher Baba appears on the seventh, but Jesus, who because of his cultural environment had to retain some concern for miracles and dualistic attitudes, was embodied as a Master on the sixth plane. The appealing devotional writing of Meher Baba is pure Sufi celebration of intoxication with the wine of God's love, and of the comparison of the love of God with the love of fair women, and displays the charm of the babbling fools of this love.

To a remarkable extent, the lovers of Meher Baba carry to the streets of our cities this Sufi love. A meeting of Meher Baba followers I attended was held in the back room of a Meher Baba bookstore. From the outside the store appeared drab, and it was located in a "skid row" block. But within, the rooms were enlivened by many giant posters of the Master's beaming face, and by the harlequin dress of his devotees who were mostly young and of the new generation of seekers. About twenty-five were present, seated on couches and cushions in a big circle.

The unofficial leader, a bright-faced young man with a brown beard, opened the meeting by remarking that the center needed certain objects, including a vacuum cleaner and refrigerator. He then said that recently he had been with his wife to a natural childbirth class. It was in a Catholic hospital. During a break he wandered into the bookstore and picked up a paperback copy of *The Little Flowers of St. Francis*. He had apparently been unfamiliar with this classic before, but remembering that Baba had said St. Francis was the only Perfect Master the West had produced, he read this delightful and moving collection of incidents in the life of the saint of Assisi. Finding it real "heart stuff," full of the divine fool's love of God and man, he wanted to share it. He read aloud several incidents from the book, such as the conversion of Brother Bernard and the taming of the wolf of Gubbio. The group discussed the stories. Several had read Nikos Kazantzakis's novel about St. Francis. One boy, who could not have been more than twelve or thirteen, remarked that Francis's saying to Brother Leo that perfect joy is found in suffering for God reminded him of the same theme in the life of the Tibetan mystic Milarepa. Parallels in Baba's teachings were also continually brought out.

Next another member of the group read an installment of a continuing Sufi love story—one of those stories of wine and romance which can be taken on two levels. A little earlier, an obviously very drunk denizen of the neighborhood had wandered in, slouched down on the floor, and sat dozing. As the Sufi story was being read, he roused himself, looked at the reader, and broke in, saying, "Shcuse me, I wanna ask you a question. Are you happy?"

The reader with some aplomb smiled at him and said, "Yes. I'm happy because Baba is happy."

The visitor replied, "Who's Baba?"

"Baba is like our father."

"I'm sorry," he said.

"That's all right. Thank you, friend." The word of thanks seemed to amaze the guest as he sank again back into a stupor.

The group, like most religious groups centered around affective experience, is informal with emphasis on the creation of a fellowship of coequal love.[7] Baba insisted he did not want to found an organization or "religion," and that there be no central structure. The original center at Meherabad, near Poona, India, publishes a magazine. There is a Baba center at Myrtle Beach, South Carolina, where Baba himself spent time on one of his five visits to the United States. A San Francisco organization, Sufism Reoriented, makes Meher Baba as avatar a very important part of its vision, but is concerned with the main Sufi tradition too. In general, though, the followers of Baba form only scattered groups, usually meeting in Meher Baba bookstores (run by enthusiasts without much financial profit) or private homes. No permission to organize or join is needed save a love for Baba, and a delight in hearing and talking about him.

Unquestionably the movement is on the decline today in part because of the death of Baba, in part because of the diminishing of the drug and mysticism culture which fed into it during its revival in the sixties. Unless the expectations of the remaining faithful turn out to be vindicated, it will probably continue to decline. But it deserves to be remembered as one of the most touching and quixotic of mankind's spiritual adventures.

Reading Selection: The Meher Baba Movement

In the following intriguing passage, the Master Meher Baba himself purports to describe his own consciousness for those who are not yet able to intuit it directly. The sense of mission, the bhakti-sufi sense of divine playfulness are there. To allow one like this to work in oneself is, for Baba's lovers, joy and the promise of more joy.

Believe that I am the Ancient One. Do not doubt that for a moment. There is no possibility of my being anyone else. I am not this body that you see. It is only a coat I put on when I visit you. I am Infinite Consciousness. I sit with you, play and laugh with you; but simultaneously I am working on all planes of existence.

Before me are saints and perfect saints and masters of the earlier stages of the spiritual path. They are all different forms of me. I am the Root of every one and every thing. An infinite number of branches spread out from me. I work through, and suffer in and for, each one of you.

My bliss and my infinite sense of humour sustain me in my suffering. The amusing incidents that arise at the expense of none lighten my burden.

Think of me; remain cheerful in all your trails and I am with you helping you.

Meher Baba, *The Everything and the Nothing*
(Sydney, Australia: Meher House Publications,
1963), p. 56.

---

6. Subud

The religion called Subud does not advertize and has not much been in the news in recent years, but nearly everyone with any knowledge of the religious counter-culture has heard of it. Everywhere in this world it has a certain reputation as the most "far out," or the most "deep in," of them all.

In most of the seventy-some United States cities with Subud centers, the only notice of the organization is a modest listing in the telephone directory, often without an address. By calling this number, inquirers will be able to find the time and place of Subud's only corporate act of worship, the *latihan*.

This soft Indonesian word points to the land of origin of this movement, but scarcely anything of its dynamics. When the inquirer locates the address he has received on the phone, he will probably find himself at a drab hotel or house in a nondescript section of town on a weekday night. Upon entering, he will see a gaggle of people in old clothes. He would scarcely realize that some of them are students, professors, psychologists, doctors, and executives, as well as misfits and rejecters of society.

The visitor will be met by someone called a "helper." The "helper" will tell him what the *latihan* is. It may seem to the visitor quite different from anything he has previously known as a spiritual exercise. Members enter a large darkened room. They first stand there with eyes closed. They allow themselves to be completely open to the motions of the Spirit. This leads very quickly to external manifestations as each person gets into his "exercise": shouting, crooning, jumping and leaping about, weeping, glossalalia. Men and women have *latihan* in separate rooms.

Only those who have been "opened" are permitted to be in the room. Visitors and probationers sit outside the door. They can hear the sound of the *latihan* but see nothing. The visitor will probably find fifteen or twenty minutes of listening unforgettable. There is a strange luring attraction to the sound of total spiritual expression. It is the sound of earliest childhood, the child leaping and crying about the nursery, free to shout and weep, and the primitive festival, the return to chaos and renewal. One hears animal sounds, sounds of frenzy and joy, and deep, utterly strange and moving wordless hymn-like chants. Sometimes the action is individual; sometimes all move in one direction around the hall, moving and singing in concert as though participating in some great cosmic dance. Despite the darkness and the emotionality, members of the *latihan* never collide with each other. As though led by a sixth sense they move gracefully around and past their companions.

There is a feeling of being pulled almost magnetically toward the *latihan*, if susceptible to it, as toward a vortex. It is the discovery of total freedom, of whole return expressed through positive forms. Members say that participation in *latihan* twice a week—the norm—leads to the opening up of the person one really is, the person as he is known to God. It leads to purification, to the falling away of undesirable habits, and to an acquisition of buoyancy and power. Some report that they have received physical and emotional healings in the *latihan*. Others claim that they have received clear and unmistakable guidance in personal decisions, guidance that may have seemed contrary to prudence at the time, but which has turned out in the end to be right.

The originator of this movement is an Indonesian name Muhammad Subuh, now generally called "Bapak," a conventional Javanese term meaning "father." He was born in 1901, and it is said that his childhood was marked by strange psychic occurrences. This, and a prophecy of early death, led him to seek out spiritual teachers as a young man. In Indonesia these are not hard to find. Bapak contacted many sages of the dervish and Sufi traditions. But none satisfied him, and some allegedly claimed his was a destiny beyond their ken, and reversed custom by paying the applicant honor. So Bapak took up family life and a minor government job.

Then, on his twenty-fourth birthday in 1925, as he was strolling with friends on a dark moonless night, Bapak had a new and clearly initiatory experience. A sphere of light brighter than the sun manifested above him and seemed to enter through the top of his head. He felt filled with coursing, vibrating light. It is said the preternatural light was visible miles away. For three years after, he felt an experience like that of the *latihan* trembling through him frequently, so that he was always full of joy and energy.

Inexplicably, when he was twenty-seven in 1928, the spontaneous *latihan* stopped. Bapak passed through a period of confusion, a "dark night of the soul," in his interior life, even though his outward life as a government official and husband and father continued normally, and he was beginning to acquire a reputation as a counsellor.

This stage ended on his thirty-second birthday, when Bapak's mission was revealed to him. He was to pass the experience he had received to others. This unfolding restored Bapak's own spiritual life, and gave him an all-consuming vocation. Leaving his former work, Bapak henceforth devoted himself entirely to the movement he called Subud. Unlike other methods, the Subud experience, he teaches, can be communicated wholly and entirely by "contact," and others can immediately receive—if the receiver's intellectual mind does not interfere—the same energy he received when the illumination greater than the sun descended.

From 1933—the real birthday of Subud—until after the Second World War, Subud spread very quietly on the island of Java. But it had won the attention of a few Europeans, and beginning in 1956 it moved rapidly around the world. Since then Bapak has spent most of his time travelling and visiting one center after another.

In countries like Britain where Gurdjieff's teachings had been strong, Subud cut a particularly wide swath through the adherents of the south Russian philosopher. The situation is vividly described in the autobiographical book by Anthony Bright-Paul, *Stairway to Subud*. Gurdjieff had paved the way by mysterious allusions to a coming Indonesian teacher, and some of his followers had felt that no real headway could be made until the "higher emotional center" was opened. When Bapak arrived in Britain with Subud, the Gurdjieff center of Coombe Springs were swept by enthusiasm for the *latihan*. With almost indecent speed its leader, J. G. Bennett, and his followers laid aside the words, talk, heavy intellectual exposition, and techniques involving arbitrary discipline and grueling manual labor of Gurdjieffism for the release of the *latihan*. One is reminded of Krishnamurti's equally radical rejection of the intricate intellectualism of Theosophy and the dilemma this created for his devotees. Shortly after, in 1959, Subud was well launched with an International Congress held in England. A few days after the Congress, the well-known Hungarian actress Eva Bartok gave Subud a burst of favorable publicity by being "opened" by Bapak and in the process being healed of childbirth complications.

The word Subud is derived from the Sanskrit *susila*, meaning living according to the will of God, *budhi*, the principle of enlightenment in man, and *dharma*, teaching. Its verbal expression, found primarily in the writings of Bapak, is what is implied by this—that there is a higher, purifying, and joyous consciousness into which one can be opened, and which gives its own definition of human reality. Bapak and most Subud followers definitely believe in God, though without excessive talk about his nature. What is required is complete surrender to his will and his gifts. This surrender in the *latihan* room is what makes the experience work. Bapak says, "We do not have a teaching, there is nothing we have to learn or do, because all that is required of us is complete surrender. A person who claims to know the way to God is really one who is anticipating God's gifts without having received them." But if one surrenders, God will give immediate guidance, and every person will find the right way toward God for himself.

"Opening," the initiation by which this happens, is no elaborate ritual, although the present preparatory requirements in the United States—that one has registered as a probationer and attended *latihan*, without entering the room, once a week for three months—are relatively rigid. Usually something like this is done at an "opening": the probationer meets with a "helper," who may read some words from Bapak to him in a cloak-room, then goes into the *latihan* room with him and says, "Close your eyes and begin."

The *latihan* room will be bare with a rug on the floor. The *latihan* itself will be initiated by a "helper" saying, "Begin," and ended when he says, "Finish." "Helpers" may go to the homes of sick members to assist them in experiencing *latihan* there.

Subud has three kinds of meetings: the *latihan*, business meetings, and the *salamatan*. The organization of Subud is not complex, but each center does have a Board of Directors (distinct from the "helpers," spiritual guides, appointed by Bapak or his representatives), and regional and national boards. There is a periodical, publishing house, and conventions. The *salamatan* is a feast held from time to time. Usually Subud people are convivial and enjoy these occasions. Everything is discussed except the "meaning" of Subud, for some Subud members have a certain anti-intellectual bias and greatly resist such talk. These persons do not respond warmly to outside investigators, though others do.

Subud shares with the seemingly converse Gurdjieff tradition with which it is oddly linked in the West—and with the alternative reality tradition—a belief that if one finds the right key or technique, one can "short" oneself into a very different and higher kind of consciousness which makes life suddenly meaningful. Its technique is perhaps the most open and direct, reminding one of such recent psychotherapeutic methods as primal therapy. Unlike others, it does not provide a given symbol system, visual or verbal, to associate with the new consciousness. Perhaps one could say the *latihan* is its own symbol, or that it provides a clearing in which the person can erect his own symbol evoked out of newly released parts of the unconscious.

Reading Selection: Subud

This passage by a westerner who experienced Subud after being very active in the Gurdjieff movement, when Bapak (Pak Subuh) first brought it to England, enables one to experience the latihan *in company with the leader himself and several Indonesians of Muslim background as well as Western novices.*

The whole of that Whit weekend, except for its culmination on the Monday evening, has now been blotted from my memory. I can remember only that sometime on Monday afternoon, about fifteen men gathered upstairs in Mr. Bennett's study, prior to being "opened." He gave us a very brief introductory talk. We were to take off our shoes and ties and watches. We were simply to stand and to be open in our feelings. If we experienced the spontaneous arising of movements within our bodies we were not to resist but simply to follow. We were not to make any effort to control our mental associations, but were to let them wander freely, constraining nothing.

We then filed downstairs to the dining room, the floor of which had been covered by a number of new carpets, and the curtains had been drawn. We were placed in a rough sort of circle in the room. Pak Subuh was already in the room, together with a number of other Indonesians. I recall a very fine exquisite odour, such as I had never smelt before.

Pak Subuh said a few words in Indonesian that were translated haltingly by one of the Indonesian helpers. He said something about coming to the true worship of God, and that in the way of Subud we should not use our thoughts for meditation but simply receive. Then, "Close your eyes and we begin."

Almost at once a number of people began a very strange singing. They sang quite independently, but it did blend in a curious way. The singers also seemed to be moving about in the room. Someone else began to pray in a loud voice in a language that I presumed to be Arabic. The words "Akbar Allah" were repeated a great number of times. But if I simply say prayed in a loud voice, such as one has heard from a priest or muezzin, this would give entirely the wrong impression. This prayer seemed to be heaved from the very depths of his being, as if he was in an agony of remorse, sorrow and supplication. It had a strong effect upon my feelings and I began to feel very small and utterly unworthy. At the same time I began to be afraid and I tensed up. I heard a friend on my left crash to the ground. At the other end of the room someone began to weep, as if he would burst in two. Yet another began to laugh as if at the most huge joke in the world. And still others were obviously moving about quite rapidly, to judge from the panting and the feet padding on the floor.

The longer the exercise lasted the more afraid I became, till I was holding on to myself, determined to resist anything that might come. Suddenly, one word was called out—"Finish!"—and the pandemonium stopped. I opened my eyes and saw that six or seven of my friends were still standing as I was, while the rest had obviously been moving about. A half-hour had passed.

I went next door to put on my shoes and jacket. A friend tried to catch my eye with a questioning look, but I avoided him. I quickly gathered my things together and went down to the station to catch the train to London. Four of us shared the same compartment who had been to the exercise, but not one of us spoke a word.

ANTHONY BRIGHT-PAUL, *Stairway to Subud*
(New York: Dharma Book Company, Inc.,
1965), pp. 165–66.

7. The Unified Family

This small but remarkable group, founded in Korea, bearing Christian, Spiritualist, and "New Age" overtones, has been tempered by the apocalyptic events of our time. Perhaps it would be well to begin by describing an introductory meeting of the group.

In major cities throughout the world, The Unified Family, sometimes called the Unification Church, has houses which are typically both communal living places for young, single members, and meeting places for the whole group. It is one of these homes the visitor would approach for a Sunday afternoon or weekday evening meeting. A pleasant, lively circle of perhaps twenty or twenty-five people, mostly young, will make the guest feel at home. He will be given a hymnbook containing religious songs in folk and popular style. Someone will play a guitar, and the circle will sing for some thirty minutes such songs as "Joyful, Joyful We Adore Thee" and "The Morning Light is Breaking." Then most persons in the circle will tell in simple words what the movement has meant to them, and deep unstructured prayer will be offered by the leader and several members. The visitor will be offered an opportunity to attend a series of lectures on the Divine Principle, a necessary step before he learns more of the secret of the joy of the circle, and the reason for the obvious profound love of God it shares. After the meeting many of the members will probably go out on the streets to invite strangers to attend the lecture, especially on college campuses and even in churches.

The secret of this group's joy is information regarding the work of God in our day revealed by a Korean sage, Sun Myung Moon. Born in Korea in 1920, Moon paralleled the cruel sufferings of his country in the past half-century with religious passions and sufferings of his own. At age sixteen, he believed that Jesus appeared to him on Easter day and told him to complete the mission that was begun nearly 2000 years ago. For nine years after this vision, Moon felt himself engaged in a bitter struggle against Satanic forces who spiritually and physically tortured him. Finally, by persevering, he discovered the secret crime Satan had committed in the Garden of Eden. He then believed himself called to establish the foundations of the Kingdom of Heaven. Unfortunately, it was now 1945, and the site he chose was in Pyongyang, which became the capital of Communist North Korea in the same year. No sooner had Moon gathered a small following for his religious movement than he was arrested by the Communists. According to The Unified Family account, he suffered terrible tortures in a labor camp, yet sustained the faith of his fellow prisoners until his escape to South Korea in 1954. There he began to speak of a Divine Principle which should rule all of life. In 1958, he established a Divine Principle religion.

This movement in Korea has all the marks of a Far Eastern new religion of the Japanese type. It has scores of thousands of members and, showing strong traces of the traditional shamanism of the Korean countryside as well as of missionary Christianity, it places no small emphasis on clairvoyance, clairaudience, healing, and spiritualistic phenomena. Believers feel spiritual fire and electricity, and communicate mediumistically with spirits, Jesus, and God.

In 1959 a Korean lady named Miss Young Oon Kim came to the United States as a graduate student at the University of Oregon and an envoy of the teachings of Sun Myung Moon. She established the original American houses. Of Christian background like Moon himself, she presented an English translation and adaptation of Moon's doctrines in her book *The Divine Principle and Its Application*.

In this country Miss Kim's book is the primary authority for The Unified Family. Its teaching seems rather more abstract, and more evangelical, than the Korean religion. But it is no doubt true to Moon's convictions and manner. It tells that the universe is founded on certain laws establishing the right relations of things, of which the most fundamental are Polarity and the Four Base Relationships. All things come in pairs: God and man, male and female, inward and outward. Within the polarities is a proper fourfold hierarchy: God, as head; Male and Female, coequal in the middle; the Child, on the bottom as New Life. As one might have expected, the secret sin which Moon perceived Satan to have committed in the primal Garden was to have sexual relations between himself and Eve. This caused a shattering reversal of the Four Base Relationships, for it put Satan instead of God on top.

Because of this deed, man has been separated from God, and conflict and turmoil have followed him. The Bible is explained by The Unified Family in these terms. Throughout the Old Testament, man failed to restore the right order of the Four Base Relationships; even Jesus, in the New Testament, failed to do so because he was crucified. But now, the mission is about to be finished. We are at the dawn of a new era when the crime of Satan will be exposed by a man with a new name from a nation new in spiritual history. In our century, three significant events marking the end of the old dispensation have occurred as Satan has striven archetype against archetype with God. During World War I, Kaiser Wilhelm was the Satanic imitation of Adam. During World War II, Hitler was the Satanic imitation of Jesus. Finally, Communism represents the absolute culmination of Satan's world. In these apocalyptic last days the polarities of good and evil are vividly set out. But since 1960 the forces of evil have been on the defensive and the New Age has begun, even though Communism must yet be defeated. Then a new highly spiritual day can open for man, restored to a familyhood of right order.

The members of The Unified Family are the first of this new paradise of total restitution. There are about 10,000 of them in the United States, with headquarters established in Washington, D.C. They seem independent and cooperative persons. Decisions are referred to the Directors of each house, usually a youngish man and wife, but they act more like coordinators or camp counselors than parent figures; that role is reserved for Moon himself, who occasionally visits the United States.

In their own way, The Unified Family people participate in the widespread expectation of a new and far better age to be ushered in by a momentous spiritual event now anticipated by only a few, which is part of the climate of so many new groups—from UFO cults to Baha'i. The Unified Family is unique, however, in that it is based on an interpretation of the Christian Bible by a non-westerner. Non-Western Christian cults, while common enough in the "Third World," have very rarely brought their message to those lands whose missionaries first gave them that Bible which they now read in new ways. Certainly The Unified Family is the most important of this sort among the nonethnic minority religious movement scene in America. It is more in the emissary than exemplary tradition owing to its evangelical style of communication and the suffering prophet pattern of the founder's life. And so if not strictly a cult as I have defined the term, it seems of sufficient interest to warrant inclusion in this book.

Reading Selection: The Unified Family

The curious account which follows is from a book by the well-known Spiritualist medium, the late Arthur Ford. It exemplifies the connection between Sun Myung Moon's movement and Spiritualism. Later Mr. Ford held sittings at which Mr. Moon was present. Here the questioner is Anthony Brooke, a British writer interested both in Spiritualist communication and Mr. Moon's mission. "Fletcher" is Arthur Ford's control on the spirit plane; the words attributed to him are coming through Ford in trance. Since it appears that Ford and his circle were familiar with Moon before this seance, these words are not of evidential value so far as Spiritualism is concerned, but they do present an interpretation of Moon's mission and some measure of his influence.

ANTHONY BROOKE: Could you say anything about the significance of Mr. Moon in relation to any other individual in the flesh today?

FLETCHER: You mean in interpersonal relationships?

ANTHONY BROOKE: What can you tell us about Sun Myung Moon?

FLETCHER: His mission is as a teacher, a revealer. At the end of an age always there must be a few, sometimes even one, who will become the voice of this Intelligence—Creative Mind—which you call God. His relationship is to the rest of the world what that of many have been in the past. Abraham spoke and became the voice of God for a tribe. Moses spoke and became the voice of God for a nation. Jesus spoke and became the voice of God for the whole world. But the Anointed One cannot die— God cannot die. And the effort that is necessary now and the divine purpose for which Mr. Moon (is) brought into your consciousness is simply stated in this way, "It is necessary (he is the voice of inspiration, guidance) to restore to mankind an understanding of his full nature and his relationship to God."

And out of the shambles of a crumbling civilization and above the cries of distress that you hear in every part of your world today, there is a plan slowly and definitely unfolding to restore man to the state of perfection which is necessary if he is to live happily and handle wisely the instruments that materialistic science has wrested from this mysterious and growing universe.

Restoration not of anything of the past simply because it belongs to the past, but restoration of the basic truths out of which all civilizations and all religions have grown.

There have been many and each of them has been solitary until he has touched and inspired others—and gradually the pyramid spread out. He is not the first, nor the last. But for the present moment he is, in my estimation, a most important spiritual light that shines in the darkness of your confused world. . . .

And he has the rare quality of projecting himself, which isn't a miracle really. It's simply an employment of techniques which swamis, yogis, and holy men have known and which the saints have known for projection until you become real and visible to your devotees or people whom you need in order to further the kingdom. Mr. Moon in deep meditation can project himself and be seen just as Jesus has been able to project himself and be seen by the saints. This is one of the marks of the messiahs always.

Notes

1 The thirteen numbers of this magazine published in 1940 and 1941 by the Buddhist Society of America have been reprinted with a foreword in a bound volume called *Cat's Yawn* (New York: First Zen Institute of America, 1947).

2 Philip Kapleau, *The Three Pillars of Zen* (New York and Tokyo: John Weatherhill, Inc., 1965).

3 For further material on these practices, see H. Byron Earhart, *A Religious Study of the Mount Haguro Sect of Shugendo* (Tokyo: Sophia University, 1970).

4 Jacob Needleman, *The New Religions* (New York: Doubleday & Company, Inc., 1970), p. 170.

5 Needleman, *The New Religions*, Chapter 7, gives a fascinating account of one Tibetan Center in the West, the Tibetan Nyingmapa Meditation Center in Berkeley, California, founded by the refugee lama Tarthang Tulku in 1969. Another lama, Chogyam Trungpa Rinpoche, leads two centers, the Tail of the Tiger in Barnet, Vermont, and Karma Dzong in Boulder, Colorado. They publish a beautiful magazine, *Garuda: Tibetan Buddhism in America.* Probably the best introduction to the actual practice of Tibetan methods in a Western setting is John Blofeld, *The Way of Power* (London: George Allen & Unwin, 1970). The books of Lama Govinda, Alexandra David-Neel, David Snellgrove, Herbert Gunther, and W. Y. Evans-Wentz have also been very influential and sympathetic, but not always uncritical, presentations of the Tibetan heritage.

6 Aleister Crowley, of all people, seems to concur with this view of the communication role of the greatest religious founders, among whom he placed himself. He writes, "In recorded history we have scarcely had a dozen Magi in the technical sense of the word. They may be recognized by the fact that their message may be formulated as a single word, which word must be such that it overturns all existing beliefs and codes." John Symonds and Kenneth Grant, eds., *The Confessions of Aleister Crowley* (New York: Bantam Books, 1971), p. 420. He gives as examples the Buddha's "anatta," Muhammad's "Allah," and his own word "Thelema," given through him by Aiwass, which means "will" and which he says upsets totally the concept of the dying God.

7 For a discussion of the role of the Meher Baba movement in the counter-culture, see Thomas Robbins, "Eastern Mysticism and the Resocialization of Drug Users: The Meher Baba Cult," *Journal for the Scientific Study of Religion*, VIII, No. 2 (Fall 1969), 308–317. Robbins believes that the Baba movement appeals particularly to persons who defined their drug experience in mystical terms and offers a "worldly asceticism" which affords a means of reentry into the nonmystical secular world.

nine

Retrospect and a Glance at the Future

Beginning with an exploration of the venerable Theosophical tradition, we have moved, as if on pilgrimage, through a long series of American groups representing what we have called the alternative reality tradition in the West. Some have been large, and some small. Some seem as futuristic as the movie *2001*, and visiting others is more than anything else an exercise in Victorian nostalgia. Some have probably seemed attractive to the reader, others bizarre, still others quite repulsive. Some will doubtless not survive more than a few years, others may be part of the American scene for centuries.

A number of common motifs, however, have run through the vignettes of these cults. Over and over again we have heard of a new age, with a new messiah and a new message. The reader may in fact have tired of this parade of new messiahs, and fallen into cynicism about it. "If there are so many," he may ask, "can any of them be true?"

Cynicism, though, would not show full sensitivity to the message of an age of many messiahs. First of all, they and the response to them show a feeling that we are in a time of spiritual change and creativity. Each claims, in his own way, that a new dispensation is at hand and a new kind of spiritual man is about to emerge. And being in the exemplary alternative reality tradition, which takes words and claims to objective truth more lightly than do science, reason, Christianity, or Islam, the seeming incongruity of a plurality of messiahs and avatars is felt less sharply in the cult world. The important thing is not whether a symbol is "true" or "false," but the interior realization of a new state of consciousness. All symbols, including the person of the messiah, become

297

symbols of the self as initiated and realized. This is not always said, but seems to be understood in the cult world, for people move blithely from one earth-shaking revelation to another, requiring at one time the openness of an irenic and tolerant cult, at another the character-hardening experience of an intolerant "true believer" movement. The groups we have studied are groups which take care of people in this process of self-initiation in a time of great spiritual change.

I have endeavored, for the sake of clarifying the background of the new groups, to point toward an alternative reality tradition in the West. It has its source in the Platonic sense of wonder at the whole of being, of which man is a part, with shamanism behind it, just as the Judaeo-Christian tradition has its source in the sense of the numinous personal presence of the Other. These two sufficiently distinct emotional experiences give rise to the phenomena of religion, and inspire (respectively) the exemplary and emissary styles of religious communication.

In virtually all cases the new groups have represented the exemplary style of religious life and communication in a society which has otherwise been accustomed to the fire of the emissary manner, whether burning harshly or with the soft glow of a white mystical candle.

These groups are not normatively Judaeo-Christian. The means of ultimate transformation they offer is quite outside the ministry of the Mosaic Law or the work of Christ—even nominally in most cases. They present the transformation of interior initiation. One wakes up as did the Buddha to the solid light of the crystal within, which is simply there and can be found, and has no particular connection to an outside personal God, a past historical event, or an externally imparted message. We could ask if a new type of spiritual man is emerging—the proto-mutants, perhaps, of which the Prosperos speak.

The answer would have to be "yes" *and* "no." It is tempting, of course, to take the new groups at their own evaluation as harbingers of a new age of mystical religion, when the East (or the gnosis) shall dominate the West spiritually even as the West has overwhelmed the East in material culture. It is easy in this day of vastly accelerated mass communications to make an ephemeral movement of a few dozen souls appear momentous, until the next enthusiasm is in the forefront. But the implications are not simple. Only an ignorance of history could lead to the feeling that spirituality of the alternative reality type is really more widespread in America today than at many other points in European and American history. Regardless of publicity, the total number of people affected by all the movements in this book do not represent more than a few percent of the population of America, and the percentage is not likely to grow much in the future.

Yet statistics are no very meaningful clue to the significance of movements like these. If the mass communications of McLuhan's "global village" can magnify out of proportion movements of little statistical scale, the media's creations, like those of dreams and imagination, have a life of their own. In a day of omnipresent communication, a report of a handful of American Hindus flashed across the nation instantaneously makes American society more pluralistic than it was the day before. A new option is irreversibly there; whether many accept it or not, none can totally forget its presence. The cults will not convert America as Arabia was converted to Islam or as Britain was to Christianity. It is questionable whether nationwide shifts like this, very rare in any case, can conceivably happen again, given the degree of individualism now available in religion. Today, it is political and economic theories, rather than religions, that have the power to unify peoples, provoke wars and persecutions, and sweep across continents.

What the cults are doing is contributing to the formation of a Protean or expansive man whose spiritual life is not tied to a monolithic culture or self-identity. They are changing the meaning of religion from a single commitment to a series of experiences or awareness of a possible series of options whose very presence subtly changes the tone of religious activity even if many are left untried. The fact that many of the cult groups claim they are "not a religion," even though they deal in religious values, indicates some sensitivity to the fact that they are part of a change in the traditional meaning of religious identity. Rosicrucianism and Theosophy have long made it possible, by not being "religions," for people to combine one sort of relationship to Protestant Christianity with another to the "ancient wisdom."

If a new kind of spiritual man is emerging, it will not be a cult man precisely. After all, since cults provide a spiritual means of expressing alienation, and since the mystic, however valued by a culture, is always a singular individual, cults could hardly attain majority status. A pluralistic society, by logical necessity, will always have minorities, which will inevitably feel "alienated." There is much reason to think that after the irreversible discovery of history, for reasons of cultural lag and the dynamics of compensatory psychology, it is the minority which is likely to identify itself spirituality through initiatory, mystical—what we have called alternative reality—symbols.

But in a pluralistic society alternatives will not be laid out in polarized terms; it will not be a matter of two alternatives, the majority and the minority, between which a person must make a holistic choice. The media and the free nature of the society will see to it that most people are sufficiently exposed to the spectrum of choices that each will, in some way, in greater and lesser degree, become a part of him. He will within himself be both majority and minority, establishment and alienated, historical and mystical, know the principal and the alternative reality. The new spiritual man will not be man converted to Proclus or Buddha, but man within whom they, and also Moses and Christ and Faust, can coexist more comfortably than before—though not necessarily with equal value.

On a shorter range, changes are always afoot. In the seventies, it appears that alienation will not take the same religious forms as in the sixties. There seems to be a more critical attitude toward oriental and mystical religions, and a resurgence of fundamentalist Christianity. Three factors are involved: the rise of a sense of the sacredness of nature, a growth of American nativism in religion, and a move toward desiring punctiliar simplicity in religious experience. Other new movements today do not necessarily represent fundamentalism or provincial nativism, such as The Mythopoeic Society, concerned with the Christian fantasy writing of Charles Williams, C. S. Lewis, and J. R. R. Tolkien.

In part the new movements represent a Western response, a westernizing adjustment, toward the strong, anarchic spiritual forces of the sixties. Despite the desire of a minority to express total alienation, there is a limit to how discontinuous a new spirituality can be to its cultural environment. The reaction has been a predictible revival of American nostalgia. It has taken the form of a new vogue for evangelical, fundamentalist religion—probably the last thing most observers of the sixties would have expected, but then as H. G. Wells once pointed out, common people love nothing more than to fool the prophets. The nostalgia aspect of it is evident from the plain farm overalls favored as dress by some of the new Christians, the old-fashioned hymns, the rural communes, and above all the simple, nonintellectual nature of the religion which seems to yearn for a time in American history when, it is presumed, both life and decisions were less ambiguous, when it was easier to assimilate oneself to an archetype.

Thus it is often emphasized that Jesus is the one absolute answer. Instead of having to work one's way through the endless fantastic worlds of the drug experience or the *Tibetan Book of the Dead* or the Hindu pantheon, and rather than make the shaman's quest to far away lands full of stolen souls, one is offered a straightforward immediate ecstasy in Jesus greater than all these riches. In a sense, it is the ultimate statement of the "now generation" in spirituality. In many cults, because of the monistic immanence of the divine, immediacy is promised. But expectation devours immediacy, and the movement becomes an interiorized apocalyptic hope. The hope is for an impossibly vast and world-transforming mystical experience, or rather a subjective experience which will seem to transform the world because it transforms the individual's vision. In Christianity the transformation is exteriorized; it will really happen in the Day of the Lord many now await. There is a sense in which only the emissary style can truly deliver immediacy, for any exemplar can only initiate the individual into a process which promises interior change. But the emissary can declare it a fact, and if he is convincing, it is a fact.

There was reason for the outburst of non-Judaeo-Christian cults. What is not often realized is that despite the love of some of them for scientific-sounding terminology, most of them are in pertinent ways more anti-scientific than anti-Christian. They are really opposed to the Judaeo-Christian tradition only insofar as it has seemed to "fellow-travel" with the scientific and technological world view, giving it aid and comfort and, indeed, with its historical and dominational view of the human vocation, bearing ultimate responsibility for it. This is evident in the readiness of the counter-culture to embrace other aspects of Christianity: the fashionable (if seldom read) mysticism of Eckhart and St. John of the Cross, St. Francis, Fundamentalism.

The non-Judaeo-Christian cults have sensed in the West an underestimation of man for all its pride in man's achievements. They have sensed, better than many theologians, that despite fiery surface struggles, the scientific outlook—rationalistic, seeing man isolated from the universe, a strange conscious being who is in an alien world and can only wrest knowledge and power and pleasure from it by exercise of reason and will —is tied to the Judaeo-Christian tradition like Jacob to Esau. They have felt the same thing in once-fashionable Western existentialism—a view of man as an alien outcropping of consciousness in a dead cosmos. But it is only because he had put blinders on his mind and soul, through his rationalism, science, and emissary religion, they say, that Western man has unnecessarily put himself in this box. The cults, wanting to experience man as continuous with nature, his mind continuous with the universal, have protested against this depersonalized antiseptic cosmos which devalues the infinite meaning of both rich and paltry experiences of consciousness. They challenge the inability of Western man to value "in-between" states of mind not directed to things and problem-solving or words and concepts.

But the kind of answers the cults have given will receive more careful scrutiny. People want solid answers. There is reaction against the mere appeal of exoticism, and simple gimmicks—macrobiotic diet, chants, techniques, bare metaphysics—which allegedly unlock the wealth of the alternative reality tradition. These have all been tried in the sixties, and have left many still unsatisfied. A certain reaction against Asia—perhaps a result of the Vietnam War—has come to pass. Many Americans are tired of that continent and not especially eager to get new wisdom from it. It is recognized, rightly, that most traditional Asian societies have not in practice done a very good job either of meeting human needs or of conserving natural resources and natural beauty. A feeling is setting in that we must search our own tradition and our own creativity, and find our own solutions to our problems.

But the new spirituality will not be merely traditional. Western tradition, it is also recognized, is not of itself adequate to the present. The "now generation" insists that religion has to be experiential. Tradition is not enough. But tradition does lend great support to a religious expression that is endowed with the positive emotional valuation which age gives and which creates feeling of nostalgic yearning. These feelings move easily into feelings for the sacred; the sense of "otherness" induced by the emotionally charged past becomes a sense of the numinous. This transition is a mainstay of religion. "Ritual perpetuation of the past" is the essence of rite (and of rhetoric as rite).

All these concerns seem to have produced two new movements which have not yet found a synthesis. First is the "Jesus movement." During 1970 and 1971, a number of young people who had tried drugs, Eastern cults, the occult, free love, and communes were converted to evangelical Christianity. Without abandoning much of the externalia of their former lives—dress, argot, communalism—they accepted the "high" that acceptance of Jesus gives and moved into Christian communes and "street Christian" chapels. In Laguna Beach, several members of Krishna Consciousness switched to a Christian commune. This new Christianity is characterized by a fervent street evangelism, fundamentalist theology, and an apocalyptic expectation of the imminent coming of Christ. It is also marked by a negative attitude toward most conventional Christian churches, whether conservative or liberal. Many, for example, have little use for the ordinary Sunday morning service. Worship happens spontaneously. Someone picks up a guitar and begins singing, or is moved to pray or speak in tongues. This may occur in the middle of the night, or on Wednesday afternoon, as well as on Sunday morning. For some, the new Christianity is no doubt an expression of the same "generation gap" which has led others to cults. Probably many people felt a secret guilt about throwing off the beliefs of their family and culture, and in the new Fundamentalism have brought it back in a manner calculated also to express a gulf between themselves and the conventional Protestant or Catholic affiliations of their parents.

But others are disturbed by a motif which is of continuing importance, and is better expressed, it seems, in the new culture of the sixties than in conservative Christianity. That is belief in the sacredness of nature. The new sense of the sacredness of nature is a real religious phenomenon, for the sense of the sacredness of what is left unspoiled as it was before the hand of man was felt in the world has all the connotations of the religiously sacred—the temple, the holy mountain. These are spots where one has direct communion with the roots of reality, and where consciousness is changed. Rage against blasphemers of these spots is as intense as against profaners of a holy sanctuary. In a real sense, this is a new motif, especially in the West. It has roots in romanticism, but has gone beyond aesthetics for large numbers of people only more recently. For archaic man, and for most religion through the ages, nature has been real, but not in itself sacred. It has been rather the "enemy," identified with primordial chaos, which man subdues to create the sacred as ordered human society—the city with the temple in its midst. The shaman or prophet may go into the wilderness, but not so much because its beauty is sacred, as because there he may prove his mettle by doing battle with the strange inhuman spirits who dwell there, or by meeting God in strange and novel ways. The Bible begins with a garden, but ends with a city, the heavenly Jerusalem, as image of the Kingdom of God.

Now, however, in a return to a new form of cosmic religion, nature has become the sacred and the city the profane. This new discovery is in some ways related to the revival of monistic cosmic religion by the cults, but only peripherally. It was really a new discovery of modern man, and like all real religious discoveries it was unexpected, yet in hindsight not unpredictable. It was not actually likely that the "secular city" would become the sacred, for the sacred is always that which is hidden, inaccessible, rare—which has the quality of "otherness." At one time human society was as chancy as God, fragile before all the vicissitudes of war and famine and plague. Now it has become the common; what is left of nature gives a sense of the rarity and uncanniness of the numinous, and it is enhanced by the sacral feelings induced by nostalgia.

These two new movements have some themes continuous with those of cults: the search for a simple and sure key, a reaction against "ritual" (which despite the resurgence of magic and Neo-Paganism is still disdained by most contemporary seekers), the discovery of the cosmic as bearer of the sacred. But there are some new notes: the simple key has, in the Jesus movement, been made even more radical, as is possible with a return to the emissary mode. Acceptance of Jesus requires not even chanting or meditation; it is a simple, spare, punctiliar act of faith, which promises immediate joy. It is more apocalyptic than even the Aquarian Age, with its mystical and evolutionary overtones. It is tied to a new American spiritual nostalgia. The sacredness of nature is more and more becoming something which can no more fit the categories of archaic or Asian religion (though it may draw symbols and inspiration from them) than those of emissary Western religion.

An unstable dialectic is therefore set up: traditional emissary faith versus cosmic hierophany; nostalgia versus an antipathy to the technology to which the values of that past gave rise. But the dialectic will not be settled with the absolute victory of one side or the other. All of this occurs to Protean man in the context of pluralistic society. It is inevitable that the resolution will be as much within as between people, and will take the shape of new creations from out of the maelstrom of the new Hellenistic era. There may be some grounds for synthesis, though they have not yet been much explored in popular religious culture.

Figures like Satya Sai Baba remind us that Jesus can be venerated as an oriental holy man with at least as much authenticity as the conventional Western deculturized Christ. Even more promising, a full recovery of the eschatological heritage of biblical Judaism and Christianity could recover a sense of cosmic hierophany linked far more to future hope than past nostalgia, and could see the sacred in nature as, through Christ and the continuing work of God, far more a sign of coming glory than a pathetic remnant of a dying past. The great trump card Christianity holds over all Eastern and alternative reality faiths is that however harder it may be to believe, with its sudden and miraculous new heaven and earth, it also makes by far the greatest promises.

It is likely these and other possibilities will be explored, and that what religion brings will again be what is least expected. Religion, despite occasional predictions of its demise, seems a perenniel attribute of man. It is needed to fill a certain void caused by lack of communication with his environment in the widest sense, boundless space and time, and by awe at the unlikely fact of his possessing consciousness in a seemingly inert universe. There must, religion seems to say, be more that is directly pertinent to him in the limitless depths of this environment, on both the dimensional and mental planes, than appears on the surface.

Americans expect much from religion. Foreign observers often insist that America is the most religious nation in the world. If so (and of course no generalization of this sort means much) it is not because America is tied to traditional religion to the same extent some Asian nations still are, but because Americans—unlike modernized people in some other countries—seem unable to become completely and happily secular. Even while multiplying secular sources of happiness, they continue to expect religion to produce happiness, they set up poles of time and place as sacred, they feel religious guilt, they use religion as justification for everything from national policy to individual vocation, they look for it to handle personal disappointments and sorrows. In terms of expectation, America is perhaps a very religious country. For this reason, it will continue to be a very creative country religiously.

Bibliography

This bibliography is intended to provide some starting points for the student of cult movements. Naturally, the whole body of the literature on topics like the Kabbalah and Madame Blavatsky cannot be cited here. It is hoped that enough is included to assist the reader who wishes to pursue further some matters touched upon in this book. In general, scholarly studies rather than official or advocacy literature of the groups themselves are listed here. In cases where published research is scanty, some items of historical or general interest from the news media are cited. Some groups are not included in the bibliography because there seems to be no significant literature about them outside of their own publications which the student would obtain through contacting the group.

CHAPTER ONE
IN QUEST OF NEW RELIGIONS

ATKINS, GAIUS G., *Modern Cults and Religious Movements*. Old Tappan, N.J.: Fleming H. Revell Company, 1923.

BELLAH, ROBERT N., *Religion and Progress in Modern Asia*. New York: The Free Press, 1965.

BRADEN, CHARLES S., *These Also Believe: A Study of Modern American Cults and Minority Religious Movements*. New York: The Macmillan Company, Publishers, 1949.

BRADEN, WILLIAM, *The Private Sea: LSD and the Search for God*. Chicago: Quandrangle Books, Inc., 1967.

BRIDGES, HAL, *American Mysticism: From William James to Zen*. New York: Harper & Row, Publishers, 1970.

CATTON, WILLIAM JR., "What Kind of People Does a Religious Cult Attract?" *American Sociological Review*, XXII (October 1957), 561–66.

CLARK, ELMER T., *The Small Sects of America*. New York: Abingdon-Cokesbury, 1949.

DOHRMAN, H. T., *California Cult: The Story of "Mankind United."* Boston; Beacon Press, Inc., 1958.

ELIADE, MIRCEA, *Cosmos and History*. New York: Harper & Row, Publishers, 1959.

——, *From Primitives to Zen*. New York: Harper & Row, Publishers, 1967.

——, *Mephistopheles and the Androgyne: Studies in Religious Myth and Symbol*. New York: Sheed and Ward, Inc., 1965.

——, *The Sacred and the Profane*. New York: Harper & Row, Publishers, 1961.

——, *Shamanism: Archaic Techniques of Ecstasy*, Bollengen Series LXXVI. Princeton: Princeton University Press, 1964.

Festinger, Leon, Henry W. Riecken, and Stanley Schacter, *When Prophecy Fails*. Minneapolis: University of Minnesota Press, 1956.

Glock, C. Y., "The Role of Deprivation in the Origin and Evolution of Religious Groups," in *Religion and Social Conflict*, eds. R. Lee and M. Marty. New York; Oxford University Press, 1964.

Hedgepeth, William, and Dennis Stock, *The Alternative: Communal Life in New America*. New York: P. F. Collier Inc., 1970.

Hoult, Thomas, "A Functional Theory of Religion," *Sociology and Social Research*, XLI (March 1957), 277–80.

———, *The Sociology of Religion*. New York: Dryden Press, Inc., 1958.

Johnson, Benton, "Church and Sect," *American Sociological Review*, 28, No. 4 (August 1963), 539–49.

Knudten, Richard, ed., *The Sociology of Religion: An Anthology*. New York: Appleton-Century-Crofts, 1967.

Lifton, Robert Jay, "Protean Man," in *The Religious Situation*, ed. Donald R. Cutler. Boston: Beacon Press, Inc., 1969, pp. 812–28.

Lommel, Andreas, *Shamanism: The Beginnings of Art*. New York: McGraw-Hill Book Company, 1967.

Mann, W. E., *Sect, Cult, and Church in Alberta*. Toronto: University of Toronto Press, 1955.

Martin, David A., *Pacifism: An Historical and Sociological Study*. London: Routledge and Kegan, Paul, 1965.

Maslow, Abraham, *Toward a Psychology of Being*. New York: Van Norstrand-Reinhold Books, 1968.

———, *Religion, Values, and Peak Experience*. Columbus: Ohio State University Press, 1964.

Mathison, Richard R., *Faiths, Cults, and Sects of America: From Atheism to Zen*. Indianapolis: The Bobbs-Merrill Co., Inc., 1960.

McLuhan, Marshall, *Understanding Media: The Extensions of Man*. New York: Signet Books, 1964.

Moberg, David, "Potential Uses of the Church-Sect Typology in Comparative Religious Research," *International Journal of Comparative Sociology*, II (March 1961), 47–58.

Orr, John B., and F. Patrick, Nichelson, *The Radical Suburb: Soundings in Changing American Character*. Philadelphia: Westminster Press, 1970.

Redekop, Calvin, "Decision-Making in a Sect," *Review of Religious Research*, II (Fall 1960), 79–86.

Roszak, Theodore, *The Making of a Counter-Culture*. New York: Doubleday & Company, Inc., Anchor Books, 1969.

Salisbury, W. Seward, "Faith, Ritualism, Charismatic Leadership, and Religious Behavior," *Social Forces*, XXXIV (March 1956), 241–45.

Stark, Werner, *The Sociology of Religion* (4 volumes). (London: Routledge and Kegan, Paul, 1966.

STRENG, FREDERICK J., *Understanding Religious Man*. Belmont, California: Dickenson Publishing Company, Inc., 1969.

STRUNK, ORLO JR., ed., *Readings in the Psychology of Religion*. New York: Abingdon Press, 1959.

SWEET, W. W., *American Culture and Religion*. Dallas: Southern Methodist University Press, 1951.

TALMON, YONINA, "Pursuit of the Millennium: The Relation Between Religious and Social Change," in *Reader in Comparative Religion*, eds. William Lessa and Evan Vogt. New York: Harper & Row, Publishers, 1965.

TOCH, HANS, and ROBERT ANDERSON, "Religious Belief and Denominational Affiliation," *Religious Education*, LV (May-June 1960), 193–200.

———, *The Social Psychology of Social Movements*. Indianapolis: The Bobbs-Merrill Co., Inc., 1965.

TROELTSCH, ERNST, *Social Teaching of the Christian Churches*. New York: The Macmillan Company, Publishers, 1931.

VAN DER LEEUW, GERARDUS, *Religion in Essence and Manifestation*. New York: Harper & Row, Publishers, 1963.

WACH, JOACHIM, *Sociology of Religion*. Chicago: University of Chicago Press, 1944.

———, *The Comparative Study of Religion*. New York: Columbia University Press, 1958.

WEBER, MAX, *The Sociology of Religion*. Boston: Beacon Press, Inc., 1963.

WEISE, LEOPOLD VON, and HOWARD BECKER, *Systematic Sociology*. New York: John Wiley & Sons, Inc., 1932. See especially pp. 624–42, "Four Types of Religious Organization."

WIEDEMAN, GEORGE, "The Importance of Religious Sectarianism in Psychiatric Case Study," *American Journal of Psychotherapy*, III (1949), 392–98.

WILSON, BRYAN, "An Analysis of Sect Development," *American Sociological Review*, XXIV (February 1959), 3–15.

———, *Sects and Society: The Sociology of Three Religious Groups in Britain*. London: William Heinemann, 1961.

YINGER, J. MILTON, "Religion and Social Change: Functions and Dysfunctions of Sects and Cults Among the Disprivileged," *Review of Religious Research*, IV (Winter 1962), 65–84.

———, *Religion, Society, and the Individual*. New York: The Macmillan Company, Publishers, 1957.

———, *The Scientific Study of Religion* (New York, The Macmillan Company, 1970).

ZAEHNER, R. C., *Mysticism Sacred and Profane*. New York: Oxford University Press, 1961.

ZETTERBERG, HANS, "The Religious Conversion as a Change of Social Roles," *Sociology and Social Research*, XXXVI (January 1952), 159–66.

CHAPTER TWO
THE HISTORY OF
ALTERNATIVE REALITIES IN THE WEST

WILSON, COLIN, *The Occult: A History*. New York: Random House, Inc., 1971.

A. *The Hellenistic Period*

BUTLER, E. M., *The Myth of the Magus*. New York: The Macmillan Company, Publishers, 1948.

CONYBEARE, F. C., trans., *The Life of Apollonious of Tyana*. New York: The Macmillan Company, Publishers, 1912.

CREMER, FRIEDRICH, *Die Chaldaischen Orakel und Jamblich De Mysteriis*. Meisenheim am Glan: A. Hain, 1969.

DILL, SAMUEL, *Roman Society from Nero to Marcus Aurelius*. London: The Macmillan, Company, Publishers, 1904.

DODDS, E. R., *The Greeks and the Irrational*. Berkeley: University of California Press, 1951.

GRANT, FREDERICK C., *Hellenistic Religions*. New York: Liberal Arts Press, 1953.

GRANT, ROBERT M., *Gnosticism and Early Christianity*. New York: Harper & Row, Publishers, 1966.

JONAS, HANS, *The Gnostic Religion*. Boston: Beacon Press, Inc., 1963.

MEAD, G. R. S., *Echoes from the Gnosis*. London: Theosophical Publishing Society, 1908. Vols. VIII–IX, *The Chaldean Oracles*.

PHILIP, JAMES A., *Pythagoras and Early Pythagoreanism*. Toronto: University of Toronto Press, 1966.

SCOTT, WALTER, *Hermetica*. Oxford, England: Clarendon Press, 1924–36.

TARN, WILLIAM W., *Hellenistic Civilization*. New York: World Publishing Co., 1961.

VAN MOORSEL, GERARD, *The Mysteries of Hermes Trismegistus*. Utrecht: Kemink & Zoon, 1955.

B. *The Middle Ages*

BUTLER, E. M., *Ritual Magic*. Cambridge: Cambridge University Press, 1949.

DEGIVRY, GRILLOT, *A Pictorial Anthology of Witchcraft, Magic, and Alchemy*. New York: University Books, 1958.

ELIADE, MIRCEA, *The Forge and the Crucible*. New York: Harper & Row, Publishers, Inc., 1962.

HUGHES, PENNETHORNE, *Witchcraft*. London: Longmans, Green and Co., 1952.

MURRAY, MARGARET, *God of the Witches*. New York: Doubleday & Company, Inc., Anchor Books, 1960. (First published 1933.)

RUNCIMAN, STEVEN, *The Medieval Manichee*. Cambridge: Cambridge University Press, 1960.

SCHOLEM, GERSHOM G., *Major Trends in Jewish Mysticism*. New York: Schocken Books, Inc., 1967.

———, *On the Kabbalah and its Symbolism*. New York: Schocken Books, Inc., 1969.

SUMMERS, MONTAGUE, *The Geography of Witchcraft*. New York: University Books, 1958.

WILLIAMS, CHARLES, *Witchcraft*. New York: Meridian Books, 1959.

C. *The Renaissance*

ALLEN, DON CAMERON, *Doubt's Boundless Sea: Skepticism and Faith in the Renaissance*. Baltimore: Johns Hopkins Press, 1964.

HARGROVE, JOHN, *The Life and Soul of Paracelsus*. London: Gallancz, 1951.

JACOBI, JOLANDE, *Paracelsus: Selected Writings*. New York: Pantheon Books, Inc., 1951.

D. *The Rosicrucians*

CRAVEN, JAMES BROWN, *Doctor Robert Fludd*. Kirkwall, Scotland: William Peace & Son, 1902.

DEBUS, ALLEN G., *The English Paracelsians*. New York: Franklin Watts, Inc., 1966.

JONES, MERVYN, "The Rosicrucians," in *Secret Societies*, ed. Norman Mackenzie. New York: P. F. Collier, Inc., 1971.

MAGRE, MAURICE, *Magicians, Seers, and Mystics*. New York: E. P. Dutton & Co., Inc., 1932.

SHELLEY, PERCY BYSSHE (1792–1822), *St. Ivryne or The Rosicrucian: a Romance* (1811).

STOUDT, JOHN JOSEPH, *Sunrise to Eternity: A Study in Jacob Boehme's Life and Thought*. Philadelphia: University of Pennsylvania Press, 1957.

WAITE, A. E., *The Brotherhood of the Rosy Cross*. New York: University Books, 1961.

———, ed., *The Works of Thomas Vaughan*. New York: University Books, 1968.

YATES, FRANCES AMELIA, *Theatre of the World*. London: Routledge and Kegan, Paul, 1969.

E. *The Eighteenth Century*

COOPER-OAKLEY, ISABEL, *The Count of Saint-Germain*. Blauvelt, New York: Rudolf Steiner Publications, 1970. (Originally published 1912.)

DUMAS, F. R., *Cagliostro*. New York: Grossman Publishers, Inc., 1968.

JONES, MERVYN, "Freemasonry," in *Secret Societies*, ed. Norman Mackenzie. New York: P. F. Collier Books, Inc., 1971.

KATZ, JACOB, *Jews and Freemasons in Europe 1725–1939*. Cambridge: Harvard University Press, 1970.

PILK, FRED, et al., *Pocket History of Freemasonry*. New York: International Publications Service, 1969.

SWEDENBORG, EMANUEL, *The World of Spirits and Man's State After Death*. New York: Swedenborg Foundation, 1940.

TOKSVIG, SIGNE, *Emanuel Swedenborg, Scientist and Mystic*. New Haven: Yale University Press, 1948.

TROWBRIDGE, W. R. H., *Cagliostro*. London: Allen & Unwin, 1910.

WAITE, A. E., *New Encyclopedia of Freemasonry* (2 vols). New York: University Books, 1970.

———, *The Unknown Philosopher: The Life of Louis Claude de St. Martin*. Blauvelt, New York: Rudolf Steiner Publications, 1970.

WALMSLEY, DONALD MENRO, *Anton Mesmer*. London: Hale, 1967.

F. *Spiritualism*

ANDREWS, ERNEST DEMING, *The People Called Shakers*. New York: Oxford University Press, 1953.

BROWN, SLATER, *The Heyday of Spiritualism*. New York: Hawthorne Books, Inc., 1970.

CROSS, WHITNEY R., *The Burned Over District: The Social and Intellectual History of Enthusiastic Religion in Western New York*. New York: Harper & Row, Publishers, 1965.

FORNELL, EARL W., *Unhappy Medium: Spiritualism and the Life of Margaret Fox*. Austin: University of Texas Press, 1964.

NELSON, GEOFFREY K., *Spiritualism and Society*. New York: Schocken Books, Inc., 1969.

NORDHOFF, CHARLES, *The Communistic Societies of the United States*. New York: Dover Publications, Inc., 1966.

PRICE, ROBERT, *Johnny Appleseed, Man and Myth*. Gloucester, Massachusetts: Peter Smith, Publisher, Inc., 1967.

G. *Theosophy*

BUTT, G. BASEDEN, *Madame Blavatsky*. London: Rider and Co., 1925.

GREENWALT, EMMETT A., *The Point Loma Community in California, 1897–1942: A Theosophical Experiment*. Berkeley: University of California Press, 1955.

NEFF, MARY K., *Personal Memories of H. P. Blavatsky*. Wheaton, Illinois: Theosophical Publishing House, 1937, 1967.

"New Messiah in Tennis Flannels," *Literary Digest*, June 26, 1926, p. 37.

OLCOTT, HENRY STEELE, *Old Diary Leaves: The True Story of the Theosophical Society*, Series I-IV. Adyar, Madras, India: Theosophical Publishing House, 1895–1910.

On establishment of Point Loma and rivalry of Theosophical Organizations, see *New York Times*, February 12, 1897, p. 2; April 5, 1897, p. 2; June 28, 1897, p. 7; March 19, 1897, p. 7.

On Krishnamurti's break with Theosophical organization, see *New York Times* August 4, 1929, II, p. 22; August 6, 1929, p. 4; August 11, 1929, IX, p. 11.

SINNETT, A. P., *The Occult World*. London: Theosophical Publishing House, 1881, 1969.

H. *New Thought*

BRADEN, CHARLES S., *Spirits in Rebellion: The Rise and Development of New Thought*. Dallas: Southern Methodist University Press, 1963.

ENGLAND, R. W., "Some Aspects of Christian Science as Reflected in Letters of Testimony," *American Journal of Sociology*, LIX (March 1954), 448–53.

GRISWOLD, ALFRED WHITNEY, "New Thought: A Cult of Success," *American Journal of Sociology*, XI (November 1934), 309–18.

———, "Inspirational Religious Literature: From Latent to Manifest Functions of Religion," *American Journal of Sociology*, LXII (1957), 476–81.

JUDAH, J. STILLSON, *The History and Philosophy of the Metaphysical Movements in America*. Philadelphia: Westminster Press, 1967.

PFAUTZ, HAROLD, "Christian Science: A Case Study of the Social Psychological Aspects of Secularization," *Social Forces*, XXXIV (March 1956), 246–51.

SCHNEIDER, LOUIS, and SANFORD DORNBUSCH, *Popular Religion: Inspirational Books in America*. Chicago, Illinois: University of Chicago Press, 1958.

I. *Eastern Imports*

LANDAU, RON, *God Is My Adventure*. London: Unwin Books, 1935, 1964.

NEEDLEMAN, JACOB, *The New Religions*. New York: Doubleday & Company, Inc., 1970.

THOMAS, WENDELL, *Hinduism Invades America*. New York: Beacon Press, Inc., 1930.

CHAPTER THREE
NEW VESSELS
FOR THE ANCIENT WISDOM

A. *Theosophy*

BARKER, A. T., ed., *The Mahatma Letters to A. P. Sinnett*. London: Rider and Company, 1933.

BLAVATSKY, HELENA PETROVNA, *Collected Writings*. Boris de Zirkoff, compiler (10 volumes), varying dates and publishers.

BRADEN, CHARLES S., *These Also Believe: A Study of Modern American Cults and Minority Religious Movements*. New York: The Macmillan Company, Publishers, 1949.

GUÉNON, RENÉ, *Le Théosophisme: histoire d'un pseudo-religion*. Paris: Editions traditionelles, 1965.

JUDAH, J. STILLSON, *History and Philosophy of the Metaphysical Movements in America*. Philadelphia: Westminster Press, 1967.

LILJEGREN, STEN BODVAR, *Bulwer-Lytton's Novels and Isis Unveiled*. Cambridge: Harvard University Press, 1957.

RANSOM, JOSEPHINE, *A Short History of the Theosophical Society*. Adyar, Madras, India: Theosophical Publishing House, 1930.

B. *Full Moon Meditation Groups*

BAILEY, ALICE A., *Works*. New York: Lucis Publishing Company, varying dates.

———, *The Unfinished Autobiography of Alice A. Bailey*. New York: Lucis Publishing Company, 1951.

JUDAH, J. STILLSON, *History and Philosophy of the Metaphysical Movements in America*. Philadelphia: Westminster Press, 1967.

C. *Anthroposophy*

BARFIELD, OWEN, *Romanticism Comes of Age*. London: Anthroposophical Publishing Co., 1944.

HARWOOD, A., *The Faithful Thinker*. London: Hodder and Stoughton, 1961.

LANDAU, RON, *God Is My Adventure*. London: Unwin Books, 1935, 1964.

D. *Order of the Pleroma and Modern Gnosticism*

ANSON, PETER, *Bishops at Large*. London: Faber and Faber, 1964.

E. *The "I Am" Movement*

BRADEN, CHARLES S., *These Also Believe: A Study of Modern American Cults and Minority Religious Movements*. New York: The Macmillan Company, Publishers, 1949.

BRYAN, GERALD B., *Psychic Dictatorship in America*. Los Angeles: Truth Research Publications, 1940.

McGAUGHEY, H. G., "Another One in Los Angeles: The I Am Movement," *Christian Century*, August 31, 1938.

"Mighty I Am," *Time*, February 28, 1938, p. 32; *New York Times*, January 21, 1941, p. 7.

F. *The Liberal Catholic Church*

ANSON, PETER, *Bishops at Large*. London: Faber and Faber, 1964.

BRADEN, CHARLES S., *These Also Believe: A Study of Modern American Cults and Minority Religious Movements*. New York: The Macmillan Company, Publishers, 1949.

DART, JOHN, "Liberal Catholic Church Preaches Free Conscience," *Los Angeles Times*, March 24, 1969.

CHAPTER FOUR
THE DESCENT OF THE MIGHTY ONES

A. *Spiritualism*

BRADEN, CHARLES S., *These Also Believe: A Study of Modern American Cults and Minority Religious Movements*. New York: The Macmillan Company, Publishers, 1949.

BROWN, SLATER, *The Heyday of Spiritualism*. New York: Hawthorne Books, Inc., 1970.

CARMER, CARL LANSON, *Listen for a Lonesome Drum*. New York: Farrar and Rinehart, 1956.

CRENSHAW, JAMES, *Telephone Between Worlds*. Los Angeles: DeVorss & Company, 1950.

FORNELL, EARL W., *Unhappy Medium: Spiritualism and the Life of Margaret Fox*. Austin: University of Texas Press, 1964.

GOODSPEED, EDGAR T., *Modern Apocrypha*. Boston: Beacon Press, Inc., 1956.

JUDAH, J. STILLSON, *History and Philosophy of the Metaphysical Movements in America*. Philadelphia: Westminster Press, 1967.

NELSON, GEOFFREY K., "The Spiritualist Movement: A Need for the Redefinition of the Concept of Cult," *Journal for the Scientific Study of Religon*, VIII, No. 1, 152–60.

———, *Spiritualism and Society*. New York: Schocken Books, Inc., 1969.

WHITE, EDITH A., *A Spiritualist Sect in Nashville*. New York: Vantage Press, Inc., 1970.

B. *UFO Movements*

BUCKNER, H. T., "Flying Saucerians Linger On," *New Society*, September 9, 1965.

———, "The Flying Saucerians: An Open Door Cult," in *Sociology and Everyday Life*, ed. Marcello Truzzi. Englewood Cliffs, N.J.: Prentice-Hall, Inc., 1968.

CATOE, LYNN E., *UFO's and Related Subjects: An Annotated Bibliography*. Washington, D.C.: U.S. Government Printing Office, 1969.

CONDON, EDWARD, *Scientific Study of Unidentified Flying Objects*. New York: Bantam Books, Inc., 1969.

DRAPER, H., "An Afternoon with the Space People," *Harpers*, September 1960, pp. 37–40.

FESTINGER, LEON, HENRY W. RIECKEN, and STANLEY SCHACTER, *When Prophecy Fails*. Minneapolis: University of Minnesota Press, 1956.

JACKSON, J. A., "Two Contemporary Cults," *The Advancement of Science* (June 1966).

Jung, Carl G., *Flying Saucers: A Modern Myth of Things Seen in the Sky.* New York: Signet Books, 1969.

"Out of This World: Convention of the Amalgamated Flying Saucer Clubs of America," *Newsweek,* November 7, 1966, p. 38.

Reeves, Bryant, and Helen Reeves, *Flying Saucer Pilgrimage.* Amherst, Wisconsin: Amherst Press, 1957.

Sable, Martin H., *UFO Guide: 1947–1967.* Beverly Hills: Rainbow Press, 1967. (Bibliography)

Valee, Jacques, *Anatomy of a Phenomenon.* New York: Henry Regnery Company, 1965.

Chapter Five
The Crystal Within

A. *Gurdjieff*

Anderson, Margaret C., *The Unknowable Gurdjieff.* London: Routledge and Kegan, Paul, 1962.

De Hartmann, Thomas, *Our Life With Mr. Gurdjieff.* New York: Cooper Square Publishers, Inc., 1964.

Gurdjieff, G., *All and Everything.* New York: Harcourt, Brace & World, Inc., 1950.

Lefort, Rafael, *The Teachers of Gurdjieff.* London: Gollancz, 1966.

Nott, C. S., *Teachings of Gurdjieff, The Journal of a Pupil.* London: Routledge and Kegan, Paul, 1961.

Ouspensky, P. D., *In Search of the Miraculous.* New York: Harcourt, Brace & World, Inc., 1949.

———, *The Fourth Way.* London: Routledge and Kegan, Paul, 1957.

Pauwels, L., *Gurdjieff.* New York: Samuel Weiser, 1969.

Peters, Fritz, *Boyhood With Gurdjieff.* New York: E. P. Dutton, Inc., 1964.

Walker, Kenneth, *A Study of Gurdjieff's Teaching.* London: Jonathan Cape, 1967.

"Wise Man from the East," *Time,* January 28, 1952, p. 100.

B. *Scientology*

Eisenberg, A., and H. Eisenberg, "Dangerous New Cult of Scientology," *Parents Magazine,* June 1969, p. 48.

Jackson, J. A., "Two Contemporary Cults," *The Advancement of Science* (June 1966).

Malko, George, *Scientology: The Now Religion.* New York: Delacorte Press, 1970.

O'Brien, Helen, *Dianetics in Limbo.* Philadelphia: Whitmore Publishing Company, 1966.

PHELAN, J., "Have You Ever Been a Boo-hoo?" *Saturday Evening Post,* March 21, 1964, p. 81.

"Victory for the Scientologists," *Time,* February 14, 1969, p. 76. See also *New York Times,* February 6, 1969, p. 39.

C. *Astrology*

HOWE, ELLIC, *Urania's Children: The Strange World of the Astrologers.* London: Kimber, 1967.

McINTOSH, CHRISTOPHER, *The Astrologers and Their Creed.* London: Hutchinson, 1969.

New York Times, 1969: January 12, VI, p. 22; April 16, p. 52; September 28, VII, p. 42; November 23, XIV, p. 1.

CHAPTER SIX
THE EDENIC BOWER

A. *Neo-Paganism*

GRAVES, ROBERT, *The White Goddess.* London: Falser, 1959.

STEVENS, HENRY BAILEY, *The Recovery of Culture.* New York: Harper & Row, Publishers, 1953.

B. *Witchcraft*

GARDNER, GERALD, *Witchcraft Today.* New York: Citadel Press, 1970.

GREELEY, A. M., "There's a New-Time Religion on Campus," *New York Times Magazine,* June 1, 1969, p. 14.

MURRAY, MARGARET, *The God of the Witches.* New York: Doubleday & Company, Inc., Anchor Books, 1960.

ROBERTS, SUSAN, *Witches, U.S.A.* New York: Dell Publishing Company, 1970.

SCHURMACHER, EMILE, *Witchcraft in America Today.* New York: Paperback Library, Inc., 1970.

SETH, RONALD, *Witches and Their Craft.* New York: Taplinger Publishing Co., Inc., 1968.

TINDALL, GILLIAN, *Handbook on Witches.* New York: Atheneum Publishers, 1966.

C. *Ceremonial Magic*

BARDON, FRANZ, *Initiation into Hermetics.* Kettig uber Koblenz: Osiris-Verlag, 1962.

———, *The Practice of Evocational Magic.* Graz-Puntigam, Austria: Rudolf Pravica, 1967.

BURLAND, C. A., *The Magical Arts.* New York: Horizon Press, Inc., 1966.

BUTLER, W. E., *Apprenticed to Magic.* London: Aquarian Press, 1962.

CAVENDISH, RICHARD, *The Black Arts.* London: Routledge and Kegan, Paul, 1967.

CROW, W. B., *Witchcraft, Magic, and Occultism.* Los Angeles: Wilshire Book Company, 1968.

CROWLEY, ALEISTER, *Magic in Theory and Practice.* New York: Castle Books, n.d.

KING, FRANCIS, *Ritual Magic in England.* London: Neville Spearman, 1970.

LEVI, ELIPHAS (A. L. Constant), *Transcendental Magic.* New York: Samuel Weiser, 1970.

————, *History of Magic* New York: Samuel Weiser, 1970.

MATHERS, S. L., *The Sacred Magic of Abra Melin.* New York: Wehman Brothers, 1948.

REGARDIE, ISAREL, *The Golden Dawn* (2nd ed.). St. Paul: Llewellyn Publications, 1970.

————, ed., P. R. STEPHENSEN, *The Legend of Aleister Crowley.* St. Paul: Llewellyn Publications, 1970.

————, *My Rosicrucian Adventure.* Chicago: Aries Press, 1936.

SYMONDS, J., *The Great Beast.* New York: Roy Publishers, Inc., 1952.

————, *The Magic of Aleister Crowley.* London: Muller, 1958.

SYMONDS, J., and K. GRANT, eds., *The Confessions of Aleister Crowley.* New York: Hill and Wang, Inc., 1970.

WAITE, A. E., *The Book of Ceremonial Magic.* New York: University Books, 1961.

D. Satanism

LaVEY, ANTON, *The Satanic Bible.* New York: Avon Books, 1969.

LYONS, ARTHUR, *The Second Coming: Satanism in America.* New York: Dodd, Mead & Company, 1970.

RHODES, H. T., *The Satonic Mass: A Sociological and Criminological Study.* New York: Citadel Press, 1955. (Reprint, Wehman.)

CHAPTER SEVEN
THE GANGES FLOWS WEST

A. The Vedanta Society

BRIDGES, HAL, *American Mysticism: From William James to Zen.* New York Harper & Row, Publishers, 1970.

ISHERWOOD, CHRISTOPHER, ed., *Vedanta for Modern Man.* New York: P. F. Collier, Inc., 1962.

————, ed., *Vedanta for the Western World.* Hollywood: Marcel Rodd, 1946.

————, *Ramakrishna and His Disciples.* New York: Simon & Schuster, Inc., 1965.

SCHNEIDERMAN, LEO, "Ramakrishna: Personality and Social Factors in the Growth of a Religious Movement," *Journal for the Scientific Study of Religion,* VIII, No. 1 (Spring 1969), 60–71.

THOMAS, WENDELL, *Hinduism Invades America.* New York: Beacon Press, Inc., 1930.

YALE, JOHN, ed., *What Vedanta Means to Me.* London: Rider, 1961.

B. *The Self-Realization Fellowship*

"Guru's Exit," *Time,* August 4, 1952, p. 57.

THOMAS, WENDELL, *Hinduism Invades America.* New York: Beacon Press, Inc., 1930.

C. *The Maharishi Mahesh Yogi's Transcendental Meditation Movement*

Campbell, Anthony, M.D., *Seven States of Consciousness: A Vision of Possibilities Suggested by the Teaching of Maharishi Mahesh Yogi.* New York: Harper Torchbooks, 1973.

EBON, MARTIN, *Maharishi the Guru.* New York: New America Library, 1968.

"The Good-Time Guru," *Newsweek,* May 15, 1972, pp. 14–15.

"Guru," *Newsweek,* December 18, 1967, p. 44.

HEDGEPETH, W., "Non-drug Turn-On Hits Campus," *Look,* February 6, 1968, p. 68.

HORN, P., "Visit With India's High-Powered New Prophet," *Look,* February 6, 1968, p. 64.

LAPHAM, L. H., "There Once Was A Guru From Rishikesh," *Saturday Evening Post,* May 4, 1968, p. 23; May 18, 1968, p. 28.

LEFFERTS, B., "Chief Guru of the Western World," *New York Times Magazine,* December 17, 1967, p. 32.

"Merseysiders at the Ganges," *Time,* March 1, 1968, p. 25.

NEEDLEMAN, JACOB, *The New Religions.* New York: Doubleday & Company, Inc., 1970.

TART, CHARLES T., "A Psychologist's Experience with Transcendental Meditation," *Journal of Transpersonal Psychology,* 2 (1971), 135–40.

WAINWRIGHT, L., "Invitation to Instant Bliss," *Life,* November 10, 1967, p. 26.

WALLACE, ROBERT KEITH, "Physiological Effects of Transcendental Meditation," *Science,* 167 (March 27, 1970), 1751–54.

WALLACE, ROBERT KEITH, and HERBERT BENSON, "The Physiology of Meditation," *Scientific American,* February 1972, pp. 85–90.

"Yogi on the Beach," *Newsweek,* May 13, 1968, p. 111.

D. *Krishna Consciousness*

LEMBKE, DARYL, "Krishna Cult—The Chant Goes On," *Los Angeles Times,* January 11, 1970, p. B.

SINGER, MILTON B., ed., *Krishna: Myth, Rites, and Attitudes.* Honolulu: East-West Center Press, 1966.

E. *Satya Sai Baba Movement*

"God-Possessed," *Newsweek*, November 17, 1969, p. 110.

CHAPTER EIGHT
THE EAST IN THE GOLDEN WEST

A. *Western Zen*

BENOIT, HUBERT, *The Supreme Doctrine.* New York: Viking Press, Inc., 1968.

BRIDGES, HAL, *American Mysticism: From William James to Zen.* New York: Harper & Row Publishers, 1967.

GRAHAM, DON ALFRED, *Zen Catholicism.* New York: Harcourt, Brace & World, Inc., 1963.

GUSTAITIS, ROSA, *Turning On.* New York: The Macmillan Company, Publishers, 1969.

KAPLEAU, PHILIP, *The Three Pillars of Zen.* Boston: Beacon Press, Inc., 1967.

NEEDLEMAN, JACOB, *The New Religions.* New York: Doubleday & Company, Inc., 1970.

SARGEANT, W., "Profile: Dr. D. T. Suzuki," *The New Yorker*, August 31, 1957, p. 34.

SUZUKI, D. T., *Zen Buddhism.* New York: Doubleday & Company, Inc., Anchor Books, 1956.

WATTS, ALAN, *The Way of Zen.* New York: Pantheon Books, Inc., 1957.

"Zen," *Time*, February 4, 1957, p. 65. See also *Time*, May 26, 1958, p. 65; July 21, 1958, p. 49; February 23, 1959, p. 52.

"Zen, With a Difference: Tassajara Monastery in California," *Time*, October 18, 1968, p. 80.

Zen Center of San Francisco, *Wind Bell*, VIII, Nos. 1–2 (Fall 1969). (Issue devoted to history of Zen Centers in America.)

B. *Nichiren Shoshu*

BRANNEN, NOAH S., *Soka Gakkai, Japan's Militant Buddhists.* Richmond: John Knox Press, 1968.

DATOR, JAMES ALLEN, *Soka Gakkai, Builders of the Third Civilization: American and Japanese Members.* Seattle: University of Washington Press, 1969.

FLAGLER, J. M., "A Chanting in Japan," *The New Yorker*, November 26, 1966, pp. 37–87.

OKAMOTO, RICHARD, "Japan: A Booming Economy Has Spawned a Militant New Religion," *Look*, September 10, 1963, pp. 15–17.

"The Power of Positive Chanting," *Time*, January 17, 1969, p. 51.

C. *Meher Baba*

"Jai Baba," *The New Yorker,* June 21, 1969, pp. 28–31.

NEEDLEMAN, JACOB, *The New Religions.* New York: Doubleday & Company, Inc., 1970.

PURDOM, CHARLES B., *The God-Man: The Life, Journeys, and Work of Meher Baba.* London: Allen and Unwin, 1964.

ROBBINS, THOMAS, "Eastern Mysticism and the Resocialization of Drug Users: The Meher Baba Cult," *Journal for the Scientific Study of Religion,* VIII, No. 2 (Fall 1969), 308–17.

D. *Baha'i*

"Baha'i's 100th," *Newsweek,* May 11, 1953, p. 60.

GAVER, JESSYCA, *Baha'i Faith.* New York: Award Books, 1968.

"Heretics in Islam," *Time,* June 6, 1955, p. 68.

"In the Hands of the Hands," *Time,* December 9, 1957, p. 87.

KEENE, JAMES, "Baha'i World Faith: Redefinition of Religion," *Journal for the Scientific Study of Religion,* VI, No. 2 (Fall 1967), 221–35.

"Nine Hands," *Newsweek,* June 27, 1960, p. 94.

"Tempest in a Temple," *Newsweek,* June 6, 1955, p. 50.

E. *Subud*

NEEDLEMAN, JACOB, *The New Religions.* New York: Doubleday & Company, Inc., 1970.

Addresses of Groups

The following current (1972) addresses of groups discussed in this book are provided to assist those who may wish to undertake further investigation of particular groups.

CHAPTER THREE

NEW VESSELS FOR THE ANCIENT WISDOM

Theosophy

The Theosophical Society in America, Box 270, Wheaton, Illinois 60187.

The Krotona School of Theosophy, Route 2, Box 4-B, Ojai, California 93023.

The Theosophical Society, Post Office Bin C, Pasadena, California 91109.

The United Lodge of Theosophists, 245 West 33rd Street, Los Angeles, California 90007.

Full Moon Meditation Groups

Lucis Publishing Company and the Arcane School, 866 United Nations Plaza, Suite 566–7, New York, N.Y. 10017.

Meditation Groups for the New Age, P. O. Box 566, Ojai, California 93023.

Other Groups

Anthroposophical Society in America, Rudolf Steiner Information Center, 211 Madison Avenue, New York, N.Y. 10016.

The Rosicrucian Fellowship, Oceanside, California 92054.

Rosicrucian Order (AMORC), Rosicrucian Park, San Jose, California 95114.

The Order of the Pleroma, B.C.M./Consortium, London, W.C.1, England.

Sophia Gnostic Center, 1265 No. Alexandria Avenue, Los Angeles, California 90029.

"I Am" Movement, Saint-Germain Press, Inc., 8411 Stony Island Avenue, Chicago, Illinois 60617.

Liberal Catholic Church, St. Alban Press, P. O. Box 598, Ojai, California 93023.

CHAPTER FOUR

THE DESCENT OF THE MIGHTY ONES

National Spiritualist Association of Churches, P. O. Box 147, Cassadaga, Florida 32706.

George W. Van Tassel, College of Universal Wisdom, P. O. Box 458, Yucca Valley, California 92284.

Understanding, Inc., P.O. Box 206, Merlin, Oregon 97532.

Amalgamated Flying Saucer Clubs of America, 2004 North Hoover Street, Los Angeles, California 90027.

The Aetherius Society, 6202 Afton Place, Hollywood, California 90028.

CHAPTER FIVE
THE CRYSTAL WITHIN:
INITIATORY GROUPS

The Gurdjieff Foundation, 123 East 63rd Street, New York, N.Y. 10021.

The Prosperos, 1441 Fourth Street, Santa Monica, California 90401.

Church of Scientology of California, 2005 West 9th Street, Los Angeles, California 90006.

World Headquarters, The Institute of Ability, 617 N. Larchmont Avenue, Los Angeles, California 90004.

Builders of the Adytum, 5105 North Figueroa Street, Los Angeles, California 90042.

The Church of Light, P.O. Box 1525, Los Angeles, California 90053.

CHAPTER SIX
THE EDENIC BOWER: NEO-PAGANISM

The Church of the Eternal Source, P.O. Box 7091, Burbank, California 91505.

Feraferia, Inc., P.O. Box 691, Altadena, California 91001.

The Church of All Worlds, P.O. Box 2953, St. Louis, Missouri 63130.

OTA, P.O. Box 3341, Pasadena, California 91103.

Church of Satan, 6114 California Street, San Francisco, California 94121.

The Crystal Well, P.O. Box 18351, Philadelphia, Pennsylvania 19120 (Wicca periodical).

CHAPTER SEVEN
THE GANGES FLOWS WEST

Vedanta Press and Bookshop, 1946 Vedanta Place, Hollywood, California 90028.

Self-Realization Fellowship, International Headquarters, 3880 San Rafael Avenue, Los Angeles, California 90065.

Students International Meditation Society, 1015 Gayley Avenue, Los Angeles, California 90024.

Sivananda Yoga Society, 5178 St. Lawrence Blvd., Montreal, P.O., Canada.

International Society for Krishna Consciousness, 61 Second Avenue, New York, N.Y. 10003.

Satya Sai Baba Center, "Sai Nilayam," Tecate, California 92080.

CHAPTER EIGHT
THE EAST IN THE GOLDEN WEST

Cimarron Zen Center, 2505 Cimarron Street, Los Angeles, California 90018.

Zen Center, 300 Page Street, San Francisco, California 94102.

Kailas Shugendo, 2139 Pine Street, San Francisco, California 94115.

Tail of the Tiger Community (Tibetan Buddhism), Star Route, Barnet, Vermont 05821.

Tibetan Nyingmapa Meditation Center, P.O. Box 4182, Berkeley, Ca. 94704.

Nichiren Shoshu of America, 1351 Ocean Front, Santa Monica, California 90401.

Baha'i National Spiritual Assembly, Wilmette, Illinois 60091.

Meher Baba Bookstore, 31 W. Union Street, Pasadena, California 91101.

Sufism Reoriented, Inc., 1290 Sutter Street, San Francisco, California 94101.

Subud North American Inquiry Section, P.O. Box 453, Cooper Station, New York, N.Y. 10003.

The Unified Family, 1611 Upshur Street, N.W., Washington, D.C. 20011.

CHAPTER NINE
RETROSPECT AND A GLANCE
AT THE FUTURE

The Mythopoeic Society, P.O. Box 24150, Los Angeles, California 90024.

index

Abilitism, 176–78
  emphasis on communication, 177
  offshoot of Scientology, 176
  relating exercise, 177
"About the Sivananda Yoga Society and
  Yoga Philosophy," quoted, 238–39
Adams, Frederick, 194. *See also* Feraferia
Adamski, George, 143. *See also* UFO
  cults
A.E. (George Russell)
  member Theosophical Society, 97
  poem quoted, 98
Aetherius Society, 150–55
Albigensianism, as dissent from Chris-
  tianity, 54
Alchemy
  Jung on, 56
  prima materia, 57
  in Renaissance, 57
All and Everything, G. Gurdjieff, 159,
  162. *See also* Fourth Way Schools,
  Gurdjieff
  quoted, 163–64.
Amalgamated Flying Saucer Clubs of
  America, 145–49
Anabaptists, 20
Angelucci, Orfeo, 142. *See also* UFO
  cults
Anthroposophy, 106–10
  alternative to Judeo-Christian tradi-
  tion, 3, 89
  Christian Community Church, 108

  founded 1912, 107
  "law of seven," 107
  "right-wing" Theosophy, 92
  Waldorf Schools, 108
Apocalyptic, defined, 38n
Apollonius of Tyana
  expression of Theosophical Sixth Ray,
  95
  leader of Hellenistic cult, 46
  magus, 50
  Pythagorean, 52
  wandering philosopher, 44
Aquarian Age, apocalyptic direction in,
  29
Aquarian Gospel of Jesus Christ, 138.
  See also Spiritualist Church
Aristotelian Schoolmen, in Renaissance,
  58
Ashmole, Elias, linked to Masons and
  Rosicrucians, 63
Astrology
  Church of Light, 183
  in Renaissance, 57
Astrology Is Religion's Road Map,
  quoted, 185
Autobiography of a Yogi, 82
  quoted, 229–31
Aura, 122–23
  defined, 126
Axis mundi
  as basic religious symbol, 11
  sacred mountain as, 263

323